FROM THE ARRIVAL OF HUMANKIND TO THE BIRTH OF A NATION

Volume One of *The Oxford History of the American People* begins with the origins of humankind in North America and concludes with the first difficult, profoundly significant years of the infant United States. It charts the development of Indian civilizations on the continent, the era of European discovery, exploration and conquest, and the quickening tempo of colonial competition and conflict that resulted first in English supremacy and then in American independence. Here, brought to life by a master historian, is a drama of change and transformation unequaled in the annals of world history.

The Oxford History of the American People
Volume One: Prehistory to 1789

"A splendid book!"   —*New York Times*

"Sparkling, living history, brimming with personality, bright with anecdote . . . the product of America's most fastidious historian."   —*Saturday Review*

"With an extraordinary measure of . . . vigor and daring [Professor Morison] combines a great mastery of factual detail garnered in his long lifetime of teaching and writing, all embellished by a literary grace and fluency unexcelled among contemporary American historians."
—*Book Week*

SAMUEL ELIOT MORISON was one of this nation's most distinguished historians. A two-time winner of the Pulitzer Prize—for his biographies of Christopher Columbus and John Paul Jones—he also was the U.S. Navy's official historian, writing the acclaimed fifteen-volume *History of United States Naval Operations in World War Two*.

THE OXFORD HISTORY OF THE AMERICAN PEOPLE

Volume One, *Prehistory to 1789*

Samuel Eliot Morison

A MERIDIAN BOOK

MERIDIAN
Published by the Penguin Group
Penguin Books USA Inc., 375 Hudson Street, New York, New York 10014, U.S.A.
Penguin Books Ltd, 27 Wrights Lane, London W8 5TZ, England
Penguin Books Australia Ltd, Ringwood, Victoria, Australia
Penguin Books Canada Ltd, 10 Alcorn Avenue, Toronto, Ontario, Canada M4V 3B2
Penguin Books (N.Z.) Ltd, 182–190 Wairau Road, Auckland 10, New Zealand

Penguin Books Ltd, Registered Offices: Harmondsworth, Middlesex, England

Published by Meridian, an imprint of Dutton Signet, a division of Penguin Books USA Inc.
Published by arrangement with Oxford University Press, Inc. For information address
Oxford University Press, Inc., 200 Madison Avenue, New York, N.Y. 10016.
Previously published in a Mentor edition.

First Meridian Printing, August, 1994
10 9 8 7 6

REGISTERED TRADEMARK—MARCA REGISTRADA

LIBRARY OF CONGRESS CATALOGING-IN-PUBLICATION DATA
Morison, Samuel Eliot, 1887–1976.
    The Oxford history of the American people / Samuel Eliot Morison.
        p.   cm.
    Contents: v. 1. Prehistory to 1789—v. 2. 1789–1877—v.
3. 1869–1963.
    ISBN 0-452-01130-2 (v. 1).—ISBN 0-452-01131-0 (v. 2).—ISBN
0-452-01132-9 (v. 3)
    1. United States—History.   I. Title.
E178.M855   1994
973—dc20
                                                94–14636
                                                CIP

Printed in the United States of America

TO MY BELOVED WIFE

PRISCILLA BARTON MORISON

WHO HAS HELPED ME TO UNDERSTAND

THE MOVING FORCES IN THE HISTORY

OF OUR NATION

I find the great thing in this world is not so much where we stand, as in what direction we are moving. . . . We must sail sometimes with the wind and sometimes against it, — but we must sail, and not drift, nor lie at anchor.

Oliver Wendell Holmes *The Autocrat of the Breakfast Table* (1858)

The role of government and its relationship to the individual has been changed so radically that today government is involved in almost every aspect of our lives.

Political, economic and racial forces have developed which we have not yet learned to understand or control. If we are ever to master these forces, make certain that government will belong to the people, not the people to the government, and provide for the future better than the past, we must somehow learn from the experiences of the past.

Bernard Baruch, presenting his papers to Princeton University, at the age of 93. *The New York Times,* 11 May 1964

Preface

THIS BOOK, in a sense, is a legacy to my countrymen after studying, teaching, and writing the history of the United States for over half a century.

Prospective readers may well ask wherein it may differ in form and content from other American histories of similar length. Politics are not lacking; but my main ambition is to re-create for my readers American ways of living in bygone eras. Here you will find a great deal on social and economic development; horses, ships, popular sports, and pastimes; eating, drinking, and smoking habits. Pugilists will be found cheek-by-jowl with Presidents; rough-necks with reformers, artists with ambassadors. More, proportionally, than in other histories, will be found on sea power, on the colonial period in which basic American principles were established, on the American Indians, and the Caribbean. I am offering fresh, new accounts of the Civil War and the War of Independence. A brief account of the parallel history of Canada, so near and dear to us, yet so unknown in her historical development to most citizens of the United States, has been attempted.

Having lived through several critical eras, dwelt or sojourned in every section of our country, taken part in both world wars, met and talked with almost every President of the United States in the twentieth century, as well as with thousands of men and women active in various pursuits, I have reached some fairly definite opinions about our history. At the same time, I have tried when writing about great controversial issues, such as war and peace and the progressive movement, to relate fairly what each side was trying to accomplish.

Since this is not primarily a textbook, but a history written for my fellow citizens to read and enjoy, footnote references, bibliographies, and other "scholarly apparatus" have been suppressed. Readers may take a certain amount of erudition for granted! Of course nobody, much less myself, can possibly read every printed source and monograph on American history from the beginning through 1964. This is particularly true of social history, comprising ideally, though impossibly, all human activities. Consequently, I have depended for particular subjects

on the information and advice of experts, some my colleagues or former pupils, many my friends, but others who were strangers; and it has been most gratifying to find people so generous with their special knowledge. Moreover, having learned from my naval experience the value of oral testimony by participants, I have sought out, talked with, and profited by conversations with many of the civilian and military leaders of the past fifty years. These, excepting a few who wish anonymity, are named in the following section on Acknowledgments.

For many years I have been interested in collecting the popular music of American history, from that of the Indians to the present. The Oxford University Press has given me the opportunity to use some appropriate tags and choruses of these at the ends of appropriate chapters, and more could have been added to the later chapters but for the reluctance of music publishers to part with copyrighted material.

The illustrations have been chosen as much for their artistic appeal as for illustrations in the strict sense. The late Dr. Harold Bowditch helped me to make the point that the English Colonies were not originally democratic, by selecting and delineating coats of arms of colonial founders to which they were entitled, and which they used on bookplates, silver, and in other ways.

One thing has deeply impressed me as I swept through the history of North America — the continuity of American habits, ways, and institutions over a period of three centuries. The seeds or roots of almost everything we have today may be discerned in the English, French, and Spanish colonies as early as 1660. Nobody has better expressed this fundamental unity of American history than George E. Woodberry in his poem "My Country."

> She from old fountains doth new judgment draw,
> Till, word by word, the ancient order swerves
> To the true course more nigh; in every age
> A little she creates, but more preserves.

SAMUEL ELIOT MORISON

44 Brimmer Street
Boston
Christmastide 1964

Preface to the New American Library Edition. The entire text has been reviewed and corrected, in the light of fresh information and of errata noted and sent in by readers. I hope they will continue to do just that! Renewed thanks are due to Miss Antha E. Card for collecting and collating these errata, and to Oxford University Press for its steady cooperation and consideration.

SAMUEL ELIOT MORISON

"Good Hope"
Northeast Harbor, Maine
July 1971

Acknowledgments

MY BELOVED WIFE Priscilla Barton Morison not only encouraged me to write this book but listened critically to the reading of draft chapters, and greatly contributed to my happiness and well being while the work was going on.

General acknowledgments are due to my secretaries during the period of writing, Diana G. Hadgis and Antha E. Card. Miss Card, especially, has helped me by repeatedly checking facts, and by research and suggestions.

To Dr. Sydney V. James, Jr., who for a year helped me by research on the Indians, the Jacksonian period, and other subjects.

To my daughters Emily M. Beck, editor of the latest edition of Bartlett's Familiar Quotations, for looking up and checking quotations, and to Catharine Morison Cooper for research on American music.

To the many naval and military officers and civilians who are mentioned in the prefaces of my earlier books, especially in the fifteen-volume *History of U. S. Naval Operations in World War II.*

To my colleagues at Harvard and other American universities, and at the Universities of Oxford, Paris, and Rome, from whom I have learned very, very much, through friendly conversation and correspondence.[1]

Special Subjects of Acknowledgment

AVIATION: Professors Secor D. Browne and Jerome C. Hunsaker of M.I.T., and Dr. J. Howard Means of Boston.

CANADA: Professor A. R. M. Lower of Queen's University, Professor John J. Conway, formerly of Harvard, and the Honorable William Phillips.

CATHOLIC CHURCH HISTORY: Professor Marshall Smelser of Notre Dame University and Monsignor George Casey of Lexington, Massachusetts.

COLONIAL PERIOD: Professors Edmund S. Morgan of Yale and

---

[1] My Balzan lecture at Rome on "The Experiences and Principles of an Historian" is printed in *Vistas of History* (Knopf, 1964).

xiii

Carl Bridenbaugh of Brown; both Professors Schlesinger and the late Perry Miller of Harvard, and the Rev. Arthur Pierce Middleton of Brookfield Center, Connecticut.

CONSERVATION: Mr. Ernest C. Oberholtzer of Ranier, Minnesota, Mr. Edmund Hayes of Portland, Oregon, Mrs. Marguerite Owen of Washington, D.C., and Professor Arthur A. Maass of Harvard.

ECONOMICS, especially the Great Depression: Professors Edward S. Mason of Harvard, Joseph Stancliffe Davis of Stanford, and Adolf A. Berle of Columbia Universities.

FEDERAL CONVENTION: Professor Henry S. Commager of Amherst College.

HORSES AND SPORTS: Mrs. Thomas E. P. Rice of Boston, Mr. Franklin Reynolds of Mount Sterling, Kentucky, Dr. George C. Simpson of the Harvard Museum of Comparative Zoology, and Mr. Colin J. Steuart Thomas of Baltimore.

ILLUSTRATIONS: Addison Gallery of American Art, Andover; American Museum of Natural History; Archives of Canada; Mrs. Bern Anderson of Newport; Atkins Museum of Fine Arts, Kansas City; Mr. David W. Barton; Boston Athenaeum; Boston Museum of Fine Arts; British Museum; Mrs. Richard E. Byrd; Corcoran Gallery, Washington; Mrs. John Duer; the H. F. DuPont Winterthur Museum; Mrs. Frederica F. Emert; the Franklin D. Roosevelt Library; Harvard University; Historical Society of Pennsylvania; Professor M. A. de Wolfe Howe of the Harvard Law School; Mrs. Mabel Ingalls; the John Carter Brown Library; Johns Hopkins University; Karsh of Ottawa; Mrs. Fred C. Kelly; The Mariners Museum, Newport News; Maryland Historical Society; the National Archives and National Gallery of Art, Washington; New-York Historical Society; Pach Brothers of New York; Peabody Museum of Cambridge; Peabody Museum of Salem; Pennsylvania Academy of Fine Arts; Princeton University; the Syracuse Savings Bank; Tennessee Valley Authority; Virginia Chamber of Commerce; United States Navy.

IMMIGRATION: Professor Oscar Handlin of Harvard.

INDIANS AND PRIMITIVE MAN IN AMERICA: Mr. Leonard Ware of the Bureau of Indian Affairs, Department of the Interior; Professor J. Otis Brew of Harvard University and the late Samuel K. Lothrop, curator of Andean Archaeology in the Peabody Museum, Cambridge.

LATIN AMERICA: Professor Roland T. Ely of Rutgers; Colonel Robert D. Heinl Jr. USMC (Ret.); the Honorable Mauricio Obregón of Colombia; the Honorable Aaron S. Brown, American Ambassador to Nicaragua.

MARITIME: Mr. Marion V. Brewington of Peabody Museum, Salem; Professor K. Jack Bauer of Morris Harvey College, Charleston, West Virginia; Rear Admiral Ernest M. Eller, Mr. Jesse R. Thomas, and Mr. Donald R. Martin of the Navy Department; Mrs. John M. Bullard of New Bedford.

MEDICINE: Drs. Paul Dudley White, J. Howard Means, and Sidney Burwell of the Harvard Medical School; Dr. J. Whittington Gorham of New York.

MUSIC AND THE FINE ARTS: Mr. Erich Leinsdorf, conductor of

the Boston Symphony Orchestra; Professor G. Wallace Woodworth of Harvard; Mr. George Biddle of New York; Mr. Joseph A. Coletti; the late Maxim Karolik; the several music publishers who have allowed me to quote snatches of their songs.

PSYCHOLOGY: Professor Erik H. Erikson of Harvard.

SUEZ AFFAIR: Marshal of the R.A.F. Sir John Slessor; the Honorable Winthrop Aldrich, former Ambassador to Great Britain.

TEXAS: the late Walter P. Webb and J. Frank Dobie of the University of Texas; Professor Allan Ashcroft of the Texas Agricultural and Mechanical University.

WITCHCRAFT: Miss Esther Forbes of Worcester.

Contents

List of Maps

MAPS BY VAUGHN GRAY

List of Songs

The Navajo war god, clad all in flint, fought the "ancient folk," or destructive forces of Nature. His flinty armor strikes lightning, in four directions, dashing the enemy into the earth, one after the other:

> Hi! ni! ya! Behold, the man of flint, that's me! / Four lightnings zig-zag from me, strike and return. / Behold the man of flint, that's me! I'm he! / Everywhere my lightnings strike they plow the foeman under! / The ancient folk with evil spells, dashed to earth, plowed under!

From *The Indian's Book* by Natalie Curtis Burlin. Reprinted by permission of Paul Burlin.

This ancient Benedictine chant was sung every evening by the sailors on Columbus's and other early voyages. Arranged by Benedict FitzGerald.

A popular French song of the reign of Henry of Navarre, sung by the French pioneers in North America. Adapted by C. M. Cooper.

A translation of Psalm 136 from the Rev. Henry Ainsworth's *Book of Psalmes,* published by a Puritan refugee in Holland in 1612, and set to a vigorous popular tune of the time. Not only the Pilgrim Fathers but other English pioneers, after landing on our shores, made this joyful noise unto the Lord.

From *The Burl Ives Song Book,* 1953, Ballantine Books, New York. Reprinted by permission of Mrs. Helen Ives.

V *Old Hundred*   **117**

From Sternhold & Hopkins *Whole Booke of Psalmes* (1652), a favorite with English Puritans. This version of Kethe's hymn from the Geneva Psalter of 1551 sets Psalm 100 to a lively tempo, which strict Puritans called the "Geneva jig."

From *The Burl Ives Song Book,* 1953, Ballantine Books, New York. Reprinted by permission of Mrs. Helen Ives.

VII *Vexilla Regis*   **155**

This ancient hymn, composed in the sixth century by Venantius Honorius Fortunatus on the occasion of a relic of the True Cross being received, was sung by the French explorers when they took formal possession of territory for the king. It is still sung at Passiontide in most Christian Churches. Julian's *Dictionary of Hymnology* (1915) lists more than twenty English translations, of which one of the best is in G. Thring's *Church of England Hymn Book* of 1882:

> Abroad the Regal Banners fly, / Now shines the Cross's mystery; / The Cross where life did death endure, / and yet by death did life procure.

From *The Hymnal of the Protestant Episcopal Church in the U.S.A.,* 1940.

VIII *Lilleburlero*   **178**

This catchy tune, ascribed to Henry Purcell, with nonsensical refrains, was the theme song of the Glorious Revolution of 1688. Bishop Burnet wrote that army and people "were singing it perpetually; and perhaps never had so slight a thing so great an effect."

X *Am I a Soldier of the Cross?*   **212**

Isaac Watts's hymn of 1724, set to an early eighteenth-century psalm tune, expresses the fervor of the Great Awakening. George Whitefield introduced Watts's hymns to the colonies on his tour of 1739–41. Mark Twain gives an amusing account of a minister "lining out" this hymn

in the old manner, in Chapter V of *Tom Sawyer*.
From *The Hymnal of the Protestant Episcopal Church in the U.S.A.,* 1940.

This stirring tune by William Boyce, with words by David Garrick, was first sung in London in the "Wonderful Year" 1759, and has been a favorite of the Royal Navy ever since.

William Billings of Boston, America's first professional musician, self-taught and uninfluenced by European fashion, composed this music in 1770, and the naïvely patriotic words in 1778.

These words, written about 1776 to the popular tune "The British Grenadier," were sung by the Continental soldiery.

This sarcastic ditty by Francis Hopkinson in 1778 celebrated an incident of the Northern Campaign. Hopkinson represented New Jersey in the Continental Congress, painted portraits, and designed the Stars and Stripes.

A popular tune, played by the bands of Washington's army when Cornwallis surrendered at Yorktown.

By Daniel George and Horatio Garnett, sung on 4 July 1789, the first Fourth since Washington's inauguration, with an accompaniment of drums and trumpets.
From Olin Downes & Elie Siegmeister *Treasury of American Song,* 1940, New York.

With these words and music Jezaniah Sumner, an obscure American musician, hailed the Enlightenment as the handmaid of Liberty, in 1789.
From Olin Downes & Elie Siegmeister *Treasury of American Song,* 1940, New York.

THE
OXFORD HISTORY
OF THE
AMERICAN PEOPLE

Volume One, *Prehistory to 1789*

I

America Under Her Native Sons

1. *The Origin of Man in America*

HISTORY IS THE STORY OF MANKIND; but when we try to tell
the story of man in America from the beginning, the lack of
data quickly brings us to a halt. There are plenty of surviving
objects which antedate the coming of Europeans, but no written records; none, except the Maya calendar, that anyone as
yet has been able to read. The historian trying to find out
when and whence man first came to America, and how he
lived during the hundreds of centuries before Europeans arrived, is like a child trying to solve a picture puzzle with only
one per cent of the pieces. Under such circumstances no two
people would make the same design. Archaeologists, anthro-
pologists, plant geneticists, and others who have gone into the
subject of man's arrival and spread in America, do not agree.
New discoveries—new pieces to the puzzle—are made almost
yearly, new methods of dating these finds are being devised,
and new patterns are set up which confuse an historian who is
used to working with dated documents, monuments, and
books.

Thus, what we mean by the history of the American People
is the history in America of immigrants from other continents.
Mainly they came from Europe, and there were many un-
willing ones from Africa, and not a few from Asia. But we
cannot ignore the "Indians," as Christopher Columbus, making one of the worst guesses in history, called the natives

31

whom he encountered on 12 October 1492. These natives first welcomed the Europeans, then fought them, and finally were subjugated by them. They gave the Europeans some of the world's most valued agricultural products—maize, tobacco, the potato, cassava, and chocolate. They taught their conquerors hundreds of skills and so frequently mated with them that millions of people in the United States, Canada, Mexico, Central and South America have Indian blood in their veins. The Indians have so influenced, indeed so transformed, the lives of white and black men in North America that we are eager to know where they came from and how their culture developed. But in this search we find little but silence, darkness, and mystery.

Nothing certain is known of the origin of man in the continent we call America. One guess is as good as another, and some speculations have been repeated so often as to acquire the force of fact. The existence of people here before the Indians has always been suspected, often asserted, but never proved. Our European ancestors entertained a low opinion of Indian culture. Hence, when they came upon a remarkable monument like an inscribed rock or a serpentine mound, or the stone temples of Yucatán and Guatemala and the cyclopean walls of Peru, they were apt to ascribe them to Phoenicians, Egyptians, or anyone but the natives. Theories of the Lost Continent of Atlantis (a literary conceit of Plato), or of a land bridge between Africa and Brazil, have been brought up to prove that Europeans or Africans were in America thousands of years before Columbus.

There is no reason to deprive the American Indians of credit for developing their own civilization. There is no doubt that they themselves, without external aid or example, designed and built the marvelous pre-Columbian monuments and sculpture of Central America, and produced the beautiful examples of goldsmiths' work, pottery, and implements which are now treasured in museums. Similarities (such as the use of the bow and arrow, pottery making, and the Mexican game *patolli* resembling the Hindu game *parchesi*) have been pointed out as evidence of a continuing contact between Asia and America. This argument assumes that the Indians were incapable of inventing anything; an argument which, in view of the unchallenged fact that they developed corn and the potato from wild plants, and made boats from birch bark, is untenable. Reversing the argument, one may point out that, if the Indian had enjoyed even occasional contact with the Old World, he would certainly have imported things that even the Maya and the Inca lacked—steel implements, the wheel, and built-up wooden boats. The Indians had no iron, no wheel in any form, and their boats were either dug out from a log or stripped from the bark of a single tree, or were rafts of reeds and balsa. The Indians of Ecuador and Peru taught themselves to sail balsa rafts, and invented the centerboard to help them point up to the wind; but, unlike the Polynesians, who were among the world's boldest sailors, they stayed close to shore.

It is generally agreed that *Homo sapiens* originated in Central Asia, whence he gradually spread into every region of the globe except Antarctica; and now he is there too. Physical characteristics of the American Indian are either definitely Mongoloid or a mixture of that with something else. They probably first began coming from Asia to America during the pleistocene, or Ice Age, which started in remotest antiquity and ended at some time between 8000 and 5000 B.C. During that era a large part of North America was covered by an ice cap which alternately advanced and retreated, each period taking thousands of years. This movement radically affected plant, animal, and human life. As the ice cap retreated, temperature rose and rain decreased until (around 8000 B.C. in the southwestern United States) the big mammals that fed on grass starved to death, and the men who hunted them died or moved on. After an arid period that lasted until about 2000 B.C., the temperature again declined, the rain returned, and the prophecy was fulfilled that "the desert shall rejoice and blossom as the rose." For about a millennium the American Southwest enjoyed more moisture than it does today. Then the climate gradually grew drier, and by the beginning of the Christian era had reached about the same degree of humidity that it still retains.

At Bering Strait, between America and Asia, only 23 miles of open water separate the northeastern cape of Siberia from Great Diomede Island. That island belongs to the U.S.S.R., but only three miles of water separate it from Little Diomede Island, which belongs to the U.S.A.; and from Little Diomede it is only another 22 miles to the Seward peninsula of Alaska. A primitive people, pressed by enemies from behind, could have crossed Bering Strait by raft. The first comers were not very advanced in culture. They brought little to mark them as humans except speech, fire, and the arts of making flint spear points and of scraping animal hides for clothing and shelter. Even that far back, they were accompanied by dogs, man's ever faithful companions.

Again assuming that the geologists are right, the last great ice cap that covered a large part of the United States began to melt about 40,000 years ago. Until then, living conditions in North America could hardly have been attractive even to Mongoloid aborigines. The ice first melted along the Northwest Coast. Studies of soil and rock formation prove that a fertile, relatively warm corridor first emerged from the ice along the Alaskan coast, and then up the Yukon, Mackenzie, and Fraser river valleys, and southeast of the Rocky Mountains. We may suppose that successive waves of immigrants from Siberia pushed down this corridor, thrusting the first comers further and further afield, into the buffalo country of the Great Plains, thence to New Mexico and Arizona. There the Cliff Dwellers maintained themselves against later invaders who, finding the cliffs too formidable, swept around them into Mexico and Central America. Some groups built dugout canoes by means of which they were able to settle the Caribbee islands. Others passed over the jungle-covered cordillera into South America, spread fanwise over that immense continent, and finally reached Patagonia, where Magellan in 1520 encountered the clumsy giants who worshipped the god Setebos and gave Shakespeare his character Caliban. These diverse branches of American Indians cannot have descended from a single group. There must have been innumerable crossings of the Strait, over thousands of years; a procession of refugees from Siberia. The Eskimo were the last to cross, and some of them stayed in Asia. We are challenged to find out what went on in this bottomless pit of American prehistory. We must assume that it took many, many thousands of years after the first coming for the continent to be peopled with tribes and nations differing as much in physique and language as do the nations of modern Europe. For the civilizations of Mexico, Peru, and Colombia to have developed from a crude hunting people can hardly have taken less time than it did for paleolithic man, the "cave man" of Europe, to develop the civilizations of Egypt and Greece.

Science has come to the aid of imagination in the shape of three methods of dating. One is known as dendrochronology. The rings on trees make a definite pattern, owing to the differing amounts of moisture and sunlight that they receive annually, and these rings persist even when the wood becomes charcoal. In a region such as that inhabited by the Pueblos of the Southwest, where wooden beams are found in varying levels under modern native buildings, the rings of a recently cut tree may be compared with those of a pueblo destroyed a century ago, and those with the rings of an earlier pueblo, and so on until we have a chain of overlapping tree-ring patterns extending over 2100 years. That does not get us very far back, as archaeology goes; but we can get much farther with the method known as Carbon 14.

Carbon 14 is an isotope of carbon formed in the upper atmosphere by the action of cosmic rays. It is continually being absorbed by all living animals and plants, but after death they ingest no more and the Carbon 14 already absorbed disintegrates at a constant rate. About 5730 years after death an organism will have lost half of its radiocarbon, in the next 5730 years half the remainder, and so on. Thus, by determining the quantity of Carbon 14 in a dead organism by special instruments, one can calculate when it died. After about eight "half-lives," 40,000 years, detection of Carbon 14 becomes very difficult, but it can be done. A "radiocarbon date," therefore, is an estimate, within a bracket of several hundred years, and its accuracy varies with the nature of the material and other conditions. Nevertheless, it is the best method of dating prehistoric samples yet devised. Findings based on it, since 1948, have upset all earlier calculations of the antiquity of man in the Americas. Very recently, Dr. John N. Rosholt has developed a third method of dating, by utilizing "daughter" products of uranium. This may prove to be more accurate.

Who the first paleo-Indians or proto-Indians were, is another matter. But archaeological finds, starting in 1926 with the one at Folsom, New Mexico, and dated by the Carbon 14 method, have taught us much about how they lived. At Folsom a party from the Denver Museum of Natural History, digging up the bones of a long-extinct type of bison, found some twenty two-inch points, laboriously chipped out of flint and beautifully fluted so as to fit on the head of a spear. These are unlike the arrowheads later made by American Indians, and also different from European Stone Age implements. Accompanying the spear points were flint rasps for scraping the hides that these people used for clothing and shelter. Since then, over twenty-five similar caches have been found, all the way from Canada down to Patagonia, and from California to Massachusetts; and the organic matter in some of them has been dated.

The Clovis finds of 1932 are some of the most important. In a region near the Texas-New Mexico border there have been excavated fluted spear points sticking into mammoths' bones, together with bone shafts for the spears. These have been carbon-dated at about 8000 B.C. The Fort Rock, Oregon, find of 1951 yielded several dozen spear points, scrapers, bone awls and drills, and a pair of sandals made of shredded sagebrush bark which, when given the Carbon 14 treatment, could be dated as having been made around 9053 B.C. The people who made these points knew the use of fire. They were hunters of big game; for, in a dozen different sites, weapons have been found sticking into or lying near the bones of Ice Age bison, hairy elephants and mammoths, jaguars, ground sloths, camels, and other big mammals that became extinct far beyond the memories of the Indians that Europeans first encountered.

Most surprising of all these finds is a pair of caves in Patagonia, excavated by Junius Bird in 1951, where human remains were found in conjunction with spear points, and bones of the primitive horse, and which the carbon test gave an average age of 8639 years. This means that somewhere around 6700 B.C., descendants of the hunter folk who had crossed Bering Strait had reached the southern tip of the American continent, traveling through forests, plains, and jungles, along rivers, valleys, arroyos, and mountain ranges, and possibly part of the way by dugout canoe. And as primitive man seldom moved unless forced by pressure of other men or savage beasts, or scarcity of food, this safari must have taken thousands of years.

It is anyone's guess when the first crossing from Asia took place; estimates run all the way from 12,000 to 25,000 B.C. The geologists put a ceiling—or bottom—on it at 38,000 B.C., at which time they believe the ice cap started to melt. But we must remember that the Bering Strait route is only one of numerous assumptions that have been made. Man may have reached America from Asia in big dugout canoes such as the Polynesians built, and such as those observed by Columbus in the Caribbean.

Somewhat more developed than the people who made the Folsom points were those of the so-called Cochise culture along the southern borders of Arizona and New Mexico. The Ventana Cave in the Castle Mountains, about 75 miles south of Phoenix, shows evidence of having been occupied continuously by Indians for thousands of years prior to A.D. 1800. Archaeologists have dug down through layer after layer of debris to one of about 2000 B.C. that contains stone mortars for grinding wild seeds. And at the other end of the continent, in Boston, a deep excavation for a skyscraper in the Back Bay uncovered an elaborately woven fish weir, which has been carbon-dated at about 2000 B.C. These two finds indicate that the primitive American was getting on, but very slowly. His great burst of material progress came not earlier than 500 B.C., even in Guatemala.

Very old human remains are rare in America because the primitive Indian (it is conjectured) exposed his dead on raised platforms, so that they disintegrated. The oldest hitherto found in America are those of the hunter folk who made the spear points, but not enough of these have as yet been discovered to establish a definite pattern. The subject is complicated by jokers who like to tease scientists by pretended finds of "cave men" in the bowels of the earth.[1]

Some of the ancient human remains that are generally accepted as genuine are: (1) The "Tepexpan man," a skeleton found in the Valley of Mexico in 1949 under an ancient lake bed and in a stratum with mammoth bones. Both geological and carbon datings of a nearby peat sample yield dates between 9000 and 10,000 B.C. The man, about sixty years old, showed no markedly primitive features, so that some scientists think that he was just another Indian of the Aztec period who happened to be buried very deep. (2) The "Midland man," a female skull and fragments of human bones with numerous spear points, a hearth, and bones of extinct species of antelope, camel, bison, and mammoth, discovered in 1953–54 at the bottom of a sand blowout near Midland, Texas. The bones are those of a woman about thirty years old, and there is nothing about them to suggest that her race was different from that of the American Indian. By using the latest uranium isotope method of dating, it seems that this woman was buried at some time between 13,000 and 17,000 B.C. She is America's oldest inhabitant, so far. (3) The "Minnesota man," the remains of a fifteen-year-old girl who fell or was pushed into the glacial Lake Pelican, Minnesota, discovered in 1931. The teeth and jaws of this young lady were of such exceptional size as to encourage the belief that here, at last, was a pre-Indian; but a careful examination of the remains by her discoverer, Professor A. E. Jenks, proves that her buck teeth are definitely Mongoloid, similar to those of modern Eskimo girls. With Miss Minnesota were found an elk-antler dagger which was probably the instrument of her death, and a small conch shell from the Gulf of Mexico, evidently the poor girl's jewelry. No carbon dating was possible, but the geographical stratum in which she was found points to a maximum age of 11,000 years.

On the basis of these few finds—a fraction of one per cent of our picture puzzle of early man in America—one may make the following tentative conclusions:

(1) At an era prior to 10,000 B.C., people of a Mongoloid type began crossing the Bering Strait from Asia to America,

[1] The "Calaveras skull" from California and the "Piltdown man" of England are noted examples of these fakes.

and after many vicissitudes spread throughout the length and breadth of the continent, reaching Patagonia by 8000 B.C.

(2) These people were racially akin to the American Indians whom Europeans later encountered, but not necessarily their ancestors. Our Indians may have come later by the same or other routes, they may have exterminated the primitive folk or assimilated them, or driven them into undesirable corners.

(3) The first comers subsisted by hunting big game, which they killed by means of spears tipped with flaked-flint or other hard stone points. Pelts of bison and other now extinct animals were dressed with stone scrapers and used for clothing and shelter, although caves were the preferred homes. These people supplemented their diet with nuts and wild seeds and, presumably, with fish, but did not plant corn or other seeds or keep domestic animals other than the dog. Ignorant of the use of metal, they correspond, roughly, to early Stone Age man in Europe.

Thus, our knowledge of man in America, and the appearance and habits of these first Americans, is recent, fragmentary, and subject to controversy. We are just beginning to let a little dim light down that bottomless well.

2. *The Indians' America*

Coming from the study of these primitive Americans to the Indians whom the first Europeans met is like stepping out of darkness into a blaze of brilliant light. For the Indians are still with us, in North, Central, and South America; their society and folklore have been studied for over four hundred years, and the results have been incorporated in thousands of volumes.

Yet, even now we cannot write "The History of America before 1492," because history presupposes a more or less continuous and dated story. Even the most advanced Indians, those in Mexico and Peru, could not write, and recorded nothing of their past except remembered myths. In that respect they were like the earliest Greeks before Hellas burst into radiant life. They knew little and cared less whence or when they came. The most that the first Europeans who questioned them could ascertain was a few leading events of a century or two back.

It challenges our imagination to re-create this unrecorded gulf of American history between the passing of the primitive hunter folk and the rise of civilized empires in Mexico, Peru, and Colombia, and the high development of the Pueblos in the southwestern United States. Most archaeologists believe

that the hunting culture of the Folsom points lasted from the
first crossing to somewhere between 500 B.C. and A.D. 500.
Within that millennium, "progress" hit the inhabitants of
America. They learned agriculture, basketry, and pottery; in
some regions they began to weave cotton and other fibers, to
build with stone, and to smelt copper with gold. The entire
race moved upward, but some groups moved much faster than
others. Those that went furthest were the Maya of Central
America, the Inca of Peru, the Chibcha of Colombia, and
the Aztec of central Mexico.

Out of the silence of the centuries, archaeologists are attempting to reconstruct the complicated Maya Empire which
was already falling apart when the first Spaniards reached
these shores. But the glistening white pyramids that rise out
of the tangled jungles of Yucatán, the ornate palaces of the
kings, the great stone courts for a game of ball that was once
played from the West Indies to Paraguay, the temples of fire
and human sacrifice, the massive walls covered with reliefs
of strange human figures, repulsive serpents, and the magnifi-
cently plumed Quetzal bird—these, although recovered physically by archaeology, still guard the secrets of that amazing
people.

Over 800 sites of Mayan cities have been discovered, but no
more than a dozen have been carefully excavated, and even
in the four that have received the most attention—Piedras
Negras, Uxmál, Copán, and Chichén Itzá—only some of the
monuments have been cleared of jungle growth. Sequences
of picture carvings, which conveyed something to the Maya as
hieroglyphics did to the ancient Egyptians, have never been
deciphered. But their carved calendar glyphs have been solved
and these afford us a few dates to the pre-Columbian history
of Mexico. The starting date of their calendar, which was
more accurate than the Julian calendar which English-speaking lands used until 1752, corresponded to 613 B.C. in our
reckoning. The Maya empire began in Guatemala, whose
stone-built cities were completely abandoned in favor of new
homes in Yucatán. There Mayan civilization reached its height
around A.D. 1100. About a century later a warrior tribe from
the north called Toltec, traditionally led by a remarkable king
named Quetzalcoatl, conquered most of the Maya and absorbed their culture, much as the Romans did that of the
Greeks. The Toltec empire fell before the onslaught of a new
warrior race from the north, the Aztec, who reached Mexico
City about A.D. 1325 and founded an empire, whose last ruler,
Montezuma II, was overthrown by Hernando Cortés. We can
date the Maya temples from their stone calendars, but we

know nothing of what happened in the Maya cities; not even the names of their prophets, priests, and kings.

In South America, other high and complex civilizations were attained by the Chibcha of the Colombian highlands, and the Inca of Peru. Yet the most striking achievements of the Indians, north and south. were in agriculture. Maize, which our European forebears called "Indian corn," they probably developed from a wild grass of the Mexican highlands. Little pod-like ears of it have been found in caves in New Mexico with objects that are at least 2000 years old. The white potato is derived from a wild tuber that grew in Peru. The cacao bean was cultivated to make chocolate as a drink and a confection, and the Indians flavored it with vanilla. Tobacco, an aromatic wild herb, was planted by the Indians and esteemed for its narcotic effects; and tobacco spread throughout the world faster than any religion. Quinine they also discovered and used as a febrifuge. Many varieties of beans and tomatoes were cultivated, cordage was twisted from sisal and henequen fiber, the wild caoutchouc tree was tapped for latex from which the Indians made rubber balls for their games, and even waterproof shoes and clothing. Indian organic chemists learned how to leach poison out of cassava so that they could cover their arrowheads with the deadly *curare* and use the flour to bake bread.

Through tens of thousands of years, successive migrations and intertribal wars raged over the surface of the Americas; empires rose and fell, arts and skills were developed, with no discernible trace of outside influence. But the Indians were never united. As among Melanesians in the interior of New Guinea today, adjoining villages spoke different languages and frequently warred with one another. A few groups of the Indians—the Iroquois confederacy in northeastern United States and the empires of Mexico, Peru, and Colombia—evolved a political organization; but the rest did not grow beyond tribal units. There is evidence of trade passing from north to south or vice versa—the products of a good pipestone quarry might be carried over 1000 miles; but in general each tribe, occupying an area covering only a few hundred square miles at most, lived in a state of permanent or intermittent hostility with its neighbors. The Indians of the same region or language group did not even have a common name for themselves. Each tribe called itself something like "We, the People," and referred to its neighbors by a word that meant "the Barbarians," "Sons of She-Dog," or something equally insulting.

Thus Europeans could impinge here and there on the New

World without arousing any general hostility. On the contrary, they were usually welcomed as allies against a nearby enemy. Firearms, little used by the first Europeans, were not responsible for their conquest of the Indians; the natives fell victims to their own disunity and primeval isolation. The principle of union, which in North America has created one of the strongest nations in modern history, was almost unknown to them. Hiawatha, a Mohawk chief who flourished around A.D. 1570 (not to be confused with Longfellow's hero), created the Iroquois League of the Five Nations; but he is an almost unique figure. Some of the most advanced tribes in North America at the period of European discovery were those of the Northwest Coast, extending from Alaska into Oregon. Their economy was based on salmon and other fish, which they learned to preserve by smoking, so that everyone had plenty to eat the year round and an abundance of leisure. The Northwest Coast Indians wove baskets so close that water and food could be boiled in them by using hot stones, built great dugout canoes, and ornamented their dwellings with carved genealogical trees, the totem poles, which told every passerby who you were and from whom descended. These Indians accumulated inherited property, and were such keen traders as to be more than a match for the first white men who came their way. Strangely enough, their culture did not extend into California, where numerous small tribes, contemptuously called "Diggers" by outsiders, lived until very recently on small game and acorn-meal bread.

In the area north of Mexico, only in New Mexico and Arizona can any long historical sequence be given to Indian life. Here a hunting nation which knew the rudiments of agriculture settled somewhere about the beginning of the Christian era. They built adobe-walled towns with apartment-house dwellings, community courts, and buildings where religious dances were held and other ceremonies practiced. These pueblos (which is merely the Spanish word for "towns") were so defensible that succeeding waves of Indian conquerors passed them by, and they have been less molested by Spaniards and Americans than other North American Indians. Today the Pueblo Indians, as we call them, afford the best example in the United States of a well-rooted Indian culture. With a tree-ring method of dating, it has been possible to establish a sequence of basket weaving and pottery for them, in different styles, from the first centuries of the Christian era to the present. In the 1300 years that elapsed between A.D. 217 (year of the oldest Pueblo roofbeam that can be dated) and 1540, when the Spaniards burst into this region, there gradually grew up what archaeologists called the Anasazi culture—from a Navajo word meaning "the old people"—and this culture is divided into six consecutive periods. In the oldest, that of the Basket Makers, the people, who lived in caves or round adobe huts, wove baskets in which they stored wild seeds and little nubbin-like ears of corn which they cultivated with a digging stick. They kept dogs and possibly turkeys, hunted with flint-headed spears, smoked tobacco in a pipe shaped like a cigar-holder, and went naked except for sandals and furs. Owing to the dry climate, and a custom of burying their dead in dry caves, many human remains of these people have been found.

In their next or second stage, the Basket Makers learned to make pottery, as Mexican Indians had done earlier; and this art spread throughout America. The proof that it did not come from Asia is that American Indians never used the potter's wheel, which the Old World possessed thousands of years earlier. The second Basket Maker people wove crude fabrics from plant fibers, the women adorned themselves with bracelets of shell, seed, and turquoise beads. The bow and arrow, another independent invention of the Indians which had earlier been adopted in the Old World, replaced the spear.

The third Pueblo period, from about A.D. 1050 to 1500, curiously corresponds to the "glorious thirteenth century" in Europe. It was the golden age of the Anasazi culture, that of the best cliff houses, great masonry-walled communal dwellings built in the open, with terraced setbacks like modernist skyscrapers, and big *kivas* like built-in drums, where the priests danced and produced awe-inspiring burps and booms. The close-woven basketry and decorated black-on-white pottery of this period are both remarkable. After 1300 the area occupied by the Pueblo civilization was seriously reduced by drought, arroyo erosion, and invasion; the people were forced into larger pueblos where there was a good supply of water, and their arts, ritual, and organization expanded. These were the ancestors of the Zuni, Hopi, Tewa, and Kere nations of today. Navajo and Apache of the Athabascan language stock moved in during the sixteenth century and absorbed the Anasazi culture, which the Navajo still maintain. These people have been very tenacious of their way of life so that nowadays at Acoma, Walpi, Orabi, Laguna, Taos, and other modern pueblos, one can observe Indians living very much as they did before the Europeans arrived.

Of the Indian history of North America east of the Rockies, even less is known because the Indians there did not stay put, like those of the pueblos. Whence came the "Mound Builders," as the older Indians of the Ohio and Upper Mississippi valleys are popularly called, we do not know. Certainly they did not arrive there until about the beginning of the Christian era. They traded with other Indians, replaced the pointed sticks with which the Anasazi tilled the earth by hoes of stone and shell; carved elaborate stone tobacco pipes into realistic pictures of birds and fish, and painted their bodies with red ochre, of which a plentiful supply is often found in their graves. They made elaborate ornaments out of shell, bone, and copper that they obtained from the Lake Superior deposits. Mound Builders were the best metal workers north of Central America before the European discovery, and even had a musical instrument—pan-pipes of bone and copper. These disappeared when they disappeared, along with the tunes that a thousand years ago resounded through the oak groves of our Middle West. Above all, these people recorded themselves by gigantic earthen mounds, often built in shapes of serpents and birds. The Cahokia Mound at East St. Louis is a hundred feet high and covers sixteen acres. Within these mounds the Indians buried their dead almost as elaborately as the ancient Egyptians did, and the contents of their tombs tell us how they lived.

At the time the first Europeans arrived, the Indians of the Great Plains between the Rocky Mountains and the forested areas bordering on the Mississippi lived partly by corn culture but mostly by hunting the buffalo on foot with bow and arrow. Although Europeans regarded all Indians as nomads (a convenient excuse for denying them the land they occupied), only the Plains Indians really were nomadic. Even they did not become so until about A.D. 1550, when they began to break wild mustangs, offspring of European horses turned loose by the Spaniards. Use of the horse gave the men mobility in pursuit of the buffalo herds, while women followed with children and baggage on *travois*, earth-trailing shafts attached to big dogs or old horses; or, in winter, on toboggans, another Indian invention.

The Algonquian language group included the Abnaki of Maine and Nova Scotia, all tribes of southern New England, the Delaware and Powhatan of the Middle states and Virginia, the Sauk and Fox, Kickapoo, Pottawatomi, and Blackfoot in the Middle West. This complex of tribes, semi-sedentary and agricultural, we know fairly well from the observations of the English and French with whom they made their first European contacts. They cultivated beans, pumpkins, tobacco, and maize which, on many occasions, saved English colonists from starvation. The Algonquin, living sociably and filthily in long bark-covered communal houses, was an excellent fisherman and hunter. He invented a light and efficient small boat, the birch-bark canoe, and the snowshoe, hunted deer and moose for their meat and skins, and trapped beaver for their fur, of which the womenfolk made smart jackets. The men went almost naked, even in winter, except for short trousers and moccasins of deerskin. These tribes produced some great and noble characters: Powhatan, Massasoit, King Philip, Tammany, Pontiac, Tecumseh, and Keokuk. The Algonquin were susceptible to Christianity and assimilated European culture better than most Indians, although some of the chiefs we have named tried to unite their people against the English and perished in the attempt.

The Five Nations (Mohawk, Cayuga, Oneida, Onondaga, and Seneca) of the Iroquois confederacy had the reputation of being the toughest fighters in North America; and they had to be, to hold their own against the Algonquin. In 1600, when first seen by Europeans, they occupied the territory from Lake Champlain to the Genesee river, and from the Adirondack Mountains to central Pennsylvania. Hard pressed when the Europeans arrived, the Iroquois survived, and even extended their dominion, partly owing to Hiawatha's league, which prevented war among themselves, and later through alliance with the Dutch and English. Their folkways were similar to those of the Algonquin. Among their famous leaders were Hendrick, Cornplanter, Red Jacket, Brant, and Logan. The Tuscarora, who in 1720 moved north and became the Sixth Nation, and the southern Cherokee, were also of Iroquoian stock. The Cherokee produced one of the greatest of American Indians, Sequoya, who invented an alphabet for his people and vitally advanced their culture.

In southeastern United States the Muskhogean stock, which included the Apalachee, Chickasaw, Choctaw, Creek, Natchez, and Seminole nations, was regarded by Europeans of the colonial era as the elite of North American Indians. They had an elaborate system of castes, from the "Suns" down to the "Stinkards," who were not allowed to intermarry. All Muskhogean tribes were planters of maize, which they accented with the annual "busk," or green corn festival; and they were expert potters, weavers, and curers of deerskin for clothing. They quickly learned from Europeans to plant orchards and keep cattle. Like the Cherokee, they for the most part were forcibly removed to Oklahoma over a century ago.

We know nothing of the development of the many and complex Indian languages before the curious Europeans tried to transpose the sounds to their own languages and write them in their own letters. The language stocks with which Europeans first came in contact in North America were those of the Pueblos (basically akin to Aztec), the Algonquian, Iroquoian, and Muskhogean. Algonquian dialects, differing no more than French from Spanish, were spoken as far north as Hudson Bay, west to the Rockies, and south to the Carolinas; but there was no mutual knowledge or connection between the widely separated tribes who spoke them. Not one of these Indian tongues has any connection with a known European or Asiatic language.

Not all Indians lived in a continual state of intertribal war, but war was part of the social pattern. Bringing back scalps was equivalent to a high school certificate for the young braves; if you didn't do it you were a despised underdog. Any Indian group that tried to shift its dominant values from war to peace was doomed to extinction by another. That is probably what happened to the Mound Builders, whose burial objects display ornaments and gadgets rather than weapons; and it is known to have happened to the Huron in Canada.

On the negative side it was the Indians' lack of union, and on the positive side it was European sea power, which enabled white men to overrun the New World. Once a European established a beachhead, he had a bridge of ships bringing supplies and reinforcements from the Old World. An isolated garrison like Columbus's at Navidad, or Raleigh's on Roanoke Island, might be wiped out; but this was no longer the eleventh century, when the Norsemen abandoned their colony because the natives were too much for them. The European invaders of the sixteenth and seventeenth centuries had the means and the determination to keep coming. The Indian was incapable of bringing up anything better than local defense forces to counterattack. Time and again he tried, but almost always he failed. Only in the remote fastnesses of the Andes and Amazonia, where Europeans have never penetrated, and in the Sierra Nevada de Santa Marta and the Isthmus of Panama, where the Cuna-Cuna managed to protect themselves, have the Indians succeeded in keeping their civilization intact. If the European discovery had been delayed for a century or two, it is possible that the Aztec in Mexico or the Iroquois in North America would have established strong native states capable of adopting European war tactics and maintaining their independence to this day, as Japan kept her independence from China.

The population of the Americas in 1500 is largely a matter of conjecture, aided by a few fragmentary estimates by early Europeans. The latest scholarly estimates of Indian population in the present area of Canada and the United States vary from 900,000 to 1,500,000; of Mexico, 3 to 4.5 million; of Central and South America and the West Indies, 4.5 to 10 million. The Indian population of the United States and Canada in 1960—counting only those who are purebloods or consider themselves Indians—was not far short of the lowest estimate of 1500; a remarkable recovery, considering the stresses to which that race has been subjected.

There is no reason to regard the North American Indian as an inferior race. Backward in many respects he was, but he has proved to have every potentiality common to other human beings. Americans of European stock, from Bishop Las Casas to Oliver La Farge, who have taken the trouble to live with the Indians and understand their ways, find them inferior to none, and superior to many in firmness and integrity of character. They were far more "rugged" than any of the Europeans who claimed to be individualists; and in contrast to the Negro, who adopted the culture of each European race that enslaved him, the Indian has firmly resisted four centuries of intense European pressure.

As children of nature who "take no thought for the morrow," and give their last bit of bread to an unknown guest, the Indians follow the New Testament better than many who profess and call themselves Christians. The names they gave to our lakes and rivers are still on the map, as are those of states like Utah, Arkansas, and Massachusetts, and cities like Keokuk and Chicago. They have mated successfully with people of European stock; it has become something of distinction in the United States to claim Indian ancestry. One President of the United States (Coolidge) and one Vice President (Curtis) had Indian blood and were proud of it.

In peace as in war the Indians have had a profound effect on later comers to America. Our culture has been enriched by their contribution. Our character is very different from what it would have been if this continent had been uninhabited when the Europeans arrived. It was a good thing for our forebears that they had to fight their way into the New World; it will be a sorry day for their descendants if they become too civilized to defend themselves. As the Algonquian warrior of old drank the blood of his fallen enemy in order to absorb his courage, so the people of America may thank the brave redskins who made their ancestors pay dear for the mastery of a continent.

ANCIENT NAVAJO WAR CHANT

II

The European Discovery of America

1. *The Heritage of Classical Antiquity*

WE NOW REACH THE FASCINATING SUBJECT of the European discovery of America. Who was the first "white man" to set foot on these shores? Where did he step off? How long did he stay? There is no reasonable doubt that Christopher Columbus made the *effective* discovery, from which all American history stems. But was Columbus really the first? And what advances, scientific or otherwise, made his voyage possible?

To answer the last question first, the 1492 discovery was the culmination of two or three centuries of maritime exploration, all based upon geographical knowledge and theory left by the ancients. A Greek named Pytheas made furthest north prior to the Christian era. In the fourth century B.C. he sailed to a point where the night lasted only two hours in the summer, and reported an island six days' sail north of Britain, where the sun shone at midnight, which he called Thule. We do not know what island he meant, but his narrative was so widely read that *Ultima Thule* became the designation for any far-off, never-never land. That is why the Danish explorer Knud Rasmussen in 1909 named his northernmost base in Greenland, Thule.

Homer and Herodotus regarded the world as a flat disc edged by the ocean, but the Pythagorean school of philosophers in the sixth century B.C. advanced a spherical theory. Aristotle took it up, and Claudius Ptolemy, a Greek geographer who lived at Alexandria in the second century of the Christian era proved it by pointing out that the shadow of the earth on the moon during an eclipse is always round, and that you can see the masts of ships at sea when their hulls are below the horizon, or the mountain tops of islands before you can see their bases. To these proofs the medieval theologians added the argument that since the sphere is the most perfect form, God must have made the world that way. The spherical globe was taught to every lad who attended a medieval university. Columbus never had to argue for it. No doubt the uneducated majority, and people who lived on flat plains far from the sea, continued to think of the earth as flat; but so do some people even today. There is still in existence a flat-earth fraternity, founded by the late Wilbur G. Voliva of Zion, Illinois.

Although a spherical world was assumed, nobody cared how big it was until Alexander the Great became master of a large part of the ancient world. Close figuring was required to march troops from Greece to India, or to send a fleet from Suez to Ceylon. Accurate maps and charts were necessary, roads had to be laid out, ocean trade routes established. So Alexander and his successors called on the scientists. A school of geography was set up at Alexandria; Hipparchas, who flourished there about 150 B.C., was the first to divide the globe into 360 degrees and to use the device of latitude and longitude in order to give co-ordinates of every place. Even earlier, Eratosthenes made a successful effort to measure the length of a degree, and so figure the size of the earth. His estimate of the circumference of the earth was nearly correct—21,420 miles instead of 24,975. Ptolemy, however, made a new set of calculations which allowed a shorter degree and estimated the world to be only about five-sevenths its true size. That was a fortunate error, because it encouraged Columbus to sail. Ptolemy's work, with the maps that accompanied it, was the geographical bible of the Renaissance and remained the basis of all geography for a century after Columbus. Strabo, a Greek geographer, wrote about A.D. 50, "Those who have returned from an attempt to circumnavigate the earth do not say they have been prevented from continuing their voyage by any opposing continent, for the sea remained perfectly open, but through want of resolution and the scarcity of provision." They were obviously defeated by the lack of really seagoing sailing vessels. Sail, in the ancient world, was an auxiliary to oar-power, and the row galleys that made both short and long voyages had to land every few days to replenish food and water for their big crews. When the Egyptian

Pharaoh Necho, around 600 B.C., sent Phoenician galleys to circumnavigate Africa, they had to stop over twice to sow and reap grain, and it took three years to complete the voyage.

By the second or third century A.D. the ancient world had lost its zest for discovery, and geographical knowledge made no advance for a thousand years.

2. Irish and Norse Discoveries

On any globe or map of the northern polar region you will note a series of island stepping-stones from Europe to America, parallel to those from East Asia to Alaska. These stepping-stones are the Shetland and Faroe Islands, Iceland, Greenland, and Baffin Land. The longest gap measures only 250 miles across; but, for small boats, these were formidable crossings over tempestuous northern waters, far more difficult than the short hops across the Bering Strait that the ancestors of the American Indians must have made. By this short route Norsemen discovered the New World about the year 1000, and an unknown Irishman probably did so even earlier.

It is an historical fact that Irishmen discovered and settled Iceland when it was empty of human life, and that Norsemen expelled them about A.D. 850. The same sagas which describe the Norse discoveries call certain lands west of Greenland, "White Man's Land," or "Ireland the Great," and add a few interesting details. An Icelander named Bjorn put to sea with a northeast wind one day in the tenth century, and never returned. Years later, Gudlief Gudlangson, driven west by a gale, landed in a country where white people rushed down to the beach and would have killed him but for their leader, whom Gudlief recognized as Bjorn, who told him that these people were rough Irish and he had better get out, which he did. The saga of Eric the Red states that natives encountered on the continent told of white people living far off who "wore white garments and yelled loudly, and carried poles before them to which rags were attached." Just what an Irish religious procession would have looked like to Indians! But if Irishmen did reach America in the ninth or tenth century, they never returned, and left no trace. Probably there were too few to contend with the natives. Some day, perchance, authentic Irish relics will be found in northeastern Canada; but until that time comes we have only these elusive stories of an Irish colony glimpsed vaguely through northern mists.

The Norse discovery of America rests on a sound basis of documentary evidence, supported by extensive ruins and remains of their colony in Greenland, and now on the American continent. These Norsemen, bold adventurers, seafarers, and colonizers, left a permanent stamp on the institutions and the architecture of England, Normandy, and Sicily. For them, as later for the Portuguese and English, the one way to wealth and independence was to follow the sea. For raiding they used the Viking warships, but for trading, the stubby, one-masted vessel some 40 to 60 feet long, called *knarr*. In the knarr they made long voyages without knowledge of the compass.

Greenland was discovered and colonized from Iceland by Eric the Red about 985 A.D. He founded two settlements on the west coast; and as the climate was warmer then than of late, cattle could be raised and some food crops grown. These Norse settlements lasted for several centuries. Sixteen churches were built, and even a small stone cathedral for the bishop. Danish excavations have uncovered the ruins of this church, of hundreds of houses, and bodies of small undernourished Europeans buried deep and clothed in fashions of the thirteenth to fourteenth century. A letter of Pope Alexander VI at the time of Columbus states that the Vatican had received no word from Greenland for some eighty years. What had happened? It seems probable that around A.D. 1400 the climate became so severe that Norwegian and Icelandic traders found voyages thither no longer profitable, and that the Norsemen in Greenland died off or were killed by the Eskimo.

Now for Vinland. Two Icelandic sagas tell how Leif the Lucky, Eric's son, on a visit to Norway in the year 1000, was ordered by King Olaf to bring Christianity to Greenland; how he missed Greenland in a storm and made a land where wild grapes and self-sown wheat grew, which he named Vinland the Good. According to one saga, he sought out Vinland after it had been discovered by Biarni Heriulfson, built huts and a large house, and there spent a winter before sailing back to his father's settlement in Greenland. The Eric family seems to have brooded over Vinland without doing anything about it; but a few years later Thorfinn Karlsefni, a Greenland trader, attempted to establish a colony there. Sailing in his knarr with wife Gudrid, 20 or 30 people and a few cattle, he crossed Davis Strait to Labrador and coasted until he found Leif Ericsson's huts. The party landed there and passed two winters which were mild enough for cattle to live outdoors. The Norsemen were disappointed at finding no wild grapes, and their relations with the natives, whom they called *skrellings* (dwarfs), were unfriendly. Karlsefni decided that the country was too dangerous, embarked his people, and sailed back to Greenland.

For over a century, Americans and Scandinavians have been trying to locate Leif's Vinland. If Leif really did find wild grapes, his Vinland could have been no further north than Nova Scotia. His topographical description fits that of northern Newfoundland better than of any other region. In 1962 the Norwegian archaeologist Helge Ingstad excavated a site at L'Anse aux Meadows facing the Strait of Belle Isle which, by carbon dating of half-burnt timbers, must have been constructed around the year 1000. There he has found the ruins of Leif's house, in design similar to the Norse houses in Greenland, and authentic Norse artifacts. All other alleged Norse relics hitherto "discovered" were either built centuries later, such as the stone tower at Newport, or are forgeries such as the "Kensington Rune Stone" and the "Beardmore Weapons," inscribed or planted by practical jokers.

If Europe had been ready for expansion in the eleventh century, and interested in finding new regions, the Norse discovery might have led to something; but Europe was not ready, and nothing that the Norsemen found suggested that Vinland was worth following up. Fish, fir trees, and wild grapes were not worth fighting natives to get. Nor did anyone suspect that Greenland and Vinland were keys to a New World. Greenland appears on several early maps both before and after 1500 as a promontory of Europe or Asia curving west over Iceland. Vinland is on no pre-Columbian map, unless the Yale Vinland Map is genuine. And nothing in the saga descriptions of Vinland could have attracted later European explorers, who were looking for gold, gems, and spices.

The Norse occupation of the American continent was ephemeral. It made no change in the balance of nature and left no trace on native folklore. Yet there is a fascination about it to this day. Across the centuries one can spare a thought for the Greenlanders, struggling against starvation in a frigid climate becoming colder, beset by bands of surly and belligerent Eskimo. During the short summer the Norsemen stare out to sea, hoping and praying for the ship that never comes. Then the winter closes in; and, knowing that no ship can get through until next spring, they do their best to survive. One by one they drop off, until none are left.

3. Genoese and Portuguese

We now shift our attention to the Mediterranean. Here was the cradle of the civilization which eventually spread into the New World; here were born and trained the seamen who brought Europe into Africa, America, and the Far East.

During the Dark Ages the Mediterranean nations were weak and poor, owing in great part to the depredations of Arab pirates on the ports of the decrepit Roman Empire. But in the eleventh century the Christian nations began pushing the "Moors," as they called the Arabs, out of Spain and Portugal, and conducting crusades to recover the Holy Land from the infidel. The crusaders' need of water transportation stimulated commerce and shipbuilding in Italian seaports and brought their people into contact with the Middle East. Genoa, the birthplace of Columbus, set up trading posts in the Aegean isle of Chios and on the shores of the Black Sea. The long overland journey of Marco Polo to Peking, and his stories told after his return, gave the late medieval world its first direct knowledge of the fabulously wealthy empire of China, and indirect knowledge of an even richer island that Marco called *Cipangu*—Japan. All this suggested that Europeans attempt to tap that wealth by sea, instead of by long and expensive camel caravans across Asia.

So far as we know, the first to make the attempt were the Vivaldi brothers of Genoa. In 1291 they led an expedition of two galleys along the West African coast; and their object, according to a contemporary chronicle, was "to reach India by an ocean route." But the Vivaldi never returned. Moslem merchants later reported that one of their ships was wrecked on the African coast and that the other landed, but its crew was enslaved.

The fourteenth century was a period of political degeneracy, civil strife, and dissension, leaving slight scope for maritime energy. But in the next century a distinct advance was made by the Portuguese. Portugal, the ancient Lusitania, was a small country but she had the right situation for dominating the Western Ocean, "Where endeth land and where beginneth sea," as Luis de Camoëns wrote. Portugal did more to enlarge the boundaries of the known world and to improve methods of navigation than all other nations of Europe combined. Today the mark of her navigators is written on the map of the world in places so remote as Cape Race, the Azores, Brazil, Angola, Mozambique, Timor, and Macao.

An able royal family, the house of Aviz, ruled Portugal in this era. A son of that house, Prince Henry the Navigator, invited Jewish, Moslem, and Christian mapmakers and astronomers to Cape St. Vincent, which he made a center for exploration "through all the watery roads." Between 1451 and 1470 his captains discovered all eight islands of the Azores, and colonized most of them. Corvo, remotest of the group, is only 1054 nautical miles from Cape Race, Newfoundland.

Why, then, did it not become a stepping-stone to America? Largely because of the westerly winds, which prevented several Portuguese mariners, who set forth from the Azores in hope of finding more and bigger islands out in the ocean, from sailing far enough to discover anything. There was a persistent legend of an island called Antilia, where Portuguese Christians, thrown out by the Moors in the eighth century, had settled, much as the Irish expelled from Iceland were said to have gone to America. But Antilia was never found, though it has left its mark on the map of America in the name "The Antilles."

Portuguese explorations of Africa opened to commerce the entire west coast and a part of the east coast of that continent. For such voyages the design of seagoing sailing ships had to be improved so that they could beat back against prevailing northerly winds; and navigation by the sun and stars had to be invented so that a sailor could know where he was. The Portuguese invented the caravel, a sharp-built vessel rigged with lateen sails and so designed that she could sail almost as close to the wind as a modern racing yacht. These were the first European sailing vessels to make progress against the wind, necessary if you were to make long voyages over wide stretches of ocean, since you could not always count on fair winds. In addition, the Portuguese developed celestial navigation. They learned how to tell latitude by measuring the height of the sun, or of the North Star, above the horizon; a method of navigation not entirely superseded to this day. The early instruments, however, were so inaccurate on a rolling and pitching ship that the Portuguese took their sights ashore whenever possible; and that helped them to map the African coast.

By the time of Prince Henry's death in 1460, trade in gold, ivory, pepper, and slaves had been opened up with the Gold Coast and Sierra Leone. African exploration was then carried forward by the prince's nephew Alfonso V, and so profitably that Portugal became the envy of Europe. The culmination came when Bartholomew Dias made one of the greatest voyages of all time. He had already been at sea six months in 1487, touching now and again on the West African coast, when he lost sight of land and was driven southeastward by a heavy gale, expecting at any moment to be cast ashore. When the wind moderated and shifted, Dias turned northward, and on 5 February 1488 his lookouts reported land on the *port* bow. Dias then knew that he had rounded the southern end of the African continent. He followed the east coast of Africa for a few days, when his seamen mutinied and he was forced to turn back, leaving the glory of actually reaching India to Vasco da Gama. On the homeward passage Da Gama sighted the promontory which his sovereign named the Cape of Good Hope.

4. Columbus's First Voyage

America was discovered accidentally by a great seaman who was looking for something else; when discovered it was not wanted; and most of the exploration for the next fifty years was done in the hope of getting through or around it. America was named after a man who discovered no part of the New World. History is like that, very chancy.

Toward the close of the fifteenth century the wings of discovery began to brush very close to the shores of America. Portuguese sailors looking for fabled Antilia may have come within a day's sail of Newfoundland. Doubtless the New World would eventually have been discovered as men became more venturesome; for instance, a Portuguese navigator named Cabral accidentally raised the coast of Brazil in 1500 when on a voyage to India. But that does not detract from the glory of Columbus, whose discovery really opened America to Europe. Most Europeans at that time were not looking for a New World, but a new way to get at the oldest part of the Old World—the Indies. By that word they meant all Asia east of Suez, together with Oriental islands such as Sumatra and Japan, of which Marco Polo had brought home tall tales. An ocean route was sought to countries of fabulous wealth in the hope of tapping them directly instead of paying tribute to a horde of caravan conductors, camel jockeys, junk sailors, Oriental brigands, and miscellaneous middlemen. But even the most practical promoters looked for something more; they hoped to convert the heathen to Christianity, whose area had been contracting since the rise of Islam. First the Arabs overran North Africa and most of Spain; now the Turks had conquered the Byzantine empire and were threatening Austria. If Europeans could only get in touch with "Prester John," as they called the Christian emperor of Ethiopia, supposed to live somewhere in the Indies, they might form a Holy League against the Turks and recover the Holy Land.

Bartholomew Dias, as we have seen, returned to Lisbon in 1488 after opening up a sea route to India around Africa. In the receiving line was a sailor destined to even greater fame. Cristoforo Colombo, as he was christened at Genoa in 1451, we know by the latinized form of his name, Christopher Columbus. A sailor since his early years, he had swum ashore

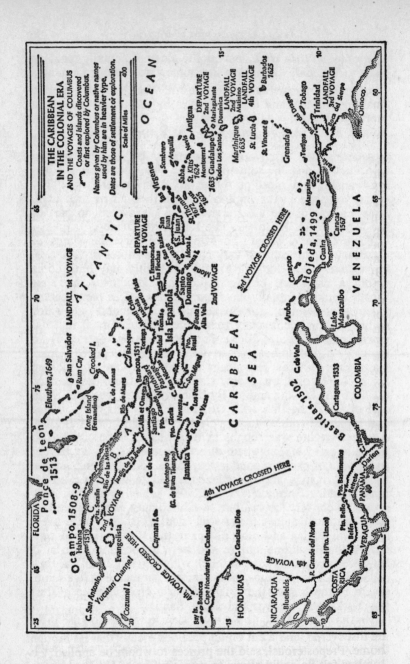

THE CARIBBEAN
IN THE COLONIAL ERA
AND THE VOYAGES OF COLUMBUS
Coasts and Islands discovered
or first explored by Columbus.
Names given by Columbus or native names
used by him are in heavier type.
Dates are those of settlement or exploration.

Scale of Miles
0   200   400

on the Portuguese coast at the age of twenty-six, after his ship had been sunk in a naval battle, and cast his lot with Portugal. In partnership with a brother he conducted a chart-making business and made voyages under the Portuguese flag north to Jan Mayen Land, south to the Gold Coast, and out to the Madeiras and Azores.

For several years Columbus had been promoting a plan for a direct ocean route to the Indies. It was simple enough—to drop down to the Canary Islands and sail due west along lat. 28° N, which according to his best information would hit Japan. Actually, that parallel does run between Japan proper and Okinawa. Since everyone agreed that the world was spherical, nobody doubted that this voyage was theoretically possible, just as nobody today doubts the possibility of landing a man on Mars. Distance was the obstacle, then as now. By air from the Canaries to Japan is about 10,600 miles; but Columbus figured out that it was less than one-fourth of that distance—2400 miles. He not only made the smallest estimate of the size of the globe in modern history; he followed Strabo in declaring that the ocean was relatively narrow and the European-Asiatic continent about twice its actual length. Thus, he calculated that Japan would be about the same distance west of Spain as are Haiti and New York. His critics, and the experts who turned him down in Portugal and Spain, were really better geographers than he; and their attitude was natural enough. For nobody suspected the existence of an American continent to bar the sea route to the Indies; and a voyage of 10,000 miles over an empty ocean, with the same distance to sail back, was more than the seamen of those days could take. The logistics problem alone would have rendered it impracticable even if the wind were fair all the way out and home.

Columbus was not the kind of man to take no for an answer. He was sure he could do it, certain that God meant him to do it; his name meant "Christ Bearer," so he was destined to carry the good tidings to heathen lands. But he also insisted on a proper reward. As a poor boy and a self-made mariner he had been pushed around all his life, and he intended to take no more of that. So he demanded three ships, the hereditary title of Admiral of the Ocean Sea, control of all trade between Spain and whatever Oriental port or island he discovered, and a cut on all precious metals that he brought home. Preposterous!, said the princes to whom he applied. Columbus felt he could afford to wait. But he might have waited until death if the intuition of Queen Isabella had not flown out to meet his supreme self-confidence and irritating conceit.

Early in 1492 it was settled between him and the joint Spanish sovereigns, Ferdinand and Isabella. On 3 August Columbus set sail from Palos in southern Spain in the ship *Santa Maria*, accompanied by two caravels owned and captained by the Pinzón brothers of Palos. All three were manned by local men and boys. He had a letter of introduction from the sovereigns to the "Grand Khan," the supposed title of the Emperor of China, and blank letters in which Columbus could insert the name of any potentate at whose dominions he touched. He had a Latin passport stating, "By these presents we dispatch the noble man Christopher Columbus with three equipped caravels over the Ocean Sea toward the regions of India for certain reasons and purposes." He shipped a learned Jew who knew Arabic, which he hoped would enable him to converse with Orientals who knew no Latin. The more you look at it, the more naïve Columbus's enterprise seems. The only solid thing about it was his faith in God and his mission. And what he asked faithfully he obtained effectually.

Columbus was not so simple as to assume that one could land in Japan or China with ninety sailors and take over the country in the name of Spain. He proposed to set up a trading post colony, the only type of colony that Europe then knew, on some outlying island off the Asiatic coast. He had visited the chief trading post in West Africa, São Jorge da Mina, where nearby black kings welcomed the Portuguese; so why should not the Chinese or Japanese roll out a Persian carpet for an honorable admiral from Spain? Actually, that is what eventually happened in the Philippines. Manila became a Spanish trading post where products of East and West were exchanged.

The most important voyage of discovery in all history was also one of the easiest, outward-bound. Columbus sailed south to the Canary Islands, there topped off with provisions, and departed thence on 6 September 1492. From earlier voyages he knew that in those latitudes his ships would be wafted along by the northeast tradewind, as they were.

After they had been out of sight of land for a full month and had logged over 2700 miles from the Canaries, the sailors threatened to force Columbus to turn back, fearing that they could never get home again. Columbus naturally was not going to be done out of his discovery after coming that far. He spoke cheering words, assured them there were plenty of provisions, appealed to their desire for gold and to their sense of honor; then set his jaw and remarked, "It is useless to complain. I made this voyage to go to the Indies, and shall continue until I find them, with God's help." Signs of land now became frequent. On 12 October 1492 at 2 a.m., a look-out in *Pinta* sighted in the moonlight a limestone cliff on what turned out to be an island in the Bahamas. Columbus named it *San Salvador*, and it is so called today. They drifted for the rest of the night, made sail at dawn, rounded the southern shore, and anchored under the lee of the land. There Columbus and his captains went ashore and in the presence of wondering natives took possession in the name of Ferdinand and Isabella.

San Salvador, the Admiral insisted, was an outpost of "the Indies," so he called the natives Indians. They were Arawaks, gentle and unwarlike, who wove cloth and made pottery; but, to Columbus's vast disappointment, possessed no gold except for a few nose plugs obtained by trade. So, picking up a few Indians as guides—they learned to speak Spanish surprisingly quickly—Columbus sailed through the Bahamas to Cuba, which his pilots, eager to please, led him to believe was the source of gold, and which he therefore assumed to be a part of China. No gold was to be found; but some of Columbus's shipmates, returning from a trip upcountry, discovered something that has created more well-being than gold. They met "many people with a firebrand in the hand, and herbs to drink the smoke thereof, as they are accustomed." These Cuban natives rolled their own cigars, which they called *tobacos*. A walking party, such as the Spaniards encountered, would carry one big cigar with a lighted firebrand; at every halt they "lit up" and everyone took a few puffs and felt refreshed. Cultivation and use of tobacco had already spread all over the Americas—Jacques Cartier at the site of Quebec in 1535 found Indians inhaling the smoke from pipes—and it was not long before Europeans carried Lady Nicotine to the Old World.

Columbus was disappointed at finding no spices of the Orient, such as cloves and cinnamon, but he noted maize and cassava, which have spread world-wide, native cotton, dugout canoes, and the hammock, which European navies soon adopted for their seamen. And at the great island which he named Hispaniola, he found the Indians wearing massive golden ornaments which they made from gold dust panned out of river beds. So, when flagship *Santa Maria* hit a reef on Christmas Eve and became a total loss, Columbus had no trouble getting volunteers to build and man a trading post ashore; everyone wanted first whack at the gold. He named the place *Navidad* (Nativity), and on 16 January 1493 the Admiral in *Niña*, accompanied by *Pinta*, began the homeward passage. In an unusually rough winter, the caravels did well to weather two bad storms and to reach Palos on 15 March 1493.

The momentous discovery had been made; yet neither Columbus nor any member of his company realized it. The Bahamas, Cuba and Hispaniola, to them, were no new world such as we mean by that phrase, but island outposts to Asia. Japan and China were just around the corner.

5. First Colonizing Attempts

Back in Spain, Columbus reported to Ferdinand and Isabella, who confirmed his titles and privileges and promptly organized a second voyage under him, with some 1200 men to colonize Hispaniola. This fleet of seventeen vessels raised the island of Dominica on 3 November 1493 and coasted along the Lesser Antilles, discovering and naming, among others, Guadeloupe, Antigua, Nevis, St. Croix, the Virgin Islands, and Puerto Rico. Thence Columbus sailed along Hispaniola where he met his first setback—the discovery that his Navidad trading post had been wiped out. The Spanish garrison, roaming about Hispaniola in search of more gold and girls, ran afoul of a stout cacique named Caonabó, who killed them and destroyed Navidad.

Columbus abandoned that site and founded a new and more ambitious colony some 75 miles east of it at a place he named Isabela. But as soon as he stepped ashore and exchanged his sea command for that of governor, he got into trouble. Spaniards had signed on for one purpose only, to get gold; but there was none nearby and the Indians brought none in. Columbus intended everybody to live at Isabela and trade only at stated seasons, under license; but he could not prevent the men slipping off to the bush and trading with a gun. The soil was excellent and food crops could be grown in a few weeks; but, as one of the Admiral's friends wrote, nobody would work the land because, as soon as they found gold could not be picked up on the beach, they all "wanted home." The trouble about trading for gold was simply that the natives of Hispaniola had little of it and wanted less. Consumer demand for the cheap trading truck that the Spaniards brought— glass beads, tinkly hawk's bells, and strips of scarlet cloth— was soon satisfied. So, in order to keep his colony going, Columbus was forced to desperate expedients. First, he required a gold tribute from every native, a tribute too great for them to collect with the best will in the world. Next, he divided up the land—with the Indians who lived on it— among the Spanish colonists. In other words, he set up a system of forced labor for private profit. At the same time the smaller islands were raided for more laborers, and Indians who refused to work were either slaughtered or shipped home to be sold as slaves. Within fifty years the natives of Hispaniola, estimated by ethnologists to have numbered around 300,000 in 1492, and those of the Bahamas too, were extinct. Slaves were then imported from Africa to work sugar and cotton plantations and sift the earth for gold.

Columbus still insisted that Hispaniola was in "The Indies," and in the spring of 1494 he explored the south coast of Cuba, hoping to contact Chinese mandarins or Japanese shoguns; but he only met more Arawaks. He turned back before reaching the westerly cape of Cuba, satisfied that it was a promontory of China. Leaving his brother Bartholomew in charge of the colony at Isabela, he returned to Spain, and with difficulty convinced the sovereigns that his discoveries were valuable. They allowed him to fit out a relief expedition, recruited partly among peasants, draftees from the army, day laborers who were paid 14 cents a day, and girls who were paid nothing since they were expected to work their passage and then find husbands. Also, a free pardon was offered to criminals in jail who would spend a year in "The Indies," but not many takers were found. Ferdinand and Isabella gave Columbus three more vessels to make another voyage of discovery, in the hope of tapping the Indies further south. But before that voyage started, England had unveiled another corner of the New World.

6. First Northern Voyages

In the West Country of England the port of Bristol enjoyed a prosperous trade with Iceland and the Azores, and became the principal breeding place for English mariners who did business in great waters. To this thriving city there came to live around 1490 a countryman of Columbus named Giovanni Caboto, whom we call John Cabot. As the man who gave England her title to all North America east of the Rockies and north of Florida, Cabot and his voyages have been the object of intense research. Yet to this day we know very little about them.

King Henry VII of England, first of the House of Tudor, had been offered Columbus's enterprise but turned it down. After hearing the results of the first two voyages, in 1496, he granted authority to John Cabot and his three sons to sail "to all parts, contreys, and seas of the East, of the West, and of the North . . . upon their own proper costs and charges." They are to "seek out, discover and finde whatsoever isles, countreys regions or provinces of the heathen and infidels . . . unknowen to all Christians," raise the English "banners and ensignes," and in return may monopolize the trade. Obviously Cabot's main object, like that of Columbus, was to set up a trading-post colony adjacent to the Indies. According to one who interviewed Cabot, he had been to Mecca in Arabia, on the main caravan route for spices from the Far East to Europe. Since England, at the end of this line, paid the highest prices for spices, it occurred to Cabot to sail west along the high, short latitudes to tap the spiceries of the Indies and undercut the camel caravans.

His expedition was small but bold, braving the high seas and strong westerlies of the North Atlantic in the little ship *Mathew,* with a crew of eighteen men. We have no details of the outward passage, only that it started from Bristol about 20 May 1497, took departure from Dursey Head, Ireland, and on Midsummer Day, 24 June, Cabot made landfall on or about the northeastern promontory of Newfoundland. The Englishmen landed and raised the banner of St. George. They saw not one native, but picked up Indian fishnets as souvenirs and reported a vast store of codfish in those waters. The weather was so warm and pleasant that Cabot was sure he had discovered a northern promontory of Asia, and that on his next voyage he could reach Japan. It was a common delusion of explorers of North America for the next hundred years or more, arriving in the American summer, warmer than that of England or France, that they had found a semi-tropical country. As the wife of an early settler of Massachusetts wrote, after the disillusion of her first New England winter, "When I remember the high commendations some have given of the place, I have thought that they wrote surely in strawberry time." John Cabot reached our shores in strawberry time.

Mathew was back in Bristol on 6 August 1497, having made the ocean passage from "the new isle" (as it was called in the royal records) to Brittany in fifteen days. This indicates that Cabot had only three weeks for exploration, and contemporary records state that he took his departure from the same promontory of northern Newfoundland where he made his landfall. Henry VII gave him a pension of £20 per annum for adding "the new isle" to his dominions. But what lay behind the rockbound coasts of that northern land? Cabot tried to find out in 1498. We know nothing more of this voyage than that he started with five ships but never returned; one returned to Ireland, the other four ships were lost with all hands.

In 1500 an Azorean, a former *lavrador* (farmer) named João Fernandes, joined some other Portuguese and two Englishmen in making a northwesterly voyage from Terceira; and because João the farmer made the landfall, they named the country "Tierra del Lavrador." The Land of the Labrador it is to this day.

Except for a few entries in the English royal accounts of presents given to seamen who brought the king an eagle, a "popinjay" (woodpecker or bluejay?) and "cat of the mountain" from the "New Founde Lande," this is all we know of English exploration in the first era of discovery. To the English of that day, it was a story of failure. No gold, no spices, no Japan; only trees, rocks, and codfish.

But the humble codfish brought northern America into fame. Catholic Europe (and all Europe then was Catholic) consumed enormous quantities of fish, and the best to cure and keep, in the absence of refrigeration, was the firm-flaked cod of northern waters. Portugal had found her passage to the Indies around the Cape of Good Hope, but she could use more fish; and by a treaty with Spain, King Manuel of Portugal claimed all newly discovered lands up to the meridian 1100 nautical miles west of the Cape Verde Islands. Assuming that the English discoveries were really within his bailiwick, he authorized Gaspar Corte Real, an Azorean, to make a voyage of discovery in 1500. That summer Corte Real rediscovered Newfoundland. On a second voyage next year he was lost, but his shipmates brought back Indians as slaves, and Venetian objects which Cabot must have left behind. Shortly after, Portuguese and French fishermen began plying their calling on the Grand Bank and curing their catches ashore. Some twenty place names on Newfoundland today, from Cape Ray to Cape Race, are of Portuguese origin. Fagundes, a Portuguese, was the first to explore the Gulf of St. Lawrence, and the post of governor of Newfoundland remained hereditary in the Corte Real family until the last of that gallant line fell fighting the Moors in 1578.

Long before that, France had picked up the ball of northern dominion. For Portugal, by that time, had a great trading empire in the East to attend to. As a missionary once remarked, "God gave the Portuguese a small country to be born in, but a whole world to die in."

7. Searching for the Strait

Largely to forestall what they feared the Portuguese might do, Ferdinand and Isabella ordered Columbus in 1498 to take a more southerly route than on his two earlier voyages, in the hope of discovering the Asiatic continent. After a sultry but otherwise easy voyage, he made an island on the last day of July which he named Trinidad, and for the first time set foot on the American continent in a harbor of what is now Venezuela, on 5 August 1498. Again he was disappointed in finding only naked Indians, not bejeweled gentlemen of Japan; but here he did find pearls. And from the vast volume of fresh water emptying into the Gulf of Paria he concluded that this was not the Indies which he had sought, but *un otro mundo*, an Other World. By this he meant that it was a land unknown to the ancients. His conception of the South America which he had discovered was that of a land mass tailing off from the Malay Peninsula, much as Indonesia actually does. And if that were so, there must be a strait through it; for Marco Polo had sailed all the way home from eastern China.

So Columbus's fourth and last voyage, in 1502–4, was largely a search for that strait. He sailed from the Canaries to Martinique, then coasted along the chain of islands to Cuba and crossed the Caribbean to what is now Honduras. He spent a very tempestuous winter exploring the coast of Central America to the Gulf of Darien, sailing into almost every navigable river or bay in the hope of finding a passage to India. But he had no luck. After a terrible bout of foul weather, he passed Christmas and New Year's, 1502–3, near the northern entrance to the present Panama Canal; but without any Indian to interpret, he never learned that he was on the narrowest part of the Isthmus. He tried to establish a trading post on the coast of Panama, but was driven off by the local Indians. Two worm-eaten and waterlogged caravels had to be abandoned, and with the other two he just managed to make Jamaica, where he was marooned for a year before being rescued.

Columbus then returned to Spain to die, despised and neglected. In the eyes of the royal court his West Indies had turned out to be useless. He alone of the early discoverers predicted their value for humanity, which is one reason why we honor him. Before he died he could declare, with no exaggeration, "By the Divine Will I have placed under the sovereignty of the King and Queen an Other World, whereby Spain, which was reckoned poor, is to become the richest of all countries."

By a strange comedy of errors, this Other or New World came to be named after a man who never commanded a voyage of discovery. Amerigo Vespucci, the most controversial character in our early history, was a Florentine who settled in Seville, where he ran a ship-chandlery business and helped to fit out Columbus's voyages. It is probable that in 1499 he joined a voyage commanded by Alonso de Hojeda, one of Columbus's captains, along the Pearl Coast to the Gulf of Maracaibo. Later he made three voyages, again as a passenger or junior officer, along the coast of Brazil. In 1504–5 there were printed in Florence what purported to be letters from him about these voyages; they were very chatty and amusing but, except for several spicy items on the manners and customs of the Indians, they might have been based on Columbus's and Hojeda's voyages. Whoever did write or compile these letters intimated that Vespucci was the captain of all four voyages and that the first, in which he (or his editor) claimed that he discovered the continent, took place in 1497, a year before Columbus's. And in Vespucci's mouth is put the significant statement, "These regions we may rightly call *Mundus Novus,* a New World, because our ancestors had no knowledge of them. . . . I have found a continent more densely peopled and abounding in animals than our Europe or Asia or Africa."

It so happened that a young instructor named Waldseemüller at the College of St. Dié in eastern France was then bringing out a fresh edition of Ptolemy, with a new map of the world. Charmed with these printed letters, he wrote in his *Cosmographiae Introductio* (1507), "Since Americus Vespucius has discovered a fourth part of the world, it should be called after him . . . America, since Europe and Asia got their names from women." The idea spread, and by 1530 every European country except Spain and Portugal was calling the New World, America. Yet it was a mistake even to credit Amerigo, or whoever wrote the letters on his alleged voyages, with a new geographical idea. His *Mundus Novus* was the same as Columbus's *otro mundo,* a continental appendage to eastern Asia. Waldseemüller, however, went a step further and joined Columbus's and Cabot's discoveries to those of the Portuguese in Brazil as one continuous continent, with Japan about 600 miles west of the Isthmus of Panama; and on his map the name AMERICA appears at about the site of Uruguay.

To give the Vespucci letters their due, they gave Europe for the first time some conception of the vast extent of South America. But nobody as yet had any knowledge of the Pacific; even Balboa who in 1513 gazed on it "with a wild surmise—silent, upon a peak in Darien," supposed that he was seeing the Indian Ocean. But Magellan took the measure of the vast Pacific.

Ferdinand Magellan, greatest seaman in the world's history, was a thirty-nine-year-old Portuguese who had already sailed near the source of spices, two little islands of Indonesia named Ternate and Tidore. The voyage there and back around the Cape of Good Hope was so long and tempestuous that he conceived the idea of finding a short way through America, and Spain financed him. He discovered the Strait that bears his name, and it took him 38 days to get through it. On 28 November 1520, says the narrative of the voyage, "We debouched from that Strait, engulfing ourselves in the Pacific Sea." By chance the great captain shaped a course that missed every settled island until he reached Guam, fourteen weeks later, with crews so hungry as to have eaten the leather chafing gear on the yards. They then crossed the Philippine Sea and sailed through Surigao Strait, scene of the great naval battle of 25 October 1944. Magellan landed on the island of Limasawa, where on 31 March 1521 there occurred an intensely dramatic encounter. The captain's Malay servant Enrique, whom he had engaged on an earlier voyage to Indonesia, made himself understood by the natives. Magellan proceeded to Cebu, converted the sultan, and on 27 April 1521 was killed at Mactan when attacking the enemies of his new ally. Of his fleet, originally five strong, *Victoria*, under Captain Juan Sebastian de Elcano, sailed home around the world, arriving 8 September 1522, three years after the voyage began, with only eighteen survivors out of 266 who started.

This voyage told Europe for the first time the width of the Pacific, and where the real Indies were situated with reference to the New World. But the search continued for another strait of easier access and navigation than Magellan's.

In the meantime Hispaniola was making good as a colony. It exported about a million dollars' worth of gold in 1512, the high point. Negro slaves were being imported to replace the wretched Indians; cattle raising and sugar planting had begun. Settlers who quarreled with the government moved on. Balboa was one of those, and Juan Ponce de Leon, granted Puerto Rico in 1501 if he could conquer it from the Indians, which he promptly did. Feeling debilitated at the age of fifty-three, Ponce embarked on a voyage in search of the fabled fountain of youth, in the course of which he discovered and named Florida at Eastertide 1513. But the fountain eluded him, and the natives were unfriendly. Spanish settlement of Jamaica began in 1510; of Cuba in 1512.

Such, in briefest outline, is the history of the earliest period of European discovery and colonization. After initial curiosity was satisfied, the New World aroused slight interest. Down to 1516, when Peter Martyr brought out the first attempt at an American history—*Decades of the New World*—there was not a single work that attained the dignity of a book; only a few pamphlets such as Columbus's *Letter* and Vespucci's *Mundus Novus*. For, from the European point of view, America was a disappointment. It blocked the western route to China, Japan, and India; its precious metals appeared to be exhausted; the spices brought home by Columbus had turned out not to be spices, and the only valuable wood found so far in the New World was guiacum, an essence of which was supposed to cure the blight inflicted upon Europe by the West Indians—syphilis. The climate was unhealthy, the native food unwholesome, even some of the fish were poisonous. Spain would have been glad to write off the New World and withdraw, but for the teasing thought that some other country might move in and make something of it.

SALVE REGINA

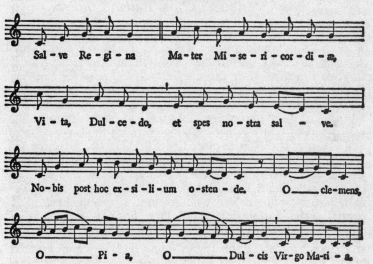

III

=====

The Spanish Century

1492-1580

1. *Spain Conquers Three Indian Empires*

WHAT NATION would put her stamp on the New World? That, we may say, was the greatest question in American history for two centuries after the discovery. We know the answer: Spain stamped America from Cape Horn up to the Rio Grande, and even beyond; but England, entering the contest late, placed the stamp of her language, law, and custom on the major part of North America, which became the United States and Canada; and France placed hers on Quebec. All three did it by colonization, a form of conquest in which a nation takes over a distant territory, thrusts in its own people, and controls or eliminates the native inhabitants. Conquest is as old as human history; but modern colonization, as we understand it, started when Europeans began that amazing expansion of trade and settlement which resulted in world dominion. This process produced lasting results in America, Australia, New Zealand, and South Africa; even in those countries of Asia and Africa which have won their independence since World War II.

We have now witnessed the fall of colonialism, affecting the world almost as deeply as did the fall of the Roman Empire. Even the words "colonial" and "colonialism" have become pejorative. But non-Indian Americans have no reason to join this hue and cry. For colonialism brought the New World into the orbit of Western civilization. Even the concepts of freedom and democracy, which almost every independent American nation, and many others too, have embraced, were imported from Europe. And the more viable of these new nations have set up governments based on the English parliamentary or the American republican system.

One may divide modern colonies into three kinds: the trading-post, the fringe colony (an enlarged beachhead on the edge of the sea), and the all-out settlement colony. The first was what Columbus tried to set up in Hispaniola. But a trading-post colony works only when planted among a realtively advanced people who are used to commerce. The Portuguese had done that among the black kingdoms of West Africa and would do it in Africa and India—where the last Portuguese colony, Goa, was grabbed by Nehru in 1962. The Portuguese never emigrated in large numbers; they merely established garrisons and left the natives alone as long as they did not try to rush the trading post and make off with the goods. But in Brazil, her portion of the New World, Portugal found she had to establish a fringe colony, just as Columbus did in Hispaniola. Both had to expand trading posts to fringes, and eventually to all-out settlements, because the natives of Central and South America were not traders; Europeans had to spread out and settle, in order to produce anything. And it was not long before all Europeans in the New World were importing African slaves to do the heavy work that Indians would not or could not do, and that Europeans were too proud or lazy to do.

The transition of the Spanish empire in America from trading post and fringe to settlement began with the conquest of Mexico in 1519–21. That date is as important as 1492 in American history, since it signaled a complete change of attitude by Europe toward the New World.

In 1519 the governor of Cuba, wishing to establish a trading post on the Mexican coast, sent an expedition of eleven ships, carrying about five hundred Spaniards under thirty-two-year-old Hernando Cortés, to set it up. His conquest of Mexico was one of the most amazing military and diplomatic feats in the world's history. The march from Vera Cruz to the great interior plateau, the audacious capture of Montezuma's lake-rimmed capital, and the defeat of a vast army on the plains of Teotihuacan, completed the ruin of Aztec power and firmly established Spain as sovereign of Mexico.

The only other conquests to be mentioned in the same breath were those of Peru and New Granada. Balboa, after

crossing the Isthmus of Panama, got word of the Inca empire
which was said to surpass even that of the Aztec in wealth
and magnificence. Spain ordered Francisco Pizarro to conquer
it. He built a fleet at Panama, invaded Peru in 1531, treacherously seized and murdered Atahualpa, the Inca emperor who
had welcomed him, founded Lima in 1535, and two years
later frustrated the last efforts of the natives to surround and
cut him off.

Cartagena, a trading-post colony founded by Pedro de
Heredia in 1533, was the jumping-off place for an expedition
under Gonzalo de Quesada which pushed up the Magdalena
river, crossed the mountains to the site of Bogotá, and over-
threw the Chibcha, third of the great native empires. Quesada
then established the government of New Granada, famous
among other things as the birthplace of Simon Bolívar, the
future liberator.

The relative ease of these conquests is explained by complete surprise, and the Spaniards' superior equipment and technique. It was as if a horde of conquerors should descend on
us from another planet with weapons that would make our
latest nuclear gimmicks of no more use than bows and arrows.
By any standards, the ruling classes of the Aztec, Inca, and
Chibcha empires were their conquerors' equals. As Cunning-
hame Graham wrote:

> Their chieftains, treated as gods, borne on the shoulders
> of their subjects, refined, intelligent, and far more rea-
> sonable in controversy than were their conquerors, boldly
> met the onslaught of a race of men who fell upon them,
> as it were, from the skies—a race of beings sheathed in
> steel, riding on animals that seemed a part of them who
> breathed out fire, as the Indians thought, taking the
> harquebus as in some way connected with the horse. With
> their poor arms and quilted cotton doublets, their poi-
> soned arrows and their fire-hardened spears, they faced
> those "children of the sun," dying in heaps, just as Leo-
> nidas and his three hundred Spartans died for their
> fatherland.

These conquests put a new face on Spanish America. Mexico, Peru, and New Granada were far more valuable than
anything Columbus had found: rich, populous native empires
with a small ruling class which the Spaniards had merely to
supplant in order to exploit the masses and extract the wealth.
Labor was there, already organized. It was as if Chinese invaders should move in on General Motors, kill all the top ex-

ecutives, and force the technicians and artisans to work for them.

Up to 1522 comparatively few Spaniards had settled in America, and most of those who did were sorry for themselves. Now that these mining empires were opened up, everyone wanted to go. Entire regions of Spain where living was hard, and the West Indies too, were depopulated in favor of Mexico, Peru, and New Granada. A census taken of the Greater Antilles in 1574 revealed that Hispaniola then contained only 1000 Spaniards—fewer than Columbus had brought over in 1493—and 12,000 African slaves; Cuba and Jamaica each had only 250 Spaniards. The islands now became agricultural, raising cotton, sugar, and tobacco for Spanish consumption, and cattle and corn for export to the American mainland.

Thus, in South and Central America the Spanish colonial system was based on the exploitation of semi-servile Indian labor and wholly servile imported African labor. Tens of thousands of Spaniards came over; but they were the plantation owners, the overseers, and the skilled artisans. The mines of Mexico and Peru were to sixteenth- and seventeenth-century Spain what oil, steel, and minerals are to twentieth-century Europe and America—the basis of nuclear power, feeders of defense and conquest.

The settlement type of colony has almost always been characterized by exploitation. That is the main reason why colonialism is so unpopular today. Europeans went to new countries primarily to get rich, and many did; but in the course of time the people they exploited, whether natives or imported slaves, had their revenge. And of the greater colonizing powers, only England, France, and the Dutch, profiting by their experience with colonial rebels, have had the wisdom to help their overseas subjects to make a peaceful transition from colony to nation.

2. *The* Adelantados *in North America*

The results of this conquest in terms of treasure were spectacular, but the prospect of more to come was infinite. It might be supposed that liquidation of three native empires would employ the energies of Spain for a century; but these conquests were only the beginning. The whole southern section of the United States from South Carolina across to California was explored by Spanish conquistadors in search of more valuable treasure, of new empires that might challenge Mexico; and for the fabled Strait of Anian which was supposed to cross North America from east to west, and might be the long-sought passage to India. These conquistadors were called *adelantados,* advancers. They were given special exploration permits by the King of Spain or the Viceroy of Mexico.

Pánfilo de Narvaez, who had been badly treated by Cortés, chose Florida for his field of glory in 1527. Most unfortunate of all conquistadors, Pánfilo lost two ships in a hurricane, landed somewhere on the Gulf coast of Florida, fought his way up to the site of Tallahassee, and retreated to the coast. There he built a fleet of boats from native wood fastened with spikes fashioned from spurs and stirrups, rigged with cordage and sails made from the hair and hides of horses eaten by his men. In these crazy craft he sailed past the mouth of the Mississippi, only to be wrecked on the coast of Texas. The survivors—Cabeza de Vaca, two other Spaniards, and a black named Esteban—spent six years among the Indians, eventually reaching Mexico with tales of wild "hunchback cows" that covered the plains as far as the eye could see, and of cities with emerald-studded walls, of which they had heard. These "Seven Cities of Cibolá" were more readily believed in than the buffalo.

In 1539 the Viceroy of Mexico sent Fray Marcos, accompanied by Esteban, up into the future New Mexico in search of the fabled Seven Cities. There they discovered the disappointing foundation of this myth, the Zuñi pueblos, and so reported. But the honest tale of Fray Marcos was so blown up by popular imagination that the viceroy now sent out the most splendid exploring expedition of all, that of Francisco Vásquez Coronado, while a co-operating fleet sailed up the Gulf of California. One of Coronado's lieutenants discovered the Grand Canyon in 1540; Coronado himself marched eastward across the panhandle of Texas into eastern Kansas, only to prick another rumor of wealthy cities and a strait. Disappointed, he returned to Mexico.

Hernando de Soto, who had served under Pizarro in Peru, obtained a grant of Florida from the king. Landing at Tampa Bay, he marched about the interior of the future Gulf states for many months, led on by tales of splendid cities. In 1541 he reached the Mississippi near Memphis, crossed to the west bank, spent the winter near the site of Fort Smith, Arkansas, returned to the Father of the Waters, and there died. His men built boats, descended the Mississippi, crossed the Gulf of Mexico, and reached Tampico in safety after an absence of over four years.

Owing to their failure to find treasure or a strait, these

Spanish explorations of North America had no immediate result; the tide of conquest turned south. Only at the end of the sixteenth century, when the frontier of Mexico had been pushed so near to the Rio Grande that conquest of the Pueblo Indians seemed desirable, did Juan de Oñate formally take possession "of all the kingdoms and provinces of New Mexico." The Pueblos promptly submitted, colonization began, and the next governor founded Sante Fe in 1609. Thus New Mexico was settled at the same time as the first permanent English colony in Virginia.

Gifts of untold value that Oñate gave to the future America were domesticated cattle and horses. Texas longhorns are descended from the cattle that he turned loose, and his mares and stallions are ancestors of the mustang or bronco. Those that Oñate turned out to graze were first killed by the Indians for food; but some converted Pueblo ranch hands who had learned to ride brought their mounts to the wild Indians beyond the Spanish pale. The latter found that horses were just what they needed to hunt the buffalo, and each other. By 1700 almost every tribe between New Mexico, the Mississippi, and Kansas had domesticated the horse, and enormous herds of wild mustangs roamed the Great Plains.

By 1600, Spain had conquered almost the whole of coastal South America except Brazil, and much of the interior as well, down to the River Plate. Thus, foundations had been laid for every one of the twenty republics of Central and South America, excepting the Argentine. No other conquest like this has there been in the annals of the human race. In one generation the Spaniards acquired more new territory than Rome conquered in five centuries. Genghis Khan swept over a greater area but left only destruction in his wake; the Spaniards organized and administered all that they conquered, brought in the arts and letters of Europe, and converted millions to their faith. Our forebears in Virginia and New England, the pathfinders of the Great West, and the French pioneers of Canada, were indeed stout fellows; but their exploits scarcely compare with those of brown-robed Spanish friars and armored conquistadors who hacked their way through solid jungle, across endless plains, and over snowy passes of the Andes, to fulfill dreams of glory and conversion; and for whom reality proved even greater than the dream.

On the institutional side, the Spanish empire more closely resembled the Roman than the British empire. All European institutions suffered a change before emerging in America, the Spanish not excepted. The English colonists of North America were able to select the more vigorous and valuable features of English political institutions, and consciously adapt them to New World needs, rejecting the useless residue of feudalism; but the Spanish colonists' institutions were selected for them at Madrid. The Spanish crown, having emerged triumphant from struggles with the nobility and the burghers, took good care that no rivals to royal authority developed in America. Proper machinery was devised to this end, in marked contrast to the lackadaisical English colonial policy. Laws for Spanish America were drafted in Spain by the Council of the Indies. The American trade, monopolized by the merchants of Seville, was regulated in minute detail by the Casa de Contratacion, the official board of trade. The New World was first divided into two great viceroyalties of Nueva España (Mexico) and Peru, to which La Plata (Argentine and Chile) and Nueva Granada (Colombia and Venezuela) were later added. They in turn were divided into eleven *audiencias,* roughly corresponding to the national boundaries of today; and these were subdivided into minor administrative units. The officials, from viceroys to alcaldes, were responsible to the king and held their posts during his good pleasure. Thus, Spanish America grew up understanding no form of government but autocracy tempered by corruption; a pattern not wholly broken today.

There is another side to the picture: first, the conversion of Indians, whose religion required the killing of thousands of innocent people annually to appease angry gods, to Christianity. From the Spanish *hidalgo* the South Americans inherit the chivalrous courtesy that one finds among their poorest people today; the Puerto Rican immigrant to New York City cherishes his *dignidad,* he cannot be pushed around. And the fine arts of Europe followed close on the trail of conquest. Lima, the "City of Kings," and Mexico City became seats of urban civilization within fifteen years of the conquest; in each a university was founded in 1551. The first printing press in the New World was set up at Mexico City in 1539. To this day an air of superb magnificence rests on the churches and palaces built by the Spaniards and their native subjects in their provincial capitals.

Thus, the Spanish empire in America had more than a century's head start on the English and French; and the results of that conquest, materially as well as spiritually, were amazing, stupendous, and the envy of every European power. Spanish prestige reached its height in the year 1580 when Philip II succeeded to the throne of Portugal as well as that of Spain, uniting under his person two empires that now stretched their arms around the world: the left arm to the west coast of Mexico, the right arm to Manila. At that time, not another nation had placed a single permanent settler on the shores of the New World.

But the end of the Spanish monopoly was near. The autumn gales of 1580, blowing up the English Channel, brought into Plymouth Francis Drake's *Golden Hind,* returning from a three-year voyage around the world, laden with the spoil of a Peruvian treasure ship, and eager for more. Only eight years later, the Spanish Armada invading England was decisively defeated. Within a few more years, Virginia and New France were well seated, and Spain could do nothing about it.

But before we relate the small beginnings of the English colonies which in 1776 became the United States, we must tell about a colony that put a permanent stamp on the Province of Quebec.

3. *The Beginnings of New France*

These were modest indeed. There is no Leif the Lucky, Cabot, or Columbus in the annals of French discovery. Humble fishermen and traders were the heralds of empire for that nation. For a century after the first Frenchman arrived in New World waters the story of New France is one of small things; petty expeditions ill-equipped by small merchants of the seaport towns, harassed by the fluctuating policy of successive kings, abandoned as soon as hope of finding gold or other quick assets was lost. Throughout her French period Canada was a trading-post and fringe colony in which the tasty codfish and luxurious peltry played the same role as the spices that brought wealth to Portugal, and the precious metals of Mexico and Peru.

French fishermen sailing in the wake of John Cabot and the Corte Real began to frequent the Grand Bank as early as 1504; but the first French voyage of discovery came twenty years later. Francis I, admirer of Italy and Spain, decided that he needed a Genoese navigator to do what Columbus and Cabot had failed to do—find a strait leading to the Indies, more practical than Magellan's. So he engaged Giovanni Verrazzano and persuaded the silk merchants of Lyons, who wanted a short sea route to China, to finance him.

Verrazzano's first port of call after the West Indies, in March 1524, was the Cape Fear river. Sailing along the coasts of the future Carolinas, Virginia, and New Jersey, he looked in at the site of New York for a day, and decided that the great river later named Hudson was no strait. He then tried

Narragansett Bay with the same result. Rounding Cape Cod, he ranged the coasts of Maine, Nova Scotia, and New Foundland. The results of this voyage were negative, from the viewpoint of the French court; but Verrazzano founded a new geographical delusion. The map of North America that his brother drafted has a narrow-waisted isthmus at Cape Hatteras, with the legend "Indian Ocean" on the other side. This northern isthmus concept persisted into the eighteenth century, when Governor Spotswood of Virginia expected to play the role of Balboa on the crest of the Blue Ridge.

Jacques Cartier, mariner of Saint Malo in Brittany, was responsible for directing the attention of France to the Laurentian region. He made two voyages to America in 1533 and 1535, sailing up the river which he named the St. Lawrence, turning back a little above the site of Montreal, wintering under the Rock of Quebec. Friendly and humorous Hurons beguiled the Frenchmen through a long, cold winter with tall tales of a Kingdom of Saguenay inhabited by white men who had mines of gold, silver, and rubies, and even grew spices; Chief Donnaconna, elaborating, declared that among them were men who had only one leg, flew like bats, and never ate. Cartier not only "bought" the whole package but persuaded the Huron chief to accompany him to France and sell it to the king, which he did. Here, thought Francis I, was the opportunity to acquire a Mexico of his own and run the King of Spain out of business. So he sent Cartier on a third voyage in 1541, with ten ships and so many people and such rich equipment that the King of Spain seriously thought of sending a fleet to break it up. This expedition pushed up the St. Lawrence, but the wealthy kingdom was always beyond the next rapid. Cartier's partner Roberval explored in boats the river now called Saguenay but found only the walls of the northern wilderness closing in on him. They returned to France with a heap of iron pyrites which they believed to be gold, and quartz crystals that they hoped were diamonds. "Canadian diamonds" became a standard joke in France, and the only tangible result of this voyage.

French efforts to colonize Canada were now suspended, owing largely to civil wars at home. But two futile attempts were made to found French trading posts on the coast of Florida, where the Spaniards had neglected to take possession. The first, by Jean Ribault, set up a pillar at the mouth of the St. John river below Jacksonville in 1562, and established a trading post on the site of the present U.S. Marine Corps reservation at Parris Island, South Carolina. That did not last long. René de Laudonnière made a second attempt, with four shiploads of French Protestants, in 1563. They located Ribault's stone column, and Jacques Le Moyne, an artist in the party, made a charming watercolor sketch of Laudonnière and Outima, chief of the Timucua Indians, fraternizing. The leader decided to pitch his trading post there, named it Fort Caroline, then returned to France for reinforcements. In his absence some of the Frenchmen stole a ship anchored in the river and went a-pirating in the West Indies. This stirred up the Spaniards, and the French left in Fort Caroline reached the verge of famine because they depended on the Indians for food. In the summer of 1565 the Spaniards caught up with them, captured Fort Caroline, and slaughtered the survivors who surrendered, every one. Spain founded St. Augustine the same year and studded the coast as far north as the Carolinas with forts and missions. For the treasure galleons returning to Spain passed that way, and it would not do to let foreigners locate at a spot whence small boats could put out and capture a becalmed ship.

The only permanent result of this short-lived French colony in Florida was the introduction of tobacco both to France and England. John Hawkins of Plymouth called at Fort Caroline and brought home a parcel of it, which he described as follows: "The Floridians have a kind of herb dried, who with a cane and an earthen cup on the end, with fire,—doe suck through the cane the smoke thereof, which smoke satisfieth their hunger."

Even though Cartier's last voyage shattered the Saguenay myth, French fishermen resorted every summer to the Grand Bank, and to cure their codfish some landed on the shores of Newfoundland and Cape Breton Island, so called by fishermen from Brittany. These landings led to trade with the Indians, who had valuable fur to barter for axes and other iron tools. Gentlemen of that era required fur for trimming coats and to make the felt of which wide-brimmed, high-crowned hats, fashionable for over two centuries, were made. So the fishermen learned to bring over a supply of cloth, axes, iron kettles, and other goods that the Indians wanted, and every fishing station became a trading post. This led to special fur-trading expeditions pushing into the Gulf of St. Lawrence, and to the establishment of a chain of trading posts—Port Royal, Quebec, Montreal, Trois Rivières—which eventually became towns or cities.

In 1590 Henry of Navarre—Henri IV whose gallant soul and bristly-bearded countenance live in the pages of Parkman —won the Battle of Ivry and brought an end to the Wars of

Religion. It was time to make an effort to colonize Canada, ahead of the English. The chosen method was natural enough in a poor country lately torn by civil strife. A monopoly of Canadian fur trade was granted to individuals or small companies, on condition that they settle a certain number of colonists per year at their own expense. The government undertook to find colonists if the company could not, by rounding up vagabonds and relieving congestion in the jails.

The immediate results of this policy were not impressive. The companies seldom complied with the terms; and when they did, the former inmates of His Majesty's prisons either died or ran away. Other fur traders in the meantime brought pressure on the king to cancel the monopoly and give it to themselves; and the monopoly so frequently changed hands that it was no longer respected. Yet one of these short-lived companies was responsible for bringing to Canada Samuel de Champlain, rightly regarded as the father of New France.

That was in 1604. A company headed by Pierre du Gua, sieur de Monts, attempted to establish a colony on the river which now divides Maine from New Brunswick. The settlement was first pitched on Dochet Island (since renamed St. Croix), for protection against the Indians. After one cold and miserable winter it was transferred to Port Royal on the Annapolis Basin in the present Nova Scotia. Champlain in a small pinnace explored the coast of "Norumbega," which later became known as New England, as far as the south side of Cape Cod, looking for a better site. He found none, because the further south he sailed, the less fur the Indians had to sell. But Port Royal did very well. A stout palisaded *habitation* was raised, a treaty concluded with the nearby Micmac sagamore, wheat and other vegetables were planted, and a jolly winter was spent by great log fires, beguiled by songs and a pageant in which the Indians took part.

4. *The Elizabethan Prelude*

Henry VII, first monarch of the House of Tudor, took over a small, weak, and war-weary England in 1485. Elizabeth I, last of that royal line, left an empire to her successor James I.

Since Henry VII had been second only to Ferdinand and Isabella in New World discovery, it may seem strange that England was slow to follow up. But there were good reasons. Cabot found no passage to India and reported nothing of value in the land that he discovered. England was afraid of Spain, and the example of what happened to the French colony in Florida deterred her from attempts to settle near the

Spaniards. The English kings were chronically broke, largely because of their dependence on Parliament for money. And England needed time to accumulate venture capital so that individuals could finance overseas enterprise.

English mariners reached America the hard way, the long way, and (as we shall see) the back way, instead of taking the short route traced by Cabot. The first big effort came in 1553 when the Muscovy Company was formed to find a northeast passage to the Indies. That was more than any ship could get through without an icebreaker, but the Muscovy Company did open a profitable trade with Russia, which at that time was hardly better known in England than the Iroquois Confederacy. The next target for English overseas enterprise was West Africa, for gold, ivory, and slaves. These led to the voyages to America by Sir John Hawkins.

Under Elizabeth I (1558–1603), England embarked on a course of expansion, spiritual and material, such as few nations have ever experienced. It was the age of Sir Philip Sidney and Shakespeare, of Sir Humfrey Gilbert and Sir Walter Raleigh, of highest skill in matters maritime, and supreme achievement in poetry, prose, and music. Yet every attempt at colonization in Elizabeth's reign failed. The efforts of Philip II of Spain (Elizabeth's brother-in-law) to rub her out as a heretic and a usurper led to a breach between the two countries, and a long war which was fought mostly on the ocean. Venture capital found it more profitable to finance privateering expeditions against Spanish treasure fleets than to search for a passage to India or set up a North American trading post. Yet, somehow, the preliminary work got done.

Sir Humfrey Gilbert was the Englishman who sparked it off. In 1566, at the age of twenty-nine, he wrote "A Discourse To Prove a Passage by the Northwest to Cathaia"; i.e. China. Eleven years later, Francis Drake departed on a voyage with the hope of finding it.

Drake had commanded a ship in Hawkins's fleet, treacherously attacked by Spaniards at Vera Cruz. He had raided the Isthmus of Panama in 1572, sighted the Pacific, and "resolved to sail an England ship in these seas." And he wished to check another unfounded geographical theory that a great Terra Australis ran around the world just below the Strait of Magellan. Sailing through that strait in the *Golden Hind,* Drake ascertained that there was no Terra Australis, only barren Tierra del Fuego. He turned north, captured a rich treasure galleon off the coast of Peru, landed at or near the place now called Drake's Bay not far north of San Francisco, and took possession of that country for Queen Elizabeth I, naming it

Nova Albion—New England. He had no doubt that the western opening of the northern strait lay nearby, and he probably sailed as far north as Vancouver Island in the search. Not finding it, he turned west, picked up a valuable cargo of cloves in the Spice Islands, and returned to England around the world. The profits of this voyage were almost $9 million in gold, and the Queen was so pleased with her share that she knighted Drake on the deck of the *Golden Hind,* which was as good as telling the King of Spain, "North America belongs to England —hands off!"

In the meantime Sir Humfrey Gilbert had obtained from the Queen a charter to discover "remote heathen and barbarous lands not actually possessed by any Christian prince or people . . . and the same to have, hold, occupy and enjoy," providing that all settlers who go out with him shall "enjoy all the privileges of free denizens and persons native of England"; and that any laws or ordinances that he may pass for his colony "be as neere as conveniently may, agreeable to the forms of the laws & policy of England." Although Sir Humfrey never made good on this grant, the last two principles, new in the history of colonization, became basic in English colonial policy. A freeborn Englishman lost no rights by moving overseas; and the lord proprietor of a colony, such as Gilbert intended to be (and Lord Baltimore and William Penn later became), could not play dictator but must govern by English law.

In June 1583 Gilbert sailed from Plymouth in command of four vessels. His prime objective was to found a trading-post colony on the Penobscot river in Maine, but first he reasserted English possession of Newfoundland. Entering St. John's harbor in August, he set up a pillar with the English arms and told the fishermen of four nations from 36 vessels which he found there at anchor, that they must obey him and the Queen. Continuing southward, he sent one ship home, lost another on Cape Sable Island; and then, discouraged, turned homeward. Gilbert sailed in the tiny pinnace *Squirrel,* which the larger vessel tried to keep in sight through raging gales and "outrageous seas." On a rough September day she closed the *Squirrel* so near that Sir Humfrey with a book in hand was heard to call out, "We are as neer to heaven by sea as by land!" The sun set, and at midnight the light on the pinnace went out, for she had been "devoured and swallowed up of the Sea," pooped and swamped.

The book that Sir Humfrey was reading on the last day of his life was undoubtedly Sir Thomas More's *Utopia,* in which is found the maxim, "The way to heaven out of all places is of like length and distance." That book, which has given its name to all other utopias, may be called the blueprint to the American dream of a good life. More's imagination fused the ideal world of Plato's *Republic* and the New World of America. He foretold that a model republic might be founded somewhere in the new countries recently discovered; and that there mankind might find what they had always sought—plenty, peace, liberty, and security, under a government of calm philosophers; a six-hour day, leaving time "for the free liberty of the mind and garnishing of the same." Will we ever attain it?

Gilbert's charter was inherited by his thirty-one-year-old half-brother, Sir Walter Raleigh, Elizabeth's favorite courtier. In 1584 Raleigh sent a reconnaissance fleet under Captains Amadas and Barlow to the future Croatan Sound, North Carolina. They brought back a glowing account of the air, soil, and Indians—"most gentle, loving and faithful, void of all guile and treason, and such as lived after the manner of the golden age." Raleigh now decided to colonize in earnest. As encouragement, the Virgin Queen knighted him and graciously permitted him to name the new land Virginia. This Virginia meant all North America that England could seize and hold, from sea to sea. Next year, Sir Walter sent out, under Sir Richard Grenville and Ralph Lane, a colonizing expedition of 108 men who settled on Roanoke Island, in what is now North Carolina. The colony included artist John White, surveyor Thomas Hariot, and a Bohemian Jew named Joachim Ganz to prospect for minerals. He found none; but Hariot's account of the expedition, illustrated by White's drawings, is the most careful description of North American natives from the pen of an Englishman in the first century of colonization. Sir Francis Drake, who had been raiding the West Indies, looked in at Roanoke Island on his way home. He found the colonists unhappy and hungry, and at their request took them back to England in June of 1586.

Sir Walter now obtained and organized "The Governor and Assistants of the City of Raleigh in Virginia." In 1587 he sent out a fresh colony consisting of 89 men, 7 women, and 11 children, in three ships, with John White as governor. This colony might have been permanent if, like the later Jamestown, it had been supported from home. But it was a bad time and a poor place to leave a small colony to its own devices. The region around Pamlico Sound had a dense Indian population, and the local tribe did not appreciate the insatiable demands of Englishmen for food and labor. It was the wrong time, too, to look for help from home. A Spanish armada was being prepared to invade England, where nobody could spare the effort to succor a tiny outpost in Virginia.

The Armada was defeated in 1588, but two years passed before anything was done about Virginia. Then Raleigh arranged for John Watts, a privateer captain; to carry supplies to his colony. They spent most of the summer of 1590 roistering about the Caribbean and only reached Roanoke in mid-August. As their commander tells the story, "We let fall our grapnel neer the shore and sounded with a trumpet a Call, and afterwards many familiar English tunes of Songs, and called to them friendly." But to these genial sounds there was no answer; and when the Englishmen landed, they found only rummaged and rifled chests, rotten maps, rusty armor, grass-grown palisades, and the word CROATOAN carved on a tree. That was the native name of the island on which Cape Hatteras is situated, about a hundred miles southward of Roanoke. The sailors refused to linger at so depressing a place, and the relief expedition returned to England.

Nobody knows what became of the "Lost Colony." The best guess is that some starved to death, and others were killed by the Indians, who adopted the surviving children. To this day the Croatoan (now called Lumbee) Indians of Robeson County, North Carolina, maintain that the blood of Raleigh's colonists runs in their veins.

Thus the sixteenth century closed like the fifteenth, without England's having planted a colony or even a trading post in the New World. It was largely the war with Spain, which lasted until 1604, which kept her back. But that war, waged mostly on the sea, was no loss to the future of English civilization. Through fighting Spaniards the English acquired confidence, wealth, and strength. They improved the designs of ships and methods of navigation. They ceased to be insular; they acquired a world ambition.

England, too, felt that she was fighting for freedom against a despotism that covered half the world, but Elizabeth I resolutely refused to send armies into the European continent. How wise she was! How different, and worse, the world might have become if the energy that the English displayed between 1550 and 1650 had turned to the dominance of Europe; if no Virginia, no New England, had been founded overseas, and England had become a military nation. But sea power has never led to despotism. The nations that have enjoyed sea power even for a brief period—Athens, Scandinavia, the Netherlands, England, the United States—are those that have preserved freedom for themselves and have given it to others. Of the despotism to which unrestrained military power leads we have plenty of examples from Alexander to Mao. So let us not write off the forays and sea battles of the Elizabethans as failures. The efforts of blithe, lusty spirits like Drake, Gilbert, and Raleigh, under that great queen whom they called Gloriana, blazed the way for the United States of America and the British Commonwealth.

VIVE HENRI QUATRE!

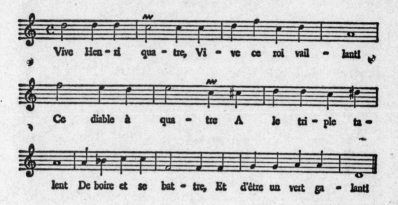

Vive Hen-ri qua-tre, Vi-ve ce roi vail-lant! Ce diable à qua-tre A le tri-ple ta-lent De boire et se bat-tre, Et d'être un vert ga-lant!

IV

Two Founding Decades

1607-1627

1. *The Setting*

ON 30 JULY 1607, owing to a royal annulment of his monopoly, De Monts with a heavy heart abandoned the French trading post so happily seated at Port Royal, Nova Scotia. Most of the colonists returned with him to France, but Poutrincourt and a handful of men remained. It must have seemed to them that all was over, that New France would now be victim of freebooters from all nations. Actually the history of Canada and the United States had just begun. Unknown to the French, a band of enthusiastic Englishmen a few months earlier had founded Jamestown, nucleus of the Old Dominion of Virginia. Champlain began in 1608, under the Rock of Quebec jutting into the St. Lawrence, the first French post in America destined to be a great city. There, more than 360 years later, the royal lilies of France are still displayed on the banners of the French-speaking Province of Quebec.

Another year passed, and the waters of the Hudson, unruffled (so far as the record goes) by any European ship since the brief visit of Verrazzano in 1524, were cloven by a little Dutch vessel called the *Half Moon,* captained by Henry Hudson. He was the herald of a short-lived Dutch empire in North America, as Cabot and Cartier were of the more permanent

English and French empires. And in 1620 a band of a hundred Pilgrims, as they called themselves, set up a trading post on the shores of Northern Virginia, which had just been renamed New England. Their Colony of New Plymouth became the second nucleus of the English American empire; and in 1625 a third was established on the island of St. Kitts in the Caribbean.

Port Royal was not dead. Madame de Guercheville, a pious lady-in-waiting to the Queen Mother of France, paid the bills for a joint fur-trading and missionary expedition to reoccupy the almost deserted post, and to establish others. Her men found Port Royal so depressed that in 1613 they set up a missionary station on the island of Mount Desert in the present State of Maine. This was wiped out the same year by Captain Samuel Argall in command of an armed ship from Virginia. He then inflicted the same punishment on Port Royal for venturing to exist on a continent claimed by England. In the valley of the St. Lawrence, French and Dutch had already taken sides in the bitter Indian rivalry of Iroquois and Huron; and the king of Spain almost decided to rub out Jamestown.

Such was the unhappy relation between the four European nations which claimed most of America north of Brazil. One could have been an optimist indeed in 1620 to predict that any good could come out of this. Nobody suspected that the seeds of democracy had already been sown at Jamestown and Plymouth, and those of the future Canadian nation at Quebec.

Fruitless as were the Roanoke colonies, the English learned from them that the seating of a colony was a highly expensive business, ruinous to any individual or small group who attempted it. Raleigh is said to have lost £40,000 in his efforts. The first twelve of the English continental colonies, and all English island colonies except Jamaica, were founded and settled by private enterprise, personal or corporate. The English crown, claiming the entire American continent north of Mexico, had neither the money nor the aptitude to found colonies. So it gave concessions to individuals and companies.

Most of the English colonies of the early seventeenth century, such as Jamestown (1607), Plymouth (1620), and Massachusetts Bay (1628), started as trading posts, owned by English merchants and settled by their employees. The first English colony to be agricultural from the beginning was Bermuda (1612), where there were no natives to trade with—only the wild hogs left by the Spaniards. In no one of these colonies was private ownership of land permitted until communal ownership proved to be a failure. Except for a few gentlemen adventurers, the original planters were hired men working under a boss called a governor, who was responsible to owners living in England. This was true of Virginia until 1616, of Plymouth until 1623, of Massachusetts Bay until 1630, and of Canada and New Netherlands until much later.

It was not, however, the English colonial intention to be satisfied with mere trading posts. In the literature of English colonization at least six main ideas are stressed: (1) England is overpopulated—"The land grows weary of its people." In the shires "the beggars are coming to town," as the old ballad states; in London the unemployed sleep in the streets. What better solution than to give the poor and unemployed a new lease on life overseas? (2) England wants markets for her woolens. What better one can be found than North America, with its cold climate? Not only settlers but Indians might be persuaded to swap furs and skins for coats and blankets. (3) England sorely needs precious metals. Surely there is as good a chance to find gold in Virginia as in Hispaniola—or Saguenay? (4) England has been paying good money to Mediterranean countries for olive oil, currants, and wine. If these could be produced in English colonies, she would be much better off. She is dependent on the Baltic countries for ship timber, tar, and cordage. Surely the Royal Navy would be better prepared if a source of supplies could be found in Virginia? (5) England needs a short route to the Indies. Maybe one can be found up one of the unexplored bays on the coast of Virginia. (6) England has the duty to propagate Protestant Christianity and prevent the Catholic Church from converting the entire native population of America. And "a place of safetie" —a Protestant refuge—might there be found "if change of religion or civil warres should happen in this Realme."

These were the basic motives of English colonization for a century and a half. And from the first it was understood that any English settlement must have English law and English liberty. The first charter of the Virginia Company (1606) declared that the colonists and their descendants would enjoy "all liberties . . . to all intents and purposes as if they had been abiding and born within this our realm of England." These became fighting words in the 1770's.

2. Virginia

As soon as James I made peace with Spain in 1604, the energy and gallantry of the English nation that had been engaged in fighting the Spaniards concentrated on setting up Virginia; and for that purpose they chose an admirable vehicle for private enterprise, the joint stock company. This combined the venture of many small investors (in the case of the Virginia Company £12 10s or about $62 in gold per share) into one joint or common stock which was administered by a governor, treasurer, and assistants elected by the stockholders at quarterly "courts" or meetings in London. Public-spirited Englishmen of all classes, laymen and divines, nobles and knights, merchants and the trade guilds of London, launched a drive for stock subscriptions; the king gave the company a charter, and on 20 December 1606, 120 colonists embarked at London in three little ships, *Susan Constant, Godspeed,* and *Discovery.* Upon their departure they were cheered by this merry ballad by Michael Drayton:

> Britains, you stay too long,
> Quickly aboord bestow you,
>   And with a merry gale,
>   Swell your stretched sayle,
> With vows as strong
> As the winds that blow you.

> And cheerefully at sea,
> Successe you still intice,
>   To get the pearle and gold,
>   *And ours to hold,*
>   VIRGINIA,
> Earth's only Paradise.

Captain Christopher Newport conducted this task force to Virginia, and the Company gave him "sole charge and command." They raised the Chesapeake Capes on 26 April 1607, after eighteen weeks at sea. Captain Newport and his council (which included Captain John Smith, George Percy, and Edward-Maria Wingfield) explored the lower reaches of Chesapeake Bay for a suitable home site, but made the usual mistake of firstcomers in America by settling on a low, swampy island. This they named Jamestown after the King, and there the people began going ashore on 14 May. They lost no time in building a fortified trading post, with wattle-and-daub thatched houses, a church, and storehouse of similar construction, which have been well reproduced in the modern National Park. They were just in time to repel an Indian attack on 26 May.

The early history of Jamestown was miserable indeed. After Captain Newport sailed for England in June, the population was 104 men and boys. Within six months 51 died of disease and starvation; and it was only Captain Smith's skill in making

friends with Powhatan—via daughter Pocahontas—and the
return of Captain Newport with a supply ship around New
Year's day, that the rest were saved. That supply ship brought
between 70 and 100 more settlers, including two women, and
five Poles who had been recruited to begin the production of
pitch, tar, and turpentine. Thus, from the start, England rejected the Spanish system of excluding foreigners from her
colony. There is no evidence that these or the forty-five other
Poles who were sent to Virginia within a few years were under
any civil disability.

The Virginia Company planned no mere trading post but a
settlement colony. The leaders had courage and vision, but the
general run of the early settlers were ill chosen; they seem to
have been divided into those who could not and those who
would not work. As Captain Smith wrote, "In Virginia, a
plaine Souldier that can use a Pick-axe and spade, is better
than five Knights." And although more men were procured,
for several years Jamestown remained a fortified trading post
where employees of the Company worked for their absentee
stockholders. No private property was allowed, hence there
was no incentive. The Company provided the colony with a
poor sort of government—a council appointed in England, of
which each member became president by turn; and under this
council's direction the people wasted time looking for gold
and failed to produce the necessary provisions to keep them
alive. They sickened on the local food that they bought from
friendly Indians, caught malaria from the hordes of mosqui-
toes, and died like flies in autumn.

Reports of those who returned to England were so discour-
aging that the Virginia Company reorganized with a new
charter in 1609. This brought in new blood and new money,
and a change of system. Lord de la Warr (from whom Delaware is named) was appointed governor of "London's Plantation in the Southern Part of Virginia," official name of the
Jamestown settlement. As the governor was not ready to leave,
Sir Thomas Gates took command of an expedition of nine
ships, the largest fleet that England had yet sent to America.
The flagship was wrecked on Bermuda, and a contemporary
account of this event inspired Shakespeare's *Tempest*. The survivors built a boat out of Bermudian cedar and in her sailed
up Chesapeake Bay in May 1610. When they reached Jamestown, they found the settlement reduced to the last stage of
wretchedness. The colonists were discouraged, diseased, and
starving; they had eaten all the livestock that skulking Indians
had not killed, and their houses were in ruins. Gates decided
to embark the survivors in ships already in the harbor and

return them to England. The entire company was on board, anchors aweigh, and sail made in June 1610, when up the river came a gig bearing Lord de la Warr, whose ships, with 300 men on board and ample supplies, were becalmed down the bay. De la Warr ordered Gates and his people ashore, vigorously took charge, and the Jamestown colony was saved from collapse or extinction.

Under De la Warr and his energetic successor, Sir Thomas Dale, strict military discipline was established and severe measures to punish laggards and delinquents were adopted. But the colony was still in a bad way. Governor Dale wrote home in 1611:

> Every man allmost laments himself of being here, and murmurs at his present state. [The colonists were] sutch disordered persons, so prophane, so rioutous, so full of treasonable Intendments, besides of sutch diseased and crased bodies which render them so unable, fainte, and desperate of recoverie, as of three hundred not three score may be called forth or imploied upon any labor or service.

He begged the king,

> If it will please his Majestie to banish hither all offenders condemned to die, it would be a readie way to furnish us with men, and not allwayes with the worst kinde of men either for birth, spiritts or Bodie.

Jamestown was still a semi-military trading post. The colonists owned no property; they were working for stockholders overseas. Twice a day the men were marched to the fields or woods by beat of drum, twice marched back and into church. They led an almost hopeless existence, for there seemed to be no future. The local Indians were no traders, had nothing but a little corn to offer; the only "cash crop" profitable in England was cedar board for wainscoting. No empire could have developed from a colony of this sort. The only thing that kept Virginia alive in these difficult years was the patriotism and deep religious faith of some of the leaders. This was well expressed by a poetical paraphrase of one of Governor Dale's reports, printed in England in 1610:

> Be not dismayed at all
> For scandall cannot doe us wrong,
> God will not let us fall.

Let England knowe our willingnesse,
For that our work is good;
Wee hope to plant a nation
Where none before hath stood.

Virginia needed more than faith and a gallant spirit to be permanent. It needed a profitable product, a system of land-holding that would give colonists a stake in the country; discipline, to be sure, but also liberty. In about eight years, 1616–24, it obtained all these. During that time the colony was transformed from an almost desperately maintained trading post, ruled by iron discipline, into something like the Virginia of the Byrds and Lees.

The first factor in this transition was tobacco. Its value for export was discovered in 1613 when John Rolfe, who married the Indian "princess" Pocahontas, imported seed from the West Indies, crossed it with the local Indian-grown tobacco, and produced a smooth smoke which captured the English market. Virginia then went tobacco-mad; it was even grown in the streets of Jamestown. We hear of one man who by his own labor raised a crop of tobacco that brought £200, another with six hired men making £1000 in one year; and the last governor sent out by the Company, Samuel Argall, who came out "with nothing but his sword," took home £3000. As early as 1618 Virginia exported 50,000 pounds' weight of tobacco to England. This encouraged settlers, but made the colony more dependent on England for supplies. To keep Virginia supplied with food, a special organization called "The Magazine" was formed by the wealthier members of the Company. It sent out food supplies and in return received the monopoly of selling Virginia tobacco in England. A fair enough solution, but politically unwise because tobacco was of ill repute with King James. At his behest Parliament would have prohibited the import of tobacco into England in 1621, had the Virginia Company not persuaded the House that this would ruin the colony.

The institution of private property was the second factor that saved Virginia. When, after seven years, the terms of the Company's hired men expired, those who chose to stay became tenant farmers and later were given their land outright. This made a tremendous difference. As Captain John Smith put it, "When our people were fed out of the common store, and laboured jointly together, glad was he who could slip from his labour, or slumber over his taske, he cared not how; nay, the most honest among them would hardly take so much true paines in a week, as now for themselves they will doe in a day." By 1617 a majority of the hardy, acclimated survivors were tenants. Within ten years tenant plantations extended twenty miles along the James river, and the total European population of Virginia was about a thousand.

The third factor that ensured the success of Virginia was political, in the broadest sense. Again it was Captain John Smith who put the issue in one sentence: "No man wil go from hence to have lesse freedome there than here"; and in the English conception of freedom the first and most important was "a government of laws, not of men." The Company ordered Governor Sir George Yeardley to abolish arbitrary rule, introduce English common law and due process, encourage private property, and summon a representative assembly. This assembly would have power, with the appointed council, to pass local laws, subject to the Company's veto.

The fourth factor was sex. There had been a few women in the colony from the first, but they stood the hardships even less well than the men and boys, and few were alive in 1620. The Company then undertook to recruit "young and uncorrupt maids" and ship them to Jamestown, where a planter who wanted a wife paid the Company 150 pounds of best leaf tobacco. Every lass promptly found a husband, and every married couple had the right to build a house for themselves, whilst bachelors continued to bunk in barracks.

All these reforms except the last were passed by the general court of the Company in England in 1618, under Sir Thomas Smyth. Sir Thomas has had a bad break from most historians; his successor, Sir Edwin Sandys, has been given the credit. Smyth was an experienced business man, governor of the Muscovy Company and director of the East India Company; but he lacked the personality of Sandys, an Oxford graduate and parliamentary leader, tolerant in religion and liberal in politics, who appeared to later Americans as a primitive Thomas Jefferson. Sandys hoped to "plant a nation, where none before hath stood"; but the less voluble and expressive Smyth may have had the same vision even though he did not talk about it.

The year 1619 brought a political upset within the Company. The small stockholders, each of whom had contributed his £12 10s, hoped to receive a dividend before they died. They suspected that the Magazine was taking all the profits while stockholders were put off with promises. So the cry went up that the Smyth party had been too long in power; and the spring election of the Company in London in 1619 was won by Sandys. As Sir Edwin Sandys had no commitments elsewhere, he was able to concentrate all his efforts on serving the Company and Virginia, and implementing the reforms of 1618.

In consequence of the votes passed by the Virginia Company in London, Governor Yeardley summoned a legislative assembly, the very first in America, in 1619; and it seems to have been elected by manhood suffrage, including that of the foreigners. The next step, equally important for the future, was to abolish the military regulations of Dale and place Virginia under the rule of law—the common law of England. That law, and orderly process to change the law, have proved to be the surest safeguards of human rights known to modern man.

Despite the new tobacco prosperity, the rate of mortality continued to be appalling. Between Easter 1619 and Easter 1620, the population fell off from about 1000 to 866. During the next twelve months, ten different ships landed 1051 more people in Virginia. But by Easter, 1621, what with deaths and the departure of the discouraged, only 843 remained alive in the colony.

Sir Edwin Sandys worried over the exclusive attention paid by the colony to tobacco, partly because a one-crop system is unhealthy for the economy (as Cuba has learned to her cost), partly because King James I was down on smoking. Sandys therefore persuaded the stockholders' meeting in London to adopt a five-year plan for Virginia. These measures were directed toward making the colony self-sustaining in food, producer of many products that England then had to purchase abroad, and a market for English goods. Vines, vintners, and olive trees were imported from France, the Company spent £5000 to establish an iron industry at the falls of the James river, sawmill workers were imported from Hamburg, and expert lumbermen from the Baltic provinces. To implement these plans more settlers were needed, and as a result of intense publicity some 4000 English people emigrated to Virginia in four years. Yet a census in February 1624 showed that only 1277 of them were still alive. "What has become of the five thousand missing subjects of His Majesty?" was asked at an investigation by the Royal Council in 1624. Except for those who returned home, they had died or had been killed in the Indian massacre of 1622.

This event, which checked Virginia when on the brink of prosperity, was due primarily to the neglect of defense by the Virginia Company and its local government. They trusted that the marriage of Pocahontas to John Rolfe would keep the Indians friendly. That it did, for a time; but Powhatan was succeeded by his brother Opechancanough who, resenting the steady encroachment of the English on his cornfields, decided to clean up. He almost did, too; in a sudden, secret onslaught, 347 colonists, at least one-third of the white population, were killed.

That calamity knocked out the five-year plan of Sir Edwin Sandys. His ambitious schemes for iron works and a college were given up, outlying plantations were abandoned, and the Virginia Company came under political attack. The king directed his attorney general to enter suit against the Company, alleging that none of its professed objects had been carried out, and the crown won, in 1624. The charter under which the Virginia colony had been seated was annulled, and the Company whose liberal policy set the pattern for English colonization was dissolved.

Virginia now became a crown colony, with a governor and council appointed by the king; but the local people welcomed the change because the king continued their representative assembly, the house of burgesses, and respected the rule of law. And under Charles I, who succeeded his father James I in 1625, a really prosperous era began.

Among the inducements to settlers offered by the Virginia Company under Sandys was this: any Englishman who agreed to take out at least 250 people at his own expense was allowed to choose a tract of unallotted land anywhere in the colony, 1250 acres or more, with powers of local self-government. These tracts, known as Hundreds or "Particular Plantations," are the origin of names such as "Martin's Hundred," "Archer's Hope," and "Bennett's Welcome" on the map of Virginia today. And, by a curious set of circumstances, this was the origin of Plymouth Colony, the first permanent settlement in New England.

3. *Plymouth Plantation*

Since 1600 there had been a number of English and French voyages along the coast of the future New England. Officially the region was Northern Virginia, granted by James I in 1606 to a Northern Virginia Company similar to the one that founded Jamestown. This company, of which the leading lights were Chief Justice Sir John Popham and Sir Ferdinando Gorges, attempted in 1607 to establish a trading post on an island inside the mouth of the Kennebec river. Raleigh Gilbert, the twenty-four-year-old son of Sir Humfrey, was the governor. They built a small vessel and sent her home with a load of mast timber, but the winter set in "extreme unseasonable and frosty," the north wind howled down-river and congealed the settlers' blood, the Indians refused to trade; and when a relief ship showed up in the spring of 1608, everyone scrambled on board and went back to merry England.

The Northern Virginia Company then employed Captain John Smith to explore the coast. He wrote an enthusiastic *Description of New England,* which was published in 1616. He praised the soil, the climate, and especially the fishing. English and French fishermen frequented the coast for the next few years, but there was no attempt to settle until the Pilgrim Fathers practically stumbled in.

These were a group of Separatists—Puritans who had seceded from the Church of England, unhappy exiles in the Netherlands. The Dutch gave them good usage, but hard living, and they wanted a place of their own to live where they could worship as they chose and also prosper. Their leader William Brewster, through a connection with Sir Edwin Sandys, got them a patent to a "particular plantation" in Southern Virginia. They intended to locate near the mouth of the Hudson (then within the boundary of Virginia and unoccupied), there to set up a trading post and fishing settlement. Poor in worldly goods though indomitable in spirit, they could raise money only by agreeing to remain in virtual servitude for seven years to a group of loan sharks in London. Owing to various delays their ship, the *Mayflower,* did not clear England until the autumn of 1620. After a rough voyage of 64 days, she made Cape Cod on 9 November. The wind headed her, and the shoals were so terrifying that the Pilgrims turned about and made Cape Cod (now Provincetown) harbor. Since this place was outside Virginia, which made their patent useless, a few rugged individualists who had joined the Pilgrims in London announced that "when they came ashore they would use their own liberty, for none had power to command them." Brewster, Bradford, Winslow, Standish, and other leaders of the expedition then drew up the famous Mayflower Compact, which almost all the adult men signed. Therein they formed a "civil body politic," and promised "all due submission and obedience" to such "just and equal laws" as the government they set up might pass. This compact, like the Virginia assembly, is an almost startling revelation of the capacity of Englishmen in that era for self-government. Moreover, it was a second instance of Englishmen's determination to live in the colonies under a rule of law. We must never forget this; for in colonies of other European nations the will of the prince, or his representative, was supreme.

After prospecting Cape Cod and deciding that it was incapable of supporting human life, the Pilgrim Fathers decided to settle at the place which Captain John Smith had already named Plymouth. On 16 December the *Mayflower* arrived there and began landing her passengers. The English had no sooner landed and built crude shelters than the "great sickness" bore in on them as it had on the Englishmen at Jamestown; and only 50 of the 102 immigrants survived. Hope returned with spring, when "the birds sang in the woods most pleasantly." *Mayflower* set sail for England on 5 April 1621, and not one of the stout-hearted survivors returned in her. With the help of a friendly Indian they learned how to plant and cultivate corn; Miles Standish taught them how to shoot game; fish, clams, and lobsters were plentiful. In October they invited friendly Wampanoag Indians to share their first Thanksgiving feast, and concluded a treaty with sachem Massasoit.

William Bradford, aged thirty-one, was elected governor after the first one died; and thereafter the Plymouth Colony had annual elections of governor and assistants. Several times the colony was at the point of starvation; it would have perished but for food bought from a Virginia shipmaster who was fishing off the coast. He also brought news of the Indian massacre of 1622 which almost finished off Virginia. This put the Pilgrims on their guard; they built a fort on the hill overlooking Plymouth harbor, and by firm diplomacy kept the hostile Indians of Massachusetts and Cape Cod at bay. In June 1625 Bradford wrote to a friend in England that the Pilgrims "never felt the sweetness of the country till this year." They managed to get along as a trading-post colony, growing corn which they traded with the Indians for beaver pelts; and by this fur trade they eventually managed to get out of debt to the loan sharks in London, to obtain a patent from the reorganized Northern Virginia Company (now the Council for New England) for their land, and even to set up branch trading posts on the Kennebec river and at the sites of the Cape Cod canal and Hartford, Connecticut.

4. New Netherland and New France

At these last two posts the Pilgrims encountered friendly rivals—Dutchmen from "the Manhatoes," the site of New York City, where the Pilgrims themselves originally intended to settle.

New Netherland, the Dutch colony which at one time comprised the entire Hudson Valley and the shores of Delaware Bay and Long Island, stems from the voyage of Henry Hudson, an Englishman in Dutch employ. In the yacht *Half*

Moon, even smaller than *Mayflower,* he sailed in 1609 up the river named after him, hoping that it would prove to be a northwest passage to the Indies; and only gave up when he reached the rapids north of the site of Albany. But he had discovered the greatest fur-bearing region in North America south of the St. Lawrence, and made friends with the local Indians by giving some of them their first taste of hard liquor. Adrien Block, Cornelis May, and other Dutch sea captains sailed thither to trade, but no real attempt to colonize was made until the Dutch West India Company was founded in 1621. This Company founded trading posts at Fort Orange (Albany) in 1624, and at New Amsterdam (New York City) in 1626. That was the year when the Company purchased Manhattan Island from the local Indians for sixty guilders' worth of trading truck—the "greatest real estate bargain in history," the sixty guilders being roughly equivalent to forty 1965 dollars.

The United Provinces of the Netherlands, having lately won their independence from Spain, were powerful and enterprising. During the seventeenth century the English regarded the Dutch as their greatest rivals and potential enemies. The two countries were very much alike in their Protestant religion, love of liberty, and other respects; but they drifted into war because of rivalry in foreign commerce. In matters maritime and many others it was difficult to "beat the Dutch." The Dutch West India Company might have planted a strong colony, a real challenge to New France and New England. But the Netherlands had no surplus population to emigrate, and the capitalists were mostly interested in wresting valuable possessions from the Portuguese in the Far East, such as the Spice Islands, Java, Malaya, and Ceylon.

The Dutch at first got along well with their English neighbors and even taught them the use of wampum, the Algonquian shell money, for trading with the natives. French Canada was a far more formidable rival to the English empire, although England did not yet know it.

Just as the founding of Jamestown in 1607 is a turning point in the history of Anglo-America, so the year 1608, when Champlain set up a trading post at Quebec, is a milestone in the history of New France. The French did not immediately abandon their posts on the Bay of Fundy, but these never wholly recovered from the effects of Samuel Argall's raid. Eventually, enough French peasants settled the Grand Pré of L'Acadie to present England with a problem, Longfellow with "Evangeline," and Louisiana with the "Cajans." But in the seventeenth century the French applied their main efforts

along the St. Lawrence and in the West Indies. Champlain, by
keeping a firm hand on Quebec, put his king in possession of
the one great valley that led from the heart of North America
to the east coast. The St. Lawrence drained the greatest source
of beaver fur on the continent; but whether the French, the
Dutch, or the English obtained the bulk of it depended on how
their colonists handled the Indians.

Champlain quickly discovered that the St. Lawrence was a
fulcrum of power politics between the Five Nations of the
Iroquois, and the Huron, Montagnais and other tribes of the
valley. He tried to secure for these neighboring Indians a firm
mastery of the great river by helping them fight the Iroquois.
Even before the Dutch occupied the site of Albany, Champlain had helped the Montagnais to win a fight with Mohawks
on the lake named after him, had explored the Ottawa river by
canoe, and reached Lake Huron where he wintered with the
Huron nation and won their allegiance. This put the Huron in
a fair way to become middlemen for the fur trade between the
French at Montreal and the Indians who trapped in the basin
of the Great Lakes. The Iroquois, determined to prevent this,
in 1624 ambushed a fleet of Huron canoes carrying fur down
the Ottawa to Montreal. That showed the French what to expect, for the Iroquois were famous for long-distance forays
and surprise attacks on Indian villages, followed by savage
scalping and the torture of prisoners.

Quebec was still a trading post, controlled by Champlain
under whatever brief monopoly had won the royal favor. He
and the fur merchants welcomed the missionaries, but wanted
no white settlers. When in 1617 Louis Hébert, a Paris apothe-
cary who had made a voyage to New France and wished to
settle there, proposed to bring out his family, he was discouraged. Champlain, not relishing the prospect of Indians hanging
around a drugstore, allowed Hébert to stay only after he had
promised not to serve the natives. For thirteen years his family
comprised the only real settlers in Canada, all the rest being
missionaries or employees of trading companies; not until
1628 did ploughing or planting begin.

Twenty-five years had then elapsed since Champlain's first
voyage, but the French hold on Canada was still so feeble
that in 1629, during a brief Anglo-French war, an English
privateer captured Quebec easily; and a Scottish laird, Sir
William Alexander (who is responsible for the name Nova
Scotia) occupied the abandoned trading post at Port Royal.
But Charles I returned both Quebec and L'Acadie to France
in return for payment of overdue installments on the dowry
of his Queen, amounting to $240,000. This was as good a

bargain for France as the Louisiana Purchase later was to be for the United States. And by 1633 Champlain was again at Quebec as governor for a new and powerful company, the Hundred Associates of New France. There on Christmas Day 1635 he died.

Samuel de Champlain was the most versatile of colonial founders in North America: at once sailor and soldier, scholar and man of action, artist and explorer. Sailors admire him, not only for exploring the rugged coast of New England without serious mishap, but for his *Treatise on Seamanship* in which his description of "The Good Captain" well applies to himself: "An upright, God-fearing man, not dainty about his food or drink, robust and alert, with good sea-legs, and in a strong voice to give commands to all hands; pleasant and affable in conversation, but imperious in his commands, liberal and courteous to defeated enemies, knowing everything that concerns the handling of the ship," and of sailors. Champlain's accounts of his coastal cruises and explorations of the interior were embellished with drawings of flora, fauna, and Indians that are not lacking in artistic merit, and accompanied by maps which were not surpassed for accuracy in fifty years. Loyal to his king and his church, he endeavored with success to lead the New Testament life in an age of loose morals; many years after his last visit to the Huron nation they were marveling at his continence. The death of this great leader closes the first chapter in the history of New France.

5. *Beginnings of the Non-Spanish West Indies*

Within the space of fifteen years English, French, and Dutch made their first settlements in the Lesser Antilles, which Columbus had discovered but the Spaniards had bypassed in favor of the big islands and the continent. After several initial failures in that region by Sir Walter Raleigh and others, Thomas Warner organized a company, and in 1624 sailed with a group of choice cutthroats to colonize St. Christopher (St. Kitts). Taking no chances with the Caribs, Warner surprised them after a drinking bout, slaughtered a number, and drove off the rest to nearby islands. His men then settled down somewhat nervously to plant tobacco, knowing that nearby islands were full of Caribs.

That same year the French, who had sailed the Caribbean for a century as pirates and privateers, began their first West Indian colony, more or less by accident. A French privateer captain whose lieutenant was named Pierre Belain D'Esnambuc, following an unfortunate encounter with a Spanish galleon, anchored in the roadstead of St. Kitts. The English settlers welcomed his men with enthusiasm, fearing a dugout canoe counterattack from nearby Nevis. That is exactly what the Caribs did. The combined English and French defense force broke up this Carib amphibious landing; and then, marvelous to relate, instead of fighting each other, divided St. Kitts amicably. The island is only 23 miles long, but the English took the middle and the French the two ends, and both found tobacco planting there very profitable.

St. Kitts was not big enough for ambitious men such as Warner and D'Esnambuc. Both sailed home to obtain royal grants. Warner received from Charles I in 1625 a patent creating him governor of the Leeward Islands with the right to colonize St. Kitts, Nevis, Barbados, and Montserrat; Louis XIII gave D'Esnambuc a patent for the middle of St. Kitts, with the right to colonize Guadeloupe and Martinique at his own expense, if he cared to try.

Warner was a little fellow without much influence, and no sooner had he obtained his Leeward Islands patent than he had to reckon with a "big shot" at the Jacobean court. This was James Hay, a Scot who followed King James to London, obtaining all manner of favors and the earldom of Carlisle. Warner, knowing Hay's power at court, attempted to use him as window dressing, but the Scot was too smart to be content with being a mere front man. He allowed Warner and his friends to raise the money; but the charter created Lord Carlisle absolute proprietor of the English Caribbee Islands from St. Kitts to Barbados, inclusive. Warner and his friends were glad to settle for permission to keep the land that they had been cultivating in St. Kitts.

In his new Caribbee Islands proprietary, Carlisle found Barbados the most profitable, and it became the wealthiest and most successful English colony in the first half of the seventeenth century. Barbados is only 300 square miles in area, but all good soil. By the end of 1629, according to Captain John Smith, no fewer than 3000 English had settled in Lord Carlisle's Caribbee Islands, most of them in Barbados but some in St. Kitts, Nevis, and Antigua. The profits from cotton and tobacco were immense, and emigration went rapidly forward.

Thus, in the twenty years 1607–27, English, Dutch, and French had firmly founded their New World empires. The French had a string of trading posts in Canada, a plantation on St. Kitts, and were about to take over Guadeloupe. The Dutch trading posts on the Hudson were about to expand into fringe colonies along its banks and on Long Island. English

Virginia was spreading rapidly along the shores of Chesapeake Bay. Plymouth Colony still bravely struggled along, and the English in the Caribbee Islands were doing very well. England, moreover, had performed a service to the future unlike that of any other country in modern times. She had planted the seeds of the common law and of representative government.

CONFESS JEHOVAH

Con - fess Je - ho - vah thank - ful - ly, for He is good;
for His mer - cies con - tin - u - eth for - ev - er.
Un - to the Lord of Lords con - fess, be - cause His mer - ci - ful kind - ness
con - tin - u - eth for - ev - er. To Him that doth, Him - self on - ly,
things won - drous great; for His mer - cies con - tin - u - eth for - ev - er.

V

New England Takes Shape

1628-1675

1. *The Puritan Movement*

PLYMOUTH COLONY was founded in 1620 by the *Mayflower*
Pilgrims, who brought Puritanism in one of its purest forms to
America. But New Plymouth would long have remained a
poor and isolated colony, and New England a mere string of
trading posts and fishing stations, but for the great Puritan
migration of the 1630's.

Puritanism was essentially and primarily a religious movement; attempts to prove it to have been a mask for politics or
money-making are false as well as unhistorical. In the broadest
sense Puritanism was a passion for righteousness; the desire to
know and do God's will. Similar movements have occurred in
every branch of Christianity, as well as in Judaism.[1] Puritanism was responsible for the settlement of New England; and
as the Congregational, Presbyterian, Methodist, Baptist, Uni-
tarian, Quaker, and other Protestant sects of the United States
are offshoots of seventeenth-century English and Scottish

[1] Jansenism in eighteenth-century France was a Puritan movement
within the Catholic Church which still has a pervasive influence in Ireland. The French Huguenots, and Scots, German, Scandinavian, and
Netherlands Calvinists were essentially Puritan in doctrine and attitude,
differing only in detail from the English Puritans.

Puritanism, it is not surprising that Puritan ways of thinking and doing have had a vast effect on the American mind and character, precursors of what is commonly called the Protestant Ethic.

The English Puritans who founded New England were nearer in doctrine to the Catholic Church than to liberal Protestant sects of the nineteenth and twentieth centuries. They agreed that man existed for the glory of God, and that his first concern in life should be to do God's will and so receive future happiness. They insisted, however, that the Catholic Church had taken a wrong turn after the fifth century by adding forms, ceremonies, and dogmas unauthorized by the Bible. The Church of England, they felt, had made a good start by repudiating Rome, but had slowed up the Reformation by retaining bishops, vestments, and ritual. Puritans proposed to worship as they imagined the early Christians did; their learned men combed through the Epistles and Acts of the Apostles to discover exactly how the primitive churches were organized. The Congregational Church in New England happened to be organized on a democratic basis, not because Puritans were in love with democracy but because leaders such as John Cotton and Thomas Hooker insisted that the First Church in Boston and the First Church of Hartford copy the exact organization of the First Church of Corinth and the First Church of Philippi, about which they knew very little, since the apostles and evangelists did not say much about them.

The English Puritans were radical, in that they proposed to get at the root of everything, no matter who or what stood in their way; but in a larger sense they were conservative, even reactionary, since their aim was to restore "the church unspotted, pure" of the early Christians and so to reform society that one could lead the New Testament life and at the same time earn a living. They wished to sweep away the practices of the Renaissance, to get back to apostolic times when the men who had seen Jesus plain were still alive. God, they believed, had dictated the Bible as the complete guide to life; the Trinity maintained a line of communication to each individual Christian through the Holy Ghost and his conscience. They were deeply impressed by a story that their favorite church father, St. Augustine, told in his *Confessions*. He heard a voice saying, *tolle et lege*, "Pick up and read." Opening the Bible, his eyes lit on Romans xiii: 12–14: "The night is far spent, the day is at hand; let us put on the armour of light. Let us walk honestly, as in the day; not in carousing and drunkenness, not in debauchery and lust, not in strife and jealousy.

But put ye on the Lord Jesus Christ, and make no provision for the flesh, to fulfil the lusts thereof."

In response to the light of conscience and the written Word, the Puritan yearned to know God and to approach Him directly without intermediary. If the Puritan rejected the ancient pageantry of Catholic worship, it was not because of any dislike for beauty. He loved beauty in women and children and, as his works prove, achieved beauty in silverware, household furniture, and architecture. He rejected ritual as a distorting screen erected by man between him and his maker. Stained-glass windows, images of the saints, organ music, and Gregorian chants, he thought, threw a jeweled, sensuous curtain between the worshippers and the Almighty. As soon as the Puritan acquired the means to beautify the exterior of his meetinghouse (as he called his church building), he did so with classic columns, Palladian windows, and spires; but the interior he preferred to leave cold and bare so as not to distract the attention of the congregation.

Puritanism spread rapidly over northern Europe, especially in Switzerland, Scandinavia, the Netherlands, and the British Isles. People seemed to acquire a longing for Bible study, extemporaneous prayer, and long, meaty sermons on duty and doctrine. We hear of men and women running from town to town to hear sermons; of churches hiring an extra preacher to deliver a sermon when their regular parson could not or would not. And Puritanism appealed to merchants because it taught that a man could serve God as well in business or a profession as by taking holy orders, and that all "callings" were equally honorable in His sight. As George Chapman expressed it in his play *Eastward Ho:*

> Whate'er some vainer youth may term disgrace,
> The gain of honest pains is never base;
> From trades, from arts, from valour, honour springs;
> These three are founts of gentry; yea, of kings.

A series of dissatisfactions with the situation in England was the main reason for thousands of Puritans emigrating to the New World. Their main grievance was religious. Puritans looked to Elizabeth I and her successor to carry through the reform and reorganize the church on an apostolic basis. Queen Bess was much too clever to do that. A large segment of her subjects had become Puritan, but many were still Catholic at heart, and would be driven into open rebellion by abolishing ritual. And James I cordially disliked the Puritans; he boasted that he would make them conform, or harry them out of the land. The Pilgrim Fathers, anticipating a crackdown, took flight to Holland and then to New Plymouth. But the great mass of English Puritans, called nonconformists, remained, hoping to reform the church from within.

Charles I, who succeeded in 1625, gave his ear to Bishop William Laud, a saintly cleric who wished to order and discipline the Church of England on a high-church pattern. He looked on Puritan practices as blasphemous; he aimed to restore candles and the cross to the altar, kneeling and chanting, and other forms of worship that had been brushed aside in earlier reigns. The government now purged the universities of Puritans and put pressure on the Puritan clergy to conform, or get out.

Not only religion but everything else was going wrong, from the Puritan point of view. In Europe, the Catholic counterreformation, implemented by Spanish power and financed by American gold, seemed to be winning. France tried to suppress her Protestants, the Huguenots; Bohemia and the Rhineland were overrun by Spanish armies. The tide seemed as irresistible as Hitlerism did three centuries later, and the Puritans suspected that Charles's Catholic queen, Henrietta Maria, was nourishing a "fifth column" in England.

The internal situation, too, dismayed the Puritans. King James, coming to wealthy England from starved Scotland, became wildly extravagant, replacing the statesmen of Elizabeth's reign by glamor boys and flatterers; the revels of his court were scandalous. His example of heavy and luxurious spending went right down the social line. Business flourished, fortunes were made in foreign trade, speculation, and through monopolies that the king conferred on his favorites. The newly rich were buying up land, all prices were inflated, fixed incomes bought less and less, foreigners like the banker Pallavicini were throwing modest farms together to make great country estates; Sir Edward Coke, the great barrister and judge, acquired over sixty manors. It was becoming increasingly difficult for the simple country gentleman or business man to hang onto his land, much less keep up with the Johnny-come-latelys. A ballad of the day tells more of this tendency than any description:

You talke of Newe England; I truly beleeve
Oulde England's growne newe and doth us deceave.
I'le aske you a question or two, by your leave:
    And is not ould England growne new?

And what is become of your ould fashiond clothes,
Your longsided Dublett and your trunck hose?
They'r turn'd to new fashions—but what the Lord knowes!
   And is not ould England growne new?

Now your gallaint and his tayllor some half yeare together
To fitt a new sute to a new hatt and fether,
Of gould or of silver, silke, cloth stuff, or lether.
   And is not ould England growne new?

New trickings, new goeings, new measurs, new paces,
New hedds for your men, for women new faces;
And twenty new tricks to mend ther bad cases!
   And is not ould England growne new?

On the political side, King Charles's attempt to govern England and levy taxes without a parliament brought Puritanism and political liberalism into alliance. By March of 1629, when Charles dismissed the last parliament to meet for twelve years, it looked as if he had succeeded in suppressing the traditional liberties of Englishmen. It was time for the weak, the indifferent, and the faint-hearted to run to cover. But the Puritan, doubting nothing and fearing no man, undertook to set all crooked ways straight and create a new heaven and a new earth. If he were not permitted to do that in England, he would find some other place to establish his City of God.

2. *The Founding of the Bay Colony*

New England was the answer. Virginia was Anglican, the Dutch had seized the Hudson, but the Pilgrim Fathers had proved that human life could be supported on a "stern and rockbound coast," and the Council for New England, to which this region had been granted, was looking for business. The Council issued several land patents in the 1620's, one to a group of Puritans who in 1628 received the coast between the Charles and Merrimack rivers, with an indefinite extension inland. Under a stout soldier named John Endecott, this group settled Salem. Next, just as modern business men buy a small concern and build it up, other groups of Puritans got control of this organization and obtained a royal charter as the "Governor and Company of the Massachusetts Bay in New England."

These men had long been talking about emigrating to America in order to set up a colony after their own hearts.

Among their leaders were Thomas Dudley, who had been captain of a foreign legion, his son-in-law Simon Bradstreet; Thomas Leverett, alderman of Boston in Lincolnshire, whose pastor, John Cotton, was one of the leading Puritan divines; Sir Richard Saltonstall and Theophilus Eaton, merchants of London; William Pynchon, Squire of Springfield in Essex; and a lawyer just turned forty, named John Winthrop. These men met somewhere in Cambridge University, of which most of them were alumni, in August of 1629 and signed an agreement to emigrate to New England within seven months, provided they could carry over the government and charter of the Massachusetts Bay Company. The reason for this important proviso was to protect themselves from the king, who otherwise might confiscate their charter, as had happened to the Virginia Company only five years earlier. And it so happened, whether by chance or design, that the Massachusetts Bay Charter did not require the stockholders to meet in any particular place. The stockholders voted for the transfer and elected John Winthrop governor. Many families sold both land and goods, and during the first six months of 1630 some fifteen ships, carrying over 1000 men, women, and children, cleared from English ports for Massachusetts. The movement gathered force as Bishop Laud put the screws on the Puritans, until by 1634 some 10,000 of them had settled in New England.

These Puritans had a definite mission—to establish a community rather than a mere colony, where they could put their ideals into practice. New England, to them, was a New Canaan which the Almighty had set apart for an experiment in Christian living. They felt, as Winthrop remarked on the way over, that they were "a city upon a hill," "with the eyes of all people" upon them; an example to prove that it was possible to lead the New Testament life, yet make a living.[1] These immigrants, organized in neighborhood groups and led by their ejected pastors, made several settlements around Boston. For a generation the fur trade was important, especially on the Connecticut river, where William Pynchon established a new Springfield. The Reverend Hugh Peter, from a fishing center in Cornwall, organized fisheries at Marblehead and found a market for dried codfish, an industry which became so important that a wooden image—"the sacred cod"—was hung up as a symbol in the assembly chamber at Boston, and is still

[1] John Winthrop, *A Modell of Christian Charity*, p. 20; quoted by President-elect John F. Kennedy in his speech to the General Court of Massachusetts, 9 January 1961, at a time when Massachusetts had become a bad example of political corruption.

there. But for several years the main business of the Massachusetts Bay Colony was raising cattle, corn, and other foodstuffs to sell to newcomers who came supplied with money and goods. The Puritans' connections with London merchants, who extended credit to their friends overseas, were essential to sustain a colony that doubled its population every year.

This system ended in 1637 when the Puritan migration stopped, owing to the troubles that heralded the English Civil War. Puritans now hoped to prevail at home, as indeed they did. This occasioned the first major American depression—the "fall of cow," as a local poet described it—which forced the Puritans to look around for other means of livelihood. These were found through shipbuilding and the West Indies trade. In the Caribbee Islands, where it paid planters to concentrate on raising tobacco and sugar with slave labor, there was a great demand for New England products—dried fish, salt beef and pork, ground vegetables, poultry, even horses—and for ships to transport them. By selling these in the West Indies, the New Englanders obtained a balance to buy goods in England. Around 1670 they began distilling West Indies molasses into rum, which replaced hard cider and home-brewed beer as the drink of the country. This West Indies trade was the main factor in New England prosperity until the American Revolution; without it the settlements on the northern coast would have remained stationary or declined.

The transfer of the Massachusetts Bay charter from London to Boston had an important influence on future American institutions. It made the colony virtually independent of England. There was no royal governor or judge, no English army garrison, no parliamentary agent; nothing to keep it in line with English colonial policy. And the form that this colonial government took, following the terms of the charter, became the standard American pattern. As a business charter, the corporation consisted of freemen (stockholders), meeting in an assembly called the general court where were annually elected, on a stated date, the governor, deputy governor, and assistants (councillors). But transfer overseas turned the company into a colonial government. The freemen were now the voters, the governor and deputy governor the two chief magistrates, and the assistants doubled as governor's council and supreme court. By 1644, owing to a typical small-town dispute over a stray sow, the general court separated into two houses, and Massachusetts Bay had something approaching a modern state government. The franchise was confined to church members in good standing; but this excluded very few adult men, and the annual election of all officials made the government responsible to the people. They exercised their power, too; on occasion electing another governor than staid and conscientious John Winthrop. One of Winthrop's friends wrote from England that people were wondering why the electorate "doe toss and tumble about" their leaders so disrespectfully.

This government was not a democracy, but an important step toward it. And a further check on autocracy was established by a body of laws and a bill of rights. Winthrop and his elected assistants, who also served as judges, liked to pass judgments based on their own intuition and the Bible. The people observed that this allowed too much discretion to the judges. Hence the Massachusetts "Body of Liberties" adopted in 1641, and the "General Fundamentals" of Plymouth Colony which may have been earlier, contained the classic safeguards of English liberty, such as jury trial, no taxation without representation, free elections, nobody to be deprived of

ARMS OF FOUNDERS OF NEW ENGLAND

life, liberty, or property save by due process of law, or compelled to incriminate himself. These are the same principles later incorporated in the Bill of Rights of the Federal Constitution. In certain aspects, the Body of Liberties was ahead of English practice. Torture and cruel and barbarous punishments were prohibited, feudal dues were abolished, foreigners were assured equal protection of the law (as they already had been in Virginia), and cruelty to animals was forbidden. Cruelty to wives, too; a husband was forbidden to beat his wife "unless it be in his own defense upon her assault!"

3. A Clutch of New Colonies, 1630–1650

The Massachusetts Bay form of government was copied in three New England colonies that sprang from the Massachusetts trunk, as well as in the older Plymouth Colony. Connecticut Colony was established by the earliest western migration in North American history. The Reverend Thomas Hooker and the Reverend Samuel Stone, and John Haynes, a wealthy landowner who had been elected governor of Massachusetts Bay, felt cramped in Cambridge and declared that the "bent of their spirits" required a move. In 1636 they marched cross-country and settled three towns, Hartford, Windsor, and Wethersfield, on the Connecticut river, which became the nucleus of Connecticut. Two years later, a company of London Puritans led by Theophilus Eaton and the Reverend John Davenport, chose New Haven as a likely site for a trading city to rival New York and Boston. Their colony of that name spread along and even across Long Island Sound. Each group of emigrants in 1639 drew up a written constitution—the Fundamental Orders of Connecticut and of New Haven, providing representative governments which served them well until 1662, when Charles II combined them under a corporate charter as the Colony of Connecticut. That charter remained the fundamental law of colony and state until 1818. The social and political institutions of both these colonies were similar in all essentials to those of the Bay.

Very different was the Colony of Rhode Island and Providence Plantations, founded by left-wing Puritans who, finding the atmosphere of the other New England colonies stuffy, protested loudly against their system of church and state. Rhode Island's founders were the Reverend Roger Williams, who has a deserved fame as an early exponent of religious liberty, Samuel Gorton, and the first woman to play a leading role in American history, Anne Hutchinson. All three, banished from

Massachusetts Bay or Plymouth as troublemakers, founded the four settlements on Narragansett Bay, which received a colonial patent from the Long Parliament in 1644, and, later, a charter from Charles II which protected them from being forcibly annexed by their orthodox Puritan neighbors. As hardly any two Rhode Islanders shared the same beliefs, and Williams floundered among a number of sects, the only possible basis for unity in that colony was religious liberty. This was accorded to all Christians. It not only worked, but slowly spread; in 1964 Cardinal Cushing, Archbishop of Boston, proposed that his Church adopt religious liberty as a principle.

Roger Williams was the most beloved of colonial founders prior to William Penn. The Indians, whose language he studied, lodging with them "in their filthy, smoky holes," adored Williams because he respected their individuality, protected them against land-hungry members of his race, and never tried to convert them unless they asked for it. Williams stoutly maintained what everyone else in his day considered a monstrous heresy: that, for aught anyone knew, the Indians' religion was equally acceptable to God with Christianity. It was typical of Williams that in the *Key to the Indian Language*, which he had printed in England, the vocabulary starts with "*Cowammaunsh*—I love you," and that his rules of grammar are interspersed with little rhymes such as:

> Sometimes God gives them fish or flesh,
>   Yet they're content without.
> And what comes in, they part to friends
>   And strangers round about.

> If nature's sons both wild and tame
>   Humane and courteous be,
> How ill becomes it sons of God
>   To want humanity!

In addition to the five Puritan colonies, two small proprietary colonies were set up in New England—New Hampshire and Maine. The future Granite State, which began as a personal estate of Captain John Mason, consisted of a few hundred people in Portsmouth, Exeter, and other settlements on tidewater. Mason eventually sold out to the crown. Maine to the Kennebec river belonged to Sir Ferdinando Gorges, who entertained grandiose schemes for a feudal domain which came to naught, and his heirs sold out to Massachusetts.

4. New England People and Institutions

Important for the development of New England, and of the Chesapeake and West Indies colonies too, were events in England itself. The troubles which led to the English Civil War, beginning in 1637, prevented Charles I from suppressing the Bay Colony as his friends and its enemies wished him to do. Civil war between "Cavaliers" (the king's party) and "Roundheads" (Parliament's party and the Puritans) broke out in 1641 and continued, except for a short truce, until January 1649, when Charles I was executed. Parliament then set up a republic, the Commonwealth of England, keeping sovereign power in its own hands. This worked so ill that in 1653 the Roundhead army created Colonel Oliver Cromwell Lord Protector of England. Oliver almost established a new dynasty; but after his death on 3 September 1658 his son and successor, Richard, proved a weakling and resigned. Charles II was restored to his father's throne in 1660 and resumed the Stuart policy of trying to govern without a parliament.

During these two decades 1640–60, England's American colonies were left very much to themselves. The New Englanders naturally sympathized with the Roundheads, but refused to go along with their fellow Puritans in England. Massachusetts even defended her neutrality in the Civil War by twice preventing a parliamentary privateer from capturing a royalist merchant ship in Boston harbor. On another occasion the Bay Colony assembly declared: "Our allegiance binds us not to the laws of England any longer than while we live in England, for the laws of the parliament of England reach no further, nor do the king's writs under the great seal go any further." The colony sent Edward Winslow to London with defiant instructions from Governor Winthrop, ending, "Our charter gives us an absolute power of government."

A striking proof of English capacity for self-government was the New England Confederation, formed in 1643. This was a loose federal union, precursor of the Confederation of 1781. The professed objects were to settle boundary and other disputes among the four member colonies of Massachusetts, Plymouth, Connecticut, and New Haven, and mutual protection against aggression by French, Dutch, or Indians. Each colony appointed two commissioners who met annually, handled Indian affairs, and had power to declare war by a vote of three to one. They managed to settle several intercolonial disputes, and in 1675–76 helped to concert military measures in King Philip's War.

The New England people, almost to a man, were English and Puritan. About the only non-Puritans to emigrate were some of the indentured servants; this class never became as important in New England as in Maryland or Virginia, though numerous enough to make trouble for the authorities. After their time was up they often hired out for wages. The only joke in Governor Winthrop's journal (and he didn't think it a joke but a piece of insolence) is the retort of a servant. His master, having been forced to sell a yoke of oxen to pay the man's wages, said he could keep him no longer, since he knew not how to find any more money. The hired man replied that he would accept cattle for wages as long as his master had any: "You shall then serve me, and so you may have your cattle again!"

The great mass of emigrants to New England were middle-class farmers, tradesmen, and artisans who had enough property to make wills—to the subsequent delight of genealogists. As Puritanism put no stigma on manual labor, and as every man, no matter how poor, could vote if he joined the church (and in Rhode Island did not even have to do that), independent yeomen and workmen became the backbone of the community. In New England you could always find a blacksmith, wheelwright, carpenter, joiner, cordwainer, tanner, ironworker, spinner, weaver, or whatnot,—to make things which the Southern colonies at that era had to import from England. New Englanders, however they differed in property and occupation, had a common belief in the Bible as the guide to life, and a uniform method of land division and settlement. When members of a village community felt crowded for space, they petitioned the colonial assembly for a new township, the ideal size being six miles square. A committee was appointed to satisfy Indian claimants, to settle on a village site and lay out lots. Home lots and the meetinghouse, which served both as church and town hall, were laid out around a village green, with a surrounding belt of planting lots for growing crops. Salt meadows on the coast, or river meads in the interior, valuable for the wild grass which could be cut and stored for winter forage, were laid out in long strips and usually cultivated in common. The rest of the township for many years remained the property of the community, where anyone could cut firewood and timber, or pasture cattle. Houses of this period, with high-peaked gables and leaded glass casement windows, bore little resemblance to the white-painted New England village of later colonial days; but the village pattern remained constant until the eighteenth century when, owing to no further danger from Indians, and the increase of population, people began laying out farms far from the central village.

Although the Puritans objected to the prevailing religious and social customs of their mother country, they were none the less loyal Englishmen, determined to embrace and perpetuate both English liberties and English culture. They had the Englishman's love of field sports, especially hunting and fishing; they bred horses for their own use and for export to the West Indies, and raced them, too. Yankee settlers of Long Island, as early as 1670, held annual horse races on Hempstead Plains for the prize of a silver cup.

One trait in which New Englanders even excelled the old country was their emphasis on education. Free popular education has been the most lasting contribution of early New England to the United States, and possibly the most beneficial. As Gertrude Stein once put it when writing on education: "In New England they have done it they do do it they will do it and they do it in every way in which education can be thought about." Compact villages made it possible to have and do, as well as talk about education. It is no accident that almost every educational leader and reformer in American history, from Benjamin Franklin through Horace Mann and John Dewey to James B. Conant, has been a New Englander of the Puritan stock.

Elementary education—the "three R's"—became a parental responsibility by act of the Bay Colony in 1642; and five years later, settlements with fifty or more families were required to appoint a schoolmaster "to teach all such children as shall resort to him to write and read." The same act of 1647 (shortly copied by Connecticut and New Haven) required towns of 100 families or more to set up a grammar school on the English model. These grammar schools took in boys at six or eight years of age and kept them for six years, during which they studied Latin and Greek grammar and literature, and arithmetic. Four of these schools—Boston Latin, Cambridge Latin, Roxbury Latin, and Hopkins Grammar School of New Haven—are still flourishing as public high schools. Ezekiel Cheever, a graduate of Emmanuel College, Cambridge, taught successively at New Haven, Ipswich, Charlestown, and Boston, wrote Latin textbooks, and died in harness at the age of ninety-two, without ever missing a day of school. To the boys of all four towns he was a kind and beloved master, and in his rhymed advice to later pedagogues he says:

> The lads with Honour first and Reason rule;
> Blowes are but for the refractory fool.

But, Oh! first teach them their great God to fear;
That you, like me, with joy may meet them here.

This religious sentiment was basic. The dynamic motive in colonial education, and in American higher education generally, until the rise of the public high school and the state university, was religious as well as humane. Boys had to learn to read in order to read the Bible, to write and speak "pieces" in order to communicate; to "cipher" in order to do business. Knowledge of Latin and Greek opened to them the best world literature and prepared them for college. Some 130 alumni of the universities of Oxford, Cambridge, and Dublin emigrated to New England before 1646. These men wanted the same advantages for their children as they had enjoyed in the old country; and now that the English universities were closed to Puritans, the only way they could obtain a supply of learned ministers for their Congregational churches, and of educated men to carry on the work of civil government, was to set up a college of their own. Without waiting for a wealthy benefactor, they went ahead and founded one through a grant of £400 by the assembly of the Bay Colony in 1636. Two years later the college opened at the new Cambridge, in a small house in a cow-yard given by the town, and was named after its earliest benefactor, the Reverend John Harvard, who, dying at the age of thirty, left the college half his fortune and a library of 400 volumes. In 1650 Harvard College was given a charter by the Bay Colony, which declared its purpose to be "the advancement of all good literature, arts and sciences."

The first president, thirty-year-old Henry Dunster, set up such high standards in the liberal arts as to attract students from Bermuda, Virginia, and England as well as the New England colonies. Throughout the depression of the 1640's the college flourished, students paying term bills with farm produce, clothing, and cattle on the hoof. Scholarships were provided, at the request of the New England Confederation, by voluntary contributions of a shilling, a peck of wheat, or a string of wampum from each family. Having no rivals in the English colonies until William and Mary College was founded in 1693, and Yale in 1701, Harvard set both the pace and the pattern for higher education in North America. The traditional four-year liberal arts course was followed, mostly in Latin textbooks. Instruction was by lectures, recitations, and Latin disputations; dormitories were provided for the students, who dined in hall with their tutors. A great show was made of commencement. Catalogues were issued, in which graduates were grouped under the year of taking their bachelor's degree. Three years more was required to study theology and take an M.A. Somewhat more than half the Harvard graduates in the seventeenth century became ministers.

The first printing press in the English colonies, and the second in North America, was set up in 1639 in the Harvard College Yard, as the former village cow-yard is called to this day. Here were printed the *Bay Psalm Book* of 1640 (now the most valuable of early Americana), the *New England Primer,* and an annual almanac compiled by some college "philomath" who was allowed to fill vacant spaces with his own poems and essays. But the amazing achievement of this press was to print the entire Bible in the Algonquian language, for which the Reverend John Eliot of Roxbury devised the first equivalents in Roman letters. This was the first Bible to be printed in the New World, and the first translation of it into a barbarous and hitherto unwritten language since Bishop Ulfila turned the Old Testament into Visigothic in the fourth century of the Christian era.

New Englanders, popular illustrators to the contrary, did not dress in black with steeple-crowned hats; they liked bright colors for clothing, furniture, and hangings. They mostly made their own furniture and silverware, both for domestic use and for "The Lord's Supper," as they and their successors call Holy Communion. John Hull, first of the colonial silversmiths, was also a pillar of the church, merchant, shipowner, and farmer. He owned vessels and traded with the West Indies, England, and Spain, lent money at interest, served as treasurer of the colony, and made the dies from which were coined the pine-tree shillings and sixpences, oldest of English colonial coinage. He melted down Spanish dollars ("pieces of eight") obtained in the West Indies trade, and from the silver bullion fashioned cups, beakers, and other articles that compare well with the best contemporary work in England; and he taught an apprentice, Jeremiah Dummer, to continue the business after his death.

Besides the arts of the husbandman and the crafts of the household, organized industry began in New England. Fullers from Rowley in Yorkshire set up a fulling mill at Rowley in the Bay Colony, where home-woven cloth could be shrunk and sheared. John Winthrop, Jr., later governor of Connecticut, in 1645 set up an ambitious and, for a time, successful ironworks at Saugus near Lynn. Here iron ore dug out of swamps and ponds, smelted with oak charcoal and flux from nearby rocks, was fashioned into pots and pans, anchors, chains, and other ironware for local needs. The men who ran it, mostly of a Welsh family named Leonard, later established other ironworks, and from these descended the iron and steel industry of the United States.

Another line of John Hull the mintmaster was horse-raising on Cape Cod and Point Judith, Rhode Island. Neat cattle, sheep, goats, and horses were brought to New England in the first wave of settlement, and the breeding of them became a leading industry. There was great demand for horses in other English colonies, especially in the West Indies, where the poorest jade could earn her keep by turning the rollers of a sugar mill. As early as 1668 the Massachusetts general court took measures to improve the breed by allowing only stallions "of comely proportions and fourteen hands in stature" to run free on the town commons; all others had to be stabled or gelded. Most of the stock imported into New England was nondescript, but there are records of sires being brought over from Leicestershire, traditional home of the English hunter, and draught mares from Flanders. Either the Galloway pony of Scotland, or the Irish hobby, a small hardy sorrel, was the ancestor of the once famous Narragansett pacer, so called because raised in Rhode Island as a saddlehorse with an easy gait. Every colonial lady expected to be provided with this comfortable means of transport, at a time when few roads fit for wheeled vehicles existed. And this breed remained famous for over a century. The great Edmund Burke in 1772 asked his friend James Delancey of New York to send him by sea "two good New England Pacers."

Puritanism, with its stress on faith and works, was an excellent implement for subduing the rugged wilderness that was New England. "An hour's idleness is as bad as an hour's drunkenness," a maxim announced by the Reverend Hugh Peter of Salem, kept people busy when the climate did not; and, "Never waste precious time" became a basic American doctrine. The congregational organization of the New England churches gave almost every man a say in religious affairs, as the town meeting did in local government. On occasions such as raising the frame of a meetinghouse, or of some individual's house or barn, the entire community participated. The legislature and magistracy, following the form of the Massachusetts Bay charter, gave the colonies a representative system and embodied the seeds of democracy.

And of nationalism, too. Other European colonists in America, whether in Canada, Virginia, New Netherland, the Caribbean, or South America, regarded themselves as Frenchmen, Englishmen, Dutchmen, or Spaniards living in America, and looked forward to returning "home." Not so the New Englanders. The first person on record to use the word *American* for a European colonist rather than an Indian was Cotton Mather, in 1684. The "Yankees," as they were called in the next century, regarded America as their home. They had convinced themselves that their work here for God and the English nation was supremely important; and was it not so? Puritanism was a cutting edge which hewed liberty, democracy, humanitarianism, and universal education out of the black forest of feudal Europe and the American wilderness. Puritan doctrine taught each person to consider himself a significant if sinful unit to whom God had given a particular place and duty, and that he must help his fellow men. Puritanism, therefore, is an American heritage to be grateful for and not to be sneered at because it required everyone to attend divine worship and maintained a strict code of ethics.

The effects went deeper and further than anyone could have predicted. Nor was Puritan influence confined to America. Albert Luthuli, a graduate of Adams College near Durban, South Africa, founded by New England Congregationalists in 1838, received the Nobel peace prize for 1960. Or, turn to Turkey. Little Ali, who attends a missionary school and goes on to Robert College in Istanbul, got his chance for an education because little John and Elihu in the colonial era attended Boston Latin or the Hopkins Grammar and went on to Harvard or Yale. And Ali's right to vote and be elected to the Turkish parliament owes much to the fact that Englishmen in New England and Virginia managed to make representative government work.

OLD HUNDRED

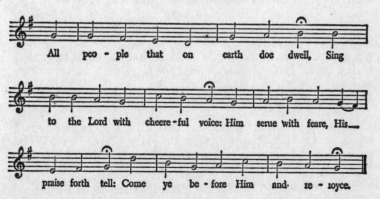

All peo-ple that on earth doe dwell, Sing to the Lord with cheere-ful voice: Him serue with feare, His praise forth tell: Come ye be-fore Him and re-ioyce.

VI

From the Hudson to the James

1626-1675

1. New Netherland and New York

NEW NETHERLAND IN 1626 consisted of three trading posts
—Fort Orange (Albany), New Amsterdam (New York), and
Fort Nassau (Gloucester, New Jersey), under the Dutch West
India Company. New Amsterdam by 1630 had neat gabled
houses, a brick church, and about 300 inhabitants. The harbor
was always full of ships and the town of sailors, since Long
Island Sound and the East river was the best route between
New England and Virginia. Beyond the wall at Wall Street,
built by Governor Dongan to keep out Indians and wolves,
stretched "bouweries," or farms. But the Company was not
interested in settlement; it wanted only enough tillage to supply with food its employees, who alone had the right to engage
in fur trade. Nevertheless several villages, such as Breukelen
and Haarlem were founded, and a number of Netherlanders
and Walloons—Belgian Protestants—came over.

Kiliaen Van Rensselaer, an Amsterdam jeweler and a stockholder of the Company, decided that fur trading alone would
never make New Netherland a proper colony. In 1629 he
persuaded the Company to issue a "Charter of Privileges to
Patroons," in order to encourage farming and settlement. A
patroon was a person who, in return for bringing out fifty peo-

ple, received a feudal domain on the Hudson, with a fifteen-mile river front, exclusive fishing and hunting privileges, civil and criminal jurisdiction, and the right to share the fur trade with the Company, which promised "to supply the colonists with as many Blacks as they conveniently can." Van Rensselaer never came over himself, but his sons did; and he provided the settlers of Rensselaerswyck with materials to build their houses and barns, and tools to begin farming. In return, he received one-third of the tenant's crop as well as income from hunting licenses and a monopoly of grinding grain at his mills. These privileges came nearer to pure feudalism than any other land system in the future United States. They continued under English rule and even outlasted the Revolution, ending only with the Rent War of the 1840's. This explains why New York became the most aristocratic of English colonies, not excepting Virginia, and the leading Tory colony in the Revolution.

New patroonships along the Hudson were established by the Courtland, Melyn, Philipse, Van der Donck, and other families. The ancestors of Martin Van Buren were tenants of Rensselaerswyck; other Dutch or Walloon families who became prominent under the Republic, such as the Van Wycks and Roosevelts, came first to "Breukelen" or New Amsterdam as farmers, clerks, or shopkeepers, and rose to merchant status in the next century. There were also settlers from outside Holland, such as Martinus Hoffman of Reval, son of an officer under Gustavus Adolphus, a founder of Esopus; and the Reverend Johannes Theodorus Polhemius of Flatbush, refugee from a Dutch colony in Brazil which the Portuguese had broken up in 1654. Englishmen from New England began to spill over into Long Island and Westchester County, where they obtained a concession of local self-government.

New Netherland, however, was a frustrated colony. The successive governors, whom Washington Irving depicted as figures of fun, were petty autocrats who ruled with a rod of iron, used torture to extract confession, and mishandled almost everything, including the Indians. The Dutch respected the powerful Iroquois Confederacy, with whom their relations were purely trading, but toward the Algonquian tribes that occupied the banks of the Hudson, Westchester County, and western Long Island they showed the same harsh unreasonableness that has made the Netherlands the most hated of all colonial powers in the present century. Governor Kieft, owing to an unprovoked massacre of the peaceful Wecquaesgeek tribe at Pavonia in 1643, sparked off a war that forced every white inhabitant to take refuge behind the wall at Wall Street.

The Dutch only won by importing Captain John Underhill from New England to lead the local militia. The company now recalled Kieft and appointed Peter Stuyvesant, who had lost a leg while storming a French fort in the West Indies.

Peglegged Peter brought energy to the company's colony, but not much judgment. The stringent regulation of gin shops and the high customs duties that he imposed kept traders away and brought stagnation to New Amsterdam. His bad temper and autocratic methods offended even the patroons, and he drove out of the colony one of the two Protestant ministers already there. A prominent settler named Adriaen Van der Donck drew up a remonstrance to the Dutch government in 1649, begging it to take over the colony and establish schools, churches, and other apparatus of civilized life. And thirty English inhabitants of Flushing protested against Stuyvesant's decree that anyone who took in a Quaker for the night would be fined fifty florins. They were commanded by the Bible, they said, to do good to all men and they wished not to offend any of Christ's children. They would, therefore, continue to shelter Quakers "as God shall persuade our consciences."

Stuyvesant established a "co-existence" policy with the surviving Indians and with the New England Confederation, concluding a treaty at Hartford in 1650 that is the basis of the present New York-Connecticut boundary. But he annexed in 1655 the weak colony of New Sweden, which the Swedish West Indian Company had established in 1638.[1] This Swedish colony, centering around Fort Cristina on the site of Wilmington, Delaware, had aroused Peter's ire by denying Delaware Bay to his traders. By 1660 New Netherland had only half the population of Connecticut. It was easy prey to an aggressor, who was not slow to appear.

Charles II, restored to the throne of England in 1660, had many friends and relations to take care of. And he hated the Dutch, despite their courteous and liberal treatment of him during his exile. So he decided to give New Netherland along with other territories to the Duke of York, and to declare war on Holland.

In March 1664, before that war even began, Charles II conferred on his brother the biggest territorial gift ever made by any English sovereign. The "Duke of York's Grant" included not only the present State of New York, but the entire region

---

[1] The Swedish colony, consisting of only 200 to 300 Swedes and Finns, brought log construction and the log cabin to America. This proved to be so well suited to pioneer housing that it spread all over the North American frontier in the eighteenth century.

between the Connecticut and Delaware rivers. Thrown in for good measure were Long Island, Nantucket, Martha's Vineyard, and the present State of Maine east of the Kennebec. The Duke promptly appointed Richard Nicolls his deputy governor, and the king gave him four frigates to help him secure his prize. Nicolls sailed into the harbor of New Amsterdam on 18 August 1664 and called upon the governor to surrender. Peter Stuyvesant, after trying in vain to persuade his subjects to resist, decided to give up without firing a shot. By the end of October the English had taken over not only New Amsterdam, which they renamed New York, but Fort Orange, which they renamed Albany, and Fort Casimir on the Delaware, which they renamed Newcastle. The province, too, was renamed New York.

The Duke at the age of thirty was now owner and ruler of a section of America destined to be the wealthiest of its size in the world. What would he do with it? His charter made him sole proprietor of this vast domain, unhampered by any requirements to obtain popular consent to his laws and regulations. The government was his to arrange as he saw fit; the unoccupied lands were his to hold, sell, or lease as he chose.

One of the first things he chose to do was to slice off a large part of his gift, the Province of New Jersey, for two friends, Sir George Carteret and Lord John Berkeley, brother to the governor of Virginia. These fortunate gentlemen became "true and absolute lords proprietors of all the Province of New Caesaria or New Jersey." Philip Carteret, cousin to Sir George, was sent over to take possession in 1665. He found the grant inhabited by a few hundred Dutchmen and English Puritans, who had settled Woodbridge and Newark. Carteret and Berkeley then issued the "Concessions and Agreements of the Proprietors of New Jersey," the most liberal grant of political privileges made by any English colonial proprietor to the people. Freedom of conscience was guaranteed, generous land grants were promised, and a representative assembly, which first met, at Elizabethtown, in 1668.

In what was left of New York (and plenty there was), the Duke's rule was fairly enlightened. He ordered Nicolls to treat the conquered Dutch with "humanity and gentleness," and made no effort to impose the English language or his Catholic religion on them. But the Duke intended to get money out of his province, and to that end drew up his own schedule of customs duties and other taxes. These made trouble. Too much water had flowed under the English bridge since 1640 for anyone to impose taxes without representation.

The Province of New York was neither racially nor geographically homogeneous in 1664, and never became so. There were a few hundred Dutch, Swedish, and Finnish settlers in the Delaware river section, the former New Sweden. On the Hudson there were Dutch villages like Haarlem, Esopus, and Rensselaerswyck, and a frontier post at Schenectady, a few miles up the Mohawk. Westchester County and Manhattan Island were covered with thrifty Dutch farms, and at the tip of Manhattan the future City of New York had about 2000 inhabitants. On Long Island a few hundred farmers, mostly English, were trying to wrest a living from the sandy soil. To keep the English happy and to attract others, the governor made free land grants on Long Island and promulgated "The Duke's Laws," founded on those of the New England colonies. But the aristocratic element in New York profited most by the change in sovereignty. James confirmed all the Dutch patroonships, and both he and the English crown made enormous grants, under the name of manors, to the Livingston, Pell, Gardiner, Heathcote, and other English and Scottish families.

Many years elapsed before New York became a happy province. On Long Island the English settlers complained that they were "inslav'd under an Arbitrary power" because they had no hand in drafting the Duke's Laws or in levying taxes. The cost of administering a government that extended from the border of Canada to that of Maryland was so great that the Duke was still in the red when a new Anglo-Dutch war broke out in 1673. In the course of that conflict New York City was recaptured by the Dutch but restored to England at the peace next year. In order to get funds to keep the government going, the Duke then instructed his hearty Irish governor, Colonel Thomas Dongan, to summon an assembly. When that met, in 1683, it enacted "The Charter of Liberties and Privileges," declaring that the assembly had the supreme legislative authority and that no taxes were to be levied without its consent. By the time His Royal Highness got around to looking over this declaration of rights, he had become His Majesty King James II, and promptly disallowed it; and New York did not obtain another assembly until 1691. James might have kept New York as his private property when he became king, but it had cost him so much trouble and brought in so little money that he considered it a liability and unloaded it on the crown. Thus New York became a royal province like Virginia, but with no assembly.

In the meantime the history of New Jersey was becoming very complicated. There were two Jersies: East New Jersey with an assembly meeting at Elizabethtown, and West New Jersey with an assembly meeting at Salem or Burlington. By 1683 East New Jersey was in the possession of twenty-four proprietors and West New Jersey belonged to three or four other men. A bad confusion in land titles, which bedeviled the province for seventy-five years, resulted from these changes. In 1702 the proprietors were persuaded to surrender their governmental powers to the crown, and East and West were united as the Royal Province of New Jersey. But the two groups of proprietors retained their property rights, and are still doing a little land business today.

2. Lord Baltimore's Province of Maryland

The most lengthy local conflict in American history is the "oyster war" between Virginia and Maryland, in which fishermen were killed as recently as 1959. It started in 1632. Charles I, cutting a slice out of northern Virginia to oblige his friend Lord Baltimore, granted him as southern boundary "the further bank" of the Potomac river down to Chesapeake Bay. This unusual grant of an entire river, right up to highwater mark on the further shore, has always been resented and disregarded by Virginia crab and oyster fishermen, despite sundry attempts over a period of three centuries to placate them.

The proprietary form of colony, in which a large extent of land with all governing powers was given by a king to an individual, is the oldest form in the English and French colonies. It was tried, as we have seen, by Sir Walter Raleigh, the French, and many others, without accomplishing anything but temporary gain and eventual loss. But the Calvert family made a success of Maryland, and their province supported them in England in grand style down to the American Revolution.

Sir George Calvert, of an old Yorkshire family, has been well described as "the most respectable and honest" of the mediocre and greedy courtiers who came into power under the early Stuarts. He aspired to build up the family fortune by a proprietary colony of his own. First he tried it in Newfoundland on the Avalon Peninsula, including the site of the World War II naval base at Argentia. After five years of this (1622–27), Calvert had to write it off as a bad investment. In the meantime, he had been converted to the Roman Catholic faith and received the title of Baron Baltimore in the Irish peerage. His new religion forced him to resign his seat on the Privy Council when Charles I became king in 1625. But the new king, who liked him personally, compensated Lord Baltimore in 1632 with a rich slice of the Old Dominion. This was the section between the latitude of Philadelphia and the south bank of the Potomac, whose commerce and fisheries he intended his friend to monopolize. The province was named Maryland, ostensibly after Queen Henrietta Maria, but really in honor of the Virgin Mary.

ARMS OF FOUNDERS OF VIRGINIA AND MARYLAND

While the Maryland charter was being processed, George Calvert died, but the king confirmed the grant to his son and heir Cecilius, second Baron Baltimore. Cecilius never visited America, but proved to be a statesmanlike colonial founder and an excellent business man. The family fortunes he hoped to recoup in Maryland. And he also intended to make his colony a refuge for English and Irish Roman Catholics, as New England had become for Puritans. Although Catholics were much more severely discriminated against in Stuart England than the

Puritans were, a far smaller proportion were willing to emigrate; never enough to make Maryland predominantly Catholic. Why more did not come is an unsolved mystery.

The second Lord Baltimore spent most of his property fitting out two ships, the *Ark* and the *Dove,* in the late fall of 1633, under the charge of his brother Leonard Calvert. The majority of the passengers were Protestants. Leonard picked up three Jesuit priests at the Isle of Wight, and after a long voyage reached the mouth of the Potomac in the spring of 1634. Profiting by the experience of Jamestown, Calvert selected a healthy town site, which he named St. Mary's, and there the two ships' companies disembarked. The colony prospered from the first; there was no "starving time," as food could be obtained from the Virginia settlements only a few hours' sail away. The neighboring Indians were weak and friendly, and the English treated them with firmness and justice.

This upper part of Chesapeake Bay which Lord Baltimore had secured for himself and his heirs is a very beautiful part of America. The land is low or gently rolling, the soil rich and fruitful; deep rivers and arms of the sea reach up into the land, both on the western and eastern shores; the waters teem with fish, crab, and oysters. Even the birds seemed to welcome the Englishmen—the oriole which "by the English there is call'd the Baltimore-Bird," says an early description, "because the Colours of his Lordship's Coat of Arms are black and yellow"; the "Mock-Bird" which "imitates all other birds," and the red cardinal "which sings like the Nightingale, but much louder."

Lord Baltimore's plan for profits was based on the headright system which had already proved a success in Virginia. To everyone who brought out servants at his own expense, he offered free 100 acres for each able-bodied man and 50 acres for each woman or child; and to those who brought out a sufficient number to rate 2000 acres he granted a manor. His gains came not from selling land but from the quitrent on it of two shillings—raised to four shillings in 1669—per 100 acres, to be paid annually forever. In practice, Lord Baltimore allowed quitrent to be commuted by a tax of two shillings on each hogshead of tobacco that the farm produced. This was collected and paid regularly (which never happened in Virginia) until the American Revolution.

The difference between a manor and an ordinary landed estate is that the lord of the manor has judicial powers. He can hold "court baron," or his steward can hold "court leet," to settle disputes between tenants and servants, and to punish them for minor offenses. Maryland lords of manors, like the seigneurs of Canada and the patroons of New Netherland, had this privilege; their Maryland grants were genuine manors, unlike the suburban estates and country restaurants which adopt the name nowadays. No fewer than sixty-two manors were granted to individuals, and about thirty more by the Lord Proprietor to himself, during the first fifty years of Maryland's existence. As examples: "St. Elizabeth's Manor" and "Cornwalleys' Crosse," each 2000 acres in St. Mary's County, to Captain Thomas Cornwallis, a councillor appointed by Lord Baltimore who came out in the *Ark;* "De la Brooke" and "Brooke Place" manors, 4100 acres on opposite sides of the Patuxent river, granted to the Reverend Robert Brooke, an Anglican clergyman who came over in his own ship in 1650 with wife, two daughters, eight sons, seven maidservants, and twenty-one manservants. Brooke sent a son to Harvard College where, after establishing a high record for undergraduate spending, he proved the value of a college education by introducing the first pack of foxhounds into Maryland. The Brooke manor house, built in 1652, and the slightly later one of "Cornwalleys' Crosse," are still standing.

The head-right system was an excellent device to keep the labor supply equal to the demand; a manor would have done its lord no good without labor to work it. Tobacco was the one great cash crop in seventeenth-century Maryland. In the old tidewater counties, rents and country doctors' bills were often paid in tobacco as late as the twentieth century.

Lord Baltimore kept an office in the City of London to deal with people who wished to emigrate, not only prospective lords of manors but servants. And for many years the majority of the white population consisted of the latter class. "Servant" in the colonial era meant about the same as employee in ours; and within the class there was as wide a variation as today between a migrant farm laborer in California and a master electrician. In the English and Dutch colonies, a servant was usually a person whose passage was paid, or assisted, in return for working for a certain number of years—usually four or five years for an adult, more for a minor. When released from this apprenticeship, the servant became a freeman like any other. An "indentured servant" meant one who had a specific contract with his employer called an indenture, because originally it was torn in two along an irregular edge. This system of exchanging the cost of passage and outfit for a few years' labor was the principal means of peopling the English colonies, and even for many years after they became independent.

Servants in Maryland—and the same is true of all English

and Dutch colonies—might be of any class, from poor gentleman to convicted felon. The average servant was a respectable
young person who wished to better himself in the New World
but could not afford the cost of outfit and passage. During the
four or five years he worked for his master, he became acclimated, learned how to grow tobacco and corn, and in many
instances learned a trade. Some maidservants were employed
in the manor house; others were dairy maids or worked hoe-
ing tobacco alongside the young men. During the term of service the servant received only food and clothing; but at the
end, each was entitled by Maryland law and custom—more
generous than those of other colonies—to fifty acres of land, a
complete suit of clothes, an axe, two hoes, and three barrels
of corn. The former servant could then set up as a yeoman
farmer, vote, and even be elected to the assembly.

Next below these respectable members of the servant class
were ex-rebels, kidnapped persons, and convicts. James I began, and Oliver Cromwell and the later Stuart kings continued,
the business of transporting to the colonies Scottish and Irish
prisoners taken in the civil wars, and this practice continued
until after the Rebellion of 1745. Most of these unfortunates
were sent to the West Indies, where their descendants form a
distinct class to this day; but some went to Virginia, Maryland,
and New England. From the earliest times a class of London
crooks specialized in "trapanning," kidnapping boys and girls.
They were "spirited" on board a colony-bound ship, whose
master sold their services on arrival to recoup himself for the
cost of transport and the kidnapper's fee. In a popular ballad
of the time, "The Trapann'd Maiden: or the Distressed Damsel," one of the victims is made to sing:

> Five years served I, under Master Guy,
>   In the land of Virginny, O,
> Which made me for to know sorrow, grief and woe,
>   When that I was weary, weary, weary, weary, O.

She tells how she has to do rough farm work from dawn to
dark and sleep on straw, "instead of drinking Beer" to "drink
the water clear," sing the children to sleep and do all that she
is bid. It does not sound too bad; but this ballad was intended
as an antidote to "The Maydens of London's Brave Adven-
tures," which promises all "merry London Girls, that are disposed to travel," that they can get rich in the gold and silver
mines of Virginia, or "have good ground enough, for Planting
and for Tilling," and live on "fare most dainty."

Finally, there were the transported convicts. The English

government under Charles II executed the worst convicts and shipped the rest to the colonies, where they had to labor for seven years to earn their freedom. Among them were juvenile delinquents, people imprisoned for nothing worse than stealing a loaf of bread, felons and habitual criminals, and highwaymen who saved themselves from hanging by "benefit of clergy"—proving that they could read. This curious exemption for the literate had come down from the middle ages, when anyone who could read was assumed to be a priest. Marylanders protested frequently against their fair land being made a dumping ground for "His Majesty's seven-year passengers," but were unable to do anything about it because the successive Lords Baltimore liked the system. And the convicts, on their part, were by no means eager for a free ride to America and subsequent hard work. These were the class of servants who gave most trouble from idleness and running away. The usual punishments for fugitives were whipping, adding months or years to their terms of service, or selling the delinquent's services to someone known to be a hard taskmaster.

There is some reason to believe that the first blacks brought into Virginia and Maryland were regarded as slaves only for life, or until baptized; for it was church doctrine that only pagans could be enslaved. However that may be, the Maryland assembly passed a "black code" in 1664, which declared any black in the colony to be a slave for life by virtue of his color. And a law of 1671, following a similar Virginia enactment, declared that neither baptism nor conversion could affect a person's bondage or freedom. Until the end of the century, slavery was no more important a factor in Maryland social life than in New York or Rhode Island; but after 1700 the importation of slaves increased, until at the time of the Revolution they numbered almost one-third of the population.

Lord Baltimore, shrewd as well as sincere, knew that as a Catholic proprietor in a Protestant empire he would have to watch his step very carefully. His instructions to his brother the governor were to "suffer no scandall or offence to be given to any of the Protestants, whereby any just complaint may hereafter be made." Catholic worship should be "done as privately as may be," Catholics should avoid arguments on religion and Protestants be treated "with as much mildness and favor as Justice will permitt." Leonard Calvert enforced these sentiments so well that at St. Mary's both Protestants and Catholics worshipped in the same building. But the proprietor had to crack down on three overzealous English Jesuits who came over in the first ships. They claimed the right to buy land from the Indians, as well as canon law privileges such as freedom from taxation, control of wills and marriages, and of being tried by an ecclesiastical court. Lord Baltimore sent over a Catholic layman to dissuade them from these pretensions, and when they refused to desist, appealed to Rome. The Vatican upheld the proprietor, and the Jesuits were sent home.

As the entire government of Maryland issued from the Lord Proprietor as fountain head, it is fortunate that Lord Baltimore, unlike the Duke of York, believed in representative government. He was, to be sure, required by his charter to obtain the "Advice, Assent, and Approbation of the Freemen of the same Province" to any laws he might enact; but how and when he should obtain this "triple-A" was left to his judgment. He appointed the governor, council, secretary, and all other officials, and the first assembly that he summoned, in 1649, consisted of twenty-one private gentlemen and four officials. As settlement spread, personal attendance at the assembly became irksome, and a representative system was worked out; after 1650 there were two houses, the council appointed by Lord Baltimore, and the elected house of burgesses. The proprietor and his governor retained the initiative in legislation; burgesses could not introduce bills. He was careful to keep all essential powers of government in family hands. Leonard Calvert's titles read like those of "Pooh-Bah" in *The Mikado:* he was governor, lord chancellor, chief magistrate, chief justice, and lieutenant general of the militia. After Leonard's death in 1647, Lord Baltimore, as a concession to the rising tide of Puritanism in England, appointed a Protestant governor, William Stone; but with the restoration of the monarchy in 1660 the chief office went back into the Calvert family. At all times in the seventeenth century, except for the decade of the 1650's, Catholics were the ruling class in Maryland, constituting a majority of the council and the permanent officials; and they governed well. Few lords proprietors ever visited Maryland, but the entire line derived a handsome revenue from the Province—some £13,000 a year around 1770.

Cecilius Calvert's astute statesmanship is again shown in the Toleration Act, which the assembly at his behest passed on 21 April 1649. This Act declared that no professed Christian should "be any ways troubled molested or discountenanced for . . . his or her religion, nor in the free exercise thereof . . . nor any way compelled to the belief or exercise of any other Religion against his or her consent." But anyone who denied the Trinity or the divinity of Christ should be hanged, and anyone who insulted the Blessed Virgin, the Apostles, or the Evangelists, should be fined or whipped. Lord Baltimore thus hoped to secure his fellow Catholics against persecution if the Protestants obtained control. Unfortunately, a community of Puritans ejected from Virginia and invited to settle near Annapolis made trouble. In alliance with William Claiborne, a Virginia trader who had been expelled from Kent Island, they rebelled, deposed Governor Stone in 1654, and attempted to repeal the Act of Toleration. The proprietor, however, handled his public relations in England with such skill that he kept his province, and after a period of turmoil the Act of Toleration was revived, only to be replaced in 1692 by the official establishment of the Church of England.

Nevertheless, the Roman Catholics had obtained a foothold in Maryland, including most of the real estate. As immigration increased, Maryland became overwhelmingly Protestant, but the Catholics have always been at the top of the social heap. Cecilius, who died in 1675, deserves high rank as a colonial founder; but good marks should also be accorded the English government which allowed and even encouraged Roman Catholics to live in Maryland without the disabilities under which they suffered at home. In no Catholic colonial empire—French, Spanish, or Portuguese—were Protestants allowed to exist, much less to acquire land and hold office. In Maryland, as earlier in Rhode Island and later in Pennsylvania, there grew up a system of legal religious toleration which became one of the cornerstones of the American republic. It was a gain for Protestants and Catholics to co-exist peaceably in the same community; this established a climate of toleration such as one does not find in countries like Spain, where a single Church has dominated the scene for centuries.

3. The Royal Province of Virginia

"Leah and Rachel, the two Fruitful Sisters," as an early chronicler called these colonies after Laban's fair daughters in Genesis, were peopled by the same sort of Englishmen who led the same sort of life; their differences were of degree rather than kind. Virginia, even after Maryland had been lopped off, remained a dominion of imperial extent, comprising at least seven later states of the Union. The younger sister's territory was always limited, and not until the census of 1960 did Rachel approach Leah in numbers—3.1 million in Maryland and 4 million in Virginia.

We left Virginia in 1624, binding up the wounds of the great Indian massacre. She was now the king's province, to dispose of as he saw fit. Charles I appointed a royal governor and council but did not disturb the other institutions that the Company had set up: the house of burgesses, the rule of law, and the head-right system for granting land. Actually, the house of burgesses until about 1660 exercised more power under the crown than it had under the Company, and the new royal regime was more popular locally than that of the Company had been, because the Company regime interfered too much in the affairs of the people—Virginians never have liked economic planning. Charles I was much too busy to do any economic planning of his own; Cromwell accorded even more self-government than the king had, so the colony was left alone to develop in a natural way.

Under this "salutary neglect," as Edmund Burke described England's old colonial policy, Virginia prospered. The total population, a little over 1100 in 1624, had risen to about 15,000, together with 300 African slaves by 1648; and by 1671 to over 40,000 according to a report of Governor Berkeley. This meant that Virginia was easily first among England's continental colonies, and second only to Barbados among all English colonies.

Owing to the prevalence of tobacco culture and the head-right system, Virginia was settled in a dispersed, decentralized manner. Here is how the head-right system worked. Upon his arrival at Jamestown, the prospective planter obtained from the colonial secretary a warrant entitling him to 50 acres of wild, ungranted land for himself and for each person brought over at his own expense; and he received another 50 acres for every person he brought in later. He did not have to convert all head-rights into land at once; they could be saved for future use, inherited by his heirs, or even sold. But if he chose to start a plantation promptly, he had to find a site for it in ungranted land, lay it out with an official surveyor, record it at the county court, and then "seat"—that is, begin to build upon or cultivate the ground. After that he received a deed, and the land was his to have and to hold, subject to a quitrent to the crown of two shillings per 100 acres.

The quitrent was more often evaded than paid, because it was nobody's business to collect it; and the tax yielded only £800 around 1700, at a time when the Lords Baltimore were getting twice that out of little Maryland. Masters of ships collected head-rights for their sailors on every voyage. Seating was often perfunctory, as under the federal Homestead Act of 1862—a few trees felled, a few furrows plowed, a shed clapped together. The indiscriminate location also had two disadvantages. It dispersed settlement, so that community life was next to impossible. Irregular or overlapping boundaries resulted from imperfect surveying, or using an "olde oake tree" as a mark. But it was a good method for equating land and labor supply; and as long as tobacco fetched a fair price in England it enabled a thrifty farmer to become a wealthy planter in a few years.

Take, for example, the case of Captain Adam Throughgood, who started life in Virginia as a boy servant. After his time was up he did so well that he returned to England and brought out wife, son, and 38 servants in 1628. Thereafter, by bringing out single men, maids, or couples, he accumulated in seven years 105 head-rights and an estate of 5350 acres. Robert Taliaferro by 1660 had acquired 6300 acres for the transport of 126 persons, 16 of them black slaves. John, the first Washington to settle in Virginia, arrived in 1657 as mate of a London ship and decided to stay. Within eleven years, in partnership with his brother-in-law Thomas Pope, he had obtained more than 5000 acres, including the estate where his famous descendant was born. One can trace the rise of John Washington not only by his increase of landholdings but by his public offices: coroner, collector of the tobacco tax, justice of the court of Westmoreland County, vestryman, burgess, and officer in the militia.

Jamestown, where every arriving and departing ship had to call, boasted a fair brick church (similar to St. Luke's, Smithfield, which has survived), and a brick State House where the assembly met, but not more than thirty other houses by mid-century. When the courts and assembly were not sitting, the town was almost deserted. A traveler of 1650, sailing up the James, the York, or another tidal tributary of Chesapeake Bay, found every few miles a clearing with a wharf, a modest mansion, a clutch of wooden cottages for servants, an orchard, kitchen garden and corn patch, and fields green with the tobacco plant. Beyond and between these plantations there was only the primeval forest in which cattle browsed and pigs rooted. Transport was largely by boat, along the natural waterways—"drowned river" estuaries up which the salt tides flowed to the line of falls. This gave every plantation a place on the tobacco pipeline to England. The Reverend John Clayton observed in a letter of 1688 that "this Conveniency" was an "impediment to the Advance of the country," because it forced ships to visit every plantation and spared the planters the necessity of sending their produce to a market town. "The Country is thinly inhabited; the Living solitary and unsociable; Trading confused and dispersed; besides other Inconveniences."

The method of trade is illustrated by the log of a small

double-ended vessel, pink *Swan* of Poole in Devonshire. She sailed 18 November 1667, and after a rough crossing sighted the Capes of the Chesapeake 25 January 1668. The wind was blowing so strong out of the Bay that she was unable to enter for ten days. She then worked up and down the Patuxent river in Maryland and proceeded to Bush river, staying there until 16 April, peddling English goods and taking on tobacco. Still not fully laden, the *Swan* visited the Magothy and Severn rivers and again the Patuxent, loading three or four hogshead from each plantation. She checked out at Lord Baltimore's custom house at St. Mary's on 25 April, cleared the Capes 8 May in company with two other tobacco ships, and after an unusually prosperous passage reached her home port a month later.

Tobacco culture was so ruinous to fertility that every planter needed reserve land. Probably no more than 100 acres of a 1000-acre plantation were under cultivation at the same time. But tobacco was the life of the Old Dominion. All prices and salaries, even of the ministers, were expressed in pounds of tobacco; and when warehouses were built toward the close of the century, warehouse receipts passed like cheques drawn to bearer today. Even the wealthiest planters handled very little hard money; all transactions were made on credit, bills paid annually when the return of the crop was made from England. There, the tobacco grown in North America was processed into pipe tobacco and snuff—cigars were not used outside the Spanish empire, and the cigarette had not been invented. North American tobacco ran to two types, the sweet-scented, ancestor of the fragrant pipe tobacco of today; and Oronoko, a strong, heavy leaf preferred by European smokers, in which Maryland specialized. Down to the 1660's the English colonies could export their tobacco in English or foreign ships to any part of Europe, where there was an insatiable demand, and the Chesapeake colonies prospered accordingly. After 1665 the English government made it increasingly difficult to send tobacco anywhere except to England (not even to Scotland before 1707, or thereafter to Ireland) or in any ship not English or colonial.

The crown levied a duty of about four cents per pound on American tobacco imported into England. This became a hardship late in the century, when the wholesale price fell to a penny a pound or even less.[1] The planter selected a London

---

[1] A part of the duty was repaid if the tobacco was re-exported to Europe; this was called the "drawback." London, for instance, imported 11.5 million pounds of American tobacco in 1678 and re-exported 5.5 million; Bristol re-exported half of what she received.

or Bristol merchant and consigned to him his entire crop along with a list of his family's needs for the next year—clothing, guns and ammunition, farm implements, furniture, horses, and servants. The merchant sold the tobacco for what he could get, and made the desired purchases, charging the planter a commission each way; and almost inevitably got the planter into debt. It was a standard joke that a son inherited his father's debts to the merchant along with his land. Yet, despite this system of economic servitude—precursor of the later pioneer farmer's dependence on grain merchants and the railroads—and crop failures, and shipwrecks, Virginia prospered. Not only did the system enable thrifty, hard-working young gentlemen like John Washington to live comfortably and become wealthy; thousands of ex-servants and poor men, using only the labor of their own families, made a fair living and enjoyed plenty of sport too.

It so happened that on the first good road built in the English colonies, from Jamestown to Governor Berkeley's plantation of Greenspring, there was a quarter-mile straightaway. The Governor and his friends adopted the habit of racing their horses along this stretch on Sunday mornings after church; and from this informal contest there developed the "quarter horse." This American strain of racehorse, bred to run that short distance at terrific speed, lacked the thoroughbred's stamina to stay for a mile or more; he was the sprinter among horses. Until recently the quarter horse was the poor man's racehorse, as he could be raced anywhere; he is now bred for formal racing and rodeos, and for handling cattle.

Another poor man's sport that started early was running foxes at night with hounds, the original American form of the fox chase. It spread all over the English colonies, followed the frontier, and is practiced to this day. On a crisp autumn night, all over the land, you would find small groups of farmers sitting around a fire in the open, passing around liquor in a jug, and talking in low voices while each man listened for the distinctive cry of his hound, running a fox in a nearby swamp or thicket.

We must now come to grips with the tradition that all white men in Virginia were "Cavaliers." That was nearly true, if we take cavalier in its then meaning of a royalist, an Englishman who, regardless of birth or rank, supported King Charles in the Civil War of 1641–49, as against the roundheads who supported Parliament and Oliver Cromwell. The humblest plowjogger who borrowed a horse and joined Prince Rupert's troop was as much a cavalier as the Duke of Norfolk. In this correct sense of the word, Virginia was nearly 100 per cent cavalier. The people sympathized with the royal cause, and were profoundly shocked by the execution of King Charles. The assembly promptly proclaimed his son in exile as Charles II, and let the world know it. Parliament's orders to discard the Book of Common Prayer were flouted; and although the assembly had to submit to a Cromwellian commission which deposed the popular governor, Sir William Berkeley, it elected him governor in 1660 when the joyful news arrived that the Cromwellian dynasty had come to an end with "Tumbledown Dick." Unfortunately for historical sanity, Virginians of the nineteenth century got the idea that cavalier meant a well-born gentleman or nobleman, a myth that in some measure contributed to secession and the American Civil War.

Who, then, were the Virginians of this half-century, 1624 to 1675? For the most part they were yeoman farmers with an upper crust of self-made men who accumulated a fortune in land. The first founders of Virginia, in the period 1607–24, were largely Oxford graduates, sons of knights or barons, men out of the top drawer of English society—like George Percy, son of the Earl of Northumberland, Lord de la Warr and his sons, and George Sandys. But few of these survived into the generation which we are now describing. They lost heart and returned to England, or died of the fever, or were killed in the massacre. The big men of 1625–45 were of middle-class origin who rose to wealth and power in Virginia itself—such as Samuel Matthews, who made his fortune by supplying tobacco ships with provisions. Most of these, too, passed from the scene, and around 1645 there arose other families of middle-class origin who became the First Families of Virginia. Such was John Carter, of unknown parentage, who arrived from England in 1645, made a fortune from tobacco, married in succession five wives who brought him more land, and left a son Robert, who became so wealthy as to be called "King" Carter. Such was the first William Byrd, son of a London goldsmith and a shipmaster's daughter, who reached Virginia in 1671 at the age of nineteen, inherited land from an uncle who preceded him, made a good marriage, got elected to the house of burgesses, purchased the plantation named Westover, built there a mansion, a shop, and a warehouse, and did very well with his tobacco crop. He imported, in his own ships, servants and all manner of goods. To the West Indies he sent provisions, grain, and barrel staves, and imported thence sugar, rum, and African slaves—in one shipment 506 slaves, most of whom he sold to his neighbors. He was also a successful Indian trader, sending goods by packhorse into North Carolina, there to obtain deerskins and furs. At the time of his death in

1704 he was rightly regarded as one of the first gentlemen of Virginia.

Among others of this class one may mention William Fitz-hugh, Giles Bland, Daniel Parke, Lewis Burwell, Thomas Ludwell, and John Page. Their class, the rising generation of tobacco aristocrats, was strengthened by the arrival of refugee cavaliers, both during and after the English Civil War. Such were William Randolph of a distinguished English family, and Richard Lee. These men formed but a small minority of the 38,000 white inhabitants of Virginia around 1675. The domi-nant feature of the country at this period was the 100- to 300-acre farm, and the typical Virginian was an English yeo-man, often an ex-servant, who worked himself, with his family and his few servants. They all had the vote and elected bur-gesses who went on record as being wholeheartedly cavalier, royalist, and Anglican.

Slavery did not become rooted in Virginia until after 1681, when according to the royal governor's estimate, there were 3000 blacks and 15,000 white servants, out of a total popula-tion between 70,000 and 80,000. Included with the blacks was a considerable number of free blacks, some of whom had be-come wealthy. In Northampton County there was a com-munity of free blacks who acquired hundreds of acres by head-rights. They imported slaves from Africa and servants from England to such an extent that the assembly in 1670 declared it illegal for blacks to own white servants. These blacks had been emancipated by their masters, partly as a re-ward for faithful service, partly because of the feeling that it was wrong to hold any man a slave, once he had professed Christianity.

The early laws of Virginia forbade playing cards or throw-ing dice—doubtless for the good Puritan motive that they "wasted precious time." There was a fine of 50 pounds of to-bacco, equivalent to a week's wages, for missing church on Sunday, when neither travel, business, nor loading of ships was allowed. Each Virginia parish was governed by a self-perpetuating vestry and two churchwardens who acted as moral policemen of the parish, like the constables of a New England town. The churchwardens presented to the county court all cases of bastardy, adultery, blasphemy, sabbath-breaking, slander, backbiting, and other "scandalous offences." County courts, composed of landowners appointed by the gov-ernor, punished by whipping, stocks, pillory, and ducking stools—rarely by imprisonment, as that was expensive and took labor out of production. The problem of five-month babies bothered Virginia like other rural societies; for where a man depended on the labor of his children, he could not take the chance of marrying a barren woman. Virginia couples caught that way had to confess premarital intercourse in open congregation while clad in the white sheet of penitence, as in New England or Old England. And there are even cases of adulterers having to wear the scarlet letter A, and of women being punished—but never executed—for witchcraft.

English men and women of that day, whether at home or in the colonies and of whatever class, expressed anger or vexation in explosive, picturesque, and bawdy language that shames the poor four-lettered profanity of today. Against this practice church and state struggled in vain. In a crusade to clean up Henrico County, 122 persons were indicted for uttering "wicked oaths," a woman was found guilty of swearing no fewer than 65 times, and John Huddlesey was imprisoned for "oaths innumerable." And there were many other indications that English tastes were the same in all latitudes. For a homely example, we find that in Virginia, as in New England, cow-kind were the favorite animals, adapting easily to the country and providing milk and traction while they lived, beef and shoe leather when they were slaughtered. We find the same pet names for cows in Virginia as in Plymouth Colony—Daisy, Bunny, Pretty, Whiteface; and for yokes of oxen, Buck and Duke, Spark and Swad.

Although Virginians honored the king and preferred to worship according to the Book of Common Prayer, their churches were conducted in a manner that would have shocked Archbishop Laud, or even a bishop of today. Parts of the liturgy were omitted, the surplice was seldom worn, holy communion was administered to the congregation sitting around a table, Puritan fashion; and there was no altar with candles and cross, which Virginians of that century regarded as faintly idolatrous.

The Anglican Church in Virginia suffered for want of ministers. Having no college like Harvard where they could be educated, and few schools, young Virginians found it too difficult to qualify for the ministry, and the colony depended on obtaining a supply from England. Young English ordinands naturally preferred a parish in Old England to roughing it in Virginia. But it is a mystery why cavalier clergy, ousted from their parishes by the Long Parliament and Cromwell because they would not turn Presbyterian like the famous Vicar of Bray, did not flock to a colony where they were desperately needed. By 1672 four out of five Virginia parishes were vacant, and two out of three which were not vacant had lay readers instead of ordained ministers. Virginia needed a bishop, as the Spanish and French governments had given to their American colonies; and there was talk of elevating the Reverend Alexander Murray, one of the most devoted and intelligent ministers in the colonies, to the episcopate; but nothing came of it.

Almost all Englishmen in the seventeenth century were interested in religion, and everyone who read anything, read works on divinity. Inventories of Virginian private libraries include a few Latin or English classics, practical works on husbandry, and a surprising number of books of Puritan theology, such as the works of the Reverend William ("Painful") Perkins, which were favorite reading in New England. The Bible was as well known and as thoroughly read in houses along Chesapeake Bay, as on the Merrimack and the Connecticut. Yet, with all these resemblances, there was a fundamental difference between Puritanism in New England and in Virginia. In the Northern colonies, it was a positive and pervasive way of life, difficult for anyone to escape. Puritanism in Virginia merely reflected the average Englishman's desire to support honesty and morality, in the absence of Anglican discipline and authority. Under conditions of dispersed settlement and immense parishes—some extending as much as 50 miles along a river—no minister could exercise much supervision. Most people in New England lived around a village green under the eye of the parson and the constable; if Elnathan Danforth was observed entering the house of Nathaniel Cotton (who had recently married a young and pretty wife) when Nate was out mowing, the whole village watched developments with keen interest. But in Virginia the parson wore out his horse, his boatmen, and his legs, merely trying to get around, and much went on that he never could know about.

In their ideas on government, Englishmen in New England, Virginia, and Maryland saw eye to eye. All would have agreed with Governor Winthrop's famous "Little Speech on Liberty," that "Democracy is . . . accounted the meanest and worst of all forms of government," and that a "mixt" or balanced government, containing monarchical, aristocratic, and democratic elements, was the best. Virginia revolted against too much monarchy in 1675, New England in 1685; Maryland rebelled against a closed aristocracy, the lord proprietor's officials. Englishmen in the Southern colonies shared the Puritans' abhorrence of arbitrary power and dislike of undignified government. As early as 1618 the Virginia Company, in order to "beget reverence" among the common people, ordered Governor Gates to hire a personal guard, and the governors of Massachusetts Bay were always attended on public occasions by militiamen carrying halberds. This tradition of dignity in government lasted well into the early Republic but was largely lost under Jacksonian Democracy, which considered dignity incompatible with popular rule, and clowning more profitable than ceremony.

Governor Berkeley, in one of his many outbursts, thanked God that Virginia had no printing press or free school. The former was true, and a pity, too; aspiring young writers had no chance to have their verse or prose published, short of London. But there were endowed free schools in Virginia. The Syms School, established under a bequest of Benjamin Syms, was in operation by 1647; and the Eaton School twelve years later. Combined as the Syms-Eaton High School of Hampton, they are still in existence. And one finds in the records occasional mention of "old field schools," erected in some worn-out tobacco field, to teach children within riding or rowing distance the three R's. Wealthy planters depended on obtaining imported Irish or Scots schoolmasters to teach their children, and were not interested in public education.

Governor Berkeley tried to persuade Maryland and North Carolina to stop growing tobacco for a year in the hope of lessening the supply and raising the price, but Maryland refused to co-operate, and overproduction continued. "Forty thousand people are empoverished," Berkeley wrote in his *Discourse or View of Virginia*, "in order to enrich little more than forty merchants in England." In 1668 the price reached an all-time low—a farthing a pound at the wharf. This was due not only to overproduction but to the English prohibition of direct export to the continent of Europe. The English government, far from affording the colonial tobacco growers relief, such as lowering the customs duty of twopence a pound, scolded Virginia for her one-crop system and ordered the planters to pay more attention to cereals, timber, and the recalcitrant silkworm. Charles II received an annual revenue of £100,000 from the tobacco duty by 1675. But American farmers had to wait almost three centuries for price support.

Thus, during the first fifteen years of the reign of Charles II, Virginia, formerly a land of opportunity, had become a relatively poor and discontented community. Something was bound to happen; and, as we shall see in a later chapter, a minor Indian war and a young aristocrat named Nathaniel Bacon sparked off a serious rebellion.

VII

<hr>

Empires of the South and North

1625-1675

1. *The Carolinas*

CHARLES II, "THE MERRY MONARCH," most popular king that
England ever had, was also the shiftiest. He had more brains
than he cared to use, and the bright side of that defect, so far
as the colonies were concerned, was an inclination to let them
alone. No English subsidies bolstered the prices of colonial
products, no royal bounty succored the settlers when they
were starving, no royal troops helped defend them against
Indians and pirates; on the contrary, this king disciplined but
one colony, Massachusetts Bay, and that after repeated provocation. The colonies were allowed to grow any old way, which
in the long run made them stronger than bounty-fed, regi-
mented French Canada.

This king can hardly be said to have had a colonial policy.
There was a drift toward closer control of colonial trade and
government; but if a colonial assembly sent the right person
to talk to the king, with a pocketful of money for important
officials, it could get away with almost anything. For instance,
Governor John Winthrop, Jr. of Connecticut, who had access
to the king through fellowship in the Royal Society, obtained
for his colony the charter of 1662, which annexed New Haven
and made Connecticut as independent as Massachusetts. Next

year, Dr. John Clark of Rhode Island obtained a similar charter which recognized that colony's privilege of electing its own government, and protected it from partition by powerful neighbors.

Charles II was a good politician: he rewarded friends and punished enemies. His restoration set everyone who claimed a slice of the English empire to dusting off old charters, and brought in a new lot of office seekers. As there were not nearly enough plums on the government tree for all, an obvious way to reward deserving cavaliers was to create them colonial proprietors. We have already seen how this was done in the case of New York and New Jersey. A fortunate result of this policy was an expansion of that part of the English empire which became the United States. Six of the original Thirteen States were founded in the reign of Charles II, all as proprietary grants. In 1662 a group of eight promoters and politicians applied to the king for a grant of "Carolina," the region between Virginia and Spanish Florida, as a proprietary province. Their leading spirits were Anthony Ashley Cooper, later Lord Ashley and Earl of Shaftesbury, and Sir John Colleton, a wealthy Barbadian planter who sought new homes for the overcrowded white population of Barbados. Anthony, a poor cavalier, rewarded by the king with the chancellorship of the exchequer and created Lord Ashley, found that in the extravagant court he could not live on his salary. So he, Colleton, and Governor Berkeley of Virginia put their heads together and took in two important people as "front men." These were General George Monk, Duke of Albemarle, who had prepared the way for Charles's restoration, and the Earl of Clarendon, historian and statesman.

Their great talking point was the prospect of raising tropical commodities such as silk and wine, currants and olives, which had been hoped for but never realized in Virginia. And they obtained the Carolina Charter of 1663 which, with boundaries extended shortly after, gave them everything from sea to sea between the present southern boundary of Virginia and the latitude of Daytona Beach, Florida. The charter was in the form of a proprietary province, following that of Maryland, with the same limitation that all laws be consented to by the freemen and not be repugnant to those of England. In addition, it expressed the new policy of religious toleration, guaranteeing liberty of conscience to all settlers demeaning themselves quietly. The English government did not want its subjects to leave England for the colonies, and hoped to extend the empire by encouraging people to move from the older colonies to the newer, and to attract persecuted Protestants from continental Europe.

After two failures by the proprietors to establish settlements in northern Carolina, young and energetic Lord Ashley took hold and made himself the real founder. His first move, however, was oddly impractical. With the aid of his secretary, John Locke the philosopher, he drafted a curious document called, "The Fundamental Constitutions of Carolina." This was the longest, most fantastic and reactionary of all colonial frames of government. It created a Carolina nobility. Anyone who purchased 3000 acres could be a baron and lord of the manor; 12,000 acres gave the owner the title of cassique; and an owner of 20,000 acres could have the German title of landgrave. The common people could elect members of a house of commons, but no bill could become law unless consented to by a majority of the barons, the cassiques, the landgraves, and the proprietors! Naturally this constitution did not work in a pioneer society. Some forty great landowners, most of them absentees, did call themselves by the odd titles; but the house of commons (as the South Carolina assembly was called until the Revolution) ignored the requirement that every bill must pass through five winnowings, and prevented landgraves and cassiques from sitting on the governor's council by right.

The lords proprietors, having, as they fondly hoped, settled the form of government, made efforts to procure people to live under it. Three vessels were fitted out in England in the summer of 1669. Two were wrecked, but the third called at Barbados, picked up a couple of hundred emigrants, and reached Carolina in the spring of 1670. Captain Joseph West, appointed first governor of the colony, turned down Port Royal as too near St. Augustine, "in the very chops of the Spaniards," and sailed along until he reached a big bay watered by two rivers that he named the Ashley and the Cooper, after his energetic proprietor. There he established Charles Town, not far from the site of modern Charleston. And here the settlement of South Carolina really began.

For almost a quarter-century, Charleston was as unlike the romantic Charleston of the Jockey Club and St. Cecilia Assembly as Jamestown was unlike royal Williamsburg. The principal occupations were raising livestock, cutting timber or barrel staves for export to the West Indies, trading for fur and deerskins with the nearby Catawba and more distant Cherokee Indians, buying captives taken by these natives in their tribal wars and selling them as slaves in other colonies. Colleton was the only proprietor ever to live in the province; most of the

Lowdnes   Huger   Butler

Leigh   Gordon   Bull

Oglethorpe   Wright   Houston

ARMS OF FOUNDERS OF THE CAROLINAS

settlers were poor whites from Barbados whose names mean
nothing to later history. So little was accomplished in the early
years that we are tempted to carry this account beyond 1675.

In 1680 the lords proprietors persuaded a small group of
Huguenots—French Protestants—to settle near Charleston
for the express purpose of cultivating the silkworm. And a
band of rugged Scots was induced to start the settlement of
Port Royal in 1683. They were attacked by the Spaniards
three years later, since Spain claimed the whole of Carolina
and had earlier established a mission at Port Royal. The few
Scots who survived this fight took refuge on the Cooper river
above Charleston.

This attack, proving that the Spanish empire was still alive
and kicking, discouraged Englishmen from settling so near
Florida. But Louis XIV of France inadvertently provided a

high class of emigrants for South Carolina. In 1685 he repealed Henry IV's Edict of Nantes, which guaranteed toleration to French Protestants—and began to "harry them out of the land" more effectively than the Stuarts had done to the Puritans. Thousands emigrated to Prussia, England, and the English colonies, where they were welcomed. And as the Carolina proprietors were eager for Protestant settlers who knew how to cultivate olives and vines, they got the lion's share. Huguenot families such as Marion, Petigru, Huger, and De Saussure gave a special character to South Carolina society. Liberty-loving people themselves, they were none the less responsible for fastening slavery on the low coastland to cultivate rice. This proved to be the first step in the conquest of South Carolina by slave economy. Rice plantations were as much dispersed as the tobacco plantations of Virginia; but, owing to the social instincts of the French, as well as malarial fevers that prevailed in the rice country during the summer, leading planters built town houses in Charleston and developed an urban society.

Completely different in character were the first settlements in North Carolina, peopled largely by former indentured servants and other poor whites who had been squeezed out of Virginia by the low price of tobacco and the rise of slavery. They hewed out small farms along the shore of Albemarle Sound, and exported tobacco, their only cash crop, in small vessels, through the shallow inlets, thus escaping export duties and other regulations imposed by Parliament. A head-right system more generous than that of Virginia was established by the lords proprietors to encourage a superior type of settler, and with success. Owing to the great distance of the Albemarle settlements from those on the Ashley and Cooper, they were given a separate governor and an assembly which was distinctly democratic in character, one of its early laws limiting individual land grants to 660 acres.

To anticipate later Carolina history, in 1710 the proprietors attracted the attention of Baron Graffenried of Bern to the possibilities of northern Carolina. He was made a landgrave and brought out over a thousand German and Swiss settlers, besides founding the town of New Bern. His colony tangled with the Tuscarora Indians, and was almost wiped out.

Although both Carolinas were successful colonies from the viewpoint of the settlers, they disappointed the proprietors, who had expected to grow rich from selling land. Like absentee landlords almost everywhere, they were robbed by their agents. The consequence was that in 1729 all but one proprietor (Lord Granville) sold out to the crown, and the two halves then became the royal provinces of North Carolina and South Carolina. The same thing happened to every other proprietary colony in the English and French overseas empires, excepting those of the canny Calverts and the popular Penns.

2. The Non-Spanish West Indies

During this half-century, the situation in the West Indies reached an uneasy balance between Spain, England, France, and the Netherlands. Spain retained Cuba, Puerto Rico, Trinidad, and the eastern part of Hispaniola, but lost Jamaica to England and Saint-Domingue (the future Haiti) to France. The French colonized Martinique, Guadeloupe, and half of St. Kitts and a few smaller islands. The English kept the other half of St. Kitts, together with Barbados, Antigua, Montserrat, and Nevis. In the Windward Islands of St. Vincent, St. Lucia, and Dominica the Carib Indians were still strong and hungry enough to keep Europeans out.

Admiral Piet Hein of the Dutch navy pulled off in 1628 the act that every French and English corsair had dreamed of for a century past, capturing an entire Spanish treasure fleet. Lying in wait off Matanzas in northern Cuba, he took nine great galleons laden with hides, ginger, cocoa, and cochineal, and eight treasure ships carrying 200,000 pounds' weight of silver. The lot netted the equivalent of $9.7 million to the Dutch West India Company which had financed him, not counting prize money to the sailors. Profits such as these go far to explain why the Company neglected New Netherland. No "pieces of eight" up the Hudson!

The king of Spain reacted to Piet Hein's exploit by sending, in 1629, a strong squadron of thirty-five sail to the West Indies under Captain Don Federigo de Toledo, to break up rival attempts to colonize the Leeward Islands. He devastated the English and French settlements on St. Kitts and Nevis, but most of the settlers made their escape in small boats, and some returned when the dons sailed away.

Pierre d'Esnambuc was the Champlain of the French Antilles. Expelled by Don Federigo from St. Kitts, he returned to France. Cardinal Richelieu, who had a keen sense of the value of colonies, was then in power. He reorganized and combined all the little companies that had begun settlement in Canada and the West Indies into two big ones, the Company of the Hundred Associates for Canada, and the Company of the Isles for the Caribbean. The latter company now encouraged D'Esnambuc to pick up more islands, and in 1635 one of his lieutenants planted the island of Guadeloupe, now France's oldest colony. Slaves were imported from Africa, a war of extermination was waged against the Caribs, and in a few years Guadeloupe became a prosperous sugar colony. Shortly after, Martinique was occupied, subdued, and settled.

Philippe de Poincy, appointed to command all French Antilles in 1638, governed in a style that completely outshone the English. At St. Kitts he built a stone château with formal gardens, orange groves, a model sugar plantation, and a sugar mill; he was served by a hundred French lackeys besides black slaves. An armed force of 8000 men was at his disposal. Almost the sole source of wealth in these tiny islands was sugar. It was in great demand in Europe, where the canes could not be grown; and its derivative, rum, helped Englishmen to endure the rigors of life from Hudson Bay to Albemarle Sound. Coffee, cocoa, indigo, and long-staple cotton were also cultivated in the West Indies; but sugar was king, like tobacco in Virginia, and it made these islands which Spain had neglected the richest and most heavily populated parts of the New World.

Refugees from Don Federigo's attack on St. Kitts, sailing down-wind to the island of Tortuga off Hispaniola, found it inhabited by beachcombers of all nations. These were called buccaneers because they lived largely on the meat of wild hogs and cattle, which they cured by smoking on a *boucan*, a framework of green wood. The refugees taught the buccaneers to use dugout canoes to capture Spanish ships becalmed in the Windward passage. The captured vessel would then become a pirate ship, and the buccaneers found pirating more profitable than hunting. Spain did not take this lying down: there were severe reprisals and counter-reprisals. Buccaneers who grew tired of constant fighting settled on the northwest shore of Hispaniola, which around 1665 was organized as the French colony of Saint-Domingue. This, by the end of the century, became the richest European colony in the West Indies, and eventually the Republic of Haiti.

Other and more reputable Frenchmen expelled the few Spaniards who inhabited the island of Santa Cruz and renamed it St. Croix, a name that it still bears as one of the Virgin Islands of the United States. The chartered company regime in the French Antilles was wound up by Louis XIV in 1674; Martinique, Guadeloupe, and Saint-Domingue became crown colonies.

About 1630 the Dutch West India Company decided to acquire a few islands before the French and English got them all. The first they took was St. Martin's, an island that one can drive across in half an hour. The big business there for the next three centuries was extraction of salt from sea water, to supply the Dutch fisheries. French refugees from St. Kitts were already present, and the two groups, after a few fights, concluded a treaty (1638) for dividing the tiny island, along a boundary that still exists. Two hundred Dutchmen settled in Tobago in 1632, but Spain decided to make an example of them. Landing next year, the Spaniards recruited Caribs who had retreated to the other side of the island, and massacred every last Dutchman. The West India Company, by no means discouraged, decided to extend its salt-making ventures and in 1634 sent out four ships which seized the islands of Curaçao, Aruba, and Bonaire off the coast of Venezuela, and established the salt business there. Eventually Curaçao became famous for a liqueur brandy and, in the present century, for processing fuel oil obtained from Venezuela.

After the death in 1638 of the Earl of Carlisle, proprietor of Barbados, Charles I made that island a royal province and granted the planters the right to elect an assembly. As early as 1650, the sugar crop in Barbados was worth £3 million, and the population had risen to 36,600 whites and 5680 African slaves. Ten years later, the white population had fallen to 23,000, but that of the blacks had risen to 20,000. This little island, only 14 by 21 miles in area, contained more people than Virginia and had become the wealthiest English colony. Life here and in the other English Caribbean islands—Antigua, Nevis, Montserrat, and half St. Kitts—was rough and riotous. Sober merchants from England were shocked by the atmosphere of brutality and drunkenness. One of them in 1651 thus noted the invention of rum: "The chief fudling they make in the Island is Rumbullion, alias Kill-Devill, and this is made of sugar canes distilled, a hott, hellish and terrible liquor."

The planters of Barbados came from the same ambitious middle class as those who went to New England and Virginia, and their sentiments were as independent as the one and as cavalier as the other. The Barbados assembly proclaimed Charles II, and in 1657 protested against Parliament's trying to give them orders, declaring that to be under "a Parliament in which we have no representatives . . . would be a slavery far exceeding all that the English nation hath yet suffered." Parliament replied by sending a fleet to reduce Barbados to obedience. It blockaded the island, but the sailors were so weakened by scurvy and typhus that the commander granted easy terms of surrender. He agreed that no taxes be imposed in Barbados save by their assembly, and that free trade continue with the Dutch. It was this same fleet which sailed on to Virginia and deposed Governor Berkeley.

Unfortunately for Barbados, this was not its only visit from an English fleet during the interregnum. Oliver Cromwell adopted a vigorous policy of relieving Spain of her most valuable possessions. Late in 1654 he issued a ringing manifesto, written by John Milton, declaring that England was honorbound to do something to redress the cruel wrongs and injuries inflicted on Englishmen in the Caribbean for the last thirty years. In revenge he proposed to capture the island of Hispaniola and make it an outpost of Puritanism. The expedition of 50 ships, commanded by Admiral William Penn (senior of that name), carried 2500 drafted soldiers under General Robert Venables. The fleet reached Barbados at the end of January 1655. Edward Winslow, a Pilgrim Father, accompanied the fleet as a sort of political commissar. It lay off Barbados for ten weeks, consuming all available food and recruiting 5000 servants and small landowners as auxiliary troops. Then, in attacking Hispaniola, Penn and Venables violated the first requisites of success in any amphibious operation. They lost surprise, landed troops too far from the objective, gave them no naval gunfire support, and made insufficient provision for their logistic supply. The result was a fiasco. The army was routed by one Spanish cavalry troop and was only saved from massacre by a disciplined English regiment of marines.

Wanting something to show for all this expense, Penn, Venables, and Winslow decided to attack another of the Greater Antilles. Jamaica was their choice because of its strategic position, "lying in the very belly of all commerce," an ideal base from which to raid Cuba or the Isthmus of Panama and engage in clandestine trade with the Spaniards. Conquest of Jamaica was easy because there were then only about 1500 Spaniards and African slaves in the entire island, and not 200 soldiers. The forts at the entrance of Port Royal Bay were surprised, the capital (later renamed Spanish Town) was taken, and the governor forced to surrender. Guerrilla warfare continued for several years, the guerrillas being supplied and supported from Cuba; and the Spaniards' slaves retired to the rugged interior above Montego Bay called the Cockpit Country. Their descendants, the "Maroons," with some justification claim to have been the first independent republic in America, as the English government finally had to negotiate a treaty with their "king."

Spain in 1670 recognized English possession of Jamaica, which became a highly valuable colony. Cromwell and his successors peopled the island largely with petty planters and

ex-servants from the smaller islands, and with slaves from
Africa. The descendants of these slaves inherited no small
measure of the Jamaica planters' pride, and after breaking up
the British West Indian Federation by secession, have become
the ruling class of an independent Jamaica in the British
Commonwealth.

From Charleston it is a short sail to the Bahamas. Although
Columbus here discovered the New World, Spain did nothing
about the islands except to depopulate them;' Englishmen
filled the vacuum. The crown granted this group in 1670 to
the Carolina proprietors, who sent in as governor Elias Hasket,
a rough sea captain from Salem. He founded Nassau but had
to make a deal with the settlers, predominantly pirates and
buccaneers, in order to live; that displeased the proprietors,
and Hasket was deposed. After sundry vicissitudes and the
arrival of a group of respectable American loyalists, the Bahamas in 1787 became a crown colony.

Before English rule had been firmly established in Jamaica,
England waged a short war with the Dutch, at that time allies
of France and Spain. The buccaneers, more vicious than ever,
were invited to settle at Port Royal by the governor of Jamaica,
and given privateers' commissions. Their most famous exploits
were on the Spanish Main, under that prince of ruffians
Henry Morgan. In 1668 he raided Puerto Bello, slaughtered
the garrison, looted the town, and carried back to Jamaica a
quarter of a million Spanish dollars. Next year he captured
three Spanish treasure ships; and in 1670–71, with 37 ships
and 2000 fighting men under his command, he took the Castle
of San Lorenzo at the mouth of the Chagres river and marched
across the Isthmus. Old Panama, then the richest city in the
New World after Mexico and Lima, was sacked and destroyed
by his men, who put prisoners "to the most exquisite tortures
imaginable" to force them to reveal hidden treasure. Morgan's
personal share required 175 pack animals to be carried across
the Isthmus. And all this when England and Spain were supposed to be at peace! During the space of seven years, the
buccaneers sacked eighteen cities, four towns, and numerous
villages in Cuba, Hispaniola, and on the Spanish Main. The
king knighted Morgan and appointed him lieutenant governor
of Jamaica, and he died a rich and respectable planter.

8. *New France*

We left Quebec, the first permanent French settlement in
Canada, mourning the death of Samuel de Champlain in 1635.
Canada at that time was the property of a joint-stock com-

pany, the Hundred Associates. L'Acadie, the future Nova Scotia, was a chain of fishing and trading stations with about 250 settlers on the Bay of Fundy, disputed by two feudal lords. Nicolas Denys, given the entire island of Cape Breton as a feudal lordship in 1670, discovered coal deposits near the future Sydney but was unable to interest anyone in mining them.

The Hundred Associates' main object was fur trade in the valleys of the St. Lawrence and the Ottawa. They soon decided, as all colonial founders concluded sooner or later, that a trading-post empire could not exist without permanent settlement. The company then established a system of *seigneuries* or lordships, with manorial privileges, similar to the patroonships of New Netherland. A seigneur was granted anything from a few acres to 360 square miles, in return for procuring a certain number of *habitants* (settlers) who paid him a small annual rent, ground their corn at his mill, and worked for him free a certain number of days each year. This seignioral system, copied from the feudal regime in France, and meticulously planned by the crown after Canada became a crown colony in 1663, suited the habitants so well that it even survived the English conquest. But it never suited the fur traders.

Settlement in Canada advanced very slowly. In 1643, the year after a palisaded stronghold had been built at Montreal, there were not 300 Frenchmen in all New France, exclusive of L'Acadie. Seigneuries were laid out along the St. Lawrence and Richelieu rivers, where almost every habitant's farm had a frontage of from 190 to 250 yards on the water's edge and ran a mile or more inland. New France in the seventeenth century has been well described as a single village strung out along the rivers, broken only by the Rock of Quebec, center of government and of the church, by the tiny town of Trois Rivières, and the frontier trading post of Montreal.

Quebec in 1665 contained only 70 houses and 550 people. In contrast to towns in the continental colonies and the West Indies, one-quarter of this population consisted of religious— secular priests and Jesuits, Ursuline nuns and those of another order who ran the Hôtel-Dieu, the hospital. Both here and at Montreal, the church edifice was of a size and splendor that no English colonial capital could match for another century. At the head of the church in Canada was Bishop François de Laval-Montmorency, who reigned on the Rock for twenty-nine years from 1659, and remained a power in the colony until his death in 1708. Laval was an ecclesiastical statesman who defended church privileges against the state, and a stern disciplinarian who enforced a Puritanical code of manners and morals not unlike that of New England. Protestants, who had been fairly prominent in the early history of New France, were now excluded; one of them named Daniel Voil, who managed to get in, was condemned to death in 1661 for a bag of crimes including smuggling, witchcraft, and blasphemy, and was executed.

As Count Frontenac once remarked, there were but two kinds of business in New France—conversion of souls and conversion of beaver. Trading for beaver with *les sauvages,* as the French called the Indians, was the one great economic interest in Canada, corresponding to tobacco on the Chesapeake and sugar in the West Indies. All efforts of company or crown to persuade the habitants to grow a surplus of corn and cattle for export, or to build ships and set up home industries, failed for the same reason that English efforts to cultivate vineyards and silkworms in Virginia failed. Nothing paid like the big cash crop. The fur trade was conducted by young Frenchmen, called *coureurs de bois,* who penetrated deep into the wilderness by canoe, spent the winter hunting and trapping with the Indians, and collected quantities of furs. As soon as the ice melted they accompanied the Indian trappers down the St. Lawrence or the Ottawa to Montreal. One canoe could carry 600 beaver pelts, worth a gold dollar each in Montreal. As soon as the flotilla was signaled coming down river, there was a lively scrimmage among Montreal merchants for spots on the river front. Booths were set up with enticing merchandise such as muskets, blankets, kettles, and looking glasses; bars dispensed well-watered brandy, a quart of which bought a beaver pelt; and there were gaming tables where the Indian staked his pack on a few throws of the dice. The governor usually showed up to give a loyalty "talk" to the Indians, and several priests came to preach fair play and good morals; but after a day or two of trading the debauchery became such that the fathers departed. The coureurs de bois, who took a cut on this trade, grew rich if they did not squander their gains on drink and gambling, which they usually did. The business had a true "Western" appeal, and every young man of spirit in Canada got into it.

The French crown disapproved this fur-trading system; Louis XIV wanted New France to develop into a farming community like Normandy, where the people did what they were told by the seigneur, and were taught what to think by the parish priest. One reason why so many brisk young men became coureurs de bois was to get away from snoopy priests.

The clergy in French Canada exercised the most effective system of thought control ever enforced in America north of Mexico. They saw to it that no printing press ever reached French Canada.

Beyond all praise, however, was the work of the Jesuit and other missionaries, devoted and courageous men, "pallid with the air of the cloister," who to save souls braved the terrors of the wilderness, lived amid the filth of Indian villages, and faced death in its most cruel and revolting forms. French Catholics were the most successful Christians of any European nation in dealing with American Indians. They appealed to their sense of dignity and, most important, did not covet their lands. But all the missionaries' efforts broke down before the implacable hostility of the Iroquois. These Five Nations, whose fortified villages and extensive cornfields lay in central New York, were kept loyal to the English through the superior quality of English woolens and the high alcoholic content of West Indies rum. The Iroquois were largely middlemen, obtaining most of their furs from the southern watershed of the western Great Lakes, and rivals to the Huron, who acted as middlemen between the French and far western tribes. In 1648 the Iroquois conquered the Huron and tortured to death the missionaries living among them, Fathers Brébeuf and Lalemant. Father Isaac Jogues, who ventured into the heart of the Iroquois country, was also done to death. During the next few years the Iroquois almost choked New France by a blockade of the St. Lawrence and Ottawa rivers, capturing and killing every Indian they encountered bringing fur packs down by canoe. A young man named Adam Dollard led a forlorn hope of sixteen Frenchmen and five Indians against a war party of 700 Iroquois at the Long Sault of the Ottawa. All were killed; but they gave the Iroquois such a tough fight that the planned assault on Montreal was abandoned.

It was largely because they were unable to cope with the Iroquois that the Hundred Associates threw in the sponge in 1663 and surrendered their charter. Louis XIV "Le Grand Monarque," then only twenty-five years old, and his energetic prime minister Colbert, took hold promptly. Canada, including L'Acadie, now became a crown colony like Virginia but with no representative institutions. "New France lived under a regime of complete absolutism," writes Gustave Lanctot, one of Canada's latest and best historians. "Her inhabitants possessed not one political right; they were even forbidden to hold any sort of public meeting without official permission, or to solicit signatures to a petition." And the severe laws made by the French crown for Canada were enforced by implacable justice; people were tortured (forbidden in all English colonies), and even punished by mutilation.

Canada's first military governor under the royal regime was the Marquis de Tracy, an elderly but energetic soldier who arrived at Quebec in 1665 with a fleet of ships. More important, he brought advance echelons of the Carignan-Salières regiment, 1100 strong, who remained in the colony permanently and were given wives and land. No fewer than 961 girls were imported in ten years. Upon arrival they were sorted into three groups—*demoiselles* of good family, middle-class girls, and (most numerous) peasants' daughters. The plump little *paysannes* were snapped up first, as they worked hard and stood the severe winters well. Dowries were provided by a paternal king, and within two weeks of her arrival every girl found a husband. From these happy unions of soldiers and habitants with *les filles du Roi,* as the imported damsels were called, most of the millions of French Canadians of our day claim descent. But it is probable that the unconsecrated unions of coureurs de bois with young Indian girls have accounted for a goodly portion of this interesting and unique people.

Tracy lost no time in taking the first step to subdue the Iroquois. In 1666, 600 men of his regiment, an equal number of peasant volunteers, and 100 friendly Indians sailed up Lake Champlain and Lake George in 300 *batteaux* and canoes and, from the site of Fort William Henry, plunged into the wilderness that was then central New York. They accomplished little in the way of fighting, as the nimble Mohawks kept several jumps ahead of them. Food gave out and the French had to retire, but they gave the Iroquois Confederacy such a scare that it laid off attacking Canada for twenty years.

This campaign reopened the West to the French. Coureurs de bois and explorers now penetrated the country of the Potawottomi, the Sauk and Fox, and even the Sioux. Jean Talon, the intendant or civil governor, pushed this westward movement vigorously, enabled Père Marquette to set up a mission at Michilimackinac, sent the Canadian-born Louis Joliet to Green Bay, Lake Michigan, across country to the Wisconsin river, and down the Mississippi to the Arkansas. At Sault Sainte-Marie ("the Soo"), in 1671, Tracy's representative, Daumont de Saint-Lusson, in the presence of messengers from fourteen Indian tribes and with impressive ceremony, took possession of the entire west of North America in the name of Louis XIV.

English efforts to invalidate this vast claim form a large

part of American history during the eighteenth century; and the feud, inherited by the United States and British Canada, continued well into the nineteenth. It was not really ended until the settlement of the Oregon Question in 1846.

The arrival at Quebec of a new governor, Count Frontenac, in 1672, marks the end of this period of transition. There were now about 500 French settlers in L'Acadie and 7000 along the St. Lawrence between the Gaspé Peninsula and Lake St. Louis. Frontenac established a new fort on Lake Ontario at the site of Kingston; but the expansionist policy which he inherited from Talon was opposed by Bishop Laval and the priests, on the ground that coureurs de bois corrupted the innocent Indians with brandy. The church had the ear of Louis XIV, and Frontenac in 1682 was recalled in disgrace.

Nevertheless, Canada had become a respectable colony with a military strength far greater than her numbers indicated. The time was fast approaching when she would have trouble with New England and New York. And when the clash came, fortunately for New France, Frontenac once more was governor.

England had already carved a slice out of France's potential western empire in the far north. The French sent overland expeditions to capture the Hudson's Bay Company's trading posts; but English tenacity and sea power triumphed; and the Company still exists.

Thus, in the fifty years between 1625 and 1675 the French and British, rivals of the next century, were firmly established in the New World. Starting in the north, trappers of the Hudson's Bay Company were exploiting the wilderness around the great inland sea where Henry Hudson had met his death in 1610. South of them, French Canada, with a settled strip along the lower St. Lawrence, was extending her tentacles into the far west; in L'Acadie there were a few hundred farmers on the Bay of Fundy and trading posts as far east as Canso. France was superb in discovery and exploration, more enterprising than the English or Dutch in staking out empire, and more skillful than either in handling Indians. France had at least twice the population of England in 1675, and many times her wealth; yet with all these advantages she proved incapable of peopling the continental empire that she claimed. New France, including the later acquisition of Louisiana, remained essentially a far-flung chain of trading posts while the English colonies were filling up with settlers and becoming commonwealths. The main reasons for this disparity were the preoccupation of the French kings with European wars which drained their country of men and money, and their insistence on their colonists' being 100 per cent French and Catholic.

The stage was set for one of the longest and bitterest struggles for power in American history.

VEXILLA REGIS

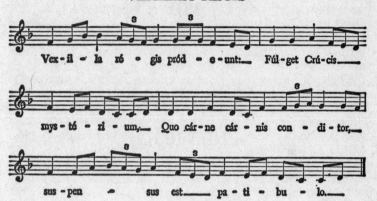

Vex - il - la ré - gis pród - e - unt:____ Fúl - get Crú - cis____ mys - té - ri - um,____ Quo cár - ne cár - nis con - di - tor,____ sus - pen - sus est____ pa - ti - bu - lo.____

VIII

Time of Troubles

1675-1691

1. *King Philip's War*

DECENNIUM LUCTUOSUM, the Woeful Decade, was the title
Cotton Mather used for the period 1685–95, when his beloved
Bay Colony lost her charter and was placed under an arbitrary government. And we may add the next earlier decade,
which began a time of troubles for New England, Virginia,
and Canada.

Hitherto, New England had suffered but one Indian war, a
short, sharp, and decisive conflict with the Pequots in 1637,
which saved the land from savage warfare for nigh forty
years. Why, then, should a war of extermination have broken
out in 1675? Explanations by contemporaries are interesting,
but hardly convincing. All agreed that it was a divine punishment on New England—but for what? Said the local clergy,
retribution for sins of the younger generation who fidgeted under
hour-long sermons, let their hair grow, wore fashionable clothes,
and drank rum. Quakers believed that war came because
Massachusetts Bay had been harsh to the Friends. Governor
Berkeley of Virginia wrote home that the New England Puritans were being punished for their sympathy with the usurper
Cromwell.

Although the Indians left no records in their defense, it is fairly certain that the underlying cause was the incompatibility of their way of life with that of the English. French Canadians could get along because their relations with the natives were mainly by way of trade, and their religion made few demands on converts. But English colonists wanted land, and it took about twenty times as much land to support an Indian as to feed an Englishman. The Algonquin tribes of New England wanted many things that the English offered, such as firearms and iron tools; but the Puritans wished to sell English civilization in one package, Congregational Church and all.

Up to a point they had an astonishing success. Missionaries such as John Eliot, John Cotton, and Richard Bourne made great efforts to teach the Indians to read their own language, printed the Bible and other books for them, and trained native preachers. The colonial assemblies segregated converts in self-governing communities, and by 1675 there was a chain of these "Praying Indian Towns" between northeastern Connecticut and the Merrimack river, with some twenty more on and near Cape Cod. The converted Indians hunted, fished, and raised their own food, and made a little cash selling game, canoes, and baskets to their white neighbors. Purchases of land from them, or from the "wild" Indians were illegal unless authorized by the colonial governments, and on several occasions overambitious realtors were heavily fined for breaking this law.

But the total number of converted Indians did not exceed 2500, out of about 10,000 in southern New England. By 1675 these "wild" Indians were beginning to feel badly crowded by the steady advance of the English frontier. They too sold land; but Indians never understood ownership of land in the English sense. Their idea of signing a deed to real estate, usually in return for a specified number of axes, kettles, and matchcoats or mackinaws, was to share it with the palefaces, not to move out; and they regarded the price as rent, to be repeated every so often. Their chiefs and medicine men resisted conversion because it undermined their authority.

The three unconverted tribes that made trouble were the Nipmuck of central Massachusetts; the Narragansett, who bordered on the bay of that name; and the Wampanoag, who inhabited eastern Rhode Island and western Plymouth Colony. The Nipmuck were being squeezed between the settlements of eastern Massachusetts and those along the Connecticut river, and dared not move west for fear of the Mohawk nation. The Narragansett, having threatened trouble in the past, had been roughly treated by the New England Confederation and were biding their time for revenge, under two able sachems named Pomham and Canonchet.

The Wampanoag, who started this war, were the original friends of the Pilgrim Fathers. Their territory had been greatly contracted by purchase, and Metacom (called King Philip by the English), chief sachem from 1662, had a taste for gay attire and ran up bills in Boston which he could only pay by selling more land. Plymouth seemed unable to prevent cattle from raiding his cornfields, or bootleggers from selling his people firewater. As he brooded over his wrongs, both real and assumed, Philip became surly and resentful. Plymouth heard from friendly Indians that he was planning a coalition against them; thrice he was haled into court and fined, which deeply offended his dignity.

War was brought on by the murder of Sassamon, a Harvard-educated Indian who had been Philip's secretary, and who tipped off Governor Winslow of Plymouth to the "king's" latest plot. The Indian murderers were arrested, tried, found guilty by a jury that included redskins, and hanged. That was too much for Philip. Indians thought it all right to kill in a fight, or to torture a prisoner to death; but to hang a man after trial violated their deepest feelings of morality. Two weeks after the hanging, on 24 June 1675, war broke out with an attack on Swansea, a frontier settlement near Philip's headquarters on Mount Hope, Narragansett Bay.

The Bay Colony came promptly to Plymouth's assistance, but their first joint operations were badly bungled. Philip, with his braves, women, and children, escaped to central Massachusetts, where they spurred into action the Nipmuck, and attacked the frontier settlements of Brookfield, Lancaster, Deerfield, and other places in quick succession. The New England Confederation declared war, bringing Connecticut Colony into the fight. By fall the westernmost settlements of Massachussetts Bay and Plymouth had been wiped out, and two striking forces sent to punish the Indians had been badly mauled. It looked as though Philip and his allies would soon drive the English into the sea.

New England presented a very grim aspect in 1675–76. The Indians, approaching stealthily through the surrounding forest, would burn and plunder every dwelling, barn, or mill, and kill or mutilate all livestock that they could not use, while the men in the designated garrison houses, where the villages gathered for defense, took potshots at them. The air was filled with terror-inspiring warwhoops, and the shrieks of tortured animals and people. This went on until the Indians retired, glutted with food and plunder, or the garrison was relieved by a troop of horse or company of infantry. The Indians, well supplied with muskets, bullets, and powder, were dead shots. They were waging total war, which the English could not do. Farmers had to plow, sow, reap, and feed stock; women had to cook, tend children, and milk cows; some soldiers had to guard each settlement so that normal activities could continue. As the Indians rubbed out one village after another, each community wanted to take the defensive and send no more striking forces into the woods where they were apt to be ambushed and slaughtered.

No outside help reached New England. Governor Andros of New York even took advantage of the situation by trying to annex a slice of Connecticut; Governor Berkeley of Virginia refused to allow a vessel sent from Boston to buy corn; King Charles II sent neither men nor money, although he could spare a fleet and 1000 soldiers to put down Nat Bacon in Virginia. Only in far-off Dublin a Protestant congregation passed the hat and sent a generous contribution to war victims in Boston.

Several factors saved New England. The Indians were not united. Pequot and Mohegan remained loyal to Connecticut; Wonalancet, the Penacook sachem in the north, remained neutral; and a large number of Praying Indians helped the English as scouts and fighters, teaching them proper tactics. This in spite of the fact that hundreds of the converted natives, unjustly suspected (like the Japanese-Americans on the West Coast in 1942) of being a "fifth column," were miserably interned on an island in Boston Harbor. And many others were killed by cowardly hoodlums. The Indians had no firm leadership—King Philip's role being largely that of an inciter to action—and no concerted plan; their warfare was all of the hit-and-run variety. The confederate New England colonies were under able governors—John Leverett, who had fought under Cromwell, John Winthrop, Jr., and Josiah Winslow. And the Confederation, taking a desperate step, decided in the fall of 1675 on a preventive war against the Narragansett, who were harboring Wampanoag refugees.

An army of over 1000 officers and men under Governor Winslow was transported by sea to a devastated settlement on Narragansett Bay. Winter closed in early that year; and on 19 November the army marched through snow, guided by a friendly Indian, to a "hideous swamp" in the present township of South Kingstown, Rhode Island. There some 3000 Narragansetts were entrenched behind a triple palisade and blockhouses. In the early afternoon the van of the English army forced an entrance through a breach. Murderous gunfire flung back their first onslaught, killing five company commanders; but the rest pressed in, and all afternoon there was desperate fighting. No quarter was given on either side, the Indian wigwams were set afire, and about two-thirds of the enemy were killed or burned to death; the rest escaped. As light faded over this grim scene, and snow began to fall, Winslow gave orders to retire, and the weary survivors filed off through the woods, carrying their wounded comrades. They reached the Bay at two in the morning, having marched 36 miles and fought savagely for three hours within the space of a single day.

This was the toughest battle, not excepting Bunker Hill, ever fought on New England soil. The English losses were severe (eighty killed, including eight out of fourteen company commanders); and, owing to a breakdown in the service of supply, the survivors spent a Valley Forge winter at Wickford, Rhode Island. But it was worth the cost. The Great Swamp Fight broke the power of the Narragansett.

The war was not yet over. Canonchet escaped, and ambushed Captain Michael Pierce's company near Pawtucket; only one Englishman and nine friendly Indians survived to be put to torture. Canonchet then burned Rehoboth and Providence, telling Roger Williams, who parleyed, that he would never make peace until Plymouth Colony was wiped out. But his number was nearly up. Two weeks later, on 3 April 1676, Canonchet was ambushed and captured by a mixed company of English and friendly Indians. When told that he was to be put to death he said, "I like it well; I shall die before my heart is soft or I have said anything unworthy of myself." Pequot warriors shot him and sent his head to Hartford as a token of their fidelity to the English.

The war was still raging in central Massachusetts, but the English by now had learned to keep the enemy on the move so that he had no chance to strike back or even to obtain food. King Philip, too proud to give up, retired to his original home at Mount Hope, there to sell his life dear. His position, betrayed by an Indian whom he had offended, was surrounded by Captain Church's company, and when Philip tried to break loose (12 August 1676) he was killed on the run by a member of the Pocasset tribe who had joined his enemies.

Some Indians escaped to the northern wilderness, and a few even made their way to the Illinois country; but most of the enemy surrendered or were captured. The women and children were parceled out to white families as servants; warriors were sold as slaves in the West Indies and on the Barbary Coast of Africa. In Maine, where the Abnaki forced the evacuation of every English settlement, the war only ended in the spring of

1678, and by treaty, not unconditional surrender. These Indians retained their lands and their strength, and as allies of the French fought against the English in later colonial wars.

New England had won, at tremendous cost. Twenty years elapsed before all the destroyed villages were resettled, forty before the frontier advanced. In the meantime these colonies suffered other disasters, from the hands of kings and the powers of darkness.

2. Nat Bacon's Rebellion

What might have been an Indian war in Virginia similar to King Philip's, developed by chance into a rebellion led by a young Englishman. This strange turn was caused by a very different economic and political situation from that of New England. While the seaports from New York to New Hampshire were prospering through trade with the West Indies, the one-crop settlements on Chesapeake Bay were suffering from low prices for tobacco. In 1668 it reached the all-time low of a farthing (half a cent) a pound; and by 1675 had not recovered even to a penny. Taxes fell very heavily on poor people, while most of the ruling class, as members of the council, were tax-exempt. Northern colonial governments, annually elected, gave the New Englanders opportunity to ventilate grievances and correct abuses; but in Virginia there had been no election for fourteen years. In a wave of loyalty over the restoration of Charles II the colony had chosen a house of burgesses so pleasing to Governor Berkeley that he merely adjourned it from year to year. This "Long Assembly" even outlasted the Long Parliament of England. The Governor kept the burgesses loyal to himself by giving almost every member an office of profit or honor, often two or more. He appointed the councillors and county judges. The parish vestries, corresponding roughly to town meetings in New England, had become self-perpetuating, and for the most part were composed of the same men who made up the county courts. Thus, Sir William Berkeley, now nearly seventy years old, had the entire machinery of Virginia government in his hands.

The Indian situation, however, was similar to that of New England. Virginia as yet had made no attempt to convert the natives within her borders, but after Opechancanough's second rebellion in 1644 she had given reservations to a number of small tribes—the Pamunkey, Nottaway, Appomattox, and a dozen others. Owing to the growth of English population, these reservations had become enclaves surrounded by white people, who were constantly encroaching. By 1675 there were only

3000 or 4000 of these subject Indians, constantly dwindling. Berkeley treated them as king's subjects whom he was bound to protect; but the lower order of white people regarded them as vermin to be exterminated.

On the southwest border of Virginia, at the confluence of the Dan and Staunton rivers, lived the Occaneechee, a small tribe who acted as middlemen in the fur and deerskin trade between Virginia, the Carolinas, and the West. On the northern frontier were the Susquehannock. These, when dwelling on the river named after them, had been allies of Lord Baltimore against their ancient enemies the Seneca. But in 1674 Maryland let them down by making a separate peace with the Seneca, who then forced the Susquehannock to move south to the Potomac. Their presence there was a danger both to Maryland and Virginia.

In July or August 1675 three Virginia settlers were murdered by Indians. Both colonial governors called out the local militia; Virginia's contingent was commanded by Lieutenant Colonel John Washington, ancestor of the first President of the United States; and Maryland's by Major Thomas Truman, who was not an ancestor of the thirty-third President. On the north bank of the Potomac, near the site of Fort Washington and almost opposite Mount Vernon, Washington and Truman found the Susquehannock entrenched in a palisaded fort like that of the Narragansett in Rhode Island. The Indians sent out five chiefs to parley. An angry colloquy took place with the white officers, at the end of which the five chiefs were taken away and killed, by whose order is uncertain.

That unjust act, contrary to immemorial usage, sparked off an Indian war. The embittered Susquehannock broke into roving bands which attacked one plantation after another on the Virginia frontier, even more vulnerable than that of New England. Indian warfare was assuming the sadly familiar pattern that lasted for two centuries. If a white man could not find the right Indian to punish, he killed any Indian, feeling that the fewer there were the better; and the Indians similarly avenged themselves on any paleface they encountered.

Governor Berkeley, indignant at the outrage against the Susquehannock, and fearful of provoking a general war like King Philip's (of which he had heard the gory details), adopted the defensive strategy of building a chain of mutually supporting forts around the settled part of the colony. Frontier planters and Indian-haters were indignant; the word went around that Berkeley "doth not take a speedy course and destroy the Indians," owing to his "love to the Beaver"—he being an Indian trader. People who felt that way soon found a leader in Nathaniel Bacon.

This young man, variously estimated by later historians as a torchbearer for democracy and a desperate rabble-rouser, was cousin to the famous Lord Bacon. He had been withdrawn from the University of Cambridge for "extravagancies," and in 1673 packed off to Virginia, complete with bride and the generous sum of £1800 from a wealthy father. A cousin to Lady Berkeley, young Bacon was warmly welcomed by the governor and appointed to the council at the age of twenty-eight. He bought two plantations on the James river above William Byrd's "Westover," and was by way of becoming a member of the ruling clique, when the overseer of his upper plantation was killed in a Susquehannock raid. Bacon's anger rose, and when he appeared before a muster of militia they cried with one voice, "A Bacon! a Bacon!" This went to the fellow's head. He was persuaded to assume command and lead the militia against the Indians. But, instead of going after the guilty Susquehannock, the militia, in typical frontier fashion, attacked the friendly, fur-trading Occaneechee, accusing them of harboring enemy fugitives, and killed their chief Persicles.

That exploit made Bacon a popular hero and began the rebellion. The lower order of white men, and a few great landowners like William Byrd who had plantations near the frontier, flocked to his standard. Governor Berkeley denounced him as "Oliver Bacon," but issued writs for a new assembly, the first since 1662. This body redressed several popular grievances such as plurality in offices and self-perpetuating parish vestries, and declared war on all neighboring Indians. Bacon appeared at Jamestown, made his submission to the governor, and was pardoned. He returned to his plantation; but, finding Indians still on the loose, cried "Treachery!," raised the country, marched on Jamestown, and forced the governor to flee to the Eastern Shore. Bacon now became a rebel indeed, summoning all true and loyal Englishmen to support him, setting up a *de facto* government, and denouncing the Berkeley clique as "sponges" who "have sucked up the Publik Treasure," "unworthy Favorites and juggling Parasites."

Back and forth rocked the fortunes of war. Bacon captured two ships on the James and organized them as a rebel navy. Berkeley called out the loyal militia of the Eastern Shore and begged King Charles to send him an army of regulars. Bacon planned to secure Virginia until a fair hearing of the people's grievances could be had in London; he hoped to capture Berkeley and send him home to be tried for failure to protect the colonial frontier. For a few months, "General" Bacon was

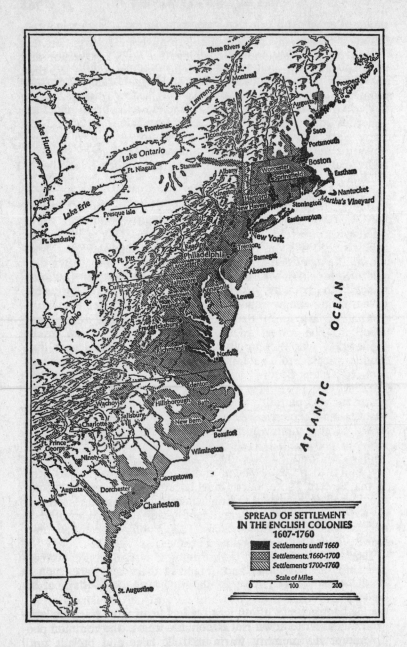

SPREAD OF SETTLEMENT
IN THE ENGLISH COLONIES
1607-1760

Settlements until 1660
Settlements, 1660-1700
Settlements 1700-1760

Scale of Miles
0   100   200

master of all Virginia except the Eastern Shore. But he had no chance to win in the end. The Cromwellian usurpation was too recent for anyone to challenge the king's governor and get away with it; and Virginia's total population was less than 50,000. In vain Bacon exacted an oath of allegiance to himself and confiscated the property of loyalists. On sober second thought, many of the very men who had bawled, "A Bacon!" shrank from opposing their monarch's lawful representative, and deserted. And, marvelous to relate, the seventy-year-old governor managed to defeat the twenty-eight-year-old "general," with no assistance from home.

Bacon concentrated the remnant of his army, including servants and even slaves, at Gloucester on the York river. Desperately he talked of beating the "Red Coates" who were on their way, and of creating out of Virginia, Maryland, and North Carolina a free state allied with the Dutch or the French. In Maryland a rebellion had broken out which Bacon hoped might spread and help his cause. But Charles, third Lord Baltimore, nipped it in the bud and hanged the leaders before any liaison with Bacon could be effected.

At his last stand, near Yorktown, Nat Bacon came down with a severe attack of the "bloody flux" (dysentery) and there died miserably on 26 October 1676. His followers buried his body secretly so that it would not be subjected to the indignities inflicted on the corpses of Canonchet and Cromwell, and the rebellion flickered out.

Following the usual procedure against defeated rebels, the Governor court-martialed and hanged all the gentlemen on Bacon's side whom he could lay hands on—twenty-three in all. Most of this work had been accomplished when a fleet arrived from England, bringing 1100 troops and a royal commission to find out what was wrong with Virginia. It also brought a general pardon from Charles II to the rebels, and an order for Berkeley to come home and give an account of himself. The governor returned to England in June 1677 and died there, before having a chance to lay his case before the king. Charles II, far from appreciating what his loyal servant had done, remarked, "that old fool has hang'd more men in that naked Country, than he had done for the Murther of his Father."

Although every effort was made by the new Virginia aristocracy to write down Nat Bacon as a knave, the common people kept his memory warm in folk tales and ballads until historians dared to do him justice.

Nat Bacon's bones	The rich and proud
They never found,	Deny his name,
Nat Bacon's grave	The rich and proud
Is wilderground:	Defile his fame:
Nat Bacon's tongue	The proud and free
Doth sound! Doth sound!	Cry shame! Cry shame![1]

Bacon's rebellion accomplished some good. Most of the reform legislation was re-enacted by the next assembly. No later royal governor dared rule through such a close, tight oligarchy as did Berkeley; but the basic trouble, the low price of tobacco, continued to harass the colony. And this brief civil war contributed to building up an aristocracy of survivors. William Fitzhugh, one of them, wrote in 1687 that he missed "spiritual helps and comforts," that Virginia was no place to bring up a gentleman's son. "Good education of children is almost impossible, and better be never born than ill-bred," a sentiment in which Virginia gentlemen of every generation concur. But transferring the capital to Williamsburg, where the College of William and Mary was founded in 1693, marked the dawn of a better day in the Old Dominion.

3. *The Dominion of New England*

In 1677 the New England colonies had barely begun to recover from King Philip's War, and on the Maine frontier the war was not even finished. Some settlements had been abandoned altogether; in others the black ruins of houses and barns were being cleared away and new ones built. In the seaports, crowded with "displaced persons" who had no other place to go, ships laid up during the war were being repaired and merchants were begging their London correspondents for fresh credit.

At this juncture the Lords of Trade, a committee of the Privy Council appointed by Charles II to deal with the English colonies, informed the Massachusetts Bay authorities that they must accept royal officials to enforce obedience to the Acts of Trade. A reasonable enough request; but the Bay government stubbornly maintained its own theory of virtual independence. After trying to appease Charles II with a gift of "ten barrells of cranberries, two hogsheads of special good samp, and three thousand of cod fish," delicacies hardly suitable for the merry monarch's table, the general court replied in words that carry one back to the old Puritans, and forward

[1] By Archibald MacLeish, reprinted with his permission.

to Samuel Adams and James Otis. "Wee humbly conceive," they said, "that the lawes of England are bounded within the four seas, and doe not reach America. The subjects of his majesty here being not represented in Parliament, so we have not looked at ourselves to be impeded in our trade by them."

The king chose to ignore this challenge. For several years he did nothing to curb this stubborn "Bay horse," except to send out a customs collector named Edward Randolph, who was thrown every time he tried to mount; illegal traders whom he arrested were always acquitted by the local courts. The English government finally concluded that in order to bring Massachusetts within the imperial system its charter must be revoked. And that obstacle was cleared by the High Court of Chancery in 1684.

Charles II died before making new arrangements about Massachusetts Bay. The next king, James II, gave Joseph Dudley, son of an old Puritan governor, a commission to rule Massachusetts, New Hampshire, and Maine, which now became the Dominion of New England. Sharing his authority were royal councillors, all of whom except Edward Randolph were New Englanders; but no assembly.

The practical effect of this change of government was to transfer political power from the Puritan oligarchy of the Bay Colony to an embryo Tory party. Joseph Dudley, the leader of this group, was a healthy young man who revolted against the grim atmosphere in which he had been brought up; and to his way of thinking were many merchants and Anglicans who wanted closer cultural and commercial ties with England. A minister who came over with Dudley celebrated the first Anglican service in Boston in 1686. Little by little, the customs of merry England, long proscribed in New England, began to creep in. When a maypole was set up in Charleston, the Reverend Increase Mather felt that the devil was indeed marching to victory in the Puritan citadel.

Dudley did not last long, as he refused to split with Randolph the proceeds of confiscating illegal imports. In December 1686, James II replaced him by the governor of New York, Sir Edmund Andros, and annexed Plymouth Colony, virtually independent for sixty-six years, to the Dominion. And James did not stop there. Like all Stuart kings an enemy to representative government, he decided to erect all colonies north of Maryland into a single viceroyalty. Rhode Island and Connecticut were annexed to the Dominion in 1687; New York and the Jersies next year; and the axe was about to fall on Pennsylvania when James II was deposed.

4. *La Salle*

In New France, successive governors refused to regard the
Five Nations as an English satellite state, and sent one punitive
expedition after another against them, usually with slight success. French explorers and traders then sought ways to get
around them, into the West.

Greatest of these French explorers was Robert Cavelier de
la Salle, who emigrated to Montreal at the age of twenty-three,
obtained a seigneury on Lake St. Louis, and entered the fur
trade. He learned the language of the Indians, became their
friend, and decided to penetrate the great West. First, with an
Indian guide, he followed portages across the future State of
Ohio and descended the Ohio river to the site of Louisville.
In 1679 he built a vessel on the Niagara river near Buffalo and
sailed her to Green Bay, Lake Michigan; then paddled around
that lake in a canoe; built a fort and left a garrison at the site
of St. Joseph, Michigan; paddled up the St. Joseph river to
its south bend near the present campus of Notre Dame University, carried over to the "Theakiki" (Kankakee) river, and
paddled down the Illinois as far as Starved Rock. That hill he
fortified, to defend friendly Indians against roving Iroquois.
Then, back to Fort Frontenac (Kingston, Ontario) by canoe
and carry, 1000 miles in 65 days. During the next winter season he retraced the greater part of this journey by canoe and
on foot.

In the last month of 1681 his greatest adventure began. With
23 Frenchmen and 31 Indians, mostly refugees from King
Philip's War, he struck out from St. Joseph fort for the Mississippi. As the rivers were frozen, the party made sledges on
which they dragged their canoes across "the divine river,
called by the Indians *Checagou*," and down the Illinois. On
6 February 1682 they joined the majestic stream of the Mississippi. Down they paddled, past the mouths of the Missouri
and the Ohio, and the Chickasaw Bluffs. "More and more they
entered the realm of spring. The hazy sunlight, the warm and
drowsy air, the tender foliage, the opening flowers, betokened
the reviving life of nature."[1] La Salle placated the fierce
Quapaw, the cultured Taensa, the Natchez, and every other
nation he encountered. On 6 April, after sailing past the site
of New Orleans, he reached the point where the Mississippi
separates into three channels. He and his men, divided into
three parties, reached the Passes in three days, and met at a
spot of dry ground on the Gulf of Mexico. There, with due

[1] This and other quotations about La Salle are from Francis Parkman's
masterly biography of him.

religious ceremony, La Salle displayed the white banner of the Bourbons and took possession of "this country of Louisiana . . . in the name of the most high, mighty, invincible and victorious Louis the Great, by Grace of God King of France and of Navarre." Louisiana he defined as the valley of the Mississippi including all its tributaries. No claim so stupendous had been made by any European monarch since the voyages of Columbus.

Returning to Quebec, where he found the new governor unsympathetic, La Salle went on to France, where he gained the king's ear. Louis XIV, who at first regarded La Salle's descent of the Mississippi as "wholly useless," now decided to seize and hold Louisiana to annoy the king of Spain, his enemy for the time being. So he gave La Salle four ships, a company of soldiers, and both men and women emigrants, with orders to build a fort on the lower Mississippi "whence we may control the continent." This expedition, which started in 1684, was fraught with disaster. The fleet overshot the Passes by 400 miles—for La Salle had no means of finding the longitude of the spot where he had taken possession. He landed on the shores of Matagorda Bay, Texas, marched inland, and built a fort on a prairie bordering on the Garcitas river. The Frenchmen found plenty of buffalo for food, and friendly Indians of the Cenis tribe, but knew not where they were. So La Salle, with a few men, set forth overland to find the Mississippi. At a point near the site of Navasota, Texas, on 18 March 1687, he was murdered by mutineers, and the body of the man who had staked out an empire for France was stripped, dishonored, and left to the wolves and the vultures.

5. Revolutions and Rebellions of 1688–1691

These events were remote from New England and Virginia, but it was partly King James's knowledge of a French design to encircle the English colonies which persuaded him to combine all the northern ones, for purposes of defense, in one dominion. The dominion government was highly unpopular in New England. Sir Edmund Andros and his henchmen declared all land titles void unless validated for a price, and required everyone to pay the crown an annual quitrent. Taxes, instead of being voted by the people's representatives, were levied by executive fiat; selectmen and town clerks who protested were jailed; no money was provided to support schools. Cape Codders, who had spliced out their slender gains from fishing and farming by trying out stranded whales, were deeply outraged by being ordered to hand over the oil to the royal governor, on the ground that whales were "royal fish." Boston merchants who had welcomed the change of government found themselves squeezed by Johnny-come-latelys on Andros's council and deprived of their accustomed lines of trade.

Andros proved to be an efficient military leader when bands of Indians led by French officers from Canada began to attack settlements on the New England frontier. But the people allowed him no credit for this. To the general run of New Englanders and New Yorkers, already accustomed to look for the cloven hoof in any action of Governor Andros, his military policy seemed evidence of a Catholic plot between James II and Louis XIV to hand over New York and New England to the French. England had recently been in a turmoil over a cooked-up "Popish Plot" in which Titus Oates played a role similar to that of Joseph McCarthy in the communist scare of the 1950's. Many colonists now imagined that there was a similar plot to turn all North America over to Rome. For, were not James II, Lord Baltimore, Governor Dongan of New York, and Governor Lord Howard of Virginia, Catholics? Two hundred families of French Protestant refugees who arrived at New York in 1687–88 spread stories of what Yorkers might expect if French dragoons were turned loose on them. If they could have read the instructions of King Louis XIV to Count Frontenac, when that stout governor returned to Canada in 1689, they would have been still more alarmed. Frontenac, with French regulars and Indian allies, was to proceed south by Lake Champlain and Lake George, capture Albany, bring the Iroquois to an alliance, and in boats descend the Hudson to its mouth, where a French fleet would be on hand to help him capture the city. He was instructed to ransom the merchants and gentlemen, exact forced labor of Protestant farmers and mechanics, and to send French Protestants home to be executed.

Fortunately for the English colonies, Frontenac's invasion stalled, the French fleet never arrived, and James II was so energetic in suppressing liberty at home that the English got rid of him. "Seven eminent persons," including a son of Sir Winston Churchill of Weymouth, sent an invitation to Prince William of Orange, who had married James's Protestant daughter Mary, to come over from Holland and save England. William landed in England with a small army on 5 November 1688. For several weeks the issue was in doubt; then James II, deserted by almost everyone, fled to France, and the "damned Dutchman" entered London. Parliament, meeting in January 1689, declared that James had abdicated, adopted a

Declaration of Rights (one source of our federal Bill of Rights), and conferred the crown on William and Mary. This bloodless change of regime was ever after referred to as the "Glorious Revolution of 1688." It even made revolution respectable.

Months elapsed before this important news reached America. On 4 April 1689 a vessel arrived at Boston bearing an order of the new king and queen that "all magistrates who have been unjustly turned out" resume "their former employment." That touched off a parallel revolution in Boston. The machinelike precision with which it unrolled points to careful plans and leadership, which no one has yet unearthed. The townspeople rose, the countryside rose, Andros and some of his principal councillors were flung into jail; a meeting was held, presided over by the last governor under the Bay Colony charter. It issued a "Declaration of the Gentlemen, Merchants, and Inhabitants," drafted by the Reverend Cotton Mather, that the Dominion was dissolved and the old charter again in force. William III and Mary II were proclaimed amid such enthusiasm as the Puritan capital had never witnessed—a parade, lighted windows, barrels of wine broached in the street. A new election returned the old crowd to power, and as soon as news of these events reached Plymouth, Providence, and Hartford, they "trotted after the Bay horse" as usual, and restored their own pre-Andros governments.

In New York events took a very different course and reached a tragic end, partly because there was no charter government for a revolution to restore; partly because James II had many partisans among the Hudson river patroons.

Lieutenant Governor Nicholson, Andros's deputy for New York, was startled (to put it mildly) when news of the Boston uprising reached the city. He summoned three councillors of the Dominion, Nicholas Bayard, Stephen Van Courtlandt, and Frederick Philipse, together with the city fathers and leading officers of the local militia, to meet as an informal council. The mass of New Yorkers wanted this body to proclaim William and Mary; but the old councillors stood firm for James II. An incautious threat by Nicholson, when drunk, to burn New York City, sparked a popular uprising. Jacob Leisler, a German-born merchant and captain of the local militia, stepped forward and accepted responsibility for heading a provisional government. Delegates elected by six counties of New York and one of New Jersey met in convention at the fort near the present Battery, proclaimed William and Mary on 22 June 1689, and appointed Leisler military com-

mander of the province and acting lieutenant governor until
the new sovereigns' pleasure was known. But they reckoned
without Albany and the grandees.

William and Mary for a long time could do nothing to help
their loyal supporters in the colonies. Jacobite rebellions in
Scotland and Ireland had to be put down first. England declared war on France. Not until 30 July 1689 did the English
sovereigns come to any decision about America. In New England they accepted the situation as they found it. But they
issued orders for New York that were liable to misconstruc-
tion. Lieutenant Governor Nicholson was to act as governor
or, in his absence "such for the time being" in power "to take
upon you the government of the said Province." Nicholson
was then en route to London to try to get Leisler thrown out;
so when this letter was delivered at New York in December,
Leisler, who "for the time being" was in power, construed it as
royal permission for his government to carry on. The Albany
clique refused to go along, and the military situation was
serious.

In October 1689 Count Frontenac, arriving at Quebec,
learned of a raid on La Chine by the Iroquois, and that the
French fort on Lake Ontario had been abandoned. These
events forced him to give up the grand design for a military
descent of the Hudson and subsequent purge of Protestants.
He decided instead on the strategy of *la petite guerre*, a series
of raids on the New York and New England frontiers. The
first raid, comprising 200 French troops and friendly Indians,
eluded the Mohawks and assaulted Schenectady on the night
of 8 February 1690. They wiped out that frontier village,
killed all but thirty of the inhabitants, and carried these cap-
tive to Montreal. Albany was in such a panic that it accepted
a garrison under Leisler's son-in-law Milborne for protection.

Leisler now acted with energy and breadth of view. He
called a meeting of delegates from all colonies north of Carolina to arrange a union for defense. The three New England
colonies which responded agreed upon a joint military-naval
expedition against Canada. Leisler was to direct a military
expedition up the Hudson and Lake Champlain to Montreal;
Massachusetts was to attack Quebec by sea. This left-and-right
method of hitting Canada where it hurt was excellent strategy.
It finally worked in 1759–60 after three tactical failures, of
which that of 1690 was the first.

Leisler's expeditionary force, placed under Fitz-John Winthrop of Connecticut, where most of the troops were raised,
suffered ill fortune. By the time it reached Lake Champlain

smallpox had broken out among the troops and Winthrop retreated, to Leisler's rage and disgust.

In London, meanwhile, there were more delays. William and Mary commissioned an Irish army officer with the ominous name of Sloughter as governor of New York; but no ship could be found to take him out in proper style, as the royal navies of England and France were slugging it out in the English Channel and the West Indies. A small squadron of four or five sail finally left England for North America in November 1690 with Governor Sloughter on board, but the skipper of the flagship got lost, and one of the smaller vessels carrying a company of redcoats under Major Richard Ingoldsby reached New York first, in January 1691. Ingoldsby called on Leisler to hand over the government to him; Leisler refused, preferring to wait until the new governor arrived. With the backing of the Albany clique, Ingoldsby besieged Leisler in the old fort near the Battery. The garrison fired on the royal troops, they attacked, and after a brisk fight compelled Leisler to surrender on 17 March 1691.

Governor Sloughter, who arrived only two days later, had Leisler, Milborne, and three members of his provisional council tried for treason. The stacked court was mostly composed of the Albany councillors, with Joe Dudley, who was looking for a royal governorship, presiding. Leisler's services in keeping order and protecting the frontier availed him nothing. The fact that he had bought land with his own money to settle French Huguenot refugees at New Rochelle, helped not one bit. He had put himself in the wrong by ordering his garrison to fire on the king's troops, and on that technical point he and his friends were found guilty of treason. His enemies were out for his blood, and got it. Leisler and Milborne were sentenced to a traitor's death. On 16 May 1691, on the site of City Hall Park, they were hanged by the neck, their bodies cut down while still alive, their bowels ripped out and burned before their faces, their heads cut off, and their bodies quartered. "The shrieks of the people," said a bystander, "were dreadful." The crowd carried off locks of Leisler's hair and bits of his garments as precious relics.

"These were the days of wrath and utter darkness," as a later petition of the New York assembly described this time of savage retaliation against a devoted servant of the people. After repeated efforts by the popular party, Parliament reversed the attainders of Leisler and Milborne. Their mutilated bodies were disinterred and given Christian burial, and in 1702 the assembly granted an indemnity to the heirs.

But that was not the end. New York politics for the next generation was divided between Leislerians and anti-Leislerians, and the last sparks of the feud had not died out when the American Revolution broke. Nicholas Roosevelt, first of that family to be in politics, was elected alderman because he had supported Leisler.

6. War and Witchcraft

The Glorious Revolution of 1688 in England saved both English and colonial liberties from a second Stuart despotism, but the English paid for their freedom by being dragged into war against France and Canada. In Europe it was called the War of the League of Augsburg; in America, King William's War.

Count Frontenac, who had a healthy respect for the Iroquois, left the New York frontier alone after the destruction of Schenectady; the New England frontier took the rap. For the past generation French missionaries and traders had been infiltrating the Maine wilderness to establish missions and trading posts among the Abnaki. In the summer of 1689 parties of Indians, led by French officers, began a series of raids on New England frontier settlements, and all forts and settlements on the coasts of Maine and New Hampshire were captured by the French and Indians before autumn. *La petite guerre,* as the French called it, looked pretty big to the frontiersmen.

These events aroused the feeling in New England tersely expressed by John Pynchon of Springfield: "We shall never be at rest till we have Cannida." Or, as Cotton Mather put it in classical style, *Canada delenda est.* To destroy Canada as a French colony became an objective of Massachusetts Bay, relentlessly pursued for seventy years. It is no wonder that the Canadians always referred to English colonists as "les Bastonnais," or that French kings planned the destruction of Boston.

The Boston authorities had the sound strategic sense to strike at the main centers of French power, Port Royal and Quebec, rather than to disperse their forces to defend a long frontier. Accordingly the Bay Colony, as the first offensive of King William's War, sent a small naval force in April 1690 to attack Port Royal, under the leadership of Sir William Phips.

This man was one of twenty-six children born to a poor fisherman's family on the Kennebec river in Maine. On a voyage to the West Indies, he became bitten by a bug that has made thousands of victims—hunting for sunken treasure. And, to this day, he has been the only person to make a real success of it. From a ship outfitted in England, he discovered the wreck of a Spanish treasure galleon north of Hispaniola and made the greatest haul ever retrieved from the ocean bottom— gold and silver bullion worth at least a million dollars. And, what was more, he got it safely to England despite his cut-throat crew, whose mutinous attempts he cowed with bare fists and a club. Each stockholder received a dividend of 8000 per cent; James II, delighted with his share, which was enough to build two capital ships for the Royal Navy, knighted Phips. Returning to Boston, Sir William led an expedition against French L'Acadie. He captured Port Royal with little trouble in May 1690, and brought the French governor to Boston as prisoner, together with plenty of loot. The colonial authorities, assuming that Quebec, too, would be easy meat, set up a sec-ond expeditionary force for Phips to command. It was too ambitious for one small colony, with no aid from England to undertake, and it started late through waiting for ammunition from England which never came. Phips's fleet of chartered merchant ships, carrying 2200 volunteers, mostly fishermen, reached Quebec on 7 October. Owing to the previous failure of Fitz-John Winthrop to reach Canada overland from New York, Count Frontenac was able to concentrate his slender defense forces on Quebec. They defeated the undisciplined Yankee landing force, and Phips decided to retreat.

Now all good effects of the Port Royal campaign were un-done. The Abnaki and Penacook Indians went on the warpath, raided Haverhill, and destroyed Wells and York in Maine, and the French recovered Port Royal.

This Quebec fiasco, proving to the satisfaction of the Eng-lish government that the Bay authorities were incompetent in military matters, ended all chance of the provisional govern-ment of Massachusetts being recognized as permanent. Wil-liam and Mary in 1691 created the royal province of Massa-chusetts Bay with a governor appointed by the king, but with a charter which guaranteed an annually elected assembly. Sir William Phips, who happened to be in London trying to get support for a second attack on Quebec, was made the first royal governor of Massachusetts Bay, an office that his mili-tary incompetence had done much to create. His bailiwick in-cluded the old Bay and Plymouth colonies, together with Maine. Rhode Island and Connecticut, which had resumed government under their old charters, were not disturbed, and New Hampshire became a separate royal province.

The inauguration of Phips as governor (16 May 1692) occurred when the "Woeful Decade" of New England was at its nadir. King William's War was going full blast. The expense of the Quebec expedition of 1690, which the Massachusetts government had hoped to finance from loot, had forced that colony to issue paper money—a new device in the English-speaking world which undermined credit and increased poverty. The frontier was in grave danger and farmers were able to tend crops only at the risk of their lives. Worst of all, the new governor had to face the Salem witchcraft delusion.

Almost everybody in the Western world, including divines and men of science, then believed that a person could make a bargain with the devil, by virtue of which he could visit good or ill on friends or enemies. There had been 44 cases of witchcraft and three hangings in Massachusetts Bay before 1692; a few cases, too, but no executions, in Canada and Virginia.

To the already vast literature on witchcraft the Reverend Cotton Mather, boy wonder of the New England clergy, contributed a book on *Memorable Providences,* describing a case of alleged witchcraft in Boston for which a poor old woman was executed, and telling how he had handled the accusing children to prevent a witch-hunting epidemic. The second edition of this "how to do it" book, filled with data on how the "possessed" were expected to behave, got into the hands of a group of young girls in a poor settlement near Salem. More or less as a prank, they accused a half-Indian, half-Negro family slave of being a witch. She, flogged by her master into a false confession to save her skin, accused two respectable goodwives of being her confederates. The "afflicted children," finding themselves the objects of attention, and with the exhibitionism natural to young wenches, persisted in their charges for fear of being found out, and started a chain reaction. Governor Phips's appointment of a special court to try the witches only made matters worse, for the chief justice (William Stoughton) and his colleagues were not trained in the use of evidence and became panic-stricken themselves. Innocent people whom the girls accused implicated others to escape the gallows. They confessed broomstick rides, flying saucers, witches' sabbaths, sexual relations with the devil, and everything which, according to the book, witches were supposed to do. Honest folk who declared the whole thing nonsense were cried out upon for witches. It was a situation not unlike that which arose at the height of Joseph McCarthy's power. In 1952, if you criticized Joe, you were a communist sympathizer; in 1692, if you criticized the witch court or tried to help an accused kinsman, you were in league with the devil.

This vicious business continued through the summer of 1692 until fourteen women and five men had been hanged, and one man, Giles Corey, pressed to death for refusing to plead guilty or not guilty. At least four died in jail of the fever that swept through it; and one poor child, jailed with her mother who was hanged, went out of her mind. Some 55 others saved their skins by pleading guilty and accusing others. The frenzy was not halted until the witch-finders began to go after prominent people such as the Boston clergy, wealthy merchants, and Lady Phips. On the sound if tardy advice of Increase Mather and other clergymen, the assembly dissolved the special court on 12 October 1692 and released some 150 prisoners who were awaiting trial.

Although the Salem witchcraft scare was small compared with the contemporary ones in Europe, and the condemned witches were hanged, not burned to death as in Europe; and despite the fact that twenty years later the Massachusetts courts annulled the convictions and indemnified relatives of the victims, it was a stain on the community that time has never erased. The records reveal an appalling moral cowardice on the part of ministry and gentry, and of credulity and hatred among the common people. It was one of those times, unfortunately more rather than less numerous in the present century, when the safeguards of liberty, religion, and plain decency are ripped asunder by fear and passion, and the evil in human nature, whipped up by demogogues and tyrants, is given full sway. The one admirable thing that stands out is the integrity of those who preferred death with an easy conscience to saving their skins by implicating the innocent.

The dreary war dragged on. There were no more big expeditions, but frontier raids by French and Indians on Dover, Andover, Groton, and Kittery; the fort at Pemaquid, Maine, was captured and destroyed. In vain the Massachusetts assembly begged King William to help them in this "languishing and exhausting war," with ammunition, a naval force or, best of all, the capture of Quebec, "that unhappy fortress from which issue all our miseries." The king was too busy in Europe to heed. He ended his war in 1697 with the Treaty of Ryswick, but left his American subjects to end their war as best they could; and in New England it continued for two years more.

LILLEBURLERO

Le - ro, le - ro, lil - le - bur - le - ro,

Lil - le - bur - le - ro, bul - le - na la,——— Le - ro, le - ro,

lil - le - bur - le - ro, lil - le - bur - le - ro, bul - le - na la.

IX

Pennsylvania and the West Indies

1688-1700

1. *Penn's Holy Experiment*

No COLONY OR STATE of the Union so well fits Emerson's dictum, "An institution is the lengthened shadow of one man," as Pennsylvania. William Penn not only founded it but obtained settlers from Europe and firmly established the principle of religious liberty which is a cornerstone of the American political system. The Penn tradition still exerts a beneficent influence, even as his statue on top of City Hall dominates Philadelphia. Of our colonial founders he was one of the most able, and, with Roger Williams, the best loved.

William Penn, born in 1644, was the indulged son of a wealthy father, Admiral Sir William Penn, conqueror of Jamaica and friend both to Charles II and his brother the Duke of York. At an early age young William showed an interest in religion which puzzled his parents. Expelled from Christ Church, Oxford, for a prank which indicated his contempt for Anglicanism, he was first well thrashed by the Admiral, then sent on a grand tour of the European capitals. Upon returning to London he read law, then went to Ireland to look after the confiscated estates that Charles II had given to his father. On a visit to Cork, young William listened to a discourse by a Quaker preacher on the text from 1 John v. 4, "There is a faith that overcometh the world"; and the Friends' faith overcame him.

The Quakers, destined to have an influence on American life far greater than their numbers, were a left-wing Puritan sect founded by George Fox in England around 1650. The Puritans had substituted the authority of the Bible for that of the church; Fox, while he respected the Bible, found the direct word of God in the human soul. For him, no ministry was necessary. His followers, believing that all men were equal, called themselves the Friends. Hence their insistence on addressing everyone as "thee" and "thou" (at that time used only to children or inferiors), and refusing to take their hats off, which got them into trouble everywhere. They took literally the commandment "Thou shalt not kill," and so ran afoul of war-waging governments.

Some 3000 Quakers were imprisoned in England during the first two years of Charles II's reign; yet, like the early Christians, they gathered strength from persecution, and victory from defeat. They spread throughout the British empire and into Holland, Germany, and even Russia. Severe laws were passed against Quakers in every colony except Rhode Island. Everywhere else they were whipped and imprisoned. In New York they were tortured; in Boston, hanged.

Finally by passive resistance the Friends won a grudging toleration in most of the English colonies. In England, by 1670, the sect had acquired a socially recognized position; and as Quakers had taken no part in the Civil War, they were regarded with more favor by Charles II than any other dissenting body. Thousands of converts were made among members of the middle class who had been repelled from Puritanism by the rule of Cromwell's major-generals.

Tolerated though they were, many Quakers wished to emigrate for the same reason that Puritans had fifty years before—to get away from the corrupt society of England. Quaker communities were founded in Rhode Island, in the back part of Plymouth Colony, on the island of Nantucket, and in North Carolina. The political situation in England was not unlike that fifty years earlier, which impelled the great Puritan migration. Throughout society there was extravagance and corruption; and the body politic was shot through with plots and counterplots. Anything seemed likely to happen, from a Cromwellian comeback to Louis XIV conquering England and treating English Protestants as he had the Huguenots. It was time for peaceably minded people to leave.

Admiral Sir William Penn, reconciled to his son, left him a small fortune at his death. In 1676, in company with George

Fox, William traveled through northern Europe. There he ascertained that thousands of Quakers and other non-tolerated Protestant sects were eager to emigrate to America if they could have a colony of their very own where they could carry out their ideals of the good life. The old admiral had been a friend of the Duke of York and had even lent him large sums of money. A tactful reminder of this eased young Penn's application for a slice of the Duke's enormous grant, and in March 1681 he obtained the magnificent proprietary province that bears his name, together with a charter from Charles II guaranteeing his possession of it.

ARMS OF FOUNDERS OF THE MIDDLE COLONIES

William Penn wasted no time; in 1682 he issued a tract called *Some Account of the Province of Pennsylvania,* which lacked the lyric enthusiasm of the booster pamphlets of early Virginia and New England and broke all canons of real estate promotion by modesty rather than overstatement. He told what sort of people he wanted, and gave instructions for the journey and outfit. He offered complete religious liberty and easy terms for land—50-acre head-rights as in Virginia, 200-acre tenant farms at a penny an acre rent; and for £100 you could have a 5000-acre country estate with a city lot in Philadelphia thrown in. *Some Account,* translated into German, French, and Dutch, circulated widely on the European continent. Thus the population of Pennsylvania quickly became cosmopolitan, although the majority of earliest settlers were English and Welsh Quakers. Penn himself came over in 1682 and laid out Philadelphia in checkerboard fashion, a reflection of the tidy Quaker mind that has had a permanent influence on American city planning.

The neighborhood of Philadelphia was no wilderness. Several hundred Swedes and Finns, survivors of the short-lived colony of New Sweden, were already there; and, owing to the food that they produced, Pennsylvania passed through no pioneering hardships. In two years' time, Philadelphia contained 357 houses. The population of the province in 1685 was not far from 9000. Germans of the Mennonite sect, mostly linen weavers from Crefeld, settled Germantown in 1683 with Francis Daniel Pastorius, a learned minister whom Penn had met on his European tour. Welsh Quakers founded Radnor and Haverford. A corporation of English Quakers, called the Free Society of Traders, stocked a general store in Philadelphia, organized whale fishing in Delaware Bay, established brick kilns, tanneries, glass works, and trade with the West Indies. Almost the complete apparatus of English civilization was transplanted in a remarkably short time and extended to non-English peoples as well. William Penn could declare in 1684 without exaggeration: "I have led the greatest colony into America that ever any man did upon a private credit, and the most prosperous beginnings that were ever in it are to be found among us."

Although he was not averse to creating a valuable estate for his heirs, Penn looked upon his province mainly as a holy experiment. The founders of New England took the same view of their colonies; but there was a difference between their ideas and Penn's. Their object was to establish a particular sect and way of life; Penn's was to give liberty to any religion, and to many ways of life. The Puritans assumed that human nature was intrinsically evil, and framed laws to keep down sin and crime; Penn believed in the essential goodness of human nature and framed laws with that principle in mind. But, after experimenting, their respective law codes became very similar.

In Pennsylvania, following a crime wave in 1698, the assembly passed and the proprietor accepted a new code so severe that the English Privy Council rejected most of it; whilst in New England the laws moved toward liberality and mercy. Both Puritans and Quakers regarded government as something more than a means to keep the peace and protect property; it was an agency in moral training. But the Puritans, like medieval churchmen, regarded government as the sword of St. Paul to uphold Christianity, whilst the Quakers, like Roger Williams, believed that a man's religion was nobody's business but his own.

Penn's charter was proprietary, like Lord Baltimore's, with a few essential differences. The crown reserved the right to hear appeals from colonial courts, to disallow acts of the assembly, and to appoint customs officials; the province was also required to obey the Acts of Trade and Navigation. This charge was more honored in the breach than the observance, since Quakers, like Puritans or Anglicans, held smuggling to be no sin. But William Penn was as free as any colonial proprietor to write his own frame of government. He wrote three in succession, modifying them to suit the people and his own tastes.

Everything went well in the local government when Penn was in Philadelphia as his own governor in 1682–84. He was a man of great charm and persuasiveness, still under forty, tall and athletic, able to impress Indians with his prowess at running and leaping. He entertained lavishly and well; he appreciated a fine horse, a well-built ship, and a handsome woman. But when the proprietor returned to England to mend his political fences, the colonial government almost blew up. The acting governor, Thomas Lloyd, quarreled with John Blackwell, an old soldier whom Penn sent over as governor. Blackwell, "driven by yells and jeers from the Council chamber at Philadelphia," consoled himself with a humorous description of Quakers as people who *prayed* for their neighbors on First Day (Sunday), and *preyed* on them the other six days of the week.

Penn made a worthy and successful effort to be just to the Indians of his province, although there never was a treaty "under the elm tree at Shackamaxon," the scene immortalized by a painting of Benjamin West. Of this treaty Voltaire wrote that it was the only one in history not ratified by an oath, yet never broken. One may say that had it been made, it was broken, since one of the slickest deals ever put over by Europeans on Indians was the famous "walking purchase."

In order to cash in on an alleged Indian sale to William

Penn in 1686 of a tract of land "as far as a man can go in a day and a half," Thomas Penn, the second lord proprietor, had a good trail cleared, hired the three best runners in the Province, and started them off at dawn one September day accompanied by pacers on horseback and a few Indians to see fair play. The Indians, after vainly trying to persuade the runners to walk, gave up in disgust before noon; as one of them said, "No sit down to smoke, no shoot squirrel, just *lun, lun, lun* all day long." One runner quit, the second fell into a creek and was drowned; but the third, at noon of the second day, grasped a sapling which was then declared to mark the end of the one and one-half days' walking. This exploit gave the Penn family half a million acres of Indian cornfields and hunting grounds.

In 1699 William Penn returned to Philadelphia after an absence of fifteen years, and in 1701 issued his third frame of government, called the Charter of Privileges. Under it the proprietor appointed both governor and council, but the legislative power was lodged in an assembly consisting of four members from each county. This charter served as the constitution of Pennsylvania until 1776. The "Three Lower Counties," the future State of Delaware, had been purchased by Penn from the Duke of York, but were overlooked in the royal charter. The Charter of Privileges allowed these three counties to have their own assembly, but their governor was always the same as Pennsylvania's.

Penn now hastened back to England to forestall another attack on his propriety. In that he was successful, but his business affairs went from bad to worse. With Lord Baltimore he had a vexatious boundary controversy which was not settled until their respective heirs agreed on a line—latitude 39° 43' 26"—which surveyors Mason and Dixon began to run in 1764. Penn was cheated by most of his agents. None of the governors he appointed were any good. He ran deeply into debt and was even confined in debtors' prison for a few months. And for six years before his death in 1718 he was a hopeless invalid.

Although Pennsylvania was hospitable to all peoples and races and many, especially German sectarians, came over in the eighteenth century, the tone and temper of the province was set by English-speaking Friends. These were of the second generation of Quakers who had sloughed off the frenzy and fanaticism of Fox's early converts, yet retained the serenity, the high ideals, and the sturdy pacifism that are the finest flowers of their sect. Although their light-of-conscience faith tended to make them deficient in public spirit, the Quakers had the same ambition as the Virginians and New Englanders to transplant the finer things of English civilization. That they did remarkably quickly. By 1700 Philadelphia had outstripped New York as a cultural center, which was not difficult, and was pushing Boston for first place. It was the first English colonial town after Boston to have a printing press, and the third to set up a newspaper. Penn himself founded Penn Charter School in 1689, and Quaker compassion provided Philadelphia with the best hospitals and charitable institutions in the English colonies. James Logan, scientist and classical scholar who came over as Penn's secretary in 1699, accumulated the best collection of books in the English colonies after Cotton Mather's.

Pennsylvania was a portent of the America to be. Maryland had tried religious toleration but repealed her famous law in 1692; Rhode Island made religious liberty work on a small scale among English people only; but Pennsylvania was the first large community since the Roman Empire to allow different nations and religious sects to live under the same government on terms of equality. It is true that the Holy Experiment was not as successful as Penn had hoped. Quarrels among governor, council, and assembly distressed him. "For the love of God, me, and the poor country," he once wrote to Thomas Lloyd, leader of the opposition, "do not be so litigious and brutish!" Yet, for all that, English, Irish, and Welsh Quakers, Anglicans, Roman Catholics, Scots-Irish Presbyterians, and Germans of four or five different sects, managed to live in the same city and province, enjoying equality one with another; and, if not precisely in a state of brotherly love, at least not flying at one another's throats. Pennsylvania, as a successful experiment in the life of reason, deeply interested the liberals of eighteenth-century Europe. They held up the province as an illustration of their belief that man could lead the good life without monarchy, feudalism, or religious uniformity.

2. The Colonies in 1700

By the dawn of the eighteenth century most of the English colonies had acquired the character they long retained, even as states. At first glance the area of continuous settlement shown on our map is not impressive. Only a fringe of territory, nowhere more than fifty miles from the seacoast or a navigable river, had been brought under cultivation or settlement. It was fairly continuous from York, Maine, to Albemarle Sound, North Carolina. Thence to the settled fringe along the South

Carolina coast there was a gap of 250 miles where the Indians were still undisturbed.

The best estimates of the population of the English colonies in 1700 are as follows:

New Hampshire	10,000		
Massachusetts Bay	80,000		
Rhode Island	10,000		
Connecticut	30,000	New England	130,000
New York	30,000		
New Jersey	15,000		
Pennsylvania and Delaware	20,000	Middle Colonies	65,000
Maryland	32,258		
Virginia	55,000	Chesapeake Colonies	87,258
North Carolina	5,000		
South Carolina	7,000	The Carolinas	12,000
Jamaica	50,000[1]		
Barbados	71,000[2]	West Indies	121,000

[1] Of this number, only 5000 were white.
[2] Probably 60,000 of these were slaves. There must have been some 2000 more English and 10,000 more slaves in the Leeward Islands, but no figures are available.

French Canada was still a string of farms, seldom more than one deep, along the St. Lawrence to Montreal, up the Richelieu river to Lake Champlain, and into the Minas Basin of L'Acadie. Its estimated population was 6200.

In the continental area, a scanty population had set the main patterns of government and society for the future United States. Every English colony had an elective assembly, and all except South Carolina had local self-government. Control from England would shortly be pressed, but it had not yet become oppressive. English culture had been transferred to America. The continental colonies now had two colleges: Harvard and William and Mary, with Yale about to be born; primary education was available for almost all white boys in the more closely settled regions north of Maryland. The printing presses of Boston had a greater output than any English city except London, and Philadelphia would soon be in the running. Religious exclusiveness, originating at opposite ends of the Protestant spectrum in Massachusetts Bay and Virginia, was breaking down. Religious liberty as practiced by Roger Williams and William Penn was becoming general. And the colonies were emerging with chins up from their troubled quarter-century, confident of the future, proud of their English liberties and heritage, and determined to protect them against all comers.

Racial homogeneity, too, had broken down. Slavery was established in every colony and strongly entrenched beyond likelihood of peaceful abolition in Virginia, South Carolina, and the West Indies. New York was still half Dutch. Scots, Irish, Germans, and French Protestants were pouring in.

The chief subject of anxiety among thoughtful North Americans in 1700 was war. England seemed poised on the edge of a struggle with France and Spain for control of both Europe and the Western Hemisphere. It would have been rash optimism indeed in 1700 to predict that England would win or that the United States, formed from the old thirteen English colonies, would aggressively push against Spanish America by war and diplomacy to the Pacific Ocean.

By 1700, England had placed her stamp on what proved to be the most valuable part of North America, as Spain had done in Central and South America; it was a powerful enough stamp to impress the immigrants from other countries. Above all, English concepts of liberty and self-government had been planted. This was the essential, outstanding fact which has made that section of North America which nobody wanted in 1600, the nucleus of the United States.

3. *The Revolution Settlement*

William and Mary became joint sovereigns of England and Scotland by virtue of a parliamentary bargain which the House of Commons never allowed them to forget. They were required to govern through and by Parliament, respect the traditional liberties of Englishmen, and support the Church of England. They did so well that, in accordance with the Act of Settlement of 1701, Mary's sister, Princess Anne, succeeded to the throne on the death of William III the following year. This, the first change of English rulers since 1625 to be unaccompanied by civil tumults, set a precedent for all later accessions. For Englishmen were heartily sick of tyrannical governments, five of which they had experienced in the preceding seventy years. As for rights, and liberties, Parliament had already passed the

Habeas Corpus Act (27 May 1679) which prevents government prolonging indefinitely the detention of suspects in jail. Later it passed a law giving judges tenure during good behavior instead of at the king's pleasure. These two acts, with the Declaration of Rights of 1689, which confirmed Magna Carta and similar documents, gave England a modern bill of rights, except for free speech and a free press, which had to wait.

The English colonies shared almost all these benefits. They too were pleased to have no brawl over the succession; almost everyone from Maine to Barbados supported William and Mary. There were no Jacobite rebellions such as Scotland experienced in 1715 for "James III," and again in 1745 for "Bonnie Prince Charlie." Americans were pleased to be assured that there would be no more tampering with colonial charters, or attempts to abolish elected assemblies. But the colonies never became as completely self-governing as the realm of England; nor did they expect to be.

Almost everything that England did or did not do about her colonies until about the year 1774 can be referred to trading considerations. It was, essentially, a commercial empire. The general theory, common to all European nations but strictly enforced only by Spain and France, was that colonies existed for the exclusive benefit of the homeland. They should trade exclusively with her, produce such raw materials as she wanted, consume her wares, and not compete with her manufactures. She, in return, owed them protection. Although the first Navigation Act was passed in 1651, England did not get around to enforcing this "mercantile system" in the colonies until the reign of William and Mary. Except with respect to the Chesapeake Bay tobacco trade, Americans had hitherto traded pretty much where and how they pleased.

This mercantile system, which the colonies were expected to obey, and to which they successfully adjusted their economy, was expressed in a series of acts of Parliament known as the Acts of Trade and Navigation. The basic principles of these Acts were as follows:

1. Exclusive Navigation: All commerce between England and her colonies had to be conducted in vessels built, manned, and owned in England or the colonies. This principle greatly encouraged colonial shipbuilding; by the time of the American Revolution, some 25 per cent of the British merchant marine was colony-built. Most nations, including the United States, apply the same principle today; a French ship or airliner can take freight from New York to France, but not from New York to San Francisco.

2. The Entrepôt Principle: This meant that colonial trade with foreign countries should normally be conducted through the home country. England was much more liberal in this respect than other nations. On the outgo side, the laws "enumerated" certain products such as tobacco, sugar, and cotton, and, later, timber and furs, which could be exported from the colonies only to England or to another English colony. The purpose was to give English merchants the monopoly of processing and distributing colonial products to other countries. On the incoming side, colonies could import foreign merchandise only by way of England; it must be handled in an English port before going to America. Exceptions were made to accommodate certain colonial interests. The salt fish of New England could be taken anywhere, and the rice of South Carolina could be exported directly to southern Europe. In return, the colonies were allowed to import fruit, salt, and wine directly from the Mediterranean or the Azores and Madeira. And, although Scotland to 1707 and Ireland even later were "foreign countries" so far as these laws were concerned, the colonies were allowed to import "servants, horses and provisions" from them directly. This entrepôt principle created no hardship for the colonies, once they were adjusted to it, because the enumerated products enjoyed a monopoly in the English market, and the English government paid bounties to certain producers. And, since customs duties on foreign goods imported into England were in part repaid when re-exported to the colonies, Americans sometimes obtained such goods more cheaply than did the English.

The enforcement of the Acts of Trade and Navigation, as well as of all other acts relating to the colonies, was entrusted to political means. All proprietary colonies except the two belonging to the Penns and the Calverts became royal provinces; and of the corporate colonies only Hudson's Bay, Rhode Island, and Connecticut retained their charters. All royal governors, appointed by the king, were expected to enforce acts of Parliament both by executive means, and by vetoes over acts of colonial assemblies that conflicted with them. And the judges of colonial superior courts did not hold office during good behavior, as in England, but at the king's pleasure. Cases could be appealed from the highest court in a colony to the Privy Council in London, but this was expensive and seldom exercised. And a law of 1696 required all cases under the Acts of Trade and Navigation to be tried by royally appointed admiralty judges, without a jury. This prevented colonial juries from acquitting their friends engaged in smuggling.

The most effective means of control was royal disallowance. Acts of colonial assemblies, although duly passed and signed by the governor, could be disallowed by the Privy Council after a hearing. About 5.5 per cent of all colonial acts were thus revoked. The right was exercised judiciously, many of the disallowed laws being attempts to discriminate against religious sects, or against other colonies; but it caused great irritation.

The British government (as it should be called after the Act of Union with Scotland in 1707) included neither a colonial secretary nor a colonial office until 1768, when Lord Hillsborough was appointed the first secretary for the colonies. All colonial business went through a committee of crown appointees, called the Board of Trade and Plantations. This in general handled colonial business justly and intelligently, although it had no power of decision. The colonies were not represented on this board or in the House of Commons, but almost every colony kept a salaried agent in London to defend its interests and protest against unfavorable legislation.

Britain undertook to defend her colonies in time of war with fleets and armies, and Parliament usually repaid a good part of the colonies' war expenditures.[1] But it did not attempt to tax them directly until 1765, when the Stamp Act started the trouble that led to the American Revolution.

This system was neither unjust nor oppressive; rather, it was inadequate and ineffective to secure its professed object, welding the empire into an economic and political unit. For the most part, the colonies took it for granted, and under it colonial commerce increased and the people prospered. From the English point of view, however, the system was very unsatisfactory. There were several big cracks in it, one of them being Rhode Island, which elected her own admiralty judge, ensuring tolerance to smugglers. The same went for Pennsylvania, where in William Penn's absence his governor winked at a surreptitious trade with the Dutch. Governor Bellomont reported that in New York "the administration of justice . . . goes upon crutches," and "our noble English laws" are "miserably mangled and prophaned." In South Carolina the assembly had the nerve to pass a law subjecting the admiralty judge to suits and penalties for his decisions! The Board of Trade in 1701 reported to the House of Commons that the entire colonial system should be overhauled, the power of assemblies curtailed, and that of the crown increased. But before Parliament got around to doing anything about it, William III

[1] For instance, in Queen Anne's War, 1702–13, Massachusetts Bay spent £87,434 and got back £34,689; New York spent £84,098 and got back £56,150.

died, Anne succeeded to the throne, and a war began that involved all Europe and the colonies.

4. Queen Anne and Her War

Queen Anne, thirty-seven years old at her accession, though not of the caliber of the two Queens Elizabeth, was no cipher in government. A plump and amiable woman, she was deeply religious, but a glutton; at her first communion the Archbishop of Canterbury felt obliged to remark, "Your Highness must not drink it *all!*" She married Prince George of Denmark, an amiable nincompoop of whom her uncle Charles II once remarked, "I have tried Prince George drunk and I have tried him sober, and there is nothing in him." They never managed to produce a healthy child, and left no descendant to inherit the throne. But by a curious turn of fate this average, kindly woman, so middle class in her tastes that she insisted on friends calling her "Mrs. Morley," enjoyed one of the most glorious reigns in English history. Hers was the "Augustan age" of English literature—Addison, Steele, Defoe, and Swift; the *Tatler* and *Spectator,* and Alexander Pope, who saluted her thus:

Here thou, great Anna! whom three realms obey,
Dost sometimes counsel take, and sometimes tea.

Two months after her accession Europe was plunged into the War of the Spanish Succession. An imbecile king of Spain died without issue. Rival heirs were a grandson of Louis XIV, who backed him up, and a Bavarian prince, who was supported by England, Austria, and other powers. In this war General Churchill distinguished himself in the battles of Ramillies, Oudenard, Malplaquet, and Blenheim, and was rewarded with the dukedom of Marlborough; England captured Gibraltar and rounded out her American empire with Nova Scotia and Newfoundland. A war futile in its immediate objects, since the Bavarian prince died in the course of it and the grandson of Louis XIV got the throne after all; but the Treaty of Utrecht that ended this war in 1713 inaugurated thirty years of peace and became a landmark in modern history.

In America this conflict was called Queen Anne's War. And since Spain was an ally of France, there was conflict on the southern frontier, where a curious chain reaction had taken place. La Salle's accidental incursion into Texas when he was looking for the Mississippi stimulated Spain to establish her first mission in Texas, near the Neches river, in 1690: a few years later, she placed a garrison at Pensacola on the Gulf

coast of Florida. Her purpose was to pinch out Louisiana, but
Louisiana refused to be pinched. Louis XIV countered by
sending Le Moyne d'Iberville and a group of pioneers to found
Biloxi, in the present state of Mississippi, in 1699. And within
a year the French had founded three trading posts—Kaskaskia,
Cahokia, and Vincennes—in the Illinois country. Also, to secure the water route linking the St. Lawrence, the Great Lakes,
and the Gulf, the post at Michilimackinac was strengthened,
and its former commandant, Cadillac, was allowed to found
Detroit, key to the three upper Lakes, in 1701.

Le Moyne d'Iberville hoped to make Louisiana a southern
Canada, but he could get no support from home. French
peasants, who might have found Louisiana's climate more con-
genial than that of Canada, were forbidden to emigrate. French
Protestants would have gone over if guaranteed toleration, but
Louis XIV refused; his cardinal policy *Un roi, une loi, une foi,*
applied to the French colonies too. So, instead of using the
willing Protestants, who consequently went to swell the
strength of Anglo-America, Louis XIV allowed himself to be
persuaded by some half-witted courtier to colonize Louisiana
with Canadian coureurs de bois, as a means of persuading
these knights of the canoe and the snowshoe to become farmers. Iberville had to put them on the garrison payroll to keep
them there.

The greatest threat to Spanish dominion of the Gulf was
not this feeble attempt at French colonization, but the vigorous
young colony that centered on Charleston. South Carolina, expanding and aggressive, occupied a position in respect to the
Gulf colonies of France and Spain similar to that of Canada
toward New York and New England. There being no Appa-
lachian barrier here, the Carolinians quickly penetrated the
Gulf region and applied the French fur-trading technique; except that on this frontier the desired Indian product was deerskin, not beaver. The Yamassee, nearest tribe to South Carolina, became her faithful ally and protected her from overland
attack, just as the Iroquois protected New York.

France, threatened both by thrusting Carolinians and Spanish Pensacola, shifted her garrison from Biloxi to Mobile in
1702, concluded an alliance with the Choctaw, and egged on
the Creek nation to attack the Yamassee. When Queen Anne's
War broke out, Le Moyne d'Iberville begged his king to send
ships and soldiers to throw the English out of Carolina. All
that Louis XIV did, for the moment, was to send out a ship-
load of *filles du Roi* (who in this case were also *filles de joie*)
to keep the Mobile garrison happy. Iberville returned to France
in search of help, and obtained command of a squadron of war-

ships and a regiment of soldiers, with orders to mop up all English colonies from south to north. First, the British West Indies; then "chase our adversaries from Carolina . . . insult New York, attack Virginia, carry help to L'Acadie and Newfoundland." This grand design fizzled because it was routed via Cuba. Iberville caught yellow fever at Havana and died, as did hundreds of his sailors and soldiers; the survivors returned to France.

England was equally backward in supporting Carolinian pleas for men and ships to mop up Pensacola and Mobile. In 1707 the Charlestonians themselves, with Chickasaw allies, burned Pensacola town but failed to capture the presidio, predecessor of the fort that held out for the Union right through the Civil War. But without ships the English in South Carolina could not accomplish much except to rescue their sister colony, North Carolina, from a severe attack in 1711 by the Tuscarora. This Tuscarora war dragged on for several years, ending in the removal of that tribe to western Pennsylvania and New York, where they became the sixth nation of the Iroquois Confederacy. Their descendants still have a small reservation near Niagara Falls, of part of which they have been robbed to make a reservoir, after an unsuccessful appeal to the Supreme Court of the United States (1960).

The Treaty of Utrecht, which ended Queen Anne's War in 1713, left the vague frontier between Carolina and Florida exactly where it had been in 1700. The founding of Georgia in 1733 was the first sign of interest by the English government in its southern American frontier.

There were only twenty-seven French families in all Louisiana in 1717. Next year Le Moyne de Bienville, Iberville's brother, founded New Orleans at a strategic position to control the river traffic.

New York remained neutral during the first half of Queen Anne's War, mainly because the Albany fur traders wished to continue their contraband traffic with Canada. So the New England frontier took the rap, suffering a series of raids by Abnaki Indians led by French officers. This *petite guerre* was big enough to wipe out the Maine coastal settlements for the third time, to destroy Deerfield and carry its inhabitants into captivity, and to render northern New England insecure for settlement.

Joseph Dudley had now reached the goal of his ambition, the royal governorship of Massachusetts Bay. Acting on a tactical suggestion of the Reverend Solomon Stoddard of Northampton, he set up a system of frontier patrols. Select companies of the militia were equipped with snowshoes and moccasins for winter service, and bounties were given to farmers to raise hounds "to discourage and keep off the Indians in ranging and scouring the woods." But Dudley did not limit his strategy to defense. He had the right idea, that the only way to render life secure in northern New England was to destroy the bases of French power in North America.

Massachusetts first struck at Port Royal in L'Acadie, base for the French privateers which were preying on New England fishermen and traders. An attack in 1707 failed, but another, in 1710, was successful. Dudley now cooked up with General Francis Nicholson a sales campaign in fancy dress. Four sachems of the Iroquois Confederacy were sent to London, to plead with Queen Anne for men, money, and ships to throw the French out of Canada. Under the chaperonage of Major Peter Schuyler of Albany, the sachems, wearing match-coats, feather headdresses, and full war paint, were presented to Queen Anne and made their plea through an interpreter. They saw the sights of London, heard a sermon by the Bishop, dined with William Penn, attended a cockfight, and stopped the show when they entered a theater to see *Macbeth*. And they managed to return safely to New York.

This really worked. The English government prepared a big operation against Quebec for the summer of 1711. Unfortunately, before it could be organized, Queen Anne had dismissed her Whig ministry and installed a Tory one, with her crony Mrs. Masham as the power behind the throne. The new favorite's incompetent brother was now promoted brigadier and made joint leader of an expedition against Canada with Admiral Sir Hovenden Walker, who sailed his fleet up from the West Indies for that purpose. This expedition was even more of a disgrace than Sir William Phips's of 1690. On 16 September, when 100 miles short of Quebec, the Admiral and General decided that winter was coming on, and they had better retreat. Several of the ships were wrecked, with great loss of life. This disaster prevented General Nicholson, who was leading an overland expedition against Montreal, from getting further than Lake George.

There was also plenty of fighting in the West Indies. By this time the buccaneers were dead, or had turned respectable; battles were between naval fleets, regular soldiers, and island militia. In August 1702 Du Casse of the French navy defeated a British fleet under Admiral Benbow off Santa Marta, a battle which lasted intermittently for six days. Benbow lost it because two of his captains flinched and he himself was mortally wounded. It was typical of the gentlemanly warfare of this century that, before he died, Benbow received this message from

Du Casse: "Yesterday I had no better hope than to be taking supper in your cabin, as your prisoner. As for those cowardly captains of yours, *hang them up*, for, by God, they deserve it!" And two were shot after they returned to England. But this was the one blue-water victory for France. The British navy captured Gibraltar, Minorca, and Argentia in Newfoundland. The French navy, which Louis XIV had neglected, engaged largely in commerce destroying, *la guerre de course*, a strategy which eventually lost France her American empire.

In this war the value of navies was first clearly recognized —"the noiseless, steady, exhausting pressure with which sea power acts, cutting off the resources of the enemy while maintaining its own." And a governor of Barbados wrote, "All turns upon the mastery of the sea. If we have it, our islands are safe, however thinly peopled; if the French have it, we cannot hold one of them." British mastery of the sea forced Louis XIV in the Treaty of Utrecht to cede Newfoundland, Nova Scotia, Gibraltar, and Minorca to England, together with the right to participate in the *asiento*, the slave trade with Spanish America. Before Queen Anne's reign, England was *a* sea power; after 1713 she was *the* sea power, and long so remained.

"Never since the heroic days of Greece has the world had such a sweet, just, boyish master," wrote Santayana two centuries later, when British sea power was beginning to totter. "It will be a black day for the human race when scientific blackguards, conspirators, churls and fanatics manage to supplant her."

X

Growth and Development

1713-1750

1. *Expansion and Business*

THE TREATY OF UTRECHT inaugurated an era of peace and
expansion for England's continental colonies. Their population
had grown from about 85,000 in 1670, to 360,000 in 1713. By
1754 it had quadrupled again to about 1,500,000. This increase
owed much to heavy migration of non-English people—Irish
and Scots, Germans and French—favored by a liberal natural-
ization act of the British Parliament in 1740. Only two new
continental colonies, Nova Scotia and Georgia, were founded
between 1713 and 1754, but the area of settlement almost
tripled. In the North it spread into the hilly interior of New
England, the region west of the lower Hudson, and central
Pennsylvania. In the Southern colonies it spread into the piedmont, the area between the fall line of the rivers and the Blue
Ridge and Smoky Mountains. And the manner of settlement,
as we shall see, created new tensions.

High prices prevailed in Europe for colonial products, especially tobacco, rice, and sugar. The last-named primarily helped
the West Indies, but the continental colonies, which provided
the islands with lumber, livestock, and provisions, indirectly
profited.

Before 1713 there had not been a real town on the continent between Philadelphia and Charleston. Norfolk now grew up as an outlet for the lumber and naval stores of North Carolina. Baltimore, founded in 1730, soon became a principal point of export for the wheat of Maryland and Pennsylvania. Philadelphia countered in 1733 by building the "Great Road" to the mouth of the Conestoga river, Lancaster County. For wagon traffic over this road in farm products, draft horses were bred from the Dutch and Flemish stock brought over by early settlers; and the Conestoga wagon, which eventually became the covered wagon of the Oregon trail, was developed.

Prosperity and a new influx of population greatly enlarged the ranks of the colonial gentry. Both they and the middle class benefited by enlarged educational facilities. By 1713 there were only three colleges in the continental colonies. The College of New Jersey (Princeton) was founded in 1746, mainly to serve Middle-colony Presbyterians. Anglican King's College (Columbia) was founded at New York in 1754; Philadelphia College (University of Pennsylvania) at Philadelphia in 1749; Codrington College at Barbados in 1745. The publication of newspapers, little four-page weeklies though they were, increased the diffusion of knowledge, as did printing and publishing. But no colony south of Maryland had a printing press before 1730.[1]

The settled frontier expanded fast. In New England the old system of laying out new townships to groups of actual settlers broke down in favor of wide belts of speculative townships. In the Middle and Southern colonies, land began to be sold outright by assemblies, proprietors or speculators, instead of being granted by the head-right system.

In the province of New York, the population grew relatively slowly, partly because of the Six Nations, partly because the patroons and their successors engrossed so much land along the Hudson that settlers could come in only as tenants, which immigrants did not like. Lords of the manor paid no quitrents and dodged most of their other taxes by influence with the assembly. Ulster County in the lower Mohawk valley was settled largely by Scots-Irish; but there was not much room for

---

[1] The first colonial town outside New England to have a printing press was Philadelphia in 1685; the second, New York in 1693. Next in order were New Castle, Delaware (1724), Annapolis, Maryland (1726), Williamsburg, Virginia (1730), Charleston, South Carolina (1732), Newbern, North Carolina (1751), Hackensack, New Jersey (1755), Savannah, Georgia (1762). The earliest newspapers were the *Boston News-Letter* (1704), *Boston Gazette* (1719), Philadelphia *American Weekly Mercury* (1719), New York *Gazette* (1725), Annapolis *Maryland Gazette* (1727), Boston *New-England Weekly Journal* (1727), Newport *Rhode Island Gazette* (1732), and Charleston *South-Carolina Gazette* (1732).

expansion while the Iroquois Confederacy had to be respected, and among the thirteen colonies New York had to yield sixth place in population to North Carolina in 1760. Virginia was then first in population, Massachusetts Bay second, and Pennsylvania third.

Owing to the connections that William Penn had made in Germany, Philadelphia became the principal port of entry for foreigners. Mostly indentured servants, but including a number of people of substance and learning, they took up land in York and Lancaster counties, creating the prosperous farms and built the great barns that are still a feature of the landscape. The German immigrants belonged mainly to sects which were discriminated against at home: Mennonites, Moravians, Dunkers (German Baptists), Pietists (Puritanic Lutherans), and others. On their heels came Scots-Irish from Ulster who were under pressure by Catholics and by restrictive legislation of the British Parliament. These hardy people fanned out into the frontiers of all colonies from Maine to Georgia.

Crossing the Atlantic in a sailing ship could seldom be a pleasure before the clipper-ship era, but it was never tougher than in the eighteenth century. Gottlieb Mittelberger, who came to Philadelphia in 1750, described the misery during his voyage:—bad drinking water and putrid salt meat, excessive heat and crowding, lice so thick that they could be scraped off the body, sea so rough that hatches were battened down and everyone vomited in the foul air; passengers succumbing to dysentery, scurvy, typhus, canker, and mouth-rot. Children under seven, he said, rarely survived the voyage, and in his ship no fewer than thirty-two died. One vessel carrying 400 Palatinate Germans from Rotterdam in August 1738 lost her master and three-quarters of the passengers before stranding on Block Island after a four-month voyage.

Many foreigners who landed at Philadelphia, as well as indentured servants whose terms were up, migrated into the upper country of Maryland, Virginia, and North Carolina. This settlement of the southern piedmont began in 1716, at the instance of Governor Spotswood of Virginia, who led a gay cavalcade of gentlemen, whom he dubbed "Knights of the Golden Horseshoe," to explore the Shenandoah valley. That part of the valley between the Blue Ridge and the Alleghenies belonged to the Northern Neck grant of six million acres which Charles II had given to Lord Culpeper, whose heir, the Earl of Fairfax, gave George Washington his first job as a surveyor. Fairfax sold land at rates that attracted immigrants from Pennsylvania, or let it on 99-year leases at £1 per 100 acres, while the Penn family was charging £15 10s and the Calverts £5, for the same amount of land. Migration from Pennsylvania and down the Shenandoah spilled over into the piedmont of Virginia and the Carolinas, peopling that region with Presbyterians and German Moravians who worked without slaves and resented control of the assemblies by slaveholding Anglican planters and merchants of the lowlands.

In North Carolina, where the piedmont was opened up by the Tuscarora removal to New York, land could be had at bargain prices. The royal governors were instructed to grant 50 acres free to each settler, and Lord Granville, who held the counties bordering on Virginia, charged only three shillings for 640 acres. It was he with whom Bishop Zinzendorf of the Moravian (United Brethren) sect contracted for the purchase of 100,000 acres for £916, a sale which resulted in the settlement of the Wachovia tract, centering on Salem. The popularity of North Carolina among yeomen, who wanted a farm where they would not be overawed by great slave-operated plantations, accounts for the phenomenal 1600 per cent increase in the population of that province between 1713 and 1763.

This up-country region of Virginia and the Carolinas, sometimes called the "Old West," lay so far from markets as to be almost self-sufficient. The people imported little but iron, gunpowder, and salt, and exported mostly peltry and cattle. Huge droves of cattle were rounded up annually in cowpens (one of which gave its name to a famous battle) to be driven to Baltimore, Petersburg, or Charleston for export. At the same time, the older English stock of the Southern colonies was expanding westward from the coast. Richmond was founded at the falls of the James in 1729; Petersburg on the Appomattox a few years later.

All English colonial exports were products of farms, forests, and fisheries. The expansion of foreign and West Indies trade was enormous, even though canalized to some extent by the Acts of Trade and Navigation. Owing to French protection of brandy against the competition of cheap rum, the French sugar colonies had a surplus of molasses which they were glad to sell to Anglo-American ships for distillation into rum at every seaport. West Indian planters, both English and French, consumed quantities of pickled beef and pork from New England, New York, and Carolina; onions and potatoes from the Connecticut valley; wheat and flour from Baltimore, and fed their slaves on New England codfish and Pennsylvania corn. They built their houses from Northern pine lumber and exported their sugar and molasses in boxes and barrels put together out of pine shooks and oak staves axe-hewn in Northern forests. They rode to town on Narragansett pacers raised in Rhode Island, and ran their sugar mills with horsepower provided by superfluous "plugs" raised on New England farms. Many West Indies products were carried to England and exchanged for consumer goods for colonial consumption. Northern traders came to depend more and more on trade with the West Indies; their prosperity was conditioned by it, and any attempt to interfere with it was certain to be evaded or resisted.

Several American industries, besides distilleries, date from this period. Governor Spotswood, in addition to promoting western settlement, created an iron industry. Through his friend Baron Graffenried he obtained German iron workers, erected a settlement for them (named Germanna) at the junction of the Rapidan and the Rappahannock in 1715, and set up an iron furnace at Massaponax about five miles below Fredericksburg. At least three other furnaces had been set up in Virginia by 1732, one owned by Augustine Washington (the General's father) on the Potomac; and by 1750 the ironworks in the Chesapeake colonies were exporting over 2000 tons annually to England. In 1750 British iron interests induced Parliament to forbid colonials to establish mills for slitting bar iron into nail rods, or to set up plating forges using a triphammer, or steel tool furnaces. But this law had little effect. The prohibition was so flagrantly disregarded that Pennsylvania, New Jersey, and Massachusetts even granted bounties for new plants after the Iron Act was on the statute books. In 1775 there were actually more furnaces for producing pig iron, and forges for resmelting the pigs into bar or wrought iron, in the thirteen colonies than in England and Wales. So, even though the acts restraining manufactures were restrictive in motive, they were hardly so in practice; and before indulging in virtuous indignation over them we should remember that, before the Philippines became independent, Congress set quotas on Philippine products such as sugar, which competed with those of the United States, and that the President now has power to set quotas on a variety of foreign imports.

2. *Currency Controversies*

Far more serious handicaps to colonial trade than the Acts of Parliament were English restrictions on colonial use of money, and the attempts of colonial assemblies to get around them. No precious metals were produced in the colonies, and the balance of trade with the mother country was against them; so their want of metallic currency was constant. Yet Parliament refused to allow the export of English coin to English colonies, or to allow them to mint coinage of their own from foreign bullion that they obtained through trade with the West Indies. Colonial assemblies endeavored to meet this situation in a variety of ways. Each colony or group of colonies established a currency of account, "lawful money" as it was called, in pounds, shillings, and pence that were worth less than sterling in England. The standard for this lawful money was the Spanish milled dollar or "piece of eight," the commonest foreign coin that came into the continent from the Caribbean, and which eventually was chosen as standard for the United States silver dollar. This dollar was worth 4s 6d in terms of English sterling; but in South Carolina and Georgia it was valued at 4s 8d; in New England and Virginia at 6s; in New York at 8s, and in the other colonies at 7s 6d. This meant that a New York pound of account was worth only half an English pound sterling, and a "York shilling" only 6d sterling, or 12½ cents; in New England and Virginia a shilling meant 16⅔ cents.[1] The colonial assemblies fondly imagined that by this overvaluation of foreign coins in terms of £ s d, these coins would stay in the colonies and not be re-exported; but the only result was a corresponding markup of prices on English goods, and consignments of foreign bullion to England in order to pay for goods ordered there.

Since overvaluing the Spanish dollar and undervaluing sterling did not help the colonists, they resorted to paper money. Personal promissory notes, tobacco-warehouse receipts, and bills of exchange had long been used as currency in the colonies, even for very small sums. From this it was a short step for the colonial assemblies to issue official promissory notes to pay for unusual expenses in anticipation of tax collections. These "bills of credit" (whence we derive our phrase a dollar "bill") relieved the currency shortage in time of war. Consequently the demand grew up for issuing them in time of peace. The American farmer believed then (as in the main he still believes) that currency inflation, raising prices of farm produce, would ease his burden of debt. Massachusetts and

---

[1] Other foreign coins common in the English colonies were the half real (6¼ cents), called "fippenny" in New England and Virginia because it was worth 5d in their money of account; the English guinea, worth 21s sterling or $5; the Spanish gold pistole, worth $4; and the Spanish doubloon and Portuguese johannes, each worth $16. The "two shillings" of New York naturally became the "two bits" of the Far West, and reckoning in shillings died hard; the writer remembers Christmas wreaths being priced at "a shilling each, six for a dollar" in Boston.

South Carolina, which had borne a disproportionate share of the Queen Anne's War burden, continued issuing bills of credit after the Treaty of Utrecht. In some colonies, notably in Pennsylvania, where Benjamin Franklin urged the legitimate value of paper currency in a growing and expanding economy, issues of bills of credit were promptly redeemed, and depreciated very little. They were, in effect, a lien on future growth and prosperity, like our terrific national debt of today. But in Rhode Island, a small colony whose possibilities of future expansion were limited, one issue of bills of credit succeeded another, until prices in terms of paper money rose about thirtyfold.

South Carolina thought up another scheme that the planters liked immensely—the so-called Land Bank. Under this system the colony created a paper "bank" or heap of bills and lent them to planters on the security of their land. It was a wonderful game, practically a gift; for if the planter was unable to redeem his paper debt, he and his fellows could generally induce the assembly to stay collection or let him discharge it in produce at inflated value. Massachusetts was almost torn apart by a land bank controversy in 1741. The merchants persuaded Parliament to declare a law of 1720, aimed at the South Sea Bubble and other wildcat English schemes of that speculative era, to have outlawed the Massachusetts land bank. This act, which ruined, among others, the father of Samuel Adams, was in part responsible for a clause in the Federal Constitution against *ex post facto* laws.

North Carolina, whose population increased so rapidly at this period, became the principal colonial source of naval stores—ship timber, pitch, tar, and turpentine—which the yellow pine of the uplands yielded in large quantities. South Carolina, too, produced them; but her most valuable export was rice—42,000 barrels in 1731, tripled by 1765. Rice culture, like tobacco, required a great deal of labor before it was ready for market, and that had to be slave labor; thus South Carolina became the greatest slave-importing colony. Indigo, the other staple of this colony, introduced from the West Indies about 1740, was encouraged by a British bounty, since it was wanted in England for dyeing woolens.

3. *Colonial Society*

Colonial prosperity brought about a change in the appearance of the older towns and villages. Merchants built themselves dwellings of a style and stature before unknown, and set the fashion for a change of architecture in farmhouses as well. Prior to this era one had only the Dutch colonial and the New England colonial styles in the North. The Dutch was generally a low, brick or stone, one-and-one-half-story house with hip roof; the New England dwelling, a two-story house with roof sloping almost to the ground in the rear, massive beams, overhanging upper story, a massive central chimney with fireplaces as long as fourteen feet, and casement windows with diamond-shaped leaded panes.

About 1720 there came a marked change. Houses were painted inside and out; the roomy gambrel roof was introduced, and sash windows with small square panes. Fireplaces grew smaller as wood became less abundant, and Ben Franklin in 1740 invented and presented to the public his "Pennsylvania Fireplace," better known as the Franklin stove, which saved at least 50 per cent on fuel. Wealthy merchants built pretentious three-story mansions, usually of brick in New England and of stone in Pennsylvania. One or more chimneys were built at each end of the house, down the middle of which was a broad central hall, and in the rear a second door or Palladian window framing a formal garden. At each side of the hall were two square parlors or reception rooms, paneled and painted white. In proportion and beauty of detail, these dwellings of the colonial grandees are among the finest types of domestic architecture ever produced in America; many are still lived in after more than two centuries.

Colonial society was not what the next century would have called healthy. The hottest colonial intellectual controversy between witchcraft and Whitefield took place over inoculation for smallpox. An epidemic hit Boston upon the arrival of an infected crew from the West Indies in 1721. The Reverend Cotton Mather, who had read in the Royal Society's *Philosophical Transactions* about protecting healthy people from smallpox by inoculating them with pus from those already down with the disease, persuaded Dr. Zabdiel Boylston to try this new method. He did so, inoculating some 250 persons of whom all but six recovered, whilst nearly half the uninoculated Bostonians who caught it "in the common way" died. In spite of this obvious success, a terrific hue and cry, led by the newspaper published by Benjamin Franklin's brother, was raised against Mather and Boylston. Stones and threatening messages were hurled through their windows; they were insulted in the street and threatened with death. Dr. Boylston persisted and in the next epidemic again demonstrated the success of inoculation, which was not replaced by vaccination until 1800.

A chatty and observant traveler through the Northern colo-

nies in 1744 was Dr. Alexander Hamilton of Annapolis, the
thriving capital of Maryland. The Doctor took a dim view of
society in New York City: "To talk bawdy and to have a
knack at punning passes among some there for good sterling
wit." Boston was more to his liking:

> There is more hospitality and frankness showed here to
> strangers than either at New York or at Philadelphia.
> And in the place there is abundance of men of learning
> and parts; so that one is at no loss for agreeable conver-
> sation nor for any set of company he pleases. Assemblies
> of the gayer sort are frequent here; the gentlemen and
> ladies meeting almost every week at concerts of music
> and balls. I was present at two or three such and saw as
> fine a ring of ladies, as good dancing, and heard music
> as elegant as I had been witness to anywhere. I must take
> notice that this place abounds with pretty women who
> appear rather more abroad than they do at York and
> dress elegantly. They are, for the most part, free and
> affable as well as pretty. I saw not one prude while I was
> there.

Boston ladies had evidently learned to imitate the manners
of the Court of St. James's. This bit of conversation was reported to Hamilton by his companion Samuel Hughes, who
was strolling along King Street with a lady when Dr. Hamilton passed in the other direction: "Lord!" said she, "what
strange mortal is that?" " 'Tis the flower of the Maryland
beaux," said Hughes. "Good God!" cried the belle, "does that
figure come from Maryland?" "Madam," said Hughes, "he is
a Maryland physician." "O Jesus! a physician! deuce take
such odd-looking physicians!"

The Doctor's observations of declining Puritanism are supported from many sources. One of Benjamin Franklin's first
excursions into print was to attack the frivolity and luxury of
Harvard students, of whom a committee headed by Judge
Sewall reported in 1723, "There has been a practice of general
immoralities particularly stealing, lying, swearing, idleness,
picking of locks, and too frequent use of strong drink." Best
sellers at a Boston book auction in 1744 were Richardson's
Pamela, the satire on it called *Antipamela,* Ovid's *Art of Love,*
and Edward Fisher's *Marrow of Modern Divinity.* Note the
modern.

Colonial Americans were far more concerned with social
status than is the present generation. The very word "colonial,"
to the average Englishman, meant inferiority; so everyone with

social ambition had to prove that he was somebody, the best proof of which was to be appointed to the council of his colony. That, and ownership of several hundred acres of land, gave one a status that nothing could shake. Gentlemen unable to trace a pedigree had one made up in England, and adopted a coat of arms. The wealthiest men, who monopolized the higher colonial offices, got their sons elected to the house of burgesses and frequently visited "home," as they called England, to freshen contacts with English society.

Virginia society now became stabilized as the traditional Virginia of brave gallants and fair women, horse-races and fox hunting, six-horse coaches and ten-gallon punch bowls. The native aristocracy, which we earlier saw in process of formation, was now in its second or third generation. The planters were now building three-story brick dwellings with a porch or veranda for protection from summer heat, and detached kitchen and servants' quarters. The typical Southern mansion of this period, like Washington's Mount Vernon, had a main building with a tall colonnaded porch and two wings connected by a covered "breezeway."

To run a plantation successfully—and one man might have as many as eight or ten different ones scattered through tidewater and piedmont—called forth managerial ability. The great estates were closer together than in the earlier century, connected by good carriage roads as well as by water, and black servants were well trained, so there was constant visiting between families, and rounds of dances, fox-hunts, and card-playing. At the top of the social order was the governor, who kept court at Williamsburg. Everybody who was anybody had to be there when the assembly was sitting. This well-built little town attracted cabinet makers and other artisans, strolling companies of actors, and a dancing school and assembly. It held two annual fairs at which cattle and all sorts of merchandise were sold; and, "for the Entertainment and Diversion of all Gentlemen and others, that shall resort thereto," prizes were offered for running and leaping races, horse-racing, catching the greased pig, and marksmanship.

William Byrd the second may be taken as a good example of the Virginia gentleman of this era. Born in 1674, he was sent to England to be educated. On returning to Virginia at the age of nineteen with pleasant manners and plenty of money, he was elected a burgess. Next year he fell heir to his father's property, married into another first family, pulled down the old house and store at Westover, and built the brick mansion which is still one of the show places on the James. By this time trading was considered ungentlemanly both in

England and Virginia, so William Byrd sold his father's rum, slave, and drygoods business, and with the proceeds accumulated a library and more land. Byrd was a man of breadth, culture, and public spirit. His scientific tastes led to his election to the Royal Society of London and his appointment as surveyor-general to run the boundary line between Virginia and North Carolina. His account of this mission, *The History of the Dividing Line,* is one of the most delightful works in our colonial literature. He speculated successfully in land (always a socially reputable way to make money), but left to his son an estate not quite so valuable as the one inherited from his self-made father. His shorthand diaries, recently deciphered and published, are the records of day by day life of a Virginia gentleman at the turn of the century. They also show that he was a good scholar, reading a little Greek or Hebrew before breakfast, and doing daily calisthenics to keep himself fit.

Byrd died in 1744. The career of his son, who succeeded him in the council, damped the fame of the Byrds of Westover for over a century. William Byrd III squandered his father's property and, in order to escape the consequences, committed suicide. Westover and his father's library were sold, his sons emigrated to the upper Shenandoah valley, and the Byrd family was heard of no more until the twentieth century, when it emerged in the persons of the famous brothers Tom, Dick, and Harry: Tom, who established the apple industry in the Shenandoah; Rear Admiral Dick, the polar explorer; and Senator Harry, the gentlemanly boss of the Democratic party in Virginia.

Horse-racing, which had been practiced on short stretches for a century, the horses becoming smaller for want of new blood, received a stimulus after 1750 through the importation of colts of three famous Oriental stallions, the Godolphin Barb, the Darley Arabian, and the Byerly Turk, which had revolutionized horse breeding in England. These thoroughbreds had greater staying power than the popular quarter horses of the previous century. Selima, daughter of the Godolphin, beat all comers in the Maryland *vs.* Virginia four-mile races of 1751–52 and reigned queen of the colonial turf for years. Janus, the Godolphin's grandson, arrived in 1756 and remained at stud down to the Revolution. Fearnought, grandson both of Godolphin and the Darley Arabian, after winning six King's Plates at Newmarket, was imported in 1764 and covered mares at £10 a time— "£8 if the money comes with the mare." From these, and from Kitty Fisher, granddaughter of the Godolphin, almost every famous horse of the American turf is descended. Colonial Americans everywhere loved horse-racing, but the most intense interest was found in the Chesapeake colonies and in New York. George Washington, whose diary reveals frequent losses and few gains from betting on races, acted as steward of those at Alexandria in 1761.

White indentured servants continued to be imported, especially Germans, much sought after for their skill and industry. English seven-year convicts were not wanted but had to be accepted. Many of the servant class had as good blood as their masters. William Byrd complained, when on a journey, of having to take his daily dose of quinine in water, "by reason a light finger'd Damsel had ransacked my Baggage, and drunk up my Brandy. This unhappy Girl, it seems, is a Baronet's Daughter; but her Complexion, being red hair'd, inclin'd her so much to Lewdness that her Father sent her . . . to seek her fortune on this side of the Globe."

In every colony south of Maryland, African slaves outnumbered white servants by 1720, and the proportion continued to increase. In 1715, for instance, there were 23,000 blacks in Virginia out of a total population of 95,000; in 1756, 120,156 blacks out of a total of 293,474; and in the tidewater counties they outnumbered the whites at least two to one. North Carolina had only 19,000 slaves out of a total population of 98,000 in 1756; but in South Carolina, where the bounty-fed production of indigo opened a new area to profitable slave labor, the disproportion was so great that the assembly required each planter to keep one white servant for every twenty-five blacks, and laid a sliding scale of duties on slave importations. South Carolina suffered the severest slave insurrections of the century—the Cato conspiracy of 1739, in which some seventy-five of both races were killed, and one the following year for which 50 blacks were hanged. Of Northern colonies, New York had the largest proportion of blacks—19,883 out of a total population of 207,890 in 1771. The slaves here gave even more trouble than they did in the South. New York City became victim of a panic in 1741 which, for cruelty and sheer terror, surpassed the Salem witch-hunt. After several fires broke out, a rumor, supported by forced confessions, created the belief that slaves were conspiring with poor whites to burn the city. After a series of hysterical trials, 101 blacks and 4 whites were convicted of criminal arson, 13 blacks were burned alive, and 18 blacks and 4 white people were hanged.

Every New England colony contained blacks; Massachusetts the most (5235 out of a total population of 224,185 in 1746), but Rhode Island had the largest proportion (3077 out of 31,516 in 1749). Newport was a center of the African slave trade. Although it is part of the Southern historical myth that most of the blacks sold in the Southern colonies were brought in by "damyankees," New England ships actually held a small share of this infamous traffic.[1] The Royal African Company of London handled most of it, but every English colonial port including New York, Philadelphia, Annapolis, Charleston, Baltimore, Barbados, and Kingston, Jamaica, participated to some extent. The principal articles to exchange for slaves in Africa were rum, salt codfish, and Spanish dollars; and there is on record the instruction of a Captain Simeon Potter of Rhode Island to one of his masters, "Worter your Rum as much as possible and sell as much by the short mesuer as you can."

4. The Great Awakening in Religion

During this era there were three parallel but rival movements in religion: aggressive missionary work by the Church of England, a quiet but pervasive growth of liberal Christianity, and the Great Awakening, an emotional revival of orthodox Calvinism.

The first may be said to have begun at Yale Commencement in 1722. The Rector, the Reverend Timothy Cutler, concluded the exercises with what would seem to us an innocent enough exhortation:—"Let all the people say, Amen!" But it sent a shudder through the audience, for this was recognized as a rubric of the Book of Common Prayer, and a rumor of the Rector's having become an Anglican convert was already circulating. Next day the board of trustees held a grim meeting. Rector Cutler, tutor Daniel Brown, and the Reverend Samuel Johnson, recently a tutor, confessed that they had been convinced by reading Anglican books (given by a Harvard man!) in the Yale Library, that Congregational ordination was invalid. This created as great a sensation in the colonies as if, today, a college president should endorse communism. The trustees gave the errant brethren a month to recant; they refused, and were dismissed. Cutler and Johnson promptly went to England, where they received Oxford degrees, obtained Anglican ordination, and were sent back to be ministers, respectively, of Christ Church, Boston, and Christ

[1] The tables in Elizabeth Donnan, *Documents Illustrative of the History of the Slave Trade*, IV, 175–81, leave no doubt of this. For instance, of 146 ships bringing slaves into Virginia between 1710 and 1718, 65 belonged to England, Scotland, and Ireland, 39 to Maryland or Virginia, 20 to the British West Indies, 4 to Philadelphia, 4 to New York, 1 to South Carolina, and 13 to New England; and all cargoes of 100 or more slaves were in English vessels.

Church, Stratford, Connecticut. Backed by two well-endowed Anglican organizations, the Society for the Propagation of the Gospel and the Society for the Propagation of Christian Knowledge, they began a militant crusade for religious liberty for Anglicans in New England, for the growth of their faith, and for the appointment of one or more bishops in the English colonies. The founding of King's College (now Columbia University) in New York City in 1754 was partly a result of this drive.

In New England, the once raging fires of Puritanism were banked. People in general attended "meeting," listened to sermons or slept during them, kept holy (outwardly, at least) the Sabbath, and attempted to observe the other commandments; but they were falling away from the antique faith. Some were simply going through the recognized motions of piety. Others were becoming what was vaguely called Arminian, believing that only good works and a free catholic spirit were necessary for salvation. This movement went quietly on, culminating in the Unitarianism of the nineteenth century.

To combat so "soft" an attitude there began in 1734 among New England Congregationalists and Middle-colony and Southern Presbyterians, a revival known as the Great Awakening. This was the first important religious revival in the English colonies; no later one spread so wide or went so deep. At a time when people generally, and in the Old West in particular, were falling away from the established churches, the Awakening descended like a whirlwind to sweep up lost souls. It stimulated a fresh interest in religion, caused hundreds of new churches to be founded, strengthened the movement for religious liberty, gave the common man a new sense of his significance, and thus indirectly contributed to the American Revolution. Most important, the Great Awakening brought it about that Christianity expanded with the frontier, and that the new independent American, like the old dependent colonist, inherited a strong Christian tradition.

The seeds of the Awakening were sown in 1734 when Jonathan Edwards began to preach revivalist sermons at Northampton, Massachusetts. This man, pure and simple in his life, was an original thinker in the realms of theology and philosophy. In another environment he might have acquired the fame of George Berkeley, whose idealistic philosophy he anticipated at the age of fifteen; or of John Locke, whose *Essay on Human Understanding* he read in his sophomore year at Yale, with far higher pleasure, he said, "than the most greedy miser finds when gathering up handfuls of silver and gold from some newly discovered treasure." Equally remarkable are his boyhood notes on the habits of the flying spider, praised for their accuracy by leading entomologists of today; and his account of his conversion at the age of seventeen, one of the most beautiful records of that Christian phenomenon since St. Augustine's. Edwards might have been a naturalist or a great literary figure, but he chose theology because he believed that an exploration of the relation between man and God was infinitely more important. He would have considered our modern efforts to explore outer space as of minor importance, since their objects are merely to extend human knowledge. He looked beyond all stellar systems and galaxies, to save men's souls for eternal life.

Edwards rocked the Connecticut valley with a series of sermons that set people reading, discussing, and meditating the fundamental truths of Christianity. He recorded this revival in a pamphlet called *A Faithful Narrative of the Surprising Work of God in the Conversion of Many Hundred Souls in Northampton* (1736), which made an immense stir in the Protestant world. Edition followed edition at Boston, London, and Edinburgh. Within a year a German translation had been printed, within two years a Dutch one, and it became the classic of revivalism. The Reverend George Whitefield in far-off Savannah, Georgia, read the *Faithful Narrative* and began his amazing career as a revivalist. John Wesley read it on foot, walking from London to Oxford. "Surely, this is the Lord's doing," he wrote in his journal, "and marvelous in our eyes." Presently Wesley began to obtain the same effects with his preaching, and in a little while the Methodist Church was born. Edward's preaching at Northampton was the womb of all modern revivalism in the Protestant churches of the English-speaking world.

Whitefield preached a revival at Philadelphia (which made even skeptical Ben Franklin empty his pockets into the plate) and then made a New England crusade of 75 days, during which he rode 800 miles and preached 175 sermons. He was the first great preacher to travel widely in the colonies. His voice, unaided by amplifying devices, could carry in the open air to 20,000 people. He made violent gestures, danced about the pulpit, roared and ranted, to the huge delight of the yokels who were tired of gentlemanly, highbrow ministers from Harvard and Yale. He introduced the second stage of revivalism, in which congregations, mad with religious ecstasy, shrieked, rolled on the floor, ran amok. College exercises at Yale had to be suspended while the students held prayer meetings and compared the state of their souls. Freshmen even tried to convert their landladies!

Throughout New England and in the Middle colonies there was turmoil. Many ministers of the established churches embraced the Awakening and preached revival sermons. The majority, however, repudiated it as a vulgar travesty on religion. If they did, their congregations were apt to secede and set up "New Light" churches, many of which eventually became Baptist or Methodist. The revival probably improved people's morals and reduced the crime rate, at least temporarily. It checked the decline of Puritanism into that vague liberalism into which many sons of the Puritans have descended. It gave the common man a new interest in religion; it gave birth to three new colleges—Dartmouth, Princeton, and Brown. On the other hand, the excesses of the Great Awakening were similar to a protracted alcoholic jag. They gave the addict a thirst for more. Periodic outbursts rather than continuity, enthusiasm rather than serenity came to distinguish popular religion in Protestant America.

This Awakening was of absorbing interest to English dissenters, who kindled a backfire against the Church of England missionaries' request for a bishop. Nobody else, not even the Anglican laymen, wanted an American bishop; they feared danger to religious liberty and to lay control of the churches. Virulent pamphlets set up the Anglican bishop, in lawn sleeves, cope, and mitre, as the colonial bogyman of the 1740's, just as George III became in 1776. England decided to let that particular sleeping dog lie, which was well for imperial unity.

The backwash of reaction from the Great Awakening swept Jonathan Edwards from the pleasant village of his ministry. He had offended influential citizens by denouncing the "frolics" of their young people—which amounted to nothing worse than sleigh rides to a neighboring town to indulge in country square dances and rum-and-water. With his wife and eight children Edwards removed to the frontier settlement of Stockbridge in the Berkshire Hills, to be missionary to a small Indian reservation. There he found leisure to write *The Nature of True Virtue, Original Sin,* and *Freedom of the Will* which, together with his earlier treatise *The Religious Affections,* gave Calvinism a new lease on life. For they proved, at least to the satisfaction of people with a Puritan background, that man with no will of his own was yet perfectly free to choose a fate predetermined before he was born.

In 1757 the College of New Jersey, which had moved from Newark to Princeton and (as a result of the Awakening and a successful drive for funds) erected Nassau Hall, called Jonathan Edwards to be president. Immediately after he had been inducted into office, a smallpox epidemic broke out in the village; and within a few days New England's saint breathed his last.

Edwards's brand of revived Calvinist theology, carried forward by disciples such as the Reverend Stephen Hopkins, ran its course. The Andover Theological Seminary, formed to perpetuate it, closed its doors early in this century, and only the Evangelicals keep some measure of it alive today. But the works of Jonathan Edwards, after long neglect, are now reprinted; and today, whatever one's belief, one owes a respectful glance to that faith which made God everything and man nothing, which plunged some men into despair but to many gave fortitude to face life bravely; and, to a chosen few, the supreme joy that comes from union with the Eternal Spirit, and the supreme beauty that is the beauty of holiness.

AM I A SOLDIER OF THE CROSS?

Thy saints in all this glo - rious war, Shall con-quer, though they die; They view the tri - umph from a - far, And seize it with their eye.

XI

Wars on the Spaniards and the French

1733-1763

1. *Georgia and War in the South*

THE FOUNDATION OF GEORGIA in 1733 led to a war between England and Spain. This merged into a war with France of vital concern to the Northern colonies, and that in turn led to the foundation of the fourteenth English continental colony, Nova Scotia.

By 1730, when Louisiana had become well established, the British government, realizing its mistake in not supporting South Carolina in Queen Anne's War, promoted a new colony on the border between Carolina and Florida. Imperial ambitions were implemented by philanthropy, and the person who combined them was General James Edward Oglethorpe. A gentleman of rank and fortune who had fought the Turks in the previous war, he had since, as a member of Parliament, interested himself in the lot of the poor and unfortunate. In particular he wished to help poor debtors, who under the harsh laws of that period were confined indefinitely in jail, and to give them a fresh start in the New World. In association with other English philanthropists, and members of Parliament interested in expansion, he obtained in 1730 a charter for the Trustees of Georgia. They were made proprietors of all the land between the Savannah and Altamaha rivers, and from sea to sea.

The Trustees of Georgia, prominent in politics and business, financed the biggest publicity campaign from which any English colony ever benefited. Flattering write-ups of the healthy climate and fertile soil were paid for in London newspapers; money was raised by popular subscription, and grants were voted by Parliament. In 1733 Oglethorpe himself, as governor, founded Savannah. He brought out in ship *Ann* the first load of 114 settlers, twenty-nine of whom died within a year. A group of Germans from Salzburg were settled up the Savannah river at a place to which they gave the biblical name Ebenezer, and members of several Scots Highland clans founded Frederica on the Altamaha.[1] Oglethorpe himself determined the sites of settlements, with a view to defense against Indians and Spaniards.

Georgia did not prosper under the benevolent despotism of Oglethorpe and the Trustees, owing largely to their prohibition of slavery and of hard liquor. They granted 50 acres of land free to each charity settler, which he was forbidden to sell; but this was not enough for a subsistence farm, and the climate was such that Englishmen insisted they could accomplish nothing without rum and slaves. The example of fortunes made in South Carolina by raising rice and indigo with slave labor caused many of the more energetic Georgians to move thither, even at the cost of their land being confiscated. Although the Trustees repealed the antislavery law in 1750, allowed prohibition to lapse, and granted Georgia a legislative assembly, the settlement made slow progress. In 1752, when Georgia had only 1735 white and 349 black inhabitants, the Trustees were glad to turn it over to the crown as a royal province, like the Carolinas.

Already "the extirpation of the English from the new colony of Georgia which they have usurped" had become a Spanish objective. But the Indian nations of the Gulf region, as well as the Cherokee of the uplands, had become alienated from Spain and were successfully wooed by Governor Oglethorpe. In 1738–39 they ceded to Georgia most of their coastal lands

[1] Down to the end of September 1741, the Trustees sent over 1810 charity colonists, of whom 45 per cent were foreign Protestants (Germans, Swiss, Scots, and 2 Italians), and the rest English. The number of those rescued from jail is not known, but the prevalence of crime in the colony suggests that it was large. More than a hundred different occupations were represented, indicating that the Trustees planned a semi-industrial society. In the same period, 1021 persons came to Georgia at their own expense; and of these, 92 were Jews.

and offered to join her in a campaign to wipe out the Spanish posts in Florida.

At this point England declared war on Spain for other reasons. The English South Sea Company, a slave-trading organization recognized by Spain in 1713, had abused its treaty privilege of sending one slave ship annually to Porto Bello. It sent a whole fleet, whose cargoes were so eagerly purchased by the Creoles that Spanish trade suffered. Retaliation followed by Spanish revenue cutters, one of whose skippers cropped the ears of an English smuggler named Edward Jenkins. At a favorable moment, when English traders were urging a renewal of aggressive war against Spain, earless Jenkins was exhibited in the House of Commons; and the war, popularly called "The War of Jenkins' Ear," was declared in October 1739.

Spain began hostilities by forcibly occupying a fort which Oglethorpe had built on Amelia Island at the mouth of the St. Mary river. The General retaliated promptly. With 200 men from his own Highland regiment, 125 South Carolinians, several hundred Indian allies, and a small supporting fleet, he captured two Spanish forts at the mouth of the St. John river and boldly advanced on St. Augustine. That ancient presidio, with a population of several thousand and a strong garrison under the command of Don Manuel de Montiano, was so well defended that Oglethorpe retired in June 1740, after a siege of 38 days and one small battle. He blamed the South Carolinians, and they blamed him.

In the meantime, England had sent a fleet under Vice Admiral Edward Vernon to capture and sack Porto Bello, which was done with ease (November 1739), and another fleet around Cape Horn under Commodore George Anson to put a pincer on the Isthmus of Panama from the Pacific side. Anson's fleet, scattered by storms and decimated by scurvy, failed to make the rendezvous and returned home around the world, after capturing the Manila treasure galleon and taking temporary possession of Tinian in the Spanish Marianas. Without Anson's support, Admiral Vernon was unable to hold Porto Bello and returned to England. There he was greeted as a hero and given command of a more formidable expedition to overwhelm Cuba and the Spanish Main.

In this enterprise the English colonies from South Carolina to New Hampshire joined with enthusiasm, furnishing about 3000 volunteers under their own officers, in addition to a force of regulars provided by England. All that took time, and the expedition did not leave Jamaica until January 1741. Vernon decided to make his first objective Cartagena, on the coast of New Granada, now the Republic of Colombia. The Spaniards had made Cartagena the strongest place in South America. Vernon managed to break into the great harbor, but his assault on the castle was thrown for a loss by the Spaniards. While the warships and transports, anchored in the bay, awaited another chance to attack, yellow fever gripped the fleet, and of the 3000 colonial troops barely 1300 returned home.

Three curiously unrelated things came out of this fiasco. Among the Virginian officers who survived was George Washington's half-brother, Captain Lawrence Washington, who named his new estate on the Potomac "Mount Vernon" after the popular English admiral. Vernon's nickname, "Old Grog," was applied to the mixture of rum and water which he ordered to be issued instead of the former ration of raw rum which was rapidly knocking the sailors out. And in the course of this expedition the colonial troops for the first time were called "Americans" instead of "provincials" by the English, and referred to themselves as such.

Disaster before Cartagena prevented Oglethorpe from making another attempt on Florida and gave Spain an opportunity to retaliate. A formidable expedition of 30 ships carrying 1300 soldiers sailed from Havana in May 1742 and, after picking up more men at St. Augustine, landed on St. Simon's Island and captured the fort. General Oglethorpe, having deployed his regiment and obtained several hundred Creek warriors, fell back on Frederica, ambushed an advancing column of Spaniards at the Bloody Marsh (7 July), and threw them back in disorder. That was the nearest the Spaniards came to "laying waste South Carolina and her dependencies," as Philip V of Spain had ordered them to do. Oglethorpe now returned to England but continued his interest in Georgia, which rightly regards him as a colonial founder in a class with Calvert, Winthrop, Penn, and Shaftesbury.

This war ended in 1748 without any settlement of the disputed southern boundary. But it was no longer possible for the English colonies to squeeze out Louisiana. That French colony was there to stay, a southern anchor to the chain that the French government would endeavor to stretch from Cape Breton up the St. Lawrence to the Great Lakes, and down the Mississippi to the Gulf of Mexico.

2. Canada and War in the North

It is not surprising that the French attempted an encirclement, or that the British endeavored to check it. The strategic position of France in North America had been greatly weakened by the Treaty of Utrecht, and loss of Newfoundland, Nova Scotia, and Hudson Bay. Her strength relative to the English colonies dwindled yearly. The population of Canada, 18,119 in 1713, did indeed double by 1734, but by that time the population of the English colonies north of the Carolinas had passed the half-million mark. And, starting with the Spotswood transmontane expedition of 1718, English America was expanding westward and threatening French communications between Canada and Louisiana.

Canada, weakened and impoverished by Queen Anne's War, needed manpower above all things, to hold firm against the English. But, at a time when the English colonies were attracting thousands of sturdy Germans, French Protestants, Scots and Irish farmers and artisans, the government of Louis XV allowed a mere trickle of emigrants to go to Canada, and not of the best sort at that—young libertines of whom their families wished to be rid, smugglers, poachers, and other petty criminals. The government authorized the introduction of African slaves, but few Canadians could afford to buy them. Even the fur trade, the one profitable business in New France, was partly strangled by the king's granting a twenty-five-year monopoly in 1717 to a private company. The export of forest products to France was fairly successful, but efforts to establish a profitable trade with the West Indies were defeated by the superior know-how of New Englanders. Poverty was the lot of most seigneurs, and the superior attraction of becoming coureur de bois continued to drain off their habitants. The bishops and the Jesuits continued their secular feud with the governors and other officials. In one matter, however, Canada was definitely superior to the English colonies. She had a well-trained militia, partly paid by the crown.

French Canadian strategy during the thirty years after 1713 was defensive from their point of view, provocative from the English, and ultimately disastrous. France spent about $6 million in gold building the "impregnable" fortress of Louisbourg on Cape Breton Island, which menaced the New England fisheries but proved useless in wartime because the relatively weak French navy could not maintain communications with it, or with Canada. On the eastern flank a series of clerical and lay emissaries kept the Acadians of Nova Scotia, and the Micmac Indians, loyal to France and expecting reconquest, a policy which ended in deportation. In Maine, Canada incited the Abnaki to resist New Englanders who were resettling land whence they had been expelled during the last war, a policy which resulted in their missionary leader, Father Sebastian

Rasle, being killed, gun in hand, and his fortified Indian town of Norridgewock, on the site of Madison, Maine, being destroyed.

In the west the French were enterprising and successful. They built a fort at Crown Point on Lake Champlain, Fort Niagara near the falls, and two forts on the Wabash. And they almost exterminated the Fox or Outagamie tribe of Wisconsin, which had threatened Detroit. Pierre de la Vérendrye, in a series of Western explorations between 1731 and 1744, built forts on the Lake of the Woods and on the site of Winnipeg, and marched into the Dakotas, Montana, and Saskatchewan.

But the fate of France in North America would not be settled there. Canada's roots were in the Atlantic, the St. Lawrence was her trunk, the Great Lakes her branches, and the Western forts mere twigs. Britain well knew that if the roots were grappled by her navy, and the trunk severed at Quebec or Montreal, French Canada could not survive.

In 1744 the War of Jenkins' Ear with Spain merged into the War of the Austrian Succession (called King George's War in America), in which England and Austria were allies against France and Prussia. Governor William Shirley and Massachusetts Bay now became aggressors on the northern frontier, as Governor Oglethorpe and South Carolina had been on the southern. Shirley, a local lawyer, had been appointed governor of Massachusetts Bay in the hope that he could settle the long-standing quarrel between the king's representative and the assembly. This he did so adroitly as to calm every faction, to receive an annual salary of £1000, and to be allowed by the assembly to run a war without their interference.

Shirley conceived and carried out the siege and capture of Louisbourg by New England militia led by William Pepperell, a merchant of Kittery, Maine, and the Royal Navy supported him with a blockading squadron under Admiral Sir Peter Warren. Pepperell's army on 30 April 1745 made a successful amphibious landing a few miles from Louisbourg, established a beachhead out of reach of the 150-gunned French fortress, and conducted the campaign in a spirit of rustic frolic, defying both military discipline and principles of strategy. The troops captured an outlying battery from the rear, dragged artillery through supposedly impassable swamps, chased French cannonballs to shoot them back from their own guns, and went fishing when they felt like it. But Pepperell knew how to handle Yankee country folk, and the net effect of their pluck and enterprise was so to discourage and confuse the French commander of Louisbourg that on 16 June he surrendered both town and fortress.

The French and their Indian allies now launched retaliatory attacks on New England frontier villages and Saratoga, New York, and the Iroquois raided Canada. In 1746 France sent a fleet of almost 100 ships under the Duc d'Anville, to reconquer Louisbourg and burn Boston. It eluded the British fleet sent to intercept, but was so battered by storms and decimated by scurvy during the three months' ocean passage that it returned to France minus 3000 soldiers and sailors, including the Admiral, and without firing a shot. The "Bastonnais" regarded this a direct answer to prayer.

Diplomacy, however, lost what valor and good luck had won. In the swapping of conquests that took place at the Treaty of Aix-la-Chapelle (1748), which concluded this war with France and Spain, England returned Louisbourg to France.

Although the mainland of Nova Scotia had been under British sovereignty since 1713, the only white inhabitants were several thousand French Acadians, mostly living on the Bay of Fundy. Toward them the British acted with exemplary liberalism. No attempt was made to interfere with their language, religion, or local self-government; but they firmly declined to admit British sovereignty, and during King George's War were actively hostile or sullenly neutral. This situation could not continue after the peace, when the British government began to people the hitherto unsettled shores of Nova Scotia. In the spring of 1749 some 1400 colonists from England, mostly objects of charity like those of Georgia, were sent out under an energetic governor, Edward Cornwallis. He founded Halifax, but the hostile attitude of the French Acadians and Micmac Indians long prevented any English settlement outside Halifax and Annapolis Royal. Before the next war broke out, the British authorities, supported by Governor Shirley, decided to deport all French who lived near strategic centers. They could not suffer this hostile minority to remain on an exposed flank.

The rights and wrongs of this policy have remained a subject of bitter controversy between French Canadian and English historians to this day. The real culprit was the French government, which sent secret agents to encourage the Acadians in the belief that France would return in might to reconquer L'Acadie. It was a situation similar to Hitler's fomenting rebellion among the Sudeten Germans in Czechoslovakia in

1938, and had equally tragic results—a wholesale deportation and a refugee problem. The Acadian deportation was carried out with unnecessary hardship. Families and neighbors were separated, as Longfellow described in *Evangeline*, which is based on a real episode that he heard from descendants of refugees. Many were quartered on towns and villages in the English colonies, where they were regarded as a potential fifth column; a few went back to France; many, after the end of the war, returned to Nova Scotia but not to their own farms, which had been confiscated and given to English settlers. The happiest were those who, like Evangeline, were sent to French Louisiana, where their descendants retained their language and to this day are known as "Cajuns."

Between 6000 and 7250 Acadians were deported, and many more escaped through the woods or by sea to Canada. It is not a pretty story; but to assert, as most French Canadian historians do, that it was completely inexcusable and the first wholesale deportation in history, is to ignore the provocation, the Old Testament, and the expulsion of some 400,000 Protestants from France after the revocation of the Edict of Nantes. Recent events in Algeria, Cyprus, Palestine, and other parts of the world indicate that it is almost impossible for two utterly different racial, religious, and language groups to live peaceably in the same region, if one or the other is encouraged and stimulated by an outside power.

3. Cold War Maneuvering, 1747–1755

It may now be said, with the privilege of hindsight, that the vital stake in all wars and diplomatic maneuverings since 1700 was the American West. Who was to rule the West—England, France, or Spain? Or, as nobody could then foresee, an American republic? Yet, until well after mid-century, the West was the last thing that politicians, whether English, French, or American, thought about. From the European point of view the principal objectives were the sugar islands in the Caribbean; that is why the major naval efforts of England and France were applied in that region. New England and New York were chiefly interested in the destruction of French power on their northern and eastern boundaries. For South Carolina and Georgia, the Spaniard in Florida and his Indian allies were the greater menace. But it was in the West that a new war began, even before the previous war ended.

In 1747 Thomas Lee, president of the Virginia Council, organized the Ohio Company, with the object of acquiring half a million acres on each side of the Ohio river. Other prominent Virginians, such as Thomas Jefferson's father, organized additional land companies and employed veteran Indian traders to push trade with the Indians in the Ohio country and to extinguish their prior claims to the land. This was a threat to French communications between Montreal and New Orleans that could not be ignored. In 1749 the governor of Canada sent a fleet of batteaux and canoes, commanded by Celeron de Bienville, to take possession of the Ohio valley.

A cold war for winning the West was on, and gradually it warmed up. In 1753 Governor Duquesne built a chain of log-walled forts on the Allegheny and the upper Ohio to defend French claims. Virginia could not ignore this challenge. The French pretention to reserve the entire West north of the Ohio ran counter to her charter boundaries, and to the claims of the new land companies. Governor Robert Dinwiddie sent young George Washington to the forks of the Ohio to protest. Protest being unavailing, Dinwiddie commissioned George (aged twenty-two) lieutenant colonel of Virginia militia and in 1754 sent him with 150 men to forestall the French. But the Canadians got there first, built Fort Duquesne on the site of Pittsburgh, and at Great Meadows in western Pennsylvania confronted the Virginia militia. Washington fired first, but lost the fight and had to surrender. This being nominally a time of peace, the prisoners were released and a somewhat crestfallen George was allowed to go home.

That shot in the Western wilderness sparked off a series of world-shaking events which reached their culmination thirty years later. In 1783 Major General George Washington, Commander in Chief of the United States Army, resigned his commission after winning independence for a republic not even dreamed of in 1753.

Virginia and New England were ready for hot war in 1754, but England and France were not. The Duke of Newcastle, the prime minister, fancied that he could maintain England's western claims by a local war. In the fall of 1754 he sent General Braddock to America with parts of two regiments to do the job.

In the meantime eight of the thirteen colonies had made an attempt to agree on a plan of union for common defense. The Board of Trade instructed the royal governors to meet representatives of the Six Nations at Albany and take measures "to secure their wavering friendship"; the Iroquois, impressed by the Great Meadows affair, were wondering which side to take. Leading Americans, however, wished the congress to undertake a more ambitious task. Before it met, Governor Shirley thus addressed the assembly of Massachusetts: "For forming this general union, gentlemen, there is no time to be lost: the French seem to have advanced further toward making themselves masters of this Continent within the past five or six years than they have done ever since the first beginning of that settlement."

The Albany Congress, meeting in June 1754, spent most of its time debating that question. The Plan of Union that it adopted was the work of Benjamin Franklin and Thomas Hutchinson. There was to be a president general appointed by the crown, and a "grand council" appointed by the colonial assemblies, in proportion to their contributions to the common war chest—a typical bit of Ben Franklin foxiness, to ensure that taxes would really be paid. The president, with the advice of the grand council, would have sole power to negotiate treaties, declare war, and make peace with the Indians; to regulate the Indian trade, to have sole jurisdiction over land purchases outside particular colonies, and to make grants of land to settlers and govern the Western territory until the crown formed it into new colonial governments. The Union would have power to build forts, raise armies and equip fleets, and levy taxes for the same, to be paid into a general treasury with branches in each colony.

This plan showed far-sighted statesmanship, but looked too far ahead, recommending a closer federal union than the thirteen colonies were willing to conclude during the War of Independence. Whether the British government would have consented is doubtful; but they never had a chance to express their views. Not one colonial assembly ratified the Plan. Every one refused to give up any part of its exclusive taxing power, even to a representative body. So the war which then began was carried through under the old system. No British commander had authority to raise troops or money from a colony without the consent of its assembly. The assemblies of provinces that were not directly menaced, and some of those that were, like Pennsylvania, refused to make any substantial contribution to the common cause. Even Virginia would not allow draftees to serve outside her borders until 1758.

English and Americans always seem to begin a war that they eventually win, with a bad thrashing. This time it was Braddock's defeat on the Monongahela, a bloody battle in that part of the Western wilderness which is now a suburb of Pittsburgh. The English ministry's strategic plan was sound: to capture four forts which the French had built on debatable territory and secure them before the hot war started. These forts, from east to west, were Beauséjour at the head of the

Bay of Fundy, Crown Point on Lake Champlain, Fort Niagara at the falls, and Fort Duquesne. This last, the key to
the West, was the objective of Major General Edward Braddock, forty-five of whose sixty years had been spent in the
British army in Europe. He was given two of the worst regiments in that army, at half strength, which he was expected
to fill with American recruits to a total of 700 officers and
men each. The colonies were expected to provide additional
troops, food, wagons, and Indian auxiliaries for a march from
Alexandria, Virginia, across the Blue Ridge and the Alleghenies, and through a yet unbroken wilderness, to take Fort
Duquesne.

Governors Dinwiddie of Virginia, Sharpe of Maryland, and
Shirley of Massachusetts, enthusiasts for expelling the French
from North America, met Braddock at Alexandria to make
plans. Young George Washington became one of the General's
aides-de-camp. So many things in this campaign went wrong
that it is impossible to pin the blame on any one person; but
Braddock made the most mistakes. Although a brave and
energetic soldier, he knew nothing of wilderness marches or
battles, and refused to learn from the Virginians. Instead of
depending on pack animals for supply, he insisted on a great
wagon train; and the only colony which provided its quota of
wagons was Pennsylvania. Ben Franklin's diplomacy was
responsible. He dropped the hint that if the farmers did not
hire out their teams voluntarily, British "hussars" would come
and take them; hussars were the storm troopers of that era.
He procured some 150 Conestoga wagons, which Braddock
said was "almost the only instance of ability and honesty"
that he had "known in these provinces."

It took Braddock's army 32 days to cover the 110 miles
from Fort Cumberland to Fort Duquesne through a trackless
hardwood forest. A pioneer battalion of 300 axemen had to
cut a crude road. By 7 July the van was only 10 or 12 miles
from its destination. Braddock formed a "flying column" of
his best troops, including both regulars and provincials, and
pressed on ahead. To avoid a narrow defile, he twice forded
the Monongahela river. George Washington, late in life, said
that it was the most beautiful spectacle he had ever seen.
Scarlet-coated regulars and blue-coated Virginians in columns of four, mounted officers and light cavalry, horse-drawn
artillery and wagons, and dozens of packhorses, splashed
through the rippling shallows under a brilliant summer sun
into the green-clothed forest. Spirits were high and victory
seemed certain; if the French did not attack at the fords, they
surely never would. Rush the fort, and hurrah for old England!

But hark! What is that firing ahead, just as the last of the rear guard crosses the river?

It was a sortie from Fort Duquesne in head-on collision with Braddock's van, an engagement that neither side planned or wanted. The small French garrison at the fort had been strengthened by almost 1000 Indian warriors, who had flocked in from every part of the Old West. With the choosiness common to Indians they had refused to move the day before to ambush Braddock at the ford; but now, when the British column was safely across, they consented to go. No fewer than 637 braves, with about 150 French Canadian militia, led by 72 French officers and regulars, sortied in the early afternoon of 9 July.

Braddock had flankers out; he was not ambushed, only surprised. The head of his column saw a young French officer stop, turn, and wave his hat; immediately the English heard the Indians' war whoop, as the redskins deployed to right and left, took cover in the ravines that paralleled the road, and poured hot lead into the close ranks of scarlet and blue coats —the best targets they had ever encountered. The British troops could not see their deadly foes, but they could hear them plenty; and, never having fought Indians, were unnerved by the horrible war whoops. General Braddock, losing one horse after another, rushed about trying to rally his men; it was no use. His senior colonel and many other officers were killed, and he himself was shot in the lungs. Toward sundown, after the largely unseen Indians had mowed down scores of the huddled and almost leaderless redcoats, panic set in. The soldiers "broke and ran as sheep pursued by dogs" (so Washington recorded), abandoning wagons, artillery, and even muskets. Fortunately, the Indians were too busy scalping, looting, and torturing prisoners to pursue, or the entire flying column would have been massacred; as it was, of the 1459 officers and men engaged, 977 were killed or wounded.

Braddock died of his wounds after turning over the command to Colonel Dunbar, who made bad matters worse by abandoning Fort Cumberland and going into winter quarters at Philadelphia when the summer was but half over, leaving the Pennsylvania-Maryland-Virginia frontier completely defenseless.

4. The Seven Years' War, 1755–1763

Braddock's defeat was the Pearl Harbor of the Seven Years' War. It brought over all Indians of the Northwest to the

French side, caused the Six Nations to waver in their allegiance, threw back the effective English frontier hundreds of miles, and exposed new settlements to a series of devastating Indian attacks. Thousands of men, women, and children who had settled the Shenandoah valley in the last forty years lost all they had, and were lucky to escape with their lives.

British operations of 1755 were inept though not disastrous. Governor Shirley failed to take Fort Niagara. General William Johnson "of the Mohawks," an able Irishman who acted as liaison between the English and the Iroquois, defeated the French at Lake George on 8 September and was made a baronet; but he was unable to capture Crown Point on Lake Champlain, and the French built Fort Ticonderoga south of it. Fort Beauséjour at the head of the Bay of Fundy surrendered to Colonel John Winslow of Massachusetts after two shells from the escorting British fleet had blown up an ammunition dump, and this secured the eastern flank.

In 1756 this "Old French and Indian War," as the Americans called it, merged into the Seven Years' War in Europe, where it was France, Austria, Sweden, and a few small German states against Britain and Prussia. England supported Prussia with money and engaged in naval warfare against France (and later Spain) in the Atlantic, the Mediterranean, the Caribbean, and the Indian Ocean. There was warfare on the continent of India between French under Dupleix and English under Clive and their respective native allies; hostilities even reached the Philippines, where an English fleet captured Manila. This should really have been called the First World War; hostilities were waged over as large a portion of the globe as in 1914–18.

The next two years were disastrous for England. The Earl of Loudoun, who succeeded Shirley as British commander in chief in America, was well described by his predecessor as "a pen and ink man whose greatest energies were put forth in getting ready to begin." Virginian militia under Colonel Washington with great difficulty held the Shenandoah valley against the Indians. Canada, reinforced by 3000 French regulars, took the offensive and the Marquis de Montcalm captured Fort Oswego on Lake Ontario and Fort William Henry on Lake George. In India, Clive lost Calcutta. On the continent of Europe, England's ally Frederick the Great was defeated by the French and Austrians; and the British commander in chief, the Duke of Cumberland, surrendered an army to the French.

How things looked to a colonial philosopher, the Reverend Jonathan Edwards, may be seen in a letter that he wrote in the fall of 1756 to a friend who was chaplain to a Massachusetts regiment on Lake George:

> God indeed is remarkably frowning upon us every where; our enemies get up above us very high, and we are brought down very low: They are the Head, and we are the Tail. God is making us, with all our superiority in numbers, to become the Object of our Enemies almost continual Triumphs and Insults. . . . And in Europe things don't go much better, . . . Minorca was surrendered to the French on the 29 Day of last June; principally through the wretched Cowardice or Treachery of Admiral Byng.[1] This with the taking of Oswego . . . will tend mightily to animate and encourage the French Nation . . . and weaken and dishearten the English, and make 'em contemptible in the Eyes of the Nations of Europe. . . . What will become of us God only knows.

Yet the entire aspect of the war changed in 1758 after William Pitt became secretary of state and prime minister. This Winston Churchill of the eighteenth century had a flair for grand strategy and a genius for choosing able men. While most Englishmen regarded the American war as secondary, Pitt saw that the principal object for England should be the conquest of Canada and the American West, thus carving out a new field for Anglo-American expansion. His strategy was simple and direct. He would send no more English troops to the continent of Europe, but subsidized Frederick to fight the French there. To the British navy he gave a triple task: to contain the French fleet in its home bases, escort convoys over the transatlantic route, and co-operate with the army in amphibious operations. And he concentrated the military might of Britain and her colonies in the American theater, under young and energetic commanders. The naval part was crucial. Canada, with a population under 60,000, could not hold out against the English colonies with a population of one million, unless the French could get reinforcements across the Atlantic.

At the Battle of Dettingen, 1743, four young English officers—Jeffrey Amherst, George Townshend, Robert Moncton, and James Wolfe—had received their baptism of fire. Now the eldest was only forty-one years old and the youngest, Wolfe, was thirty-one. He was a lanky, narrow-shouldered young man

---

[1] Byng was court-martialed and shot for this, giving rise to Voltaire's quip that the British "kill an admiral from time to time to encourage the others."

with vivid red hair, the most earnest student of the art of war in the British army. In ambition, genius, and audacity, and in his fierce concentration on making himself master of his profession, Wolfe was the most Napoleonic soldier in English history. "An offensive, daring kind of war," he wrote, "will awe the Indians and ruin the French. Block-houses and a trembling defensive encourage the meanest scoundrels to attack us."

Such was his advice to Jeffrey Amherst, whom Pitt selected as commander in chief in America. Stolid and unemotional, Amherst had the right character to neutralize the impetuosity of Wolfe, his No. 1 brigadier general. These two, making a perfect team with Admiral Boscawen, in July 1758 recaptured Louisbourg, far better fortified than in 1745 and more skillfully defended. The same year, Colonel John Bradstreet, with a force of New Englanders, captured Fort Frontenac, where the St. Lawrence flows out of Lake Ontario; and Brigadier John Forbes, with George Washington on his staff, marched across Pennsylvania and captured Fort Duquesne, renaming it Pittsburgh after the great war minister.

Then came 1759, England's "wonderful year," so charged with British glory that it was said the very bells of London were worn thin pealing for victories, and British throats went hoarse bawling out "Heart of Oak." Guadeloupe in the West Indies fell to a well-conducted amphibious operation. The French power in India was destroyed, and the French fleet intended to reinforce Canada was smashed by Hawke at Quiberon Bay. Sir William Johnson and his Iroquois braves helped the British to capture Fort Niagara, key to the Great Lakes. And the campaign of Quebec surpassed all.

The British army under Wolfe was transported by a fleet of over 200 sail, commanded by Vice Admiral Charles Saunders. Entering the St. Lawrence on 6 June, Saunders appointed Captain James Cook (of later Pacific fame) to sail ahead, take soundings, and buoy a channel through the Travers, the narrow, tortuous channel between Île d'Orléans and the south shore; and then performed the amazing feat of sailing his entire fleet up to Quebec in three weeks, without a single grounding or other casualty.

General Amherst, marching overland from New York, was supposed to co-operate. He recaptured Crown Point and Ticonderoga but was too slow and methodical to get within striking distance of Quebec. Thrice in previous wars this failure in co-ordination had saved Quebec for France, and in 1775–76 and 1812–13 similar American failures kept it British. But Wolfe was not discouraged. His total force, ex-

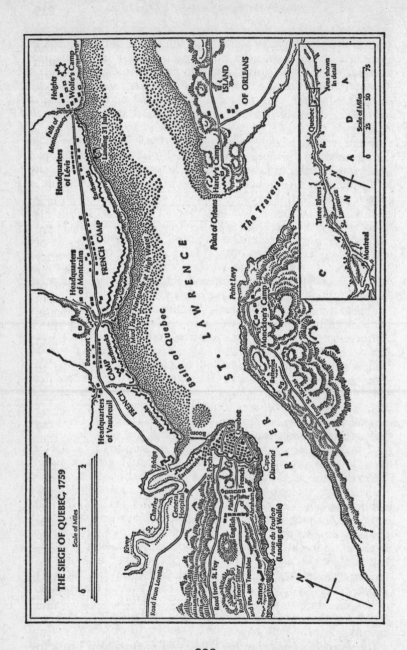

THE SIEGE OF QUEBEC, 1759

Scale of Miles

0   1   2

N

River St. Charles

Road from Lorette

Road from St. Foy

Road from Sillery and Pte. aux Trembles

Samos

Anse du Foulon (Landing of Wolfe)

Cape Diamond

Plains of Abraham

English

French

St. Roch

Earthworks

General Hospital

Bridge

Boom

Headquarters of Vaudreuil

Beauport

FRENCH CAMP

Earthworks

Headquarters of Montcalm

FRENCH CAMP

Mud flats uncovered at High Water

Headquarters of Lévis

Earthworks

Landing 31 July

Falls of Montmorency

Wolfe's Camp

Heights

Basin of Quebec

S T .   L A W R E N C E

R I V E R

Point Levy

Monckton's Camp

Batteries

Point of Orleans

Hardy's Camp

ISLAND OF ORLEANS

The Traverse

C A N A D A

Quebec

Area shown in detail

Three Rivers

St. Lawrence

Montreal

N

Scale of Miles

0   25   50   75

228

clusive of sailors and marines, amounted to only 4000 officers
and men, but included some of the crack units of the British
army. Owing to Amherst's delay, the Marquis de Montcalm
was able to concentrate some 14,000 French troops and militia
in and around Quebec. His position appeared to be impregnable. The guns of the citadel commanded the river, and the
land approach from the east was barred by two smaller rivers.

Admiral Saunders first landed a force on 27 June on the Île
d'Orléans, four miles below Quebec. Montcalm's army was
deployed along the north shore of the river, between the St.
Charles and the Montmorency, with a detachment under
Bougainville west of the city; but he neglected to secure the
south bank. Wolfe's first bold stroke was to take advantage
of this weakness and seize Point Levi, 1000 yards across the
river from Quebec, whence his guns were able to bombard
the lower town. At the same time he landed the better part of
two brigades on the north shore, just below the Montmorency
falls, to fox Montcalm (9 July). Ten days later, one of the
frigates and several smaller vessels, slipping past the guns of
Quebec under cover of a heavy bombardment from Point
Levi, sailed over twenty miles upstream to confuse Montcalm
and provide Wolfe with alternate points of attack. The British,
owing to their command of the river, were now able to select
time and place for their assault.

Wolfe first probed the Montmorency front but failed to
make any impression there. He then quietly reinforced the
up-river part of his force with men and ships, sailing them
upstream and downstream with the wind and tide, forcing
Bougainville's soldiers to march and countermarch to the
point of exhaustion. His scouts spied out a narrow defile that
led up the cliffs on the river's north bank to the Plains of
Abraham. Montcalm, thinking this route to be inaccessible,
had here posted only a small picket guard.

At sunset 12 September, Saunders put on a simulated landing
at the Montmorency front, which pulled a large part of Montcalm's force off base. Late that evening, 1700 English embarked in boats from the transports up-river, and at 2:00 a.m.
on the 13th, with a fresh breeze astern and an ebb tide under
their keels, they began floating downstream, unobserved by
Bougainville. Wolfe, in one of the foremost boats, recited
Gray's "Elegy in a Country Churchyard" to a young midship-
man, solemnly pronouncing the famous line that his own fate
would presently illustrate: "The paths of glory lead but to
the grave."

The French were expecting a convoy of provision boats to
slip down-river that night, and the British landing craft were

mistaken for them. Only one French sentry on the shore challenged, "Qui vive?" A French-speaking Scot replied, "France." "De quel régiment?" "De la Reine," replied the Scot. The sentry was satisfied.

The boats reached the bottom of the defile. Twenty-four rugged volunteers climbed up the cliff, put the French picket guard to the sword, gave the prearranged signal, and the troops jumped ashore and swarmed up the steep path, muskets slung on their backs. As fast as the boats emptied they returned to the ships or to the south shore for reinforcements. Thus, by break of day, 13 September 1759, some 4500 British were deployed on the Plains of Abraham, a grassy field forming part of the Quebec plateau, close to the walls of the citadel.

Wolfe's object was to challenge Montcalm to an open-field battle, the only kind he knew how to fight; and the French accepted. Presently white-uniformed veterans of famous regiments—La Sarre, Guyenne, Languedoc, Royal-Roussillon, Béarn—were coming on the double from the Montmorency front, rushing through the narrow streets of Quebec and deploying on the other side to face the English. At 10:00 a.m. some 4000 of them, who had formed outside the walls, advanced to the attack, flying regimental colors and cheering "Vive le Roi!" For fifteen or twenty minutes they marched, and not a shot rang out; Wolfe had learned the value of precise, accurate, and concentrated fire power. Three-quarters of his 4500 troops were deployed in one line, which waited silently until the enemy was only 40 yards away. Then the command "Fire!" rang out and the muskets crashed in a rolling roar. A second volley followed and no more were needed; the ground was already covered with French dead and wounded. Then the English soldiers charged the dazed survivors with fixed bayonets, and kilted Highlanders, shouting wildly, attacked with claymore and broadswords, completing the rout of the French. Wolfe, personally leading a picked force of grenadiers, was shot down, and only had time to order the enemy's retreat to be cut off before dying on the field of glory. Montcalm, mortally wounded in the retreat, died next day. Each side suffered about equal losses, 640 killed and wounded. Quebec promptly surrendered to the British. Never did so short and sharp a fight have so important a result.

Soon Canada was sealed off from Europe by ice, but in the spring of 1760 a reorganized French and Canadian army under the Chevalier de Lévis moved against Quebec. Brigadier Murray, commanding a small, half-starved British garrison in the city, managed to hold them off. On 9 May a warship appeared down-river, unannounced. Anxious eyes on both sides sought to make out her flag. Lévis, knowing nothing of the destruction of the French fleet at Quiberon Bay the previous November, was confident that he saw the white ensign of royal France, heralding a relief expedition. And when his aide made out a red cross of St. George on the ensign—for this ship was the van of a British fleet—the Chevalier's heart was broken. He abandoned the siege and fell back on Montreal. On 8 September 1760 after Generals Amherst, Haviland, and Murray had invested Montreal, Governor the Marquis de Vaudreuil, deserted by many French regulars and the Canadian militia, surrendered the whole of Canada to Great Britain.

In North America the war was over, except for the Pontiac conspiracy, a last flare-up by the Indians of the Ohio country who refused to accept the consequences of French defeat. In Europe, the Caribbean, and the Far East, the war lasted two years longer. A British fleet mopped up Martinique and all the French West Indies except Saint-Domingue. Spain's tardy alliance with France in 1761 gave a British naval squadron the opportunity to double Cape Horn and capture Manila. A British amphibious operation with colonial volunteers took Havana in 1762.

In that year George III, who had succeeded his grandfather George II in 1760, dismissed William Pitt, whose notions of conquest and glory had become immoderate. The king opened peace negotiations and obtained treaties with France and Spain by returning several British conquests in order to retain the most important. That was eighteenth-century war at its best. You beat your enemy, but did not try to annihilate him. Even so, the victory was too complete for the results to be permanent.

This Peace of Paris in 1763 marked the end of France as a North American power. Of the great empire won by Champlain, La Salle, and hundreds of explorers, warriors, traders, and priests, France retained only the two little islands of St. Pierre and Miquelon off Newfoundland. In the West Indies, besides a few smaller islands, she kept Saint-Domingue, Martinique, and Guadeloupe. Spain ceded to Great Britain East and West Florida, which became the sixteenth and seventeenth English continental colonies. France, in order to compensate Spain for the loss of the Floridas and Minorca, ceded to her the vast province of Louisiana, including all French claims to territory west of the Mississippi. Thus the Mississippi became a boundary between the English and Spanish empires.

Britain was now supreme on the seas, in the subcontinent of India, and in North America. English, Scots, Irish, and Americans boiled over with patriotism. "We doubt not," resolved Massachusetts Bay, "but as we are delivered from foreign Wars, we shall be equally free from intestine Divisions."

But that was too much to expect. A war may settle some things but creates new problems and tensions that beget another war.

Although Canada passed under British sovereignty, the year 1763 marks the beginning of French Canada as a self-conscious people, ill-rewarding the tolerance and justice of their English conquerors by indifference and disloyalty. Their writers created a myth to the effect that they were sold or

HEART OF OAK

Come, cheer up, my lads, 'tis to glo-ry we steer, To add some-thing more to this won-der-ful year; To hon-or we call you, as free men, not slaves, For who are so free as the sons of the waves? Heart of oak are our ships; Heart of oak are our men; We al-ways are read-y, Stead-y, boys, stead-y. We'll fight and we'll con-quer a-gain and a-gain.

betrayed by the feeble Bourbon who reigned over France. There is no truth in this. France made strenuous efforts to defend her overseas empire, but these were not enough to counteract British energy and sea power, and the superior manpower of the English colonies. Two centuries after the fall of Montreal, the Province of Quebec, with 83 per cent of its five million inhabitants Catholic and French-speaking, was nourishing ancient grievances and a party aiming at complete independence.

XII

Triumph and Tribulation

1763-1766

1. *The Thirteen Colonies in 1763*

A GREAT ENTERPRISE had been concluded in the grand manner. For a moment the British Empire was not only a political and economic unit but a moral one. English, Scots, Irish, and Americans alike bellowed patriotic sentiments and slopped over with expressions of loyalty. George III, the attractive young man of twenty-two who succeeded his grandfather in 1760, and William Pitt the Great Commoner, were as popular in America as in England. But in the long run the Seven Years' War proved to be more of a solvent than a cement. What went wrong?

The victory had been too complete. The balance of power had been upset, and the French made it their business to tip the scales the other way. One obvious way was to envenom any future dispute between England and her colonies to the point of independence. For, even though the colonists had gained in loyalty, they had also grown in confidence and strength. From their point of view, they had won the war, with a little aid from the British army and navy. Causes of dissension inherent in the English colonial system had been sharpened. The royal and proprietary governors still carried instructions to maintain the prerogative against popularly elected assemblies. The royal disallowance of colonial laws was still in effect, and on the first important exercise of it after the war—the Two-Penny Act in Virginia—Patrick Henry declared: "A king by annulling . . . laws of this salutary nature . . . forfeits all rights to his subjects' obedience," at which arose murmurs of "Treason! Treason!" Imperial sentiments proved to be temporary; colonial attitudes permanent. Americans considered their own interests first, whilst the British governing class still thought of the colonies as their property, "to be regarded in no other light but as subservient to the commerce of their mother country," as an English publicist wrote. And the conquest of Canada, the Floridas, and of numerous nations of "wild" Indians, created new administrative problems that England was ill equipped to face, and which she could not solve within the existing framework of law and custom.

One principle upon which all Englishmen then agreed was the rule of law. When in the late eighteenth century, they spoke of the "liberties of free-born Englishmen," the rule of law was in the back of their minds: resistance to Charles I in the name of law, vindication of law against James II. Colonial leaders were familiar with the works of Algernon Sidney, Harington, and Locke, who urged every Englishman to resist every grasp for power; to stand firm on ancient principles of liberty, whether embalmed in acts of Parliament or adumbrated in the "Law of Nature." Thus, in order to resist the government of George III, Americans had to prove to their own satisfaction that it was he who had broken the law. The maladroit persistence of George III and his ministers in trying to solve their administrative problems outside existing law served to smash all floating atoms of contention and produce a nuclear explosion in the political sphere.

British subjects in America, excepting of course the blacks, were then the freest people in the world, and in many respects more free than anyone today. They argued and then fought, not to *obtain* freedom but to *confirm* the freedom they already had or claimed. They were even more advanced in the practice of self-government than the mother country. There was slight pressure from ancient custom, and few relics of feudalism. Land tenure was fee simple in New England, and subject elsewhere only to a light quitrent which was generally evaded. There were no tithes to support an established church. Maximum wages were not fixed, as in most European countries, nor were the rural laborers at the mercy of tyrannical justices of the peace, as in England and Ireland. Americans were exempt from naval press-gangs. Some form of military training was obligatory, but actual service in time of war was voluntary. Since the Zenger libel case in New York in 1735, almost complete freedom of speech, press, and assembly was enjoyed.[1] Trades and professions were open to the talented— there were no guilds or corporations or exclusive professional associations; indeed, very few professional men of any sort, other than lawyers, physicians, and divines. The hand of government rested lightly on Americans. Connecticut, for three years running, levied no taxes except local rates for roads and schools. In the absence of banks, merchants lent money privately, and the frontier offered an easy escape from debt. Victory had removed the French menace to security, and would have ended the Indian menace too, had Americans been content to live east of the Appalachians. Social classes existed, but, to British visitors like Janet Schaw, a "most disgusting equality" prevailed.

It did, near the wilderness. The frontier of settlement in 1763 left the coast near the Penobscot river in Maine, cut irregularly across New Hampshire and the disputed lands which later became Vermont, pushed up the Hudson to Lake George, and up the Mohawk about 100 miles from Albany. Thence it slashed across the southeast corners of New York and Pennsylvania and hugged the Appalachians until reaching North Carolina, where again it dropped down to the sea. Scattered settlements had already been made throughout the interior of the Carolinas and eastern Georgia.

This settled area of 1763, which two centuries later had a population approaching 100 million, then included about a million and a half people, almost one-third of them African slaves. By 1775 it had increased by another million. The bulk of the population was engaged in agriculture, but visiting Europeans regarded the country as a wilderness because over 90 per cent of it was still forested. Only near the Atlantic, in sections cultivated for over a century, could one have found anything resembling the farming areas of Iowa, Illinois, or Nebraska today. Elsewhere, and especially in the South, farms and plantations lay miles apart, separated by forest.

Let us now briefly survey the British continental colonies, starting at the southern end. West Florida, defined in 1763 as old Spanish Florida west of the Apalachicola, together with

[1] John Peter Zenger, publisher of a newspaper that represented the opposition to the New York colonial government, was prosecuted for seditious libel. His friends obtained the services of Andrew Hamilton, a Philadelphia lawyer, who secured acquittal on the then revolutionary ground that truth was no libel. Although this Zenger decision was not always followed by colonial courts, it did establish the principle of a free press, which was of inestimable value to the radical party in 1764–76.

that part of French Louisiana including Mobile, Biloxi, and Natchez, had very few European inhabitants. Pensacola was still a stockaded fort; Mobile had only 112 Frenchmen. Governor George Johnstone, an energetic Scots naval officer, set up civil government at Pensacola, summoned an elective assembly in 1766, and advertised for English settlers, with good results; within ten years the population had risen to 3700 Europeans and 1200 slaves, most of them at the Mississippi end. Johnstone cemented friendly relations with the Creek and Choctaw, who ceded their lands up to a line 35 miles from the sea.

In East Florida, when the British took possession, the only settlements Spain had to show for over two centuries of rule were St. Augustine and St. Mark. In contrast to Canada, where the French habitants loved their land more than their king and preferred English allegiance to exile, the people of St. Augustine, although granted toleration, chose to leave when England took over. No Spaniard could imagine living under alien heretics. The Spanish authorities provided transportation to Havana for all white inhabitants and several hundred fugitive slaves from Georgia and South Carolina who had settled near the garrison town. South of St. Augustine, where now the palm-bordered shores are broken by eruptions of resort hotels, there were only Indians living in 1763. These were mostly the Seminole branch of the Creek nation; no white man had yet penetrated the Everglades.

Colonel James Grant, who had made two successful campaigns against the Cherokee in the last war, became the first British governor of East Florida. He had to obtain both officials and settlers from Charleston. The Spaniards, before their departure, had cashed in on land claims earlier purchased from the Indians, by selling most of them to a shady pair of land speculators, a Gordon of Charleston and a Fish of New York, who claimed 10 million acres but sold out to the crown for £15,000. Other speculators obtained land grants on condition of settling a certain number of white Protestants. Little came of these efforts, because hardly anybody then wished to live in Florida. One Robert Turnbull recruited 1500 settlers from Minorca, Greece, and Italy, and established them at New Smyrna to grow indigo; their descendants there are still called Minorcans. In addition to these, the census of 1771 showed only 288 whites and 900 blacks in all East Florida.

To travel in the 1760's from St. Augustine to Savannah or Charleston, one had to go by sea or Indian trail. Georgia had passed her heroic period; no longer did General Oglethorpe drill kilted Highlanders to raid the dons; no more evangelists like Whitefield and Wesley promoted the Kingdom of God on the Altamaha. A population of about 10,000, including a good proportion of black slaves, was engaged in planting indigo and rice.

South Carolina had passed the 100,000 mark and become very prosperous. The powerful Cherokee nation under their leader Attakullakulla or Little Carpenter, went on the warpath in 1759 but were badly beaten and forced to cede land which opened the back country to settlement. Charleston had become a gay little city with a goodly number of merchants and professional men, and a permanent theater. The wealthier Charlestonians sent their sons to England to be educated; but when it came to a showdown in 1775, your South Carolinian fresh from Christ Church or the Inns of Court became as flaming a patriot as any alumnus of Princeton, Yale, or William and Mary.

Josiah Quincy of Boston, who traveled through the Carolinas in 1773, wrote of the contrast between them: "The number of Negroes and slaves is much less in North than in South Carolina. Husbandmen and agriculture increase in number and improvement. Industry is up in the woods, at tar, pitch, and turpentine; in the fields, ploughing, planting, clearing, or fencing the land. Herds and flocks become numerous. Healthful countenances and numerous families become more common as you advance north." Many migrants from New England and the Middle colonies moved in during the expansion since 1740 and prospered at the expense of the poor "tar-heels." The back country in both Carolinas was seething with discontent, which broke out into rebellion in 1769.

In Virginia, in general, there was no middle class. If a white, you were either a First Family (F.F.V.) or a rough frontiersman. The gentry were openhanded, liberal, and hospitable; proud of their English blood. Andrew Burnaby, a clergyman who traveled through the province in 1759, observed:

They are haughty and jealous of their liberties, impatient of restraint, and can scarcely bear the thought of being controuled by any superior power. The women are, generally speaking, handsome, though not to be compared with our fair countrywomen in England. They have but few advantages, and consequently are seldom accomplished; this makes them reserved, and unequal to any interesting or refined conversation. They are immoderately fond of dancing, and indeed it is almost the only amusement they partake of.

An important accomplishment that Burnaby missed was the sound education in the ancient classics and political theory that young men obtained at the College of William and Mary. Running a plantation, serving on the council or in the house of burgesses, and reading Cicero, Polybius, and Locke gave Virginians excellent training in statesmanship.

Although progressive Virginia planters like Washington were substituting wheat for tobacco, prosperity in the Old Dominion was still largely based on tobacco. Owing to new lands being brought under cultivation in the piedmont, which could not be reached by ship, there grew up a new profession of tobacco "factors" or brokers. These, for some unexplained reason, were usually Scots connected with tobacco-processing firms in Glasgow. In 1774, for instance, William Cunningham & Co. operated six ships on the Glasgow-Chesapeake route, and maintained twenty-one agencies or stores in Maryland and Virginia, where they sold consumer goods, purchased tobacco direct from the grower, and arranged to have it carted to tidewater—sometimes by attaching a pair of shafts to a hogshead and rolling it down by horsepower. These canny Caledonians, through hard work and efficient marketing, replaced the English merchants who had handled the American tobacco crop for a century past; and, like them, were accused of depressing the price of tobacco and marking up imports. In view of the native Virginian's contempt for trade, his lack of currency and his credit requirements, he needed the brokers more than they needed him; but the antagonism that this system engendered made almost every Scot in the tobacco colonies a loyalist in the Revolution.

The Church of England was established in every Southern colony, but in none did it enjoy great influence. A clerical career did not appeal to the local gentry, and the church afforded a poor living in comparison with planting. The Two-Penny Act, which first called forth Patrick Henry's eloquence, was an attempt of the assembly to commute ministers' salaries, which had been set at 17,000 pounds of tobacco annually, at twopence a pound, at a time when it was worth sixpence.

The economic situation in Maryland was similar to that of Virginia, except that it depended less on tobacco and more on wheat, and had a growing seaport, Baltimore. That city owed its early prosperity to having waterpower close to Chesapeake Bay, making it a natural point for the grinding of grain from Maryland and Pennsylvania into flour for export. Annapolis, the capital, with tasteful brick houses and churches, was one of the liveliest little towns in North America; George Washington used to go there for enjoyment.

As travelers journeyed north from Baltimore along a tolerable road for wheeled vehicles, they found the aspect of the country changing. In Delaware, fifteen or twenty miles from Philadelphia, farms became smaller, more frequent, and better cultivated, with flower gardens and fruit trees. An Englishman crossing the Schuylkill and entering Philadelphia felt at home; the capital of Pennsylvania, remarked Lord Adam Gordon with evident astonishment, was "a great and noble city," like a large town in England, with an added Quaker primness and regularity. Some of the neatly laid out streets were paved, lined with sidewalks, lighted by whale-oil lamps, and policed at night. Philadelphia, with 18,766 people according to the census of 1760, was the largest and most prosperous town in English America. In another ten years it increased by another 10,000 and acquired some fine public buildings, including Carpenters' Hall and the State House, which would be the scene of great events in 1774–81. Philadelphia already had three semi-public libraries, a college, three newspapers (one in German), the only hospital in North America, and Benjamin Franklin. It was the only place in the English colonies outside Maryland which had a Catholic church. But the "brotherly love" principle of her founder had not worked too well. There were tensions between the English Quakers, who had the highest social standing, the German farmers, whom they regarded as uneducated boors, and the tough Scots-Irish, who had settled the frontier and back country. The province was run by an oligarchy of Philadelphia lawyers and merchants, many of them Quakers who were kept in power by a weighted system of apportionment and a property qualification for voting which excluded most of the artisans.

Proceeding north, our traveler of 1763 would cross the Delaware by ferry to Trenton and drive across New Jersey, probably spending a night at the pretty village of Princeton, where he could admire Nassau Hall, largest building in the English colonies. He crossed the Hudson by ferry from Perth Amboy to New York City. There he would find a compactly built little town, third in population in the English colonies, still bearing marks of its Dutch origin. The little city was cosmopolitan, as always, and exhibited vast differences in wealth. Not far from the stately merchants' mansions facing Bowling Green or the river were evil slums where day laborers, dockhands, and free blacks lived. There were already enough Irish in New York to celebrate St. Patrick's Day, enough Jews to maintain a synagogue, enough Scots to support a Presbyterian church, and enough Germans to maintain four churches with services in their language. Trinity and St. Paul's, the two Anglican churches, worshipped according to the Book of Common Prayer, praying daily for "George, our most gracious King and Governour."

In this royal province the franchise was so restricted by a high property qualification that not half the white men could vote, and the landed gentry controlled elections. Up-river the Livingston and Van Rensselaer manors comprised almost a million acres; the Philipse family had two manors which amounted to little less; six manors covered over half of Westchester County; 200 square miles on Long Island belonged to four families; hundreds of acres on Manhattan were owned by the Stuyvesants, Bayards, De Lanceys, and De Peysters. Instead of political parties there were rival factions whose origins can be traced to Leisler's Rebellion: the Livingston or Presbyterian, and the De Lancey or Anglican. The former, more adaptable to rising tides, produced several leaders of the pre-Revolutionary period such as John Morin Scott and William Livingston the "signer." Later, under the leadership of Aaron Burr, it merged with the Jeffersonian party.

New England was racially homogeneous, with few blacks, Irish, Scots, or Germans; and some 90 per cent belonged to Congregational churches. New England was also relatively democratic; almost every adult male had the vote, and inequalities of wealth were evident only in the seaports. Boston, with 17,000 inhabitants, was the largest town but no metropolis. There were a dozen prosperous coastal towns, each with some maritime specialty, and offshore Nantucket had already embarked in deep-sea whaling. Portland (then called Falmouth) exported lumber; Portsmouth built ships and exported white pine masts and spars to Britain; Gloucestermen fished on the Grand Bank and carried dried fish to Surinam; Salem and Marblehead ships traded with the West Indies and the Mediterranean; Newport, New London, and New Haven were deeply involved in the West Indies trade. Few rivers in New England were navigable, and the roads were few and bad. Hence the principal land transportation took place during the winter when snow lay on the ground. Farmers would then load their butter, salt provisions, wooden ware, and maple sugar on a "pung," an ox-drawn sledge, and drive it to the nearest seaport, where they exchanged these products for rum and groceries.

Social life in the country revolved around each Congrega-

tional church, and town government gave everyone a chance
to participate. Serving as selectman, or as representative in the
assembly, afforded a political training which enabled the
Yankees to concert resistance against the new imperial policy;
and, more important, to govern themselves during an upheaval.

Every seaport contained comfortable brick and wooden
houses built in the Georgian style, with excellent interior dec-
oration and well-kept gardens. The ship-owning merchants
who owned most of them shared top status with the clergy and
with a few lawyers and physicians. New England as yet had
no landed aristocracy, no leisurely country life, no shooting
and hunting in the English sense; but plenty of fishing for
sport in the rivers and for profit in the sea. The wealthiest
man in New England before the Revolution was Thomas
Boylston, a Boston merchant whose property in land, houses,
and ships was estimated at £80,000. But every seaport had a
rough working class of sailors, fishermen, and shipbuilders,
such as the caulkers who invented the political caucus. These
were easily welded by agitators into mobs, as many crown
officials and wealthy gentlemen were to learn unpleasantly,
and were always ready to "run in" a cargo without paying
duty.

Smuggling is a delicate subject. British writers on the American Revolution like to argue that it occurred because government tried to stop smuggling. It is true that the Yankees
smuggled, Yorkers and Jerseymen smuggled, Philadelphians
smuggled, and Southerners smuggled; but so did the English
smuggle, and in a big way, respectably organized. The latest
English historian of smuggling, Neville Williams, calls the
period 1713–76, "The Heyday of Illicit Trade," when smuggled tea became his nation's favorite beverage.

Apart from smuggling, however, the New England people
were law-abiding, even on the frontier. A large part of the
interior of New England was still wilderness; and much of
the rest, settled in the last twenty years, was still in the log-
cabin stage of development. But in parts that had been settled
for forty years or more, one found the village green, the spired
meetinghouse, and the white-painted dwelling built around
huge brick chimneys, that still impart charm to rural New
England. The necessities of life were plentiful and families
were large, but Puritanism had preserved a certain simplicity
and economy in social intercourse.

Although Benjamin Franklin was easily the first man of
science in the colonies—his electrical experiments printed in
1751 were hailed by the intelligentsia of Europe—the New

England colleges were centers of scientific activity. Professor John Winthrop not only taught physics, chemistry, and astronomy at Harvard, but led an expedition to observe a transit of Venus at Newfoundland in 1761. The Reverend Thomas Clap, President of Yale College, invented a new plow, maintained temperature charts, experimented with raising silk in Connecticut, promoted a spa at Stafford Springs, and observed sun spots, eclipses, and transits of Mercury with the college telescope. Throughout the country hundreds of men, many of them clergymen, were investigating natural phenomena and trying to relate them to the fundamental truths of Christianity; for science had not become so intricate as to discourage those who wished to know a little of everything.

2. The Imperial System in 1763

The loose-jointed system by which England endeavored to administer her colonies had not changed in 1763, owing to the failure of the Albany Plan of Union. Although no general opposition to this easy-going imperialism had yet been voiced by the colonies, there were several things about it that made them restless. They objected to the governor's instructions from the crown being considered mandatory. If the governor was energetic and conscientious, these instructions involved him in a row with the assembly, which naturally did not think it compatible with the liberty of British subjects that they should inflexibly obey directions from England. Nor did they like the admiralty courts, which gave verdicts without a local jury. But they particularly disliked the tenure of judges.

Tenure during good behavior (which we have for all federal judges today) had been secured in England by the Glorious Revolution of 1688; but in the colonies tenure "during the king's pleasure" prevailed. Easy-going royal governors had fallen into the practice of making judicial appointments during good behavior, to please the assemblies. The Board of Trade issued stringent instructions to stop this, and the death in 1760 of George II, voiding all royal commissions, brought on a crisis. The judges in New York and New Jersey refused to accept new commissions from George III except for tenure during good behavior. Lieutenant Governor Colden vetoed a bill of the New York assembly granting salaries to judges only on the condition of their holding office with this tenure. The Board of Trade then played a joke on New York. It obtained a royal warrant ordering the governor to appoint Benjamin Prat of Boston chief justice of the province during the king's pleasure. Colden complied; the assembly countered by voting no salary to the new chief justice. The board then ordered the governor to pay his salary out of permanent revenues. In the meantime, the other New York judges, outraged by the appointment of an imported Yankee, refused to receive new commissions from George III for king's pleasure tenure. The upshot was that poor Prat, performing the entire business of the supreme court without salary, overburdened with work and anxiety, died. The governor then found other men willing to accept judicial commissions during the king's pleasure, and the assembly gave in and paid their salaries.

In one colony after another, except North Carolina, which preferred to go without courts for several years rather than submit, the crown won this controversy, and in so doing caused a resentment which is expressed in the Declaration of Independence.[1] Americans could not understand why independent tenure of judges, a concession long since won by Englishmen, should not be extended to them. They could not grasp the English point of view that judges needed protection from the caprice and parsimony of colonial assemblies. The framers of the Federal Constitution saw both points, and provided against them.[2]

Thomas Secker, Archbishop of Canterbury, stirred up a new hornet's nest in 1763 by issuing a statement in favor of appointing colonial bishops. Presbyterian and Congregational ministers replied with hot pamphlets and passionate sermons; Anglican ministers gave as good as they got. Radical political leaders, especially Samuel Adams, made the most of the Archbishop's proposal as another instance of intended tyranny and the issue helped him to align most of the colonial clergy with the Whigs. The Reverend Jonathan Boucher, rector of St. Anne's, Annapolis, who returned to England in 1775 rather than submit to the Sons of Liberty, wrote that this controversy was the real background of the American Revolution, keeping "the public mind in a state of ferment and effervescence," and habituating the people to opposition. It certainly helped to create that "revolution in the hearts of the people" which John Adams declared to have been the real American revolution.

Although Americans found the imperial system occasionally irritating, they were not ready to do anything about it in 1763.

[1] "He has made judges dependent on his will alone, for the tenure of their offices, and the amount and payment of their salaries."
[2] Article III, Section I: "The Judges, both of the Supreme and inferior courts, shall hold their offices during good behaviour, and shall, at stated times, receive for their services, a compensation which shall not be diminished during their continuance in office."

They simply had the normal state of dissatisfaction that every free man of spirit should have with government, whatever its form. During the next twelve years of controversy, before the war started, American patriot leaders constantly referred to the situation before 1763 as the ultimate goal of their desires. John Adams even declared that at any time during the war he would have given everything he possessed to restore the old colonial system. That, however, was but a nostalgic dream. Long wars always change conditions so fundamentally that neither victor nor vanquished can ever re-create "the good old days." Never, never will they return, any more than an old man's lost youth.

In modern times we are used to war heroes and statesmen continuing in power during many subsequent years of peace. The Civil War generation governed the United States until 1901; the World War II generation governed Britain, France, the United States, and Canada for sixteen years or more. But immediately after the Peace of Paris, a new set of leaders, mostly in their twenties or early thirties, emerged in the Thirteen Colonies. Usually it was a local issue involving a constitutional question that brought them forward. Here are a few examples:—Christopher Gadsden successfully resisted an attempt of the royal governor of South Carolina in 1762 to void elections to the assembly of people he disliked. Patrick Henry and Thomas Jefferson came to the front on the Two-Penny Act and circular letter issues; Thomas McKean became embroiled with the governor of Pennsylvania; John Morin Scott led opposition to the Quartering Act; James Otis and the Adamses came forward on the Writs of Assistance and Revenue Act in Massachusetts. When old Governor Shirley, retired in England, was asked about the young troublemakers in Massachusetts, he burst out: "Mr. Cushing I knew, and Mr. Hancock I knew; but where the devil this brace of Adamses came from, I know not."

The world would soon know.

There was no American nationalism or separatist feeling in the colonies prior to 1775. Americans did not start off in 1763 like Ireland in 1798 or 1916, or Indonesia, India, and Pakistan in 1945, or the African colonies even more recently, with the conviction that they were entitled to be a separate and independent nation. They never felt, like Poland in her long, unhappy years, or Moslem dependencies in the 1950's, that they were so downtrodden by tyrannical masters as to make independence the only solution. On the contrary, Americans were not only content but proud to be part of the British imperium. But they did feel very strongly that they were entitled to all constitutional rights that Englishmen possessed in England. It took the radical leaders ten years after the Stamp Act to reach the position that Parliament had no rightful jurisdiction over the colonies, and even in the Declaration of Independence there was no complaint against the Acts of Trade and Navigation.

Thus there was nothing foreordained about the American Revolution; and historians who argue that the Revolution was inevitable can only make out a case by insisting that the Thirteen Colonies were becoming too big and self-conscious to continue as colonies. Yet Canada, which in 1960 had sevenfold the population of the Thirteen Colonies in 1776, and Australia, with four times their population, have managed to stay within the British Commonwealth; the "inevitable" argument would have made them independent long ago.[3] Nevertheless, one reason that they have remained loyal to the crown is that England, learning her lesson in time, relaxed imperial control; the American Revolution came about because she tried to tighten it.

Many interventions of the English government in colonial administration had been to protect minority groups against majorities, or small colonies against big ones; for instance, Quakers and Anglicans in New England against the dominant Puritans; Delaware against Maryland, New Hampshire and Rhode Island against Massachusetts Bay, which wanted to gobble them up; humble Georgia against proud South Carolina. The British government in the eighteenth century had a good record for religious and racial toleration. At a time when France, the German states, and even Switzerland were persecuting various Protestant sects, England welcomed foreign refugees and assisted their emigration to Pennsylvania and other colonies. Once in America they could be naturalized and enjoy all rights and privileges of British subjects, yet retain their own language, religion, and folkways, as many Pennsylvania Germans do to this day. No independence program would have got very far in the colonies before 1770, because these minority groups looked to the English government for protection. The frontiersmen in Pennsylvania and Virginia owed their safe deliverance from massacre in Pontiac's Rebellion to the British army under Colonel Bouquet, not to the militia of those colonies. American merchants and shipowners looked to the Royal Navy for protection from pirates and enemies on the high seas.

Outside the political sphere, Americans had many reasons

[3] Thirteen Colonies in 1776, 2.5 million; Australia in 1960, 10.2 million; Canada in 1960, 17.6 million.

to be grateful to Britain for contributions to their schools and churches. When Eleazar Wheelock wished to found a college in New Hampshire to educate Indians and New Hampshire frontiersmen, he knew that it would be no use to start an endowment drive in the American seaports. Instead, he dressed up a converted Indian as a parson and sent him to England to plead from the pulpit for money—and did it roll in!

When we boil down our colonial history, it is evident that by 1763 there had been worked out a compromise between imperial control and colonial self-government; between the principle of authority and the principle of liberty. King and Parliament had undisputed control of foreign affairs, war and peace, and overseas trade. Parliament canalized colonial trade into channels that it deemed profitable to all. In almost every other respect, Americans had acquired home rule. Their assemblies had secured the exclusive right to tax their constituents, to appoint officials such as colonial treasurers and fix their salaries; to commission military officers and raise troops or not as they chose; to control their own schools, churches, and land systems. They had acquired far more autonomy than Ireland then enjoyed, and infinitely more than the colonies of France, Spain, or any other country ever had before the next century. And they confidently expected to acquire more control over their destinies as they increased in population and wealth.

So, apart from minor discontents over judges and currency, Americans were satisfied with this compromise in 1763. But the government of George III was not. It had devised no method of exacting a uniform contribution from the colonies for defense. In the last war, flank colonies like New England and South Carolina, directly menaced by the French and Spaniards, had made even more effort than England expected, but the Middle colonies did far less, and Pennsylvania the least, owing to Quaker pacifism. Moreover, England had piled up a war debt, which for the eighteenth century seemed tremendous, and which had been partly incurred in conquering French Canada and Spanish Florida. It seemed reasonable that Americans who benefited from these conquests should take part of the debt off the British taxpayer's back. Hence the Revenue Act of 1764 and the Stamp Act of 1765. There were still leaks in the enforcement of the Acts of Trade and Navigation, owing largely to the fact that royal customs officials in the colonies were so few in number, and so underpaid, that they could only make both ends meet by accepting presents from smugglers.

Thus the situation between England and her American

colonies, while it had points of friction, was far from explosive. "The Abilities of a Child might have governed this Country," wrote Oliver Wolcott of Connecticut in 1776, "So strong had been their Attachment to Britain." But the Americans were a high-spirited people who claimed all the rights for which Englishmen had fought since Magna Carta, and would settle for nothing less. They were not security-minded but liberty-minded. That is why they met the attempts of the government of George III to impair these liberties, first with loyal expostulation, next with indignant agitation, finally with armed resistance.

Make no mistake; the American Revolution was not fought to *obtain* freedom, but to *preserve* the liberties that Americans already had as colonials. Independence was no conscious goal, secretly nurtured in cellar or jungle by bearded conspirators, but a reluctant last resort, to preserve "life, liberty and the pursuit of happiness."

3. *Reform and Resistance*

Successive ministries of George III tried to meet three problems at the same time: to settle what we may call the Western question (Indians, fur traders, and land speculators); to plug holes in the Acts of Trade and Navigation; and to raise money from America for defense.

The British government approached these problems piecemeal, and usually too late. Governor Bernard of Massachusetts, in a series of letters addressed to leading English politicians, pointed out that to reform the Empire, England should reform colonial governments first, strengthen her royal governors and judges by paying their salaries, confer titles of nobility on leading Americans, and admit colonial representatives to the House of Commons. The Roman Empire was held together by such methods. All were citizens of "no mean city," as St. Paul remarked on a famous occasion; Gauls, Spaniards, Jews, Greeks, and Africans became senators; Emperors Trajan and Hadrian were sons of Spaniards. But the classically educated English politicians failed to profit by this example. Baronetcies for Pepperell and Johnson were the highest honors conferred on any American, and no colonial was ever given even a minor post in the British government. English-speaking politicians always prefer piecemeal reforms to comprehensive plans. Usually that works out all right, but sometimes events catch up with and overwhelm the politicians.

The law enforcement problem was the first to be tackled.

William Pitt in 1760 ordered the Sugar Act of 1733 to be strictly enforced. That law put a prohibitive duty on molasses entering English colonies from the foreign West Indies. Since the Americans depended upon molasses from French and Spanish islands to feed their rum distilleries, the Sugar Act had been consistently evaded, usually by purchasing in Jamaica a false declaration that the molasses had been produced there. In order to enforce this unpopular law, the royal customs collectors at Boston applied to the superior court of the colony for writs of assistance. These were general warrants allowing an officer to enter any premises at any time in search of smuggled goods. As such, they were contrary to the traditional rights of Englishmen. A Boston lawyer named James Otis threw up his job as king's advocate general to argue against the issue of the writs in 1761. To young John Adams in the audience, "Otis was a flame of fire . . . the seeds of patriots and heroes were then and there sown." Otis made the significant argument, "An act against the Constitution is void; an act against natural equity is void." This invoking of a fundamental, "natural" law, "the unchangeable, unwritten code of Heaven" (as Sophocles puts it in *Antigone*), became more frequent during the next forty years. As expressed in our bills of rights, it has become basic doctrine in American law. And five years later, the British attorney general upheld Otis on the local issue.

The next problem to puzzle the ministers of George III was that of the West. Pontiac's Rebellion proved that it was not sufficient to conquer territory; something must be done to placate the Indians and defend the white frontier. Consequently, in October 1763, the king issued an important proclamation. Until further notice no colonial government could grant, and no white man take, land beyond the sources of rivers that flow into the Atlantic. This proclamation was probably intended to be temporary; but certain ministers regarded it as the cornerstone of a new policy, to discourage westward migration but encourage the peopling of Canada, Nova Scotia, and the Floridas. For in these flank colonies, as a cabinet minister declared, pioneers "would be useful to their Mother Country instead of planting themselves in the Heart of America, out of reach of Government, where from the great difficulty of procuring European commodities they would be compelled to commerce and manufacture, to the infinite prejudice of Britain." Lord Shelburne, the most intelligent of the ministers of George III in dealing with American affairs, was of another opinion; he wanted westward expansion as a safety valve; but the contrary idea became official policy.

In 1762 the ministers made another important decision, to leave a permanent garrison of 10,000 men in the continental colonies. It has often been asserted, but never proved, that this was done to create jobs for British army officers who otherwise would have been retired on half pay. General Amherst, the commander in chief in America, asked for only 6625 troops to keep the French and Indians in check; and he should have known what was necessary. When the troops arrived, most of them were garrisoned at places like Halifax and New York rather than at Pittsburgh, Detroit, and the Carolina frontier, which gave color to the charge, although the real reason was the increased expense of supplying a garrison beyond reach of water transport.

Another frontier blow-up showed that seaport garrisons were necessary to preserve order. A band of frontier hoodlums from around Paxton, Pennsylvania, furious over lack of protection during Pontiac's Rebellion by the Quaker-dominated assembly, took cowardly revenge by massacring peaceful survivors of the Conestoga tribe in Lancaster County. The "Paxton Boys" then made such dire threats against another remnant, the so-called Moravian Indians near Bethlehem, that these fled to Philadelphia. There the government quartered them in barracks and protected them by British regulars. The "Boys," 1500 strong, heavily armed and uttering "hideous outcries in imitation of the war whoop," marched on the capital in February 1764, bent on killing every redskin refugee. Philadelphia was in a panic, and it took Ben Franklin to talk the ruffians into going home, by promising more frontier protection and legislative bounties for Indians' scalps.

The first attempt of the government of George III to raise money toward defense and stop leaks in the Acts of Trade and Navigation was the Revenue Act of 1764. Its preamble stated frankly the purpose: "That a revenue be raised in Your Majesty's dominions in America for defraying the expenses of defending, protecting and securing the same." The law lowered the duty on foreign molasses from the uncollectable 6d per gallon, but levied additional duties on foreign sugar and on English or European luxuries such as wine, silk, and linen, when imported into the American colonies. It "enumerated" more colonial products such as hides and skins, which could be exported only to England, and withdrew some earlier exemptions that the colonies had enjoyed, such as free importation of Madeira wine. That favorite beverage of well-to-do Americans now became subject to a customs duty of £7 per double hogshead, as against 10s on port wine imported through England—an obvious attempt to change the drinking habits of the colonial aristocrats to profit the British exchequer.

Colonial leaders promptly seized on the declared revenue-raising purpose of this act as a constitutional point. As the New York assembly observed in a respectful petition to Parliament on 18 October, "Exemption from burthen of ungranted, involuntary taxes, must be the grand principle of every free state," without which "there can be no liberty, no happiness, no security." If Parliament got away with taxing their trade, it might proceed to tax their lands, or everything else. This seemed prophetic when Parliament on 22 March 1765 passed the famous Stamp Act.

In the meantime, a movement had begun to boycott the products taxed by the Revenue Act. This seems to have started at New Haven, as the New York *Gazette* smugly announced on 22 November 1764: "The young Gentlemen of Yale College have unanimously agreed not to make use of any foreign spirituous Liquors. . . . The Gentlemen of the College cannot be too much commended for setting so laudable an Example. This will not only greatly diminish the Expences of Education, but prove, as may be presumed, very favourable to the Health and Improvement of the Students. At the same Time all Gentlemen of Taste, who visit the College, will think themselves better entertained with a good Glass of Beer or Cider, offered them upon such Principles, than they could be, with the best Punch or Madeira." New England rum, however, did not come under the boycott.

Parliament's Stamp Act of 1765 was the first direct, internal tax ever to be laid on the colonies by Parliament; indeed, the first tax of any sort other than customs duties. It was a heavy tax, bearing on all classes and sections in America, the more so because the specified sums had to be paid in sterling. This meant that, in terms of colonial currencies, the tax was increased between 33 and 100 per cent. Almost every kind of legal paper, plea, demurrer, etc. would have to pay 3*s*, and an appeal or writ of error, 10*s*; every school or college degree diploma or donation to a school or college, £2; liquor licenses, £1 to £4 on top of the local licensing fee; a lawyer's license to practice, £10; land warrant or deed, from 6*d* to 5*s*; an appointment to office, £4. Every copy (not merely every issue) of a newspaper must pay ½*d* a sheet, and each advertisement in the same, 2*s* for each issue; and every copy of an almanac, 4*d*. Playing cards were charged a shilling a pack, and dice 10*s* a pair. All legal documents written in any other language than English must pay double duty, except in Quebec and Granada.

All offenses against the Stamp Act were to be tried in an admiralty court, where the defendant would have no benefit of trial by jury. The Act also had a high nuisance value; every sheet or document subject to the duty had to be engrossed or printed on specially stamped paper sold by the official distributors, or brought to a stamp office to be embossed with the stamp, and the duty paid. One can imagine the inconvenience and trouble this would have given the publishers of newspapers and almanacs.

That age, as Horace Walpole remarked, was one of revolt. Ireland had her "Whiteboy" riots against forced labor and absentee landlords. In London, in May 1765, there took place the Bloomsbury riots against the unpopular Duke of Bedford. While the Duke was at dinner, a mob hurled stones through his windows and would have pulled down the house and roughed him up, had they not been driven off by the Horse Guards. Jack Wilkes, arrested on a general warrant for alleged indecency, became the hero of the London mob and of the Sons of Liberty in the colonies, where town and counties were named after him. In Corsica, Pasquale Paoli unsuccessfully led a rebellion against the French and got his name, too, on the map of Pennsylvania. In Madrid there broke out *el motín de Esquilache,* a riot against the king's Neapolitan minister. Said Horace Walpole, "When the Spanish diadem totters, what royal head must not ache?"

The English colonies, chief contributors to the royal British headache, found the Stamp Act an easy mark, administered as it was by crown-appointed distributors of embossed paper which could be destroyed. Despite the few means of communication between the different colonies, their action against the Stamp Act was remarkably uniform from Halifax to Jamaica. In every continental seaport there was formed a group of middle-class citizens who called themselves "Sons of Liberty," a phrase first applied to the Americans by Isaac Barré in a speech against the Act in the House of Commons. These liberty boys, often disguising themselves as workmen or sailors, coerced distributors into resigning, burned the stamped paper, and incited people to attack unpopular local characters. On the very day (1 November 1765) that the Stamp Act came into operation, a howling New York mob led by a shipmaster, Isaac Sears, forced Lieutenant Governor Colden to take refuge on board a British warship. It then attacked the fort at the Battery, broke into the governor's coach house, destroyed his carriages, and forced the officer in charge of the stamped paper to burn it. The rabble then marched up Broadway to a country estate on the Hudson (between the present Chambers and

Warren streets), then occupied by an officer of the garrison, who had threatened "to cram the Stamp Act down the people's throats." They gutted his house, destroyed furniture, books and china, drank up the liquor, uprooted the garden, and departed carrying the regimental colors as a trophy.

In Charleston Henry Laurens, wrongly suspected by the local mob of hiding stamped paper in his house, was pulled out of bed at midnight while the house was searched by his friends, whom he recognized under blackface and sailor disguise. In Boston the stamp distributor was hanged in effigy and his shop pulled down, after which the mob turned its attention to the royal customs collectors and Chief Justice Hutchinson. It gutted their houses, burned their furniture, and tossed their books and papers into the street. The voters, in town meeting next day, expressed their "utter detestation" of this "horrid scene," but nobody compensated the victims.

Newport, Rhode Island, provided a touch of humor. There the Sons of Liberty hired an unemployed sailor named John Weber to organize a mob and terrify the local customs officials and stamp distributors. When the liberty boys tried to pay Weber off, he decided that he liked the work too much to quit, and threatened to pull down the houses of the very "patriots" who had employed him. They were rescued from this fate by the attorney general, who had Weber cast into jail and whisked out of the colony.

Except for this instance, the Sons of Liberty kept the mobs well in hand, and no blood was shed anywhere. But the Stamp Act was completely nullified. After a couple of months the courts reopened, vessels cleared and entered, and business resumed without the use of stamps. It was an amazing exhibition of what a closely knit revolutionary organization could do, anticipating the Jacobins of the French Revolution and the Bolsheviks of the Russian.

An assumption that the law was unconstitutional and void justified this violence to respectable colonists. On 30 May 1765 Patrick Henry made his famous "Caesar had his Brutus, Charles I his Cromwell" speech, after which the Virginia assembly passed a set of resolves declaring that it had "the only and sole exclusive right and power to lay taxes . . . upon the inhabitants of this Colony," who were "not bound to yield obedience to any law" of Parliament attempting to tax them. These Virginia Resolves were "an alarum bell to the disaffected" everywhere, as Governor Bernard wrote. Massachusetts summoned her sister colonies to send delegates to a congress in New York City. Nine colonies responded. This Stamp Act Congress was the first spontaneous movement toward colonial union that came from Americans themselves; and it brought together for the first time men from widely distant colonies, such as James Otis of Massachusetts, Philip Livingston of New York, John Dickinson of Philadelphia, Daniel Dulany of Maryland, and Christopher Gadsden of South Carolina. They discovered that they saw eye to eye on the need for concerted resistance against encroachments on colonial rights. And, in October 1765, they passed a set of resolutions less violent in tone than Patrick Henry's, asking Parliament to repeal the act forthwith.

Hitherto there had been loose talk on the American side of having colonial representatives in the House of Commons. The Stamp Act Congress rejected the idea as impractical because of the distance; and also, no doubt, because it realized that a handful of colonial members could not check a British majority. The idea was now shelved in favor of asserting the colonial assemblies' exclusive right to tax themselves; and the wisdom of this shift was later proved by the sad experience of Ireland under the 1800 Act of Union.

In August 1765, the Grenville ministry fell, largely because George III grew weary of hearing lectures on duty from his conscientious prime minister. An Old Whig ministry led by the thirty-five-year-old Marquess of Rockingham now came into power. Parliament, at Rockingham's instance, after a hot debate but with the king's support, repealed the Stamp Act in March 1766. It did so because the Commons were convinced that the Act could not be enforced, even by military force, against such firm and united opposition as the colonies had shown. At the same time, Parliament reaffirmed its right to tax America in the Declaratory Act, declaring that as the sovereign legislature of the British Empire it could "bind the colonies . . . in all cases whatsoever." This was an almost word-for-word copy of the Irish Declaratory Act of 1719 which held Ireland in bondage.

News of the repeal, which began to trickle into the colonies in May 1766, aroused an ecstasy of loyalty; the more so because William Pitt had moved it. In New York City repeal and the king's birthday were celebrated simultaneously; every window was illuminated, oxen were barbecued, and free beer and grog were provided for a happy crowd. The assembly voted an equestrian statue of George III and a statue of William Pitt to be erected at the Battery. Tablets or busts of "the Great Commoner" were set up at Williamsburg, even in country villages like Dedham, Massachusetts. In Boston, after the news arrived, "The Morning was ushered in with the ringing of Bells, and the Discharge of Cannon, Liberty-Tree was decorated with Flags & Streamers, and all round the Town, on the Tops of Houses, were displayed Colours and Pendants."

The Americans had won a political victory. United opposition (and not for fifty years would they be so united again) had forced the repeal. Their fundamental loyalty is proved by their neither taking notice of the Declaratory Act, nor demanding repeal of the Revenue Act of 1764. In reality the British government had taken three steps forward—Proclamation of 1763, Revenue Act, Declaratory Act—but only one back.

XIII

Crisis, Calm, and Again Crisis

1766-1774

1. *The Townshend Acts*

DURING THE GENERAL JUBILATION that followed the repeal of the Stamp Act, no serious effort was made by the British government to find out what, if anything, could be done to raise defense funds through colonial assemblies. No royal commission was sent to America to study and report; agents of the several colonies in London were not even consulted. Instead, Parliament made a fresh attempt to tax the colonies, and placed in effect a plan of imperial reorganization without consulting them.

English politics at this period are difficult to grasp, because the Whig party, dominant through the greater part of the century, had splintered into factions—as later happened to the Jeffersonian Republicans in America after the War of 1812. The faction that cared most about American affairs was known as the "Old Whigs," not from their age but because they claimed to inherit the genuine Whig principles of the Glorious Revolution of 1688. The Marquess of Rockingham, the Earl of Dartmouth, the Duke of Richmond, General Conway, Edmund Burke, and Lord Camden the chief justice, were Old Whigs; their names, adopted by American towns and counties, testify American gratitude for their efforts. But no government in England was overthrown on an American question before 1781. Ministries rose and fell largely on personal or trivial questions. One or more leaders, disgruntled because too few of their friends were given jobs, voted against the administration, the ministry had to resign, and the king asked another leader to construct a new ministry that could command a majority in the House of Commons. That happened in August 1766. The Rockingham ministry resigned, and George III called upon William Pitt, whom he had created Earl of Chatham, to construct a new one. Americans hoped for great things from a ministry headed by Pitt and including other prominent friends of America such as Isaac Barré and Lord Shelburne. Unfortunately Chatham fell ill shortly after he became prime minister, and was succeeded by the thirty-one-year-old Duke of Grafton, an amiable peer who had no sense of leadership and allowed any member of his team to initiate bills.

To quote Edmund Burke, "While the western horizon was still in a blaze with Pitt's descending glory, on the opposite quarter of the heavens arose another luminary, and for his hour became lord of the ascendant." This was Charles Townshend, chancellor of the exchequer (corresponding to our secretary of the treasury)—"a statesman who has left nothing but errors to account for his fame." Under the influence of a bumper of champagne, Townshend delivered in the House of Commons on 8 May 1767 a speech which a spectator described as "extravagantly fine. It lasted an hour, with torrents of wit, ridicule, vanity, lies and beautiful language." He taunted the former premier, still angry over the repeal of his Stamp Act. Grenville retorted, "You are cowards, you are afraid of the Americans, you dare not tax America!" Townshend replied, "Fear! Cowards! Dare not tax America! *I* dare tax America!" Grenville retorted, "Dare you tax America? I wish to God I could see it!" Townshend declared, "I will, I will!" And he did.

The Townshend Act for taxing America, passed in June 1767, was based on an unfortunate distinction made by certain colonial pamphleteers, that external taxes (customs duties), which had always been laid on goods entering the colonies, were constitutional, whilst internal taxes like the Stamp Act were not. Taking these men at their word, Parliament levied duties on certain English manufactures entering America, such as paper, glass, and paint, and on the East India Company's tea. As a concession, British duties on colonial grain and whale oil entering England were removed, which led to the first substantial export of wheat and flour from the colonies to England. And bounties were voted on colonial hemp, flax, and timber.

Although the Townshend duties afforded colonial leaders their principal talking point, far more important in the long run was the administrative reorganization that Parliament adopted at Townshend's suggestion. A big loophole in the imperial trade system was the lax collection of customs duties in the colonies. Many customs officials remained in England and appointed deputies, for a part of their salaries, to do their work. These deputies were accustomed to eke out their scanty pay by accepting gifts from importers, for turning their backs while dutiable goods were run ashore. That system now came to an end. Absentee collectors lost their jobs, mostly to conscientious, hard-working Scots, and the service was reorganized. An American Board of Commissioners of Customs was set up, with headquarters at Boston, charged with the power to issue regulations, control the collection of duties in all continental colonies, and to use the hated writs of assistance. Admiralty courts were freshly empowered to try cases under the Acts of Trade and Navigation, without a jury. The double purpose of these regulations was to raise money from America not only for defense but to create a fund from which the salaries of royal governors and judges could be paid, to render them independent of the assemblies for their salaries.

These regulations were beneficial to the royal treasury. Even though the Townshend duties on English manufactures were repealed in 1770, and despite boycotts, non-importation agreements, and the Boston Tea Party, the Commissioners of Customs collected £257,000 in ten years. Of this sum £92,000 were absorbed by administrative costs, £32,000 spent on a colonial civil list, and £83,000 remitted to England. Charles Townshend did not live to see this unexpected success of his measures. He died suddenly in September 1767 and was succeeded as chancellor of the exchequer by Lord North, of the Whig faction known as the "King's Friends."

The Townshend Acts took Americans by surprise. Their trade was in the usual depression that is apt to set in four or five years after the end of a great war. It was hard for them to find the sterling money to pay these new taxes, and the regulations of the Commissioners of the Customs required so many bonds and documents that for a time it was difficult to do business at all. But colonial leaders were hard put to find a legal argument against the Townshend duties. They wished to deny Parliament's power to tax them, yet to acknowledge Parliament's power to regulate their commerce. They were not prepared to break loose from the protective system of the

Acts of Trade and Navigation, nor could they deny that many of the new regulations were designed to stop lawbreaking. The colonial leader who came closest to resolving this dilemma was John Dickinson of Pennsylvania, who styled himself "The Pennsylvania Farmer." He was a conservative Philadelphia lawyer, born in Maryland and educated in England, neither an agitator nor a politician, but a public-spirited citizen who abhorred violence and hoped to settle all pending disputes with England by persuasion.

The twelve "Farmer's Letters" which began coming out in colonial newspapers at the end of 1767 were exactly what Americans wanted, and the loyal, respectful tone of them appealed to the Old Whigs in England. Here are some of the key passages:

> The Parliament unquestionably possesses a legal authority to regulate the trade of Great Britain and all her colonies. . . . We are but parts of a whole; and therefore there must exist a power somewhere to preside, and preserve the connexion in due order. This power is lodged in the Parliament; and we are as much dependent on Great Britain as a perfectly free people can be on another. . . .
>
> The cause of Liberty is a cause of too much dignity to be sullied by turbulence and tumult. . . .
>
> Let us behave like dutiful children, who have received unmerited blows from a beloved parent. Let us complain to our parent; but let our complaints speak at the same time the language of affliction and veneration.

The first quotation shows that Dickinson was moving, somewhat fumbling, toward the principle of federalism which became implicit in the American Revolution and explicit in the Constitution of 1787. "We are as much dependent on Great Britain as a perfectly free people can be on another." In other words, Parliament as the supreme legislature of the Empire has certain distinct powers over the colonies; but they retain the residue, corresponding to state rights. Unfortunately no responsible Englishman of that day seemed able to grasp this federal principle. William Knox, an Irishman who had lived several years in Georgia as a crown officer, had fun with Dickinson in his reply: "It is this *new invention* of *collecting taxes* that makes them burdensome to the Colonies, and an infringement of their rights and privileges."

Samuel Adams of Boston, master of the town meeting and member of the assembly, had already reached the point in his thinking that Parliament had no right to legislate for the colonies on any subject. But he was too good a politician to admit it. A middle-class Bostonian, austere and implacable, Adams alone among leaders of the American Revolution was a genuine revolutionary, resembling in several respects the communist agitators of our time. He was certainly the Western world's first orchestra-leader of revolution. He knew that voters are moved by emotion rather than logic. A master of propaganda, he realized that the general run of people prefer drama and ritual to a well-argued exposition. New England people lacked ritual in religion and drama on a stage; but Adams provided them with both in highly agreeable forms. There was dancing around the Liberty Tree (a big elm near Boston Common), the hanging of unpopular characters in effigy from its branches, serenading those whom the radicals wished to become popular, and damning the British ministers over bowls of rum punch. Adams employed classic symbols of liberty such as the Phrygian liberty cap, a liberty song with new words by John Dickinson set to the rousing tune "Heart of Oak," which everyone knew, and on every possible occasion organized a protest meeting. These devices were copied by Sons of Liberty throughout the continent; even at Charleston, where Christopher Gadsden selected a live oak as liberty tree. John Adams, after a Sons of Liberty dinner of 350 covers, attended by delegates from Philadelphia, observed that these things "tinge the minds of the people; they impregnate them with the sentiments of liberty; they render the people fond of their leaders in the cause, and averse and bitter against all opponents."

Samuel Adams, well educated in the ancient classics, thought in terms of Roman virtue, and his favorite motto, chosen from the unlikely source of Ovid's *Remedia Amoris*, was *principiis obsta*, "Take a stand at the start," lest by one concession after another you end in complete subjection. He was no orator—he had a quavering voice and a shaky hand; so he let other Sons of Liberty like Joseph Warren and the firebrand Otis make the speeches, while he wrote provocative articles for the newspapers and pulled political strings.

In February 1768, after the full impact of the Townshend Acts began to be appreciated, Adams and Otis drafted and the Massachusetts assembly adopted a circular letter to the assemblies of all other continental colonies, to call their attention to the Acts. The assembly, stated this letter, has "preferred a humble, dutiful and loyal petition to our most gracious sovereign . . . to obtain redress." The new taxes are obviously unconstitutional, but they hope that "united and dutiful supplications" of "distressed American subjects" to George III "will meet with his royal and favorable acceptance."

Although the language of this circular letter was moderate and loyal, the Grafton ministry decided to make it the occasion for a showdown. Lord Hillsborough, the new secretary for the colonies, ordered the Massachusetts assembly to rescind the letter, and Governor Bernard to dismiss them if they refused. The assembly did refuse, by a vote of 92 to 17. Samuel Adams and Sons of Liberty everywhere seized on this incident as a golden opportunity for propaganda, making the most of the patriotic ninety-two who refused to rescind. Jack Wilkes in England was still fighting to retain the seat in the House of Commons to which he had been duly elected, and his slogan was "45," the number of his scurrilous newspaper which the government had suppressed. The Boston Sons of Liberty sent him two turtles, one weighing 45 pounds, the other 47 pounds, "making in the whole 92 pounds which is the Massachusetts patriotic number." Paul Revere, silversmith, made a silver punch bowl dedicated to the "Immortal 92" and engraved all over with "Wilkes and Liberty," "No. 45," "No General Warrants," and other slogans and symbols. The South Carolina assembly voted £1500 to pay Wilkes's debts.

In Boston the chief contributor to the Sons of Liberty war chest for printing, banners, and free rum at liberty tree rallies, was a thirty-one-year-old merchant named John Hancock. The new Commissioners of the Customs therefore determined to put him out of business. He was "framed" by a prosecution of his sloop *Liberty*, falsely charged with smuggling Madeira wine. The Boston mob rescued him and his vessel, and gave the royal customs officials a very rough time, in consequence of which they retired to the castle in Boston harbor, and Governor Bernard asked for and got protection. Two regiments of the Halifax garrison were sent to Boston. Halifax inhabitants, annoyed by the loss of the soldiers' payroll, began to think that they should do a little rioting too!

The Boston radicals now overplayed their hand. When the troops arrived from Halifax and Governor Bernard refused to recall the dismissed assembly, Boston town meeting invited the province to elect delegates to a convention. This was a revolutionary act, recalling what had taken place in 1688–89. Sam Adams even buttonholed Bostonians in the street, urging them in his quavering voice to take up arms "and be free and seize the king's officers." But such towns as did send delegates to the convention warned them to do nothing rash, nor did they; and the delegates, seeing the folly of trying to resist

British troops, passed some mild resolutions and dissolved the convention.

Although the Grafton ministry failed to intimidate Boston, it dealt successfully with New York, where two regiments of the British army arrived in 1766. The Quartering or Mutiny Act of Parliament required local authorities to provide quarters or barracks for the king's troops and furnish them free with certain supplies, including beer or rum. The New York assembly boggled at paying for these beverages, but voted all other supplies for 1100 men. Lord Hillsborough announced that this was not enough, and ordered the assembly to be suspended like that of Massachusetts. In the next election, in the fall of 1769, New York voters surprisingly returned a majority of the conservative De Lancey faction, and the new assembly voted everything that the British troops required. Sons of Liberty, led by Isaac Sears and Alexander McDougall, denounced this as a "contemptible betrayal," and Governor Colden threw McDougall into prison for sedition. Even after he was released, in January 1770, New York became the scene of a serious riot. British troops cut down a liberty pole put up by the radicals and piled up the pieces in front of Sons of Liberty headquarters. A fight followed on Golden Hill, the mob using clubs and staves against the soldiers' cutlasses and bayonets, and one citizen was killed. This affair is New York's claim for having shed the "first blood of the Revolution"; but that lonely "martyr" was soon eclipsed by those of the "Boston Massacre."

2. *The Western Problem*

Although a school of American historians, working back from a time when the West was radical and the East conservative, have tried to prove that the American Revolution, too, was a Western movement, the facts are completely contrary. The American Revolution was brought about by radical groups in the seaport towns, usually in alliance with local merchants, and with planters of the Southern tidewater. The Sons of Liberty were no effete Easterners forced into rebellion by angry frontiersmen dressed in buckskin shirts and coonskin caps; they were well-educated, middle-class people who used mobs to terrify their opponents and nullify British attempts to tax and reorganize the colonies. This Revolution was made in seaports from Portsmouth, New Hampshire, to Savannah, Georgia. Here were enough people to give orators an audience, to stimulate grievances, and to organize committees; and in some there was a British garrison to cause trouble and create bitterness. The New England countryside, suspicious of seaport agitators, came slowly into the movement. "Boston folks are full of notions," was their favorite saying. Up-river New York; frontier Pennsylvania, which hated the Quaker oligarchy; the "Old West" or "back country" from the valley of Virginia into the piedmont of the Carolinas, were slow to catch fire—and many of these people never did.

Parts of the back country were full of turmoil. Their grievances, however, were not against England but against the clique that ran things in the colonial capitals. The frontier had expanded so fast since 1730 that, with the best will in the world, the colonial assemblies could not keep up with it in matters of representation and setting up courts of justice. From New Hampshire to South Carolina there were complaints that the back country was under-represented or not represented at all; that settlers had to travel hundreds of miles to attend court, that the fees required for legal business were intolerable. The assemblies and councils did not want their state houses swamped by crude frontiersmen, judges did not care to ride circuit into the backwoods, and court officers "had to live." The fee table was a survival of the middle ages when the English kings were too poor to pay salaries to sheriffs and minor officials, who supported themselves by taking fees from anyone who required their labors. Today, although the system persists in American county government, fees are relatively moderate; but the litigant in 1765 had to pay anywhere from 5s to £5 "every time he turned round," which meant that a poor man forced to go to law to defend his rights was apt to lose his shirt.[1]

Back-country discontent in the 1760's was most pronounced in the Carolinas. There, owing to thousands of pioneers from Pennsylvania pouring from the great valley into the piedmont, there had grown up a society differing in origin, religion, even race, from the people of the seaboard, and separated from them physically by a belt of pine barrens. Almost half the total population of South Carolina, and four-fifths of the white population, lived in the back country of that province in 1776. Yet the provincial government was completely cen-

[1] The fee system is one of our less recognized abuses today. Alfred E. Smith in his *Story* admits that he raked in $103,000 in fees in two years, as a minor official in New York. A study by the Associated Press in 1951 brought out the fact that the treasurer of one Indiana county collected up to $40,000 in fees; that probate judges were making more than salaried justices of state supreme courts, and that many J.P.'s were collecting thousands annually in fees for simply witnessing legal papers. And the notoriously unfair apportionment of representatives in many states led to an important Supreme Court decision in 1964.

tralized at Charleston, with neither counties nor courts in the back country, much less schools or police; a man had to own 500 acres and 20 slaves to qualify for membership in the assembly. Back-country settlers were at the mercy of border ruffians, horse thieves, and Indian raiders; a band of Creeks murdered fourteen people in the frontier settlement at Long Canes on Christmas Eve 1763, and were only driven off because Patrick Calhoun, father of John C., took command of the survivors. The people wanted government, pure and simple, and formed associations known as "Regulators" to refuse payment of taxes until they got it. They were furious to hear that the Charleston Sons of Liberty had persuaded the South Carolina assembly to lavish thousands of pounds on a statue to William Pitt, a gift to Jack Wilkes, and Christopher Gadsden's expense account attending the Stamp Act Congress, while denying schools, churches, roads, bridges, or protection to their region. In 1769 the assembly did set up six new circuit courts, and revised the fee table. But most of the Westerners' grievances in this province were still unredressed when the War of Independence broke.

In North Carolina the separation between coastal region and back country was even sharper. Here the Western grievances were not lack of government, but bad government—unequal taxation, extortion by centrally appointed judges and corrupt sheriffs, greedy lawyers, uncertainty of land titles, scarcity of hard money to pay taxes, refusal of the assembly to provide paper money or to allow taxes to be paid in produce, consequent tax levies "by distress," and government taking over poor men's farms. These grievances are strikingly similar to those of the Shays rebels of 1786 in Massachusetts; and Herman Husband, leader of the North Carolina Regulators, turns up twenty-five years later as a Whisky rebel in Pennsylvania. The five Western counties were well represented in the North Carolina assembly of 1769, but Governor Tryon dissolved that body before it could do anything about local grievances. In the meantime, the superior court at Hillsboro had been broken up by Regulators and some of the unpopular lawyers, such as Edmund Fanning, were beaten up and their houses wrecked.

Grievances accumulated for two more years, until some 2000 Regulators confronted half their number of loyal militia, on the banks of the Alamance river. There followed, on 16 May 1771, the so-called Battle of the Alamance. Only nine men were killed on each side, since most of the unarmed Regulators ran away after the first volley. But fifteen prisoners were tried for treason, and six were hanged. Governor Tryon and the army then made a triumphal progress through Regulator country and exacted an oath of allegiance from every male inhabitant.

That was the end of the War of the Regulation, the most serious internal rebellion in the English colonies since Nat Bacon's. It was put down largely by Whigs who later became Patriots. The next assembly passed some remedial legislation such as fixing maximum fees and establishing tobacco warehouses whose receipts could be tendered for taxes. But the North Carolina back country was still so discontented in 1776 that many former rebels emigrated to Tennessee to avoid taking part in the war, and others became Tories.

Back-country brawls from New Hampshire to South Carolina seem never to have interested the British government, which thereby missed a golden opportunity to win support from tough frontiersmen against the silk-stockinged Sons of Liberty and their wharf-rat mobsters. But the British government was deeply concerned with another Western problem. How far were land speculators to be allowed to encroach on the Indians' country? Would George III countenance Western expansion, or turn the Royal Proclamation of 1763 into a permanent policy?

In 1768 the two Indian superintendents who had recently been appointed made three important treaties: the Treaty of Fort Stanwix with the Iroquois, the Treaty of Hard Labour (a frontier post in South Carolina) with the Cherokee, and the Treaty of Pensacola with the Creek nation. These treaties set up a new frontier line somewhat west of the Royal Proclamation Line of 1763, not superseded until after the Federal Constitution went into effect. This new line failed to satisfy the land speculators. In 1768 George Washington and Captain William Crawford, who had accompanied him on the expedition against Fort Duquesne ten years earlier, set about obtaining deeds from Pennsylvania to a large tract in the western part of that province. Although this lay west of the Proclamation Line of 1763, Washington wrote to Crawford, "I can never never look on that proclamation in any other light (but this I say between ourselves) than as a temporary expedient to quiet the minds of the Indians and must fall of course in a few years. . . . Any person therefore who neglects the present opportunity of hunting out good lands and in some measure marking . . . them for their own (in order to keep others from settling them) will never regain it." "The scheme," he added, must be "snugly carried on by you under the pretence of hunting other game."

That sort of thing was going on all along the frontier:—

bands of "hunters" roaming the hardwood forests, blazing trees and noting landmarks, then lobbying for a grant. Washington and Crawford were small operators in comparison with the big companies then being formed. The largest and most important was the Walpole or Vandalia Company promoted by Benjamin Franklin, George Croghan, and Thomas Wharton of Philadelphia, fur-trading merchants who believed that the peltry business was about played out. The Vandalia was organized on the basis of seventy-two shares, some of which were issued free to important English politicians like the Walpoles, Lord Camden, and George Grenville. Their original modest object of acquiring one and a quarter million acres in the Ohio valley, on Franklin's advice, was swollen to ten million acres, for which they proposed to pay the crown £10,000. They had plenty of influence in London and even succeeded in getting rid of Lord Hillsborough the colonial secretary, who opposed the scheme because he was afraid it would depopulate Ireland, where he owned great estates. Some of the other schemes then pressing for crown grants were "Charlotiana," embracing most of Illinois and Wisconsin, promoted by Franklin and Sir William Johnson; General Phineas Lyman's "Military Adventurers," who asked for Kentucky and half Tennessee; and Major Thomas Mant's scheme for settling veterans on a tract covering somewhat more than the present state of Michigan. The Board of Trade and Plantations wrecked these big schemes, on the ground that "the proposition of forming inland colonies in America" was new and contrary to British interests. Let the restless Americans fill up Nova Scotia and the Floridas, where they will consume British manufactures, rather than settle on the Western waters, where the natural outlet for their products will be the Mississippi and New Orleans. This policy became official in a Royal Proclamation of 1774. It doubtless contributed toward making the big land speculators favor an independent America, which might look more kindly on their schemes.

3. *The Non-Importation Movement*

The New York assembly's cave-in and the Boston convention's collapse in 1768 convinced radical leaders that the only way they could make headway against the Townshend Acts was by co-operating with merchants to enforce a boycott of the taxed British goods. The new duties and regulations, burdensome to merchants and shipowners, gave them a common interest with the agitators. A result of this alliance was the non-importation movement of 1768–1770. Voluntary agreements were entered into by merchants, to boycott specific British or West India goods; not only those taxed but many untaxed luxuries, in order to put pressure on the British. Non-importation associations were formed in every colony and in almost every seaport. The leading merchants and, in the South, leading planters, agreed to import no British goods, or taxed tea, and to promote home industry. There began a vogue for spinning bees, wearing clothes of home-woven cloth, and brewing raspberry-leaf or Labrador tea. A freshman in the College of New Jersey, who later became the fourth President of the United States, wrote to his father that every one of the 115 Princeton students was wearing homespun. The Harvard Corporation voted to let commencers wear homespun gray or brown instead of imported black broadcloth; commencement programs were printed on locally manufactured paper. Following the earlier example of Yale students in renouncing imported wines, Harvard students made the incommensurate sacrifice of giving up tea.

Non-importation agreements were difficult to enforce, as colonial sentiment was not nearly so united against the Townshend duties as it had been against the Stamp Act. Rioting alarmed many men of property, and the strong-arm methods by which the Sons of Liberty enforced "voluntary" agreements convinced them that British taxation was preferable to mob rule. Philadelphia took almost a year to come into the movement, and in Virginia and Maryland most of the merchants were Scots who had no sympathy with colonial liberties. Loyalist newspapers published statistics proving that supposedly patriotic merchants were smuggling British goods on the side; and this weakened the resolution of merchants elsewhere. Newport backed out in October 1769, on the ground that the Bostonians were not keeping faith. And non-importation was enforced very unequally. Imports decreased 45 to 50 per cent in Boston, Pennsylvania, and New Jersey, and as much as 83 per cent in New York; but imports into Virginia, Maryland, and the Carolinas actually increased. The effect on British industry and commerce was annoying but not disastrous, as new markets for English goods were opened elsewhere.

The Duke of Grafton resigned in January 1770, and the king turned to his friend Lord North to form a new ministry. He and the king, whom Americans later regarded as monsters, were responsible for the next concession.

George III, with ten years' experience as king, would have

been called a "good guy" had he lived in the twentieth century. He was more popular in Britain and America than any English monarch since Charles II. Sincerely religious, temperate in food and drink, he had an impeccable private life; he never indulged in the clumsy frolics to which male members of the royal house of Hanover have been prone. He loved manly sports and country life, rode boldly to hounds, and ran his own farm. George was very methodical and conscientious in his conduct of public business. But of the quality of statesmanship with which kings were supposed to be born, he had none.

His object was to substitute national leadership for party government; to rescue the crown from the clutches of leading Whig families, and to be his own prime minister. By 1770 George had got the hang of English politics and had become a manipulator second to none in the kingdom. He spent so much money sustaining Lord North's ministry and supporting "friendly" members of the House of Commons that the palace servants complained of not having enough to eat. In the general election of 1780 George spent the enormous sum of £104,000 to have the "right" people elected, and succeeded. It is not correct to say that George III introduced a new system of government, or that he aimed at absolutism. He simply put himself at the head of the old Whig system and used it for what, rightly or wrongly, he believed to be the national interest. After several attempts to find a prime minister who would be responsible to him rather than to the House of Commons, he got what he wanted in Lord North—and lost an empire.

The other Whig factions did not catch on to what was going on for two or three years. By that time they had persuaded themselves that the king was trying to subvert the British constitution through corruption, and set up a royal absolutism. This explains why Burke, Pitt, Richmond, and many other leading Englishmen backed the colonists against their own government, and encouraged Americans to feel that they were fighting for liberty in England as well as in America.

George III felt no prejudice against Americans. If he had had the sense to pay them a visit, and had chased foxes in Virginia, shot quail in Carolina, and gone fishing with the Yankees, he might have won their hearts and possibly learned something about colonial quirks. He had supported the repeal of the Stamp Act, and his first gesture toward the colonies in 1770 was conciliatory. With the king's support, Lord North brought in a bill to repeal the Townshend duties except the one on tea. George insisted that, in view of the Americans' boycott of British goods, and their infractions of law and order, the tea duty must be maintained "as a mark of the supremacy of Parliament." But all Townshend duties on British goods were wiped out.

The colonial radicals wished to continue non-importation until Parliament was forced to repeal the tea duty. But they found it impossible to keep merchants in line. They had sold out their old stocks and could not continue in business without fresh goods from England. So, after news of the repeal arrived, the merchants' associations in one colony after another lifted the boycott.

On 5 March 1770, the very day that Parliament repealed the Townshend duties, a bad brawl took place in Boston. The two British regiments quartered there were having a very unpleasant time. The local radicals got out a weekly scandal sheet, *The Journal of Public Occurrences*, which they circulated throughout the colonies, describing imaginary scenes of drunkenness and outrage. The British redcoats wished to be friendly with the populace but were taunted as "lobster-backs," ambushed, and beaten up by waterside toughs. If a solid citizen of Boston, whose daughters wished more exciting company than shopkeepers and Harvard students, invited a British officer to dine, word was passed around the town, unseemly cries were heard outside the house, the guest was apt to step into something nasty when he went down the front steps, and his host was likely to find a suggestive sample of tar and feathers on his front door.

The showdown came in early March 1770 after a few soldiers, to eke out their meager pay, had taken part-time jobs in a ropewalk where the regular workmen had gone on strike. That led to a riot in which a civilian was killed. On the evening of the 5th, a group which John Adams described as "Negroes and mulattoes, Irish teagues and outlandish jacktars" began pelting with snowballs a redcoat who was standing sentry-go at the customs house on King (now State) Street. The main guard of about twenty men was called out and, with fixed bayonets, confronted a yelling mob of several hundred boys and men. After they had been taunted and stoned for half an hour, one soldier, who had been hit by a club, lost patience and fired without orders. Others followed suit; and when the smoke cleared, three men (one a sailor, another a black who was the most aggressive member of the mob) lay dead, and two more were mortally wounded.

Then what an uproar by the radicals! They named this affair the "Boston Massacre" and described it as a wanton killing of peaceable citizens by a brutal and licentious soldiery.

The continent rang with outraged screams. But news of the repeal of the Townshend duties quenched the uproar, the non-importation agreements collapsed, and a wave of prosperity set in.

From the English side came strong hints that the colonial radicals had better pipe down. The Marquess of Rockingham said that the Americans seemed determined to leave their English friends with no shadow of an excuse to defend them. William Pitt, Lord Chatham, having recovered from his illness, took his seat in the House of Lords, saying:

> I love the Americans because they love liberty, and I love them for the noble efforts they made in the last war. . . . I think the idea of drawing money from them by taxes was ill-judged. Trade is your object with them, and they should be encouraged; those millions who keep you, who are the industrious hive employed, should be encouraged. But (I wish every sensible American, both here in that country, heard what I say) if they carry their notions of liberty too far, as I fear they do,—if they will not be subject to the laws of this country,—especially if they would disengage themselves from the laws of trade and navigation, of which I see too many symptoms, as much of an American as I am, they have not a more determined opposer than they will find in me. They must be subordinate. In all laws relating to trade and navigation especially, this is the mother country, they are the children; they must obey, and we prescribe.

4. Calm and Crisis

This advice had no effect on Samuel Adams. He squeezed every ounce of propaganda out of the "Boston Massacre." The soldiers, defended by John Adams and given a fair trial, were acquitted of murder, but Sam had the "martyr" version printed in a series of articles. On each successive Fifth of March—until the Fourth of July replaced it—the Sons of Liberty staged a procession to keep up resentment against the British. One would deliver a hot oration, and relics of the "massacre" would be displayed in the window of Paul Revere, who engraved a picture of "The Bloody Massacre" which shows the soldiers in line of battle firing a pointblank volley at twenty respectable citizens.

It proved difficult to whip up resentment against Britain when the colonies were enjoying the greatest prosperity within memory. Imports into New England alone jumped from

£330,000 to £1,200,000, although the Acts of Trade and Navigation were being enforced by the efficient Commissioners of the Customs. Short harvests in Europe created a demand for American corn and wheat; and to pay for it, English specie was sent to America for the first time in history. In Boston, £8,921 in customs duties, almost twice as much as in New York, was collected in 1771; and during three years prior to the famous tea party, Boston imported almost half a million pounds of tea. The annoying regulations of the customs commissioners had been relaxed so that there was an immense traffic of sloops and schooners between colonial harbors—almost a thousand entries at Boston in 1773.

John Hancock told the royal governor that he was through with agitation. John Adams confided to his diary, "I shall certainly become more retired and cautious; I shall certainly mind my own farm and my own business." Ben Franklin, still in England, begged his countrymen to keep quiet; he pointed out that the North ministry had made a great concession and that America could well afford to bear the slight tax burden still placed upon her. New York, too, quieted down after 1770. Soldiers of the garrison could now promenade their wenches on the Battery without danger of insult or attack. Philadelphia was calm as usual. Virginia, wrote Thomas Jefferson, "seemed to fall into a state of insensibility to our situation," that Parliament still claimed power to bind the colonies "in all cases whatsoever." "Still quiet at the Southward," wrote John Adams in 1772, "and at New York they laugh at us."

Samuel Adams felt this to be a very dangerous state of affairs. "It is to be feared that the people will be so accustomed to bondage as to forget they were ever free." "Every day strengthens our opponents and weakens us," are typical statements in his letters of this period.

To the Loyalists of the Revolution, and to many conservative Americans who have since studied that era, Adams's acts and words ring false, like those of an irresponsible rabble-rouser, greedy for power. That impression is incorrect. Adams had a perfectly coherent and reasonable policy. The British government, he believed, was clinching control over colonial liberties by means of the customs duties, which enabled it gradually to put crown appointees on the royal payroll. But this issue was rather arid; rural taxpayers were apt to say it was all right with them if the king paid the governor! Adams needed a spectacular, emotional issue.

In the meantime the Boston radicals picked on their new royal governor, Thomas Hutchinson, a native-born, scholarly, middle-aged New Englander. His appointment was received with general joy as a return to the happy days of Governor Shirley. Hutchinson was a man of integrity, devoted to Whig principles within limits, always an opponent to severe British measures; but he had an unhappy faculty for rubbing people the wrong way, and of making wrong decisions. One of these was to adjourn the Massachusetts assembly to Cambridge, ostensibly to free it from pressure by the Boston mob. This succeeded in annoying the members and inconveniencing Harvard College, whose lecture rooms were commandeered; but it delighted the students, who flocked to hear the oratory of Otis and Joseph Warren, and were indoctrinated into becoming radicals themselves. When the assembly voted Governor Hutchinson a salary, he replied haughtily that the king had already taken care of that. Shortly after, news arrived that the judges of the superior court of Massachusetts were also on the royal payroll. That started Samuel Adams off on another tack. A Boston town meeting, instigated by him, inquired of the governor whether the rumor were true? He replied, in effect, that it was none of their business. The town meeting then adopted a scheme of Adams's, the appointment of a committee of correspondence to concert measures in defense of colonial liberty with similar committees in other towns and colonies. Thus began what a prominent Loyalist called "the foulest, subtlest and most venomous serpent ever issued from the eggs of sedition." It created an extra-legal organization, like the soviets in revolutionary Russia, that could be called into action when the radical leaders gave the word.

Hutchinson also indulged in a newspaper debate with Samuel Adams and his friends on constitutional principles. Both drew freely on ancient history and Latin and Greek literature. This was most imprudent on the governor's part, because not only did Adams put it over him on classical learning; he drove him into a corner, where he had to admit that Americans had no rights other than those that king and Parliament chose to recognize.

Pretty soon the radicals had a more explosive issue than judges' salaries—the *Gaspee* affair. This was a little revenue cutter commanded by a lieutenant of the Royal Navy, employed by the Commissioners of the Customs to enforce the laws in Narragansett Bay, particularly favored by smugglers. Owing to the vigilance of her commander, *Gaspee* became very unpopular with the Rhode Islanders. When chasing a smuggler, she ran aground on a sandpit below Providence; and that night (9–10 June 1772) a party of local patriots boarded her, captured the officers and crew, beat them up, and burned the cutter to the water's edge. An attack on a naval vessel has always been a very serious offense, and it is not surprising that the British government made strong efforts to arrest the culprits and send them to England for trial. The *Gaspee* affair became the signal for "agit-prop" articles in the newspapers about rights to jury trial, "worse than Egyptian tyrants," "court of inquisition," etc. The government was unable to find anyone who had taken part in burning the cutter, but the threat to bring accused traitors to trial in England became a noose around every radical's neck. And no principle of English liberty was more sacred than a man's right to trial by a jury of his own community. Hence the attempt to apprehend the *Gaspee* mob had wide repercussions. It persuaded the Virginia house of burgesses to appoint a committee of correspondence, with Patrick Henry, Thomas Jefferson, and Richard Henry Lee among the members. This was a wonderful boost for Samuel Adams's revolutionary machine; and by the early part of the year 1774 the assemblies of twelve colonies had appointed similar committees of correspondence. The machine might yet have broken down for lack of fuel, had not the North ministry come to its rescue with a tankful of explosives.

The Townshend duty of 3*d* the pound on tea entering the colonies had not been repealed, like the other duties, in 1770; and in the five years 1768–72 the thirteen colonies alone had imported and paid duty on 1,866,615 pounds of tea. At the same time, a very large amount had been smuggled in, mostly from Dutch sources. Parliament in May 1773 legalized a new arrangement designed to relieve the British East India Company from the results of its own inefficiency. It removed the duty on tea entering England and allowed the Company to be its own exporter to the colonies, doing away with middlemen. This added no new duty, but took one off; and, if enforced, would have enabled the East India Company to undersell the smugglers and give the colonial consumer cheaper tea.

It was difficult to find a constitutional issue in this device to undercut the tea-runners; but the radicals were equal to it. They had all summer to think it over, to write articles against the "illegal monopoly" given the great chartered company, and to write poems about the "pestilential herb," and "the cup infused with bane by North's insidious hand." The East India Company made matters worse by consigning their teas to "safe" merchants such as the sons of Governor Hutchinson in Boston, who were untainted by association with Sons of Liberty.

So, when the tea ships began to arrive in four continental

ports in December 1773, the Sons of Liberty were ready. In Charleston the tea was unloaded, but kept under bond in a damp warehouse; at Philadelphia and New York the masters of the tea ships were "persuaded" to turn back without entering harbor. The Boston Sons of Liberty, nettled by a criticism that Josiah Quincy had heard in the South, that "Bostonians were better at resolving what to do than doing what they resolved," determined to put on a better show. They let the two tea ships sail into the harbor. Samuel Adams summoned a convention of committees of correspondence to meet at Old South Meeting House and back up what he had planned to do. The convention sent a message to Governor Hutchinson demanding that he order the ships to take the tea back to England. This was unlawful, since the ships had already entered the customs limits. When the governor's refusal reached the mass meeting, Adams arose and said, "This meeting can do nothing further to save the country." Instantly a mob disguised as Mohawk Indians and blacks rushed down to the waterfront and emptied 342 big chests of precious tea into the harbor.

This Boston Tea Party had the calculated effect of irritating the British government into unwise acts of reprisal. Destruction of property—and tea at that—seemed to arouse John Bull far more than having a revenue cutter burned or soldiers beaten up. At a cabinet meeting on 4 February 1774, the attorney general was asked to consider whether the "late proceedings" at Boston amounted to high treason. Easy-going Lord North, bored rather than irritated, wished to avoid trouble; but the king was furious. So was English public opinion, and the North administration could not stand unless it did something. It looked as if appeasement had twice failed and that it was time for Mother England to crack down on her naughty brat. Parliament was like-minded; in spite of warnings from Burke, Barré, and even General Burgoyne, Parliament in May and June passed the so-called Coercive or Intolerable Acts. "The dye is now cast," wrote the king to Lord North. "The Colonies must either submit or triumph."

That is why this comic stage-Indian business of the Boston Tea Party was important. It goaded John Bull into a showdown, which was exactly what Sam Adams and the other radical leaders wanted.

XIV

Coercion to Independence

1774-1776

1. *The Coercive Acts*

THE BOSTON TEA PARTY needled Parliament into passing, and
George III into signing, a series of laws that Americans referred to as the Coercive, or Intolerable, Acts. These were, in
order, the Boston Port Act which virtually blockaded Boston
until it chose to pay for the tumbled tea; the Massachusetts
Government and Administration of Justice Acts, chastising
the government of that naughty province; and the Quartering
Act, which empowered royal governors to commandeer private houses in any colonial town for quartering soldiers. Asso-
ciated with these laws in the popular mind, but really directed
to an entirely different problem, was the Quebec Act.

Although passed neither in heat nor in anger—the dates of
enactment extended from March to June 1774 and all were
debated—these Coercive Acts were a pretty bald assertion of
power. Edmund Burke, writing to the New York assembly's
correspondence committee, said that the real intent of the
Boston Port Act was the necessity for "*some Act* of Power."
He was right. As Lenin once said, "The basic question of
every revolution is the question of power in the state." From
the day that unhappy law was passed, the question between
England and the Thirteen Colonies was one of power; who

would rule, or have the final say? All other questions of taxation, customs duties, and the like faded into the background. Through all stages of remonstrance, resistance, and outright war, the dominant issue was one of power—should Britain or America dictate the terms of their mutual association, or separation?

Could these opposing claims of authority and freedom ever be reconciled? We who know the outcome can little appreciate the strain of those two years from June of 1774 to 4 July 1776, on men of good will, both sides of the Atlantic. Loyalty, tradition, pride of membership in a great empire, urged the colonials to submit; but cherished principles of English liberty impelled them to take a firm stand. In England the wrench was almost as severe. Many Old Whigs and prominent merchants opposed every step in Parliament's punitive program, and braved the charge of treason in applauding America's final decision to act on James Otis's motto, *Ubi libertas ibi patria*—"Where liberty is, there is my country."

The Quartering Act was intended to ease the military occupation for redcoats, who had been forced to sleep on Boston Common. The Government and Administration of Justice Acts altered the government of Massachusetts Bay by making the council (hitherto elected by the whole assembly) appointive by the governor, to hold office during the king's pleasure. The same principle was extended to all judges, marshals, sheriffs, and justices of the peace; and the towns were forbidden their favorite indoor sport of debating colonial rights and appointing committees of correspondence. These two laws, if enforced, would have sewed up Massachusetts Bay for the king; and they aroused apprehension that similar or worse alterations would be made in the governments of other troublesome colonies.

The Boston Port Act, first to be passed, created the most widespread indignation, and more definitely showed the hand of tyranny. All customs officials were removed to Salem, and the guilty port sealed up; even boat landings were illegal. It was to remain in force until "satisfaction" were made both for the tea and for losses sustained by royal officials in the Boston riots; and also until the king decided "that peace and obedience to the laws" were restored. Again to quote Burke, "The rendering the Means of Subsistence of a Whole City dependent upon the King's private pleasure, even after the payment of a fine and satisfaction made, was without Precedent, and of a most dangerous Example." And this law was enforced by a squadron of the Royal Navy and by two regiments (soon increased to five) under General Thomas Gage, who at the same time was appointed governor and captain-general of Massachusetts Bay. The immediate effect was to start a bloodless insurrection in Massachusetts which confined the royal governor's authority to Boston and its environs. Committees of correspondence organized resistance so effectively that by the fall of 1774 the province was virtually independent, governed by an illegally elected convention.

Continent-wide, the effect was even more important. To the surprise even of the Bostonians, other colonies vied in sending food and money for the relief of the blockaded town. From South Carolina, for instance, came provisions to the value of £2700; Virginia sent 8600 bushels of corn and wheat and several hundred barrels of flour. The Old Dominion started rolling a ball which led to independence, with an assembly resolve of 24 May 1774. This resolve, drafted by Henry, Lee, Mason, and Jefferson, denounced the military occupation as a "hostile invasion," and designated 1 June, when the Port Act would go into effect, as a "day of fasting, humiliation and prayer." Governor Dunmore promptly dissolved the Virginia assembly, but before dispersing to their homes the burgesses met at the Raleigh tavern in Williamsburg and resolved that "an attack made on one of our sister Colonies, to compel submission to arbitrary taxes, is an attack made on all British America." They instructed their committee of correspondence to exchange views with similar committees in other colonies on the propriety of summoning a Continental congress. All the committees were in favor, and the First Continental Congress met at Philadelphia on 5 September 1774.

The fifty-five members of this Congress, which evolved into a federal government of a nation at war, were chosen by revolutionary conventions or committees in twelve continental colonies, from New Hampshire through South Carolina. Efforts of the extreme conservatives, whom we may now call Tories, to prevent these illegal elections were fruitless; the Continent seemed of one mind that concerted action must be taken. Congress included, besides the well-known radical leaders, a number of conservative Whigs such as the Rutledges of South Carolina, Joseph Galloway of Pennsylvania, and John Jay of New York. Peyton Randolph of Virginia was elected president of the Congress.

The Philadelphians outdid themselves in hospitality. John Adams, in addition to "generous, noble Sentiments and manly Eloquence" in Congress, enjoyed at Dr. Rush's "the very best of Claret, Madeira and Burgundy. Melons, fine beyond description"; and at Chief Justice Chew's four o'clock dinner,

"Turtle and every other thing—Flummery, jellies, sweetmeats of 20 sorts, Trifles, whip'd syllabubbs, floating islands, fools, &c. I drank Madeira at a great Rate and found no inconvenience in it." These he shared with "all the Gentlemen from Virginia" and "Mr. Carrell of Anapolis a very sensible gentlemen, a Roman catholic, and of the first Fortune in America." But Samuel Adams, when he did dine out, called for bread and milk as appropriate to Roman virtue, and a balm for his stomach ulcer.

Congress faced a delicate task. America as a whole did not want independence; every path to conciliation must be kept open. But Congress had to do something about the Coercive Acts, and also to suggest a permanent solution of the struggle between *libertas* and *imperium*. It tackled that big subject first. Galloway brought forward a plan of union which proposed to settle the power problem by establishing an American parliament parallel to the British, each to have a veto over acts of the other relating to America. While this was being debated, word reached Philadelphia, via Paul Revere's saddlebags, of the sensational Suffolk resolves of 9 September, drafted by Joseph Warren and passed by a convention of the towns around Boston. These declared the Coercive Acts to be unconstitutional and void, urged Massachusetts to form a free state until and unless they were repealed, advised the people to arm themselves, and recommended economic sanctions against Britain. This news brought Congress up short, and made debating the Galloway plan seem like discussing insurance while one's house burned. Congress encouraged the Massachusetts patriots by endorsing their Suffolk resolves, which Galloway (who eventually became a Tory), called "a declaration of war against Great Britain." His plan was then rejected.

Constructive efforts were made to solve the power problem. John Adams, James Wilson, and Thomas Jefferson wrote pamphlets advocating what amounted to dominion status—a reorganization of the British empire similar to that of the British Commonwealth prior to World War II. A colony's only connection with Great Britain would be the king, who, through his privy council, would conduct foreign relations and determine matters of war and peace, and even regulate imperial trade; but Parliament must keep hands off the colonies. This proposition went even further than the Continental Congress's resolves; so far, indeed, that it is doubtful whether even Chatham or Burke would have accepted it. But it was neither visionary nor impractical, as proved by the fact that in 1778 Lord North's government proposed to end the war and restore imperial unity on just such terms. Thus, the American Revolution was no irrepressible conflict. Everything the colonies wanted, the Old Whigs in England were ready to grant in 1775; but they were then out of office. And those in office, the coalition led by Lord North, were always too late with concessions.

The Continental Congress issued a Declaration of Rights stating that Americans were entitled to all English liberties, and citing a number of acts of Parliament of the past ten years which violated that principle. Congress then adopted a non-importation, non-exportation, and non-consumption agreement, virtually cutting off imports from Britain after 1 December 1774, and exports to Britain after 10 September 1775, if by that time the Coercive Acts had not been repealed. This agreement was called The Association. The American Revolution (as people now began to call the movement) showed a Puritan streak common to most revolutions, in a vote of Congress to encourage frugality and to "discourage every species of extravagance and dissipation, especially all horseracing, and all kinds of gaming, cock-fighting, exhibitions of shews, plays, and other expensive diversions and entertainments," including elaborate funerals. Congress also voted to give up drinking imported tea, Madeira, and port wine. But the local product, rum, was still permissible. The Congress rose on 26 October 1774, after resolving to meet again the following 10 May if by that time colonial grievances had not been redressed.

The weeks or even months then required for mail to cross the Atlantic allowed time for hotheads on both sides to cool off. But the time lag also meant that the situation got out of hand by the time England tried to do something about it. Franklin supported a common-sense suggestion to send a royal commission to find out and report what the colonists really wanted. That eventually became the normal British way to deal with imperial problems, but George III would have none of it; he told Lord North that sending over a commission would look as if he were more afraid of Congress than they of him. The next sensible suggestion came from the Earl of Chatham. On 20 January 1775 he moved in the House of Lords to withdraw the British troops from Boston. Looking "like an old Roman Senator, rising with the dignity of age, yet speaking with the fire of youth" (as one present reported), he made what is now recognized as one of the greatest parliamentary orations of all time, declaring principles that apply to the nationalist revolutions of our day as well as to those of the 1770's. The Americans, he said, will never be reconciled until the troops are withdrawn. "What is our right to persist in such cruel and vindictive measures against that loyal and respectable people?" Americans have been abused, misrepresented, and traduced in Parliament in the most atrocious manner. And how have they behaved under this provocation? "With unexampled patience, with unparalleled wisdom." The Continental Congress for sagacity, moderation, manly spirit, and honor "shines unrivalled." All attempts to establish despotism over such a mighty continental nation must be vain, must be fatal. But "there is no time to be lost. . . . Nay, while I am now speaking the decisive blow may be struck, and millions are involved in the consequence. . . . Years, perhaps ages, will not heal the wounds." And the Duke of Richmond, in the same debate, warned the Lords, "You may spread fire, sword and desolation, but that will not be government. . . . No people can ever be made to submit to a form of government they say they will not receive."

The Lords' debate was followed on 23 January 1775 by one in the House of Commons on a petition signed by hundreds of English merchants to repeal the Coercive Acts. Edmund Burke then delivered the first of his famous speeches on reconciliation with America, but the motion to repeal was lost, 82 to 197. Next, Chatham managed to have introduced in the lower house on 1 February 1775 a bill "for settling the troubles in America." The principle was to preserve parliamentary control of trade and navigation, but to recognize the Continental Congress as a legal body, competent to grant money for imperial defense. The Coercive Acts, the Quebec Act, and the tea duty would be repealed, Boston set free, colonial judges would be appointed during good behavior, and the sanctity of colonial charters guaranteed. Although this bill was no clean-cut dominion solution of the imperial problem, it conceded every practical point for which Congress had contended. If it had been passed, there would have been no war and no Declaration of Independence. But the bill was roundly defeated. The only concession Lord North's majority would make was a resolve that if any colony promised to raise what His Majesty's government considered a proper quota for imperial defense, and assume the cost of its civil list, Parliament would exempt that colony from the revenue acts. North's "conciliatory resolve" naturally failed to conciliate because, as Benjamin Franklin wrote, it left ultimate power over colonial taxation to Parliament, and did nothing about the Coercive Acts.

Time was running out. Chatham warned Parliament on 1 February, "Great Britain and America were already in martial array, waiting for the signal to engage in a contest in which . . . ruin and destruction must be the inevitable consequence to both." Joseph Warren on the 20th wrote from Boston to a friend, in London, "It is not yet too late to accommodate the dispute amicably. But . . . if once General Gage should lead his troops into the country, with design to enforce the late Acts of Parliament, Great Britain may take her leave . . . of all America." That is exactly what Gage was planning to do.

As a sign that the North ministry wanted a way out, it attempted a secret negotiation in London with Benjamin Franklin. Lord North and his friends had abused the philosopher and ousted him from his job as deputy postmaster general in America, but they looked on him as a "fixer." Three intermediaries, one a sister of Admiral Lord Howe, hinted in the course of chess games and social conversation that if Franklin would act as mediator he "might exact any reward in the power of government to bestow." They even offered him £1800 as down payment. Franklin replied that unless the Coercive Acts were repealed and the army withdrawn from Boston, even God Almighty could not bring about a reconciliation. The ministry's assumption that money and influence could settle everything so disgusted Franklin, hitherto a moderate Whig working for peace, that he became an out-and-out radical for American independence.

Lord North now introduced another coercive bill, on the fatuous assumption that it would isolate New England and make it an example. This New England Restraining Act, signed 30 March 1775, forbade the four colonies of that region to trade with any part of the world except Great Britain and Ireland, and denied their fishermen access to the fishing banks off Newfoundland and Nova Scotia. To deprive the Yankees of their fisheries was like ordering Virginians not to grow tobacco. There might have been a revolution in the name of the "sacred codfish," had General Gage not made an excursion to Concord before news of the New England Restraining Act arrived.

2. Western and Canadian Interlude

The Boston Tea Party, among other things, spoiled the game of the Vandalia and other land-speculating companies at a time when they had nearly won over the Board of Trade. But the pioneers were pushing west just the same, and Kentucky was the next scene of conflict. This "dark and bloody ground" over which many Indian tribes had hunted but where none dared dwell, was visited immediately after the French and Indian War by Daniel Boone and other "long hunters." They brought back tales of great hardwood forests, blue grass prairies, fertile meadows, and vast herds of buffalo and deer. These and other small-time speculators obtained the ear of the governor of Virginia, the Earl of Dunmore. He began granting crown lands beyond the Treaty of Fort Stanwix line to holders of land warrants issued to war veterans. This practice ran so counter to the British Western policy already laid down, that the North ministry in February 1774 ordered governors to make no land grants except in areas already ceded by the Indians, and such ceded land was to be adver lised and sold by auction. This statesmanlike plan, which Congress imitated in 1785, was bitterly resented by the speculators and alluded to as a grievance in the Declaration of Independence.

By the time these royal instructions reached America, Virginia was engaged in a war with the Shawnee nation, which had never ceded its rights over Kentucky and was rendered desperate by the long hunters killing off the game. Governor Dunmore dispatched two armed parties of volunteers to take possession of the illegally granted lands. After one party had been ambushed by Shawnee braves on the Kentucky river in July, Dunmore ordered out some 1500 militia of western Virginia, and these under Colonel Andrew Lewis, on 6 October, defeated Chief Cornstalk of the Shawnee at Point Pleasant, where the Great Kanawha river joins the Ohio. Owing to Sir William Johnson's diplomacy, the Six Nations and the Western tribes left the Shawnee to their fate, and in the subsequent peace negotiations the latter ceded all their Kentucky claims to Virginia. So ended "Governor Dunmore's War."

The Continental Congress protested vigorously against the Quebec Act of 22 June 1774. This infuriated the Americans, partly because it picked up the southern boundary of Quebec and carried it to the Ohio river, as Louis XV and the Marquis Duquesne had claimed, thus depriving the four colonies which claimed lands north of the Ohio of the territory of four future states. There were good administrative reasons for this extension. The English government at Quebec had adopted a sound Indian administrative service, Scots immigrants were sending coureurs de bois to buy furs in the Ohio country, and the advantage of having these traders controlled from Quebec, and of keeping out hunters like Daniel Boone, were obvious.

The other and more important part of the Quebec Act is generally considered a landmark of toleration. It guaranteed to the French their seignorial system and civil law, and confirmed to the Roman Catholic church in Canada the right to "hold, receive and enjoy" its "accustomed dues and rights," which included control of education. The British government should have been commended for realizing that it could never make English Protestants out of French Canadians; but the Continental Congress denounced it for "establishing the Roman Catholic religion . . . abolishing the equitable system of English laws, and erecting a tyranny there, to the great danger . . . of the neighboring British colonies." Samuel Adams for years had been conducting a whispering (or, rather, shouting) campaign that George III, like James II, tended toward "popery." So here it was—the thin end of the wedge. As a Canadian historian quipped, "To the disordered imaginations of the American patriots, the northern province loomed up suddenly like a spectre from some barbaric and vanished past." Naturally, the French of Quebec declined pressing invitations to be represented at Philadelphia and to make common cause with the American Revolution.

Nova Scotia stayed quiet through all the pre-revolutionary agitation, although her Protestant inhabitants (mostly immigrants from New England) disliked the Quebec Act. Neutrality was an old Acadian tradition, now strengthened by a religious revival started by Henry Alline, which swept through the province and aroused far more interest than the war. The Floridas were too recently acquired and thinly populated to do anything. Georgia very nearly stayed out, a southern counterpart to Nova Scotia. She was not represented in the First Continental Congress; but the energetic efforts of a small group of settlers from New England, led by Lyman Hall, brought her into the Second. The West Indian colonies were too closely tied to England by trade and consanguinity even to contemplate supporting Massachusetts.

Fear of slave insurrection also tended to keep the West Indies loyal; the population of Jamaica in 1778 was 18,420 whites and 205,261 blacks, mostly slaves. In Bermuda there was much sympathy with Congress, but the islanders, like the Nova Scotians, decided to stick to England and trade with both sides.

3. *Fighting Begins*

The Province of Massachusetts Bay became virtually independent in October 1774, when the assembly, dissolved by Governor Gage, met at Concord as a provincial congress under the presidency of John Hancock. This congress took over the government, ignoring both Gage and his newly appointed council. It appointed a new treasurer to collect taxes, and a committee of safety as a standing executive board. Boston was full of redcoats, and the harbor bristled with masts of naval vessels sent to enforce the Boston Port Act; but the governor could exert no authority outside the town. All winter long the committee of safety collected arms and munitions, organized and drilled selected militia (the minute men) for instant action, set up a system of intelligence to anticipate any British move, and prepared to resist any attempt of the royal government to take over the interior.

What made the farmers fight in 1775? Judge Mellen Chamberlain in 1842, when he was twenty-one, interviewed Captain Preston, a ninety-one-year-old veteran of the Concord fight: "Did you take up arms against intolerable oppressions?" he asked.

"Oppressions?" replied the old man. "I didn't feel them."

"What, were you not oppressed by the Stamp Act?"

"I never saw one of those stamps. I certainly never paid a penny for one of them."

"Well, what then about the tea tax?"

"I never drank a drop of the stuff; the boys threw it all overboard."

"Then I suppose you had been reading Harington or Sidney and Locke about the eternal principles of liberty?"

"Never heard of 'em. We read only the Bible, the Catechism, Watts' Psalms and Hymns, and the Almanac."

"Well, then, what was the matter? And what did you mean in going to the fight?"

"Young man, what we meant in going for those redcoats was this: *we always had governed ourselves, and we always meant to. They didn't mean we should.*"

Old men's recollections so long after the event are not regarded by historians as good sources of history, but this gaffer's estimate of the situation is supported by a contemporary report by John Howe, whom Governor Gage sent out from Boston in early April 1775 to spy out the state of the countryside. On his way back Howe called at a small house beside the road, inhabited by an old man and his wife. The man was cleaning a gun. "I asked him," wrote Howe, "what he was going to kill, as he was so old, I should not think he could take sight at any game; he said there was a flock of redcoats at Boston, which he expected would be here soon; he meant to try and hit some of them, as he expected they would be very good marks. I asked the old man how he expected to fight; he said, 'Open field fighting, or any other way to kill them redcoats!' I asked him how old he was; he said, 'Seventy-seven, and never was killed yet.' I asked the old man if there were any tories nigh there; he said there was one tory house in sight, and he wished it was in flames. The old man says, 'Old woman put in the bullet pouch a handful of buckshot, as I understand the English like an assortment of plums!' "

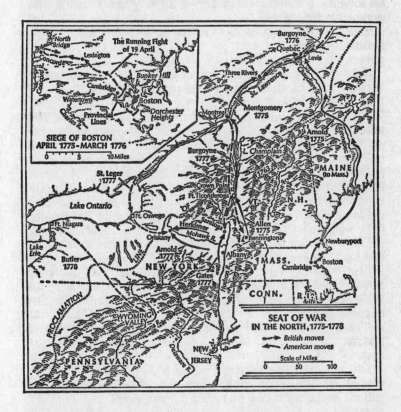

Gage did not heed the warning. To destroy patriot munitions at Concord, he dispatched a strong detail under Major John Pitcairn on the night of 18–19 April 1775. Paul Revere and other riders aroused the countryside along their route; and minute men were on the march by break of day as far away as New Hampshire and Connecticut. When Major Pitcairn, after marching his redcoats all night, reached Lexington, he found a grim band of minute men lined up on the village common parallel to his line of advance. The British halted. The Major cried, "Disperse, ye rebels, disperse!" Someone, to this day nobody knows who, fired a shot from behind a stone wall. Firing then became general, and by the time the minute men dispersed they had left eight dead on the green. Sam Adams and Hancock, when the British approached, scuttled across lots, Adams exclaiming, according to tradition, "This is a glorious day for America!" It was what he had been working toward for years—a bloody clash that would bring on independence.

The British continued their march to Concord where, as in Emerson's poem,

> . . . the embattled farmers stood,
> And fired the shot heard round the world.

And do not imagine that it failed to go round the world. The local version of an unprovoked massacre of peaceful farmers reached England eleven days before Gage's official report and raised a furor against the North government. Sent south from New England by swift expresses (Philadelphia, 24 April, Richmond on the 30th, New Bern, 7 May), the story strengthened the Patriot cause everywhere, and in Virginia and North Carolina civil war broke out. The Paris press gave full details; here were troubled waters in which France might fish with profit. In Venice the leading news sheet published an account of *la grande scaramucia a Concordia*. And, after a poet had woven the story into "The Midnight Ride of Paul Revere," it traveled the rest of the way around the world. In his opening speech at the Bandung Conference of 18 April 1955, Dr. Sukarno reminded the Asian and African members that it was the anniversary of "the first successful anti-colonial war in history," of the

> . . . cry of defiance and not of fear,
> A voice in the darkness, a knock at the door,
> And a word that shall echo forevermore!

And this first president of the Indonesian Republic concluded, "Yes, it *shall* echo for evermore!"

4. Second Congress and Olive Branch

On 10 May 1775, when all America was buzzing with the news of Lexington and Concord, the Second Continental Congress met at Philadelphia. No more distinguished group of men ever assembled in this country. The "brace of Adamses" and John Hancock came from the seat of war;

Silas Deane and Roger Sherman from Connecticut; John Jay, Philip Schuyler, and a trio of Livingstons from New York and New Jersey; Caesar Rodney, Thomas McKean, and Thomas Read, from Delaware; Samuel Chase and Thomas Johnson Jr. from Maryland; Henry, Jefferson, Washington, Lee, and Wythe from Virginia. Gadsden, Middleton, and a pair of Rutledges represented South Carolina; Joseph Hewes and William Hooper came from North Carolina; Lyman Hall and Archibald Bullock from Georgia. Pennsylvania, the key colony, had a delegation that included "farmer" Dickinson, Galloway, Robert Morris, James Wilson, and venerable Franklin. After the death of Peyton Randolph, John Hancock, a New England gentleman of fortune possessing gracious manners and an impressive signature, was chosen president.

Within a few days Congress received another startling bit of news, together with a stand of British colors to decorate Independence Hall. Ethan Allen and 83 Green Mountain Boys had crossed Lake Champlain from the Vermont side and wrested Forts Ticonderoga and Crown Point from their British garrisons; the invasion route to Canada was open. But there was no question of independence as yet, or for almost a year to come.

Besides creating a provincial army and navy and sending diplomatic agents to Europe, Congress assumed sovereign power over Indian relations—an unconscious tribute to the imperial system. It created three departments of Indian affairs, and commissioners to handle them. In September 1775 Lewis Morris and James Wilson held a council with Blue Jacket, White Eyes, Cornstalk, and other chiefs of the Shawnee, the Delaware, and the Seneca, at Fort Pitt. Strings of wampum were exchanged for the usual trading-truck gifts, and the commissioners returned to Philadelphia believing their mission had been accomplished. The Delaware, then living in southern Ohio and Indiana, honored their long friendship with Pennsylvania, and Congress in 1778 concluded its first Indian treaty with this nation—a treaty containing the interesting suggestion (never acted upon) that an Indian fourteenth colony be created in the Northwest, with representatives in Congress. But the Iroquois Confederacy remained loyal to the Great White Father in London.

Congress represented a Whig, or Patriot, bloc, whose only common ground was resistance to unconstitutional acts of Parliament. Only a few members—namely, the Lees, the Adamses, Franklin, and Gadsden—believed independence to be the only solution, and they hardly dared breathe the word; loyalty to the king and to England was still so strong. Congress took a line which left the way open to conciliation. It approved the hot war that had broken out in Massachusetts, adopted the militia besieging the redcoats in Boston as the "Army of the United Colonies," appointed Colonel George Washington commander in chief, sent Benedict Arnold across the Maine wilderness in the expectation of bringing in Canada as the fourteenth colony, and authorized other warlike acts. All in the king's name!

In order to explain this inconsistent policy, Congress issued a Declaration on the Causes of Taking Up Arms, the joint work of Dickinson and Jefferson. It assured fellow subjects in other parts of the empire, "We mean not to dissolve that union which has so long and so happily subsisted between us. . . . We have not raised armies with ambitious designs of separation from Great Britain, and establishing independent States. We fight not for glory or for conquest." But "we are reduced to the alternative of choosing an unconditional submission to the tyranny of irritated ministers, or resistance by force. The latter is our choice." The army they were fighting was not the king's army but the "ministerial army"; George III was misled by bad counselors. The majority in Congress sincerely hoped that firmness and fighting spirit on the American side would cause the House of Commons to vote down Lord North's shabby group, and that the king would call to power someone like Lord Chatham who, when he heard the news of Lexington and Concord, exclaimed, "I rejoice that America has resisted!" Almost fourteen months elapsed between the opening of the war and the Declaration of Independence.

The war extended in a mild way to other colonies, usually taking the shape of militia forcing the royal governor to take refuge on a British warship. But the provincial congresses of four Middle colonies—New York, New Jersey, Pennsylvania, and Maryland—between November 1775 and January 1776 instructed their delegates in Congress to hold out against independence.

Our generation, sadly accustomed to blitzkriegs, Pearl Harbors, and the necessity for instant decisions, finds it hard to understand why the Americans of 1775–76 took so long to make up their minds. But they were going through an emotional travail comparable only to that of the first four months of 1861. Loyalties were being torn apart. Americans were members of the greatest empire since Rome. Although the word *revolution* aroused no terrors, owing to the bloodless affair of 1688, the word *republic* did. In the past, republics had been turbulent and of short duration; they required Roman virtue to maintain, and did we have it? John Adams feared not. There was "so much Venality and Corruption, so much Avarice and Ambition, such a Rage for Profit and Commerce among all Ranks and Degrees of Men even in America," he wrote early in 1776, that he doubted whether we had "public Virtue enough to Support a Republic." No European colony had ever thrown off dependence on a mother country, or even wished to. Would we not fight among ourselves and perhaps drift into becoming a satellite of France or Spain?

Independence meant sailing forth on an uncharted sea. America was not like Ireland, Poland, or other states which cherished romantic traditions of an independent past. All the mystic chords of memory which (as Abraham Lincoln said) make a people one, responded to English names and events— Magna Carta, Queen Elizabeth, the Glorious Revolution, the Bill of Rights, Drake, Marlborough, Wolfe. Dared one break with all English memories and glories?

It was a hard choice for a man who read and thought; easy only for the savage or the illiterate. If one looked into the Bible for guidance, there was St. Peter in his First Epistle urging his flock, "Submit yourselves to every ordinance of man for the Lord's sake." As freemen, said he, you are not to use "your liberty for a cloke of maliciousness; but as the servants of God. Honour all men: Love the brotherhood: Fear God: Honour the king." What could be more explicit? Were not some of the Sons of Liberty using "liberty for a cloke of maliciousness"? There is even a touch of nostalgia in Jefferson's draft of the Declaration of Independence; "We might have been a free and a great people together."

General Washington started north from Philadelphia on 23 June 1775 to take command of the Continental army (as the Army of the United Colonies was generally referred to, even to 1783). He was met en route by the stirring news of the Battle of Bunker Hill. In May, General Gage received reinforcements which brought the British force in Boston up to 10,000, not including the sailors and marines in Admiral Graves's fleet. On 12 June Gage issued a proclamation (written by Burgoyne) to the "infatuated multitudes" who "with a preposterous parade . . . affect to hold the army besieged," promising pardon to all who would lay down their arms, except to John Hancock and Samuel Adams. Actually, the Continental army of homespun militia, which included a few good engineers, had the British hemmed in on every land side except Charlestown; and their fortifying of Breed's (not Bunker's) Hill on the night of 16–17 June 1775 brought on the battle. This was the first real standup fight between raw New England troops and British regulars; and although the redcoats won the hill, they lost 1054 killed and wounded out of 2200 engaged, against American losses of 441 out of an estimated 3200 engaged. "A dear bought victory," wrote General Clinton—"another such would have ruined us." And General Gage wrote home ruefully, "Those people shew a spirit and conduct against us, they never shewed against the French." Thus, although Bunker Hill was a tactical victory for the British, it was a strategic and moral one for the Americans. It aroused a spirit of exultation and confidence throughout the continent. Washington assumed command at Cambridge on 2 July, and began a remarkably successful job of whipping some 15,000 undisciplined militia into an army.

The Continental Congress now made a final attempt at conciliation: the Olive Branch Petition, drafted by John Dickinson and adopted by Congress 8 July 1775, largely out of respect for the author. According to John Adams, Dickinson was in a terrible quandary. "His mother said to him, 'Johnny you will be hanged, your estate will° be forfeited and confiscated, you will leave your excellent wife a widow, and your charming children orphans, beggars and infamous.' From my Soul I pitied Mr. Dickinson. . . . I was very happy that *my* Mother and *my* Wife . . . and all her near relations, as well as mine, had been uniformly of *my* Mind, so that *I* always enjoyed perfect Peace at home."

The key paragraph of the Olive Branch Petition is this:

> Attached to your Majesty's person, family and government with all the devotion that principle and affection can inspire, connected with Great Britain by the strongest ties that can unite societies, and deploring every event that tends in any degree to weaken them, we solemnly assure your Majesty, that we not only most ardently desire the former harmony between her and these colonies may be restored, but that a concord may be established between them upon so firm a basis, as to perpetuate its blessings uninterrupted by any future dissentions to succeeding generations in both countries.

Congress therefore begs the king to interpose his authority to stop the war, repeal the Coercive Acts, and bring about "a happy and permanent reconciliation."

The petition, signed by John Hancock and almost every

subsequent signer of the Declaration of Independence, was sent over in duplicate to two colonial agents, who tried without success to persuade Lord Dartmouth to present it to the king. They were informed that His Majesty would receive no petition from a rebel body. That is not surprising, since the British government had already heard of Congress's launching the Arnold expedition against Quebec, which looked like a wanton aggression against a loyal and peaceful colony. On 23 August 1775, George III proclaimed that a general rebellion existed, and that "utmost endeavours" should be made "to suppress such rebellion, and to bring the traitors to justice."

On 16 November 1775, Edmund Burke submitted a proposal for reconciliation to the House of Commons, which rejected it by a vote of two to one; and on 22 December Parliament passed an act prohibiting "all manner of trade and commerce" with the Thirteen Colonies, declaring all colonial vessels lawful prize, and their crews subject to impressment into the Royal Navy. These were logical and conventional methods for repressing a rebellion; but as one English publicist remarked, "The fate of nations is not to be tried by forms." Samuel Tucker the Dean of Gloucester, Adam Smith the economist, even Lord Barrington the secretary at war, urged that all British troops be withdrawn from America and the colonists allowed to be independent if they chose, or to state their terms for staying in the empire. It is possible that if this policy had been followed, and the worst cause of friction removed, Congress would have concluded something similar to the Statute of Westminster of the Irish Free State treaty, leaving the home government more power over America than it now has over the British Commonwealth. It is highly unlikely that there would have been any revolt in America against such a treaty, for the people did not want war, and they were not yet conscious of separate nationality. But there was not sufficient imagination in English political circles to adopt such a policy. The obstinacy of George III did not matter; he was one with his people, a good John Bull to whom it was as unthinkable to yield to this American rebellion as it had been to yield to the Scots rebellions of 1715 and 1745.

American feelings of the time were well represented by the official American flag, which was first raised by Lieutenant John Paul Jones in Commodore Hopkins's flagship *Alfred* on 3 December 1775, and by General Washington on a hill near Boston on New Year's day. It carried thirteen stripes to mark the union of the colonies, but still displayed the Union Jack in the canton as a symbol of union with Great Britain. This flag was not replaced by the Stars and Stripes until June 1777.

5. The Declaration of Independence

News of the Act of 22 December 1775, prohibiting all trade and intercourse with the Thirteen Colonies, arrived in America shortly after the appearance of a remarkable pamphlet by a middle-class English Quaker, Thomas Paine, who had been in the colonies but a short time. Paine's *Common Sense* brought the discussion to a crisis by convincing doubters and strengthening those already convinced.

His arguments against continuing the war on a loyalty basis, and in favor of declaring independence, were logical and compelling. The Association boycott on trade with Great Britain had failed, hurting America more than it did England, and hampering the conduct of the war. To obtain the wherewithal to buy munitions, trade must be resumed with the British West Indies and other parts of the world. To be successful, a war must be waged for some great object. Reconciliation on any acceptable basis was no longer possible; and if it were, there was no guarantee against a renewal by Parliament of the attack on colonial liberties. Complete independence was the only real guarantee for American liberty. Only thus could foreign aid be obtained. An independent America can trade with the whole world, manufacture what she likes, and isolate herself from Old World brawls. "A thirst for absolute power is the natural disease of monarchy," and George III, as a brutal tyrant, had violated the "compact" between him and the people to protect their rights, and so forfeited his right to their loyalty and obedience.

These arguments won over General Washington, who had been toasting the king nightly at his officers' mess in Cambridge. On 31 January 1776 he wrote to Joseph Reed of Pennsylvania, "A few more of such flaming arguments, as were exhibited at Falmouth and Norfolk, added to the sound doctrine and unanswerable reasoning contained in the pamphlet *Common Sense,* will not leave numbers at a loss to decide upon the propriety of a separation."

The "flaming argument" of Falmouth was this: The minute men of Falmouth (Portland), Maine, roughed up Captain Henry Mowatt RN and attacked his ship at anchor, after which he took revenge by bombarding the town with red-hot cannon balls which destroyed it. The burning of Norfolk, Virginia, in December 1775, was done by Patriot forces on their retreat; but they succeeded in transferring the blame to Governor Lord Dunmore and the Tories. And there were other flaming arguments.

The royal governor of North Carolina managed to enlist a

Loyalist force of 1600 Scots Highlanders, many of whom had been active in the Regulation of 1774. These were completely routed by Patriot militia at Moore's Creek Bridge near Wilmington on 27 February 1776. The result might have been different if a British expeditionary force mounted in Ireland and commanded by Lord Cornwallis had co-operated with the Loyalists, as the governor requested. Instead, Cornwallis chose to take a crack at Charleston, South Carolina. Before he arrived, the local Patriots had built Fort Moultrie, whose guns drove off the British fleet on 28 June when it tried to enter. These events removed all obstacles to the Carolinas' going for independence.

A fleet of the Continental navy of seven small ships converted from merchant vessels, under command of Commodore Esek Hopkins, sailed down to the Bahamas and captured undefended Nassau in March 1776, together with an enormous quantity of munitions. These were picked up by Washington's army when it was moving from Boston to New York.

The Canada expedition got off to a good start, but crashed against the Rock of Quebec. General Richard Montgomery led a force of about 1,000 New Englanders up the Hudson and Lake Champlain route and captured Montreal on 12 November 1775. Benedict Arnold's right punch to this left hook was a force of 600 Yankees who marched through the Maine wilderness to the St. Lawrence opposite Quebec, where they rendezvoused with Montgomery. On New Year's Eve 1775 the combined United Colonies force assaulted the citadel of Quebec, was bloodily repulsed, and brave Montgomery fell. General Washington, still besieging the British in Boston, received this depressing news on 17 January 1776. It meant that the British could now use Canada as a base, invade the Thirteen Colonies by the Champlain-Hudson route next summer, and isolate New England.

But the General was not discouraged. He occupied Dorchester Heights and forced General William Howe (who had relieved General Gage) to evacuate Boston on 17 March 1776. The American army then marched in.

The movement for independence received an important boost from a Virginia convention composed of the old house of burgesses sitting by itself after getting rid of Governor Dunmore and the council. Meeting at Williamsburg in early May, the members were outraged by the news that the king was sending 12,000 German mercenaries to put down the rebellion. On 15 May the convention instructed its delegates in the Continental Congress "to declare the United Colonies free and independent states." It then appointed a committee, presided over by George Mason, to report a declaration of rights and a plan of government for an independent state. Mason at the age of fifty-seven was regarded as the Nestor of Virginian statesmen. He hated politics and despised politicians, especially Patrick Henry; but when called upon, he always served. On this occasion he proposed, and the convention adopted on 12 June 1776, the Virginia Bill of Rights, parent of all American bills of rights. And on 29 June the convention adopted a constitution for an independent Commonwealth of Virginia.

In Congress, John Adams wrote, "By every Post and every day, Independence rolls in on us like a torrent." The Georgia delegates appeared, with full powers to vote for independence. South Carolina expelled her royal governor and voted for independence. North Carolina delegates had full powers. The Virginia resolves were read in Congress, and on 7 June Richard Henry Lee moved the Independence resolve:

> That these United Colonies are, and of right ought to be, Independent States, that they are absolved from all allegiance to the British Crown, and that all political connection between them and the State of Great Britain is, and ought to be, totally dissolved.
>
> That it is expedient forthwith to take the most effectual measures for forming foreign alliances.
>
> That a plan of confederation be prepared and transmitted to the respective Colonies for consideration and approbation.

Consideration was postponed by vote of seven colonies to five, because the delegates of New York, Pennsylvania, Delaware, and South Carolina, uninstructed by their provincial congresses, were not prepared to vote; but on 11 June, Congress appointed a committee of five to prepare a Declaration of Independence: Thomas Jefferson, John Adams, Benjamin Franklin, Roger Sherman, and Robert R. Livingston. The committee delegated to Jefferson the task of making the first draft.

Between the day when he completed his rough draft and 28 June, when the report of the committee of five was presented to Congress, many alterations were made by Adams, Franklin, and Jefferson himself. Some interesting changes were also made in the course of a debate by the whole congress. Jefferson's draft included a bitter attack on the king for disallowing acts of the Virginia assembly directed against the

African slave trade. The South Carolina and Rhode Island delegates objected, and it was deleted. The clause referring to the use of Hessians to put down the rebellion originally read, "Scotch and foreign mercenaries," since a kilted Highland regiment had already been sent to Boston. At that, the Reverend John Witherspoon of Princeton, the only clergyman in the Congress, sprang to his feet and said that he would not have the Scottish nation insulted. So the "Scotch and" was deleted.

"I turned to neither book nor pamphlet while writing the Declaration," said Jefferson; but the principles and language of John Locke's *Second Treatise of Government* (1690) were so much a part of his mind that unconsciously he thought and wrote like Locke. The basic theory of the Declaration was that of social compact, precedent and justification for government. But there are certain rights of which no government can deprive mankind; and if a prince disregards these rights and establishes a tyranny, he dissolves the compact and his subjects may throw off their allegiance. This doctrine was a godsend to tender souls among the Patriots who could not get over their duty to honor the king. It explains why the indictment of the Declaration is directed primarily against George III.

Jefferson improved on Locke, who emphasized that man entered political society to protect his property, by the statement:

> We hold these truths to be self-evident, that all men are created equal, that they are endowed by their Creator with certain unalienable Rights, that among these are Life, Liberty, and the Pursuit of Happiness.

Did Jefferson think of blacks when he wrote, "All men are created equal"? His subsequent career indicates that he did not; that in his view blacks were not "men." However that may be, the crisp challenge of the concluding paragraph allowed no exceptions:

> We, therefore, the Representatives of the United States of America [the first official use of that title] solemnly publish and declare . . . that as Free and Independent States, they have full Power to levy War, conclude Peace, contract Alliances, establish Commerce, and to do all other acts and things which independent States may of

right do. And for the support of this Declaration, with a firm reliance on the protection of Divine Providence, we mutually pledge to each other our Lives, our Fortunes and our sacred Honor.

"Sacred Honor" to Jefferson and his colleagues was no empty phrase, no echo of dying feudalism, but the proud declaration of free men that, once their word was given, it would never be broken; and none who signed that instrument ever contemplated anything else.

The committee of five reported to Congress 2 June, and its report was held over while Lee's independence resolution was debated. The first and essential clause was barely passed on 2 July, because Dickinson and Robert Morris were persuaded to stay away so that Franklin, Wilson, and John Morton could cast Pennsylvania's vote for independence. Caesar Rodney turned up to break a deadlock in the Delaware delegation; and the South Carolina members were persuaded to go along. Only the New York delegation sullenly abstained. But the principle of independence was adopted on 2 July, and the Declaration itself, after a few verbal changes had been made in committee of the whole, was adopted on the evening of 4 July 1776. Printed copies were sent next day to the former colonies, now states; and to the army. The Declaration was read from the balcony of Independence Hall on 8 July, and on the 19th, Congress voted to have the instrument signed.

If the American Revolution had produced nothing but the Declaration of Independence, it would have been worth while. The bill of wrongs against George III and Parliament, naturally, is exaggerated. Facts will not sustain many of the alleged "injuries and usurpations." But the beauty and cogency of the preamble, reaching back to remotest antiquity and forward to an indefinite future, have lifted the hearts of millions of men and will continue to do so:

We hold these truths to be self-evident, that all men are created equal, that they are endowed by their Creator with certain unalienable Rights, that among these are Life, Liberty, and the Pursuit of Happiness.

These words are more revolutionary than anything written by Robespierre, Marx, or Lenin, more explosive than the atom, a continual challenge to ourselves, as well as an inspiration to the oppressed of all the world.

CHESTER

Let Ty‑rants shake their I ‑ ron rod,

And slav‑'ry clank_____ her gall ‑ ing chains,

We fear them not, we_____ trust_____ in God,

New ‑ Eng‑land's God_____ for ‑ e ‑ ver reigns.

XV

Military and Naval Generalities

1775-1781

1. *Condition and Organization*

THE WAR OF INDEPENDENCE was not popular in America—few wars have been except the brief Spanish-American affair of 1898. Yet, even when people dislike a war, they may support it, as happened in World War II and the Korean War. In this instance a good part of the American people supported the war for independence as the only alternative to submission ("slavery" they called it); but by no standard, of that time or ours, was their support adequate. After Congress had declared independence, most of Washington's army expected to be discharged; George III should have quit when he read the ringing words of Thomas Jefferson! But the war went on. France joined as an ally in 1778, and again most American soldiers expected to go home and let the French finish the fighting; but the war went on. Many Americans were indifferent, and the Loyalist minority was actively hostile. John Adams was not heeded when he wrote in April 1776, "We shall have a long, obstinate and bloody war to go through." Most Patriots expected the war to be over in a year, and the British government had even more sanguine hopes. Had Americans been able to anticipate the length and difficulty of the war, they would probably have forced the Continental Congress to end it by compromise in 1776; even so there were sarcastic remarks about Congress risking *our* lives and fortunes to save *their* sacred honor. Conversely the British government, had it appreciated the tenacity of Washington, or foreseen the entry of France, Spain, and Holland into the war, might have conceded everything that Congress demanded.

General Washington, who had served with British regulars in the last war and respected them as a fighting force, attempted to form the Continental army on their model. The British army, with a stiff discipline enforced by flogging, was a hard and brutal service. It was recruited largely from the very young and adventurous or from ne'er-do-wells and drunkards. It may have been a mistake to try to create an American army on the British model, as the human elements to furnish that kind of army were not plentiful. But we cannot criticize Congress for not anticipating the French *levée en masse* of 1793, which created the first really national and democratic army in history. Congress made one concession to democratic social conditions by narrowing the difference in pay and privileges between officers and enlisted men. The result was to render officer procurement difficult. Almost every colony had a militia, in which all able-bodied white men were enrolled; but the militia officers were apt to be the bully boys of a neighborhood, good enough to drill yokels on a training field, but poor leaders in battle.

The best officers in the Continental army were either veterans of the previous war or young men commissioned from the ranks. Surprisingly few planters' sons in the South, or college graduates and professional men in the North, came forward to take commissions; in Maryland and Delaware, by exception, the majority of officers were local gentlemen, and the regiments of those states, by and large, were the best in the army. For naval officers the country had to depend largely on merchant mariners, and was lucky to get them away from privateering; a leading New Hampshire Patriot wrote in 1777 that if the pay and privileges of naval officers were not improved, the navy would be "officered by Tinkers, Shoemakers and Horse Jockeys." Nevertheless, in addition to Washington, America produced some field commanders in this war of whom any army could be proud—Anthony Wayne, Nathanael Greene, Henry Knox, John Eager Howard, Daniel Morgan, and Benedict Arnold; and a few naval captains who would have been an honor to any navy—Nicholas Biddle, John Barry, and John Paul Jones.

The other concession made by Congress to democracy was a short-term enlistment. This catered to the inherited English prejudice against "standing armies," and fear of the "man on horseback." Short-term enlistment is the most wasteful way to fill an army, because as soon as you get a lad trained, he is through; but America is still doing it. When a state committee in October 1776 called at Washington's headquarters to ask if one-year enlistments wouldn't do, he started from his chair and said: "Good God, gentlemen! Our cause is ruined if you engage men only for a year. You must not think of it. If we ever hope for success, we must have men enlisted for the whole term of the war." George Partridge of the Continental Congress, who told this anecdote, said that this was the only time he ever saw the General lose his self-control.

As a result of Washington's pleas, Congress before the end of 1776 authorized enlistments for three years, or for the duration. They offered liberal bounties to recruits, but found comparatively few takers, and one year continued to be the normal term under the colors. The average American hated to sign up for a longer period. Married men could not afford to, because nothing was done for dependents; and the young men's favorite contribution to the war was to turn out for a short campaign with the militia, then go home to plant the corn, get in the hay, or harvest the wheat, according to the season. Even in the first flush of enthusiasm, 1775–76, Washington was hampered by the original Yankee contingent of six-month volunteers; they felt that plenty more men were available, and should take their turn.

It must be remembered that Congress was composed of representative Americans who knew their people, and knew that Americans could be led, not driven. Their dilemma was much the same as that of Lincoln at the beginning of the Civil War. They dared not call on their people at once to make the sacrifices necessary to win a quick victory; knowing that a certain way of life, the right to choose whether or not to fight, was more precious to the people than victory, and that they had to be shown that independence could not be won by talk. Thus, we have the paradox that the same spirit of liberty which made the colonists resist George III and choose independence, was an almost fatal handicap in the fight for independence. And it would have been fatal but for George Washington and French assistance.

The Continental army consisted mainly of infantry regiments, in theory composed of 500 officers and men each, recruited in and named after one state—hence terms such as "The Massachusetts Line," "The New Jersey Line." These were called line regiments because of the battle tactics of that day—soldiers firing almost shoulder to shoulder from a line three deep. In addition, there were special corps of cavalry, artillery, engineers, and light infantry. Congress set the quotas that each state was supposed to fill, but it had no authority to draft men to fill these quotas, and no means to enforce the requisitions. This was the same system that the British Empire had used in the French and Indian wars; and, as the colonies did then, so the states now, obeyed requisitions or not as they saw fit. In general, each state passed the buck by apportioning a number of men to each county or town, and these bid against each other by offering bounties to recruits to fill their quotas.

There had been no color line drawn in the last colonial war, and the Continental army and navy followed suit. There were blacks in every line regiment and in John Paul Jones's ships. Virginian slaves who served in the armed forces were liberated at the end of the war. Rhode Island had the nerve to buy slaves to fill her quota, and send the bill to Congress. Even the South Carolina assembly authorized the recruiting of 1000 black slaves in 1780 as "pioneers, fatiguemen, oarsmen, or mariners."

In 1779, when uniforms began arriving from France, Congress passed the first uniform regulations for enlisted men. Blue coats were prescribed for all, with different-colored facings: buff for all officers and for the New York and New Jersey Line; red for the Virginia and Maryland Line, white for the New England regiments. Even after that, few enlisted men could get uniforms, for lack of supply. The general aspect of the average soldier was an eighteenth-century counterpart to Bill Mauldin's World War II cartoons, minus the helmet. He wore anything he could get, and at times that meant almost nothing. A German officer who surrendered with Burgoyne in 1777 reported that the Americans who beat him were upstanding men, slender and sinewy and of fine military bearing; but most of the officers from colonel down, and all enlisted men, wore ordinary clothes, not uniforms. A French observer commented on their "miserable, motley appearance!" Army morale undoubtedly suffered from the lack of uniforms, awards, and decorations. Not until 1782 did General Washington create the Purple Heart, to honor distinguished military service, and only three or four Purple Hearts were conferred before the end of the war.

The system of appointing and promoting officers in the Continental army was complicated. After the Battle of Trenton, Congress granted Washington power to make all promotions up to and including colonel, while Congress itself appointed the generals; but Washington usually had to consult state officials for promotions above the rank of captain. In general, troops from one state would not fight under regimental officers appointed from another. Officers' squabbles gave Washington more trouble than the discipline of enlisted men.

He had plenty of trouble, too, with the enlisted men. Leaders of the different states and sections mingled in the Continental Congress and came to appreciate each other's qualities; but it was not so with common soldiers. Provincials almost always detest people from other sections. We find the term "damn'd Yankees," later so popular in the South, used for the first time by "Yorkers" in General Schuyler's Northern army. The Yankees called the Virginians "buckskins," because Morgan's Rifles wore the frontiersman's fringed hunting shirt. In most of the line regiments from the Middle states and the South, the old-world distinctions between officers, presumed to be gentlemen, and enlisted men, were kept up. To them the fraternization between rank and file, common in the New England line regiments and in frontier units, was disgusting. When a Massachusetts colonel detailed one of his sons, a private soldier, as his batman, and allowed another son to set up a cobbler's bench to repair the men's shoes, Anthony Wayne's Pennsylvania regiment was so incensed as to attack the colonel's headquarters, destroy the bench, and drive his men from the tents with gunfire. A near-mutiny by the Connecticut Line in 1780 at Washington's Morristown headquarters was suppressed by the Pennsylvania Line, which itself mutinied the next year, killed several officers, and occupied Princeton. A mutiny in the New Jersey Line was forcibly put down by 600 troops from other states who marched down from West Point. These mutinies were not caused by treasonable intent—the Pennsylvanians even executed two British spies sent to seduce them to the king's service—but to logistic deficiencies, the lack of food, clothing, and shoes, as well as pay.

The colonial militia, which the independent states took over, included in theory every able-bodied man between the ages of sixteen and sixty. Militia turned out in great numbers whenever the British army marched inland and if properly stiffened by regulars, gave a good account of themselves. The first action of the war, at Concord, was a militia victory, pure and simple, and so was Bunker Hill. The surrender of Burgoyne would not have taken place but for the Green Mountain Boys and other militia who swarmed in to help Gates's regulars. Typical of the attitude of the average American is the story of Reuben Stebbins of Williamstown, Massachusetts. He had not seen fittin' to turn out until he actually heard the firing at Bennington. He then saddled his horse, called for his musket, and remarked as he rode off, "We'll see who's goin't' own this farm!"

The turning-out of an entire countryside to fight was new to the British. European armies marched safely through enemy country until they encountered a hostile army. Peasants and townspeople kept quiet or took to the forests and mountains, fighting was for professionals only. This phenomenon of a countryside in arms, both around Boston and in the Saratoga campaign, made British generals very loath to march far from the seacoast, where they were at the end of a logistics line maintained by the Royal Navy. After Burgoyne's surrender, and until Cornwallis cut loose in the Carolinas, no British army spent much time beyond gunfire range of the British fleet.

In 1776 the Thirteen Colonies, with a population of 2,500,000, could, within the framework of their social-economic system, have provided a regular army of 100,000. But they could never have fed and clothed so many, and 35,000 should have been enough, with militia support, to defeat the British, who never numbered more than that at any one time. The Continental army reached a top figure of 18,000 just before the Battle of Long Island, but by the end of 1776 had shrunk to 5000; by early 1778 it had recovered a strength of almost 20,000, and then declined again.

On the other hand, the war was even less popular in England than in America. Englishmen would not enlist in any appreciable numbers to fight overseas against their kith and kin; and the supply of German mercenaries was limited both by the rapacity of German princelings and the resources of the British treasury.

2. Logistics, Finance, and Foreign Volunteers

The principal reason why Washington's army, at Valley Forge and later, went hungry, unpaid, unclothed, and unshod, was no lack of supplies in the country, but the reluctance of farmers and merchants to exchange food and clothing for a Continental chit. One of the uncommemorated heroes of the war was Christopher Ludwig, a German baker of Philadelphia, who, when Congress proposed that he furnish 100 pounds of bread for 135 pounds of flour, offered to furnish as many pounds of hard bread as he was given flour, and did so. On the other hand, the merchants of Philadelphia, in 1781, refused to furnish General Greene with 5000 suits of clothes for the Southern army, although they had the cloth and the general offered them bills of exchange on France. Europe was used to armies helping themselves in wartime, and collecting from the government later, if one could; but in free colonial America the people had never experienced this, and Washington had to be pretty desperate, at Valley Forge, to "forage the country naked." The sufferings of the Continental army have not been exaggerated, but they were due to selfishness, mismanagement, and difficulties in transportation rather than to poverty or necessity.

An improvement took place after Washington persuaded General Nathanael Greene to accept the post of quartermaster general, which he did with reluctance since (as he truly remarked), "nobody ever heard of a quartermaster in history." By the spring of 1778 the army was sufficiently well fed to pursue Howe across New Jersey, but it was never properly clad until 1782. A Rhode Island colonel, writing to the governor of his state begging for more clothing, said that the condition of his men was so scandalous that they were called "the naked regiment." The Battle of Eutaw Springs was largely fought by barefooted soldiers in breech-clouts. Most American families in 1776 made their own clothing at home, and could not greatly increase the output; the well-to-do imported their clothing from England, and that supply was cut off. Wagon transportation was slow, costly, and subject to accident and depredation; the British controlled the usual sea routes from colony to colony. Supplies came from France and from prize cargoes; but clothing wears out fast in any army, and faster than usual in Washington's, where there was a shortage of tents and blankets. Procurement of blankets was a special problem since Americans, by and large, slept under quilts which were of no use to soldiers in the field. From Valley Forge General Washington wrote, "There are now in this Army . . . 4000 men wanting blankets, near 2000 of which have never had one, altho' some of them have been 12 months in service."

The medical situation in the army was so shockingly bad, even for that era of untrained "sawbones," that medical officers who survived the war got together to found American medical schools. Altogether, the private soldier of the War of Independence was so badly fed, clothed, and cared for, and often so badly led, too, that one is surprised and grateful that any continued to fight. Lafayette, De Kalb, and Von Steuben all expressed the opinion that no European army would have endured the hardships that the Americans suffered.

During most of the war, a principal source of food for Washington's army was Connecticut, where Governor Jonathan Trumbull, a business man, not only procured quantities of flour and beef but set up a cannon foundry, a shoe shop, and a plant for salvaging damaged muskets.[1] Yet the Connecticut Line was badly neglected in such items as clothing. Virginia throughout the war seemed paralyzed, so far as supplying her own line was concerned; her regiments at times were pinned down, not by the enemy, but because the soldiers had neither shoes nor clothes. Although the revolted colonies showed considerable enterprise in producing arms and munitions, these supplies were never sufficient. Military cargoes from France, which slipped through the British blockade, in large measure armed and clothed the American army that forced Burgoyne to surrender. But it was no easy matter to get supplies through that blockade. A large quantity of clothing and muskets that Lafayette persuaded the French to make for us in 1780 never reached America because Franklin could not find the merchant ships to load them or the warships to escort them.

France was also looked to for financial support. About a million dollars was advanced by the treasury of Louis XVI while France was still neutral, and about $1.6 million after she entered the war in 1778, together with about $6.4 million in loans. These, however, were but a small part of the war finance. The major financial operations were (1) bills of credit, the famous Continental currency, of which $241.5 million in face value was issued before 1781, together with state bills to the face value of $210 million; (2) domestic loans, both interest-bearing bonds known as loan office certificates in denominations of $300 up, and certificates of indebtedness for goods received or seized, amounting to about $20 million; (3) requisitions in money or in kind which were apportioned among the states on the basis of their estimated population. These yielded $5 million in paper money and $4 million worth of goods.

The loans, both domestic and foreign, as well as the states' debts, were repaid at par in the Washington administration, under Hamilton's funding scheme. But the Continental and state currency depreciated to a point where it cost more to print than it would buy. Robert Morris, appointed by Congress superintendent of finance in February 1781, at about the darkest moment of the war, succeeded in preventing a complete financial collapse. A loan of $200,000 in gold, brought over by the Frency navy, enabled him to found the note-issuing Bank of North America in November of that year,

[1] Governor Trumbell also backed the building of our first submarine, "Bushnell's Turtle," by David Bushnell of Saybrook. It was a hand-propelled, one-man job, supposed to screw a delayed-action torpedo into the side of an enemy ship; but it never succeeded in closing.

and to perform a financial miracle—putting the country on a hard-money basis before the war ended. Morris in finance accomplished as much for independence as Washington and Franklin did in their respective fields.

The officer problem was complicated by foreign volunteers. Twelve years of peace in Europe meant that many unemployed professional soldiers were eager to serve in the Continental army. They pestered Silas Deane and Benjamin Franklin, the American agents in France, for letters of recommendation. To get rid of these importunate volunteers, Franklin would give them passage money and a letter of introduction to Congress, whose president complained that French officers beset his door like bailiffs stalking a debtor. Congress appointed these soldiers of fortune to ranks as high as major general, and then left it to Washington to find something for them to do. And since Americans disliked serving under foreigners, there was nothing for most of them to do except to serve on Washington's staff, and tell him in French, German, or Polish as the case might be, that his army was lousy.

There were several exceptions. The Marquis de Lafayette was in a class by himself. A young and wealthy idealist, enthusiastic for liberty and avid of glory, he came out in 1777 in a ship equipped at his own expense; and Congress commissioned him major general in the Continental army one month before his twentieth birthday. Modest, handsome, and charming, Lafayette captivated every American with whom he came in contact, including Washington, who, before the end of the year, gave him a small independent command. The Marquis proved a brave and capable officer whom the Americans were as ready to follow as a native-born; perhaps more so, since he bought them clothing and comforts with his own money. But Lafayette's greatest service was political. The French court was flattered by the attention that the young nobleman received, and he, on a mission home in 1779, persuaded the king to send out the expeditionary force under Rochambeau which helped Washington to win the decisive Battle of Yorktown.

The Chevalier Duportail, a French engineer officer, thirty-four years old, came out in 1777 with three or four junior French engineers. Commissioned lieutenant colonel, he rose to major general and was extremely useful on Washington's staff as a designer of forts and other defensive works. Thaddeus Kosciuszko, a twenty-year-old officer of the Polish army, came to America in the summer of 1776. Pennsylvania employed him to construct forts for the defense of the Delaware river, which earned him a commission in the Continental Corps of Engineers. He designed the first fortifications at West Point.

After peace was concluded he returned home and became a national hero of Poland, in one of her many wars of liberation. Casimir Pulaski, a Polish cavalry officer, was still under thirty when Franklin advanced him the funds to sail to America. He was given the top cavalry command under General Lincoln in the Southern campaign, and fell mortally wounded when charging the British lines before Savannah at the head of his troopers.

The self-styled Baron de Kalb, a middle-aged German soldier of fortune who had fought the last two wars in the French army, was also appointed major general by Congress. He proved to be a tough and able commander. Leading his troops in the Battle of Camden, he received a mortal wound.

One of the most important foreigners to serve the American cause was Baron von Steuben, a forty-seven-year-old Prussian junker who had been on the staff of Frederick the Great. Drilling soldiers was Steuben's specialty, and one of Washington's main sources of trouble. There was no standard manual of arms, and colonial lads were not used to prompt obedience of crisp orders. Steuben drew up a manual of arms, formed a model company, drilled it himself, and in a few weeks made such smart soldiers of these men that the whole army became drill-conscious. At Washington's recommendation he was promoted major general and appointed inspector general of the Continental army. He also brought about an important reorganization. Owing to the differing responses to recruiting, some line regiments then had their full strength of 500 men, while others were down to as few as thirty. So Steuben created a new unit, the battalion of 200 men, so that the army could be maneuvered accurately. The Battle of Monmouth was the first test of this reorganized Continental army; thenceforth the Continentals were equal to the best British regulars.

3. The Weapons

Colonel von Steuben, when he reported to Washington at Valley Forge, ascertained that one infantry company might be armed with a mixture of muskets, carbines, shotguns, and rifles. He used his influence to have all foot soldiers armed with the standard infantry weapon, the smooth-bore, muzzle-loading musket with an 11-gauge (¾-in.) bore. Trained soldiers could fire a musket twice or thrice a minute; but after a few rounds they had to check to let the barrel cool off. Steuben found the bayonet unknown to Americans, and they had no defense drill against the enemy's use of that arm. British infantry frequently scored because they carried bayonets as standard equipment, and if they got near enough for a bayonet charge, usually won. And in stretches of wet weather, muskets misfired. General Washington, concerned over British superiority with the bayonet, made every effort to equip his army with them; and American bayonet tactics improved as the war progressed. Stony Point was captured in 1779 by a brilliant assault of Continental light infantry with muskets unloaded and bayonets fixed.

The rifle, introduced into the colonies by Germans and Swiss, had by 1775 become the American frontiersman's favorite weapon. It was far more accurate than the smooth-bore musket. A fair rifleman could make 40 per cent hits on a standing man at 100 yards. Morgan's Rifles, recruited from the back country of Pennsylvania, Maryland, and Virginia, formed a part of Washington's first army. But rifle never replaced musket as the standard infantry weapon, because loading the heavy, six-foot barrel required a full minute; and fighting in those days was at such close range that the enemy could bayonet a rifleman before he had a chance to reload. General Peter Muhlenberg wrote to Washington that he wanted his regiment of riflemen converted to musketry, because rifles were "of little use," on a march in wet weather. And Anthony Wayne wrote that he "would almost as soon face an Enemy with a good musket and bayonet without ammunition," as with a rifle. Nevertheless, riflemen were useful if posted on the flanks, especially on rough ground and under cover, to fire on the enemy at long range. On the British side, Major Patrick Ferguson invented a light, breech-loading rifle to which a bayonet could be fixed and which, had it gone into production, might have changed the course of the war. But the conservatism of the war office prevented that, and Ferguson, ironically enough, was killed by an American rifle ball at Kings Mountain.

Nowadays the United States Marine Corps is the elite American fighting force; but in this war the "leathernecks," as the sailors called them, were stationed on shipboard to pick off enemy gunners in close combat. The elite of Washington's army, as of the British army, was the light infantry. General Washington organized a light infantry corps in 1777, for which he selected young, agile, and dependable lads who were good shots. They wore a dashing leather helmet with horsehair crest and carried less equipment than the line. Lafayette commanded a corps of 2000 light infantry which acquired such a reputation that every ambitious young officer wished to transfer to this corps. Alexander Hamilton left Washington's staff to be a light infantry captain; Colonel Alexander Scammell left his post of adjutant general to command a light infantry corps organized shortly before the Yorktown campaign, and lost his life in the assault. Lafayette later maintained that his American light infantry were the finest troops he ever commanded, whether in America or France.

The artillery of the Continental army was commanded by General Henry Knox, a former Boston bookseller whom Washington considered the ablest and most dependable of his generals. It consisted of brass or iron muzzle-loaders, the best being captured English cannon or those imported from France, and was limited in size to what men, not horses, could pull over bad roads. A "12-pounder," a cannon that shot a round iron ball of that weight, was the caliber that all gunners wanted but did not always obtain. One- or two-gun companies of artillery, posted among the infantry or on the flanks with the riflemen, usually withheld fire until the enemy was about 400 yards distant and then let go with small balls called grapeshot; solid balls were used at shorter range. Siege artillery included howitzers to throw "carcasses" (incendiary shells) and mortars which fired exploding bombshells with slow fuses.

Cavalry was not much used by either side, largely because of the rough, wooded nature of the country. The British found that horses and their forage took up too much room on transports, and sent home from New York in 1778 one of the two cavalry regiments they had brought over. Washington, however, was able to procure enough horses to form a cavalry corps, and enough uniforms to clothe the troopers properly. The most useful mounted units were the "legions," organized in the Southern campaigns under leaders such as Pulaski and "Light Horse Harry" Lee; these troopers generally fought on foot, using horses merely for quick movement, like the European dragoons.

4. The Navies

Britain's most striking military superiority over the Thirteen Colonies lay in her navy, which might have been decisive, had France not intervened. A tight blockade of the North American coast was impossible in days of sail, but the Royal Navy, which at the onset of hostilities had 28 warships with over 500 guns and 4000 men in ports between Halifax and Florida, was strong enough to keep regular trade routes open, to operate from its Halifax and New York bases throughout the war, and from Chesapeake Bay, Boston, Newport, Charleston, and Savannah for limited periods. This meant that the British could shift troops by sea from England to America, or from one American port to another almost at will, and could deny the sea to all enemy ships except nimble privateers and frigates. And Britain had plenty of ships for patrolling the narrow seas and the Mediterranean, and escorting convoys to the West Indies, Canada, and the ports she held in the United States.

American efforts to diminish British naval superiority were divided and largely ineffective. General Washington commissioned what we might call the army's salt-water navy during the siege of Boston; and some of these little armed schooners operated into the year 1777. The army also had a fresh-water navy on Lake Champlain, organized by Benedict Arnold, which prevented the British from invading New York in 1776. No fewer than six states—Massachusetts, Pennsylvania, Maryland, Virginia, and the Carolinas—had navies of their own, to guard inland waters or prowl off shore in search of prizes. Congress, and most of the states too, commissioned privateers —about 1500 all told—to prey on enemy commerce; and, on top of all that, there was the Continental navy.

Congress, it must be admitted, had nerve to found a navy, as it did on 13 October 1775, not without opposition. Samuel Chase of Maryland said it was "the maddest idea in the world to think of building an American fleet"; but a Virginia delegate, Professor George Wythe, silenced him with an appeal to history. The Romans, he observed, built a fleet from 'scratch and managed to destroy Carthage. The first Continental fleet, which raided Nassau before the Declaration of Independence, consisted of converted merchantmen. Congress, in the meantime, had authorized the building of thirteen frigates, which it hopefully expected to be ready for sea in three months. These were three-masted square-riggers, about 125 feet long on an average, carrying a main battery of 12-pounders and a second battery of 4-, 6-, and 9-pounders. Their construction was given to several shipyards between Portsmouth and Baltimore, and former masters in the merchant marine were appointed to command them. The fate of this fleet is a sad example of what happens to an inferior sea power. Four of the frigates were destroyed on the stocks to prevent their falling into enemy hands. Frigates *Warren* and *Raleigh* were actually launched and ready for sea in the spring of 1776, but the former, together with *Providence,* was bottled up in Narragansett Bay by the British for two years; and *Raleigh,* which for want of men and guns never left port until mid-1777, was captured within a year.

Virginia, built in Baltimore and commanded by the senior American naval captain, James Nicholson, was captured even before leaving the Chesapeake; Nicholson was then given command of *Trumbull* and lost her when, after two years, she was trying to elude the British blockade of the Connecticut river. Frigate *Randolph,* commanded by Nicholas Biddle, remained inactive at Charleston for months because her crew deserted; in her next fight she blew up, killing all hands. *Hancock* was captured by the British in 1777 and renamed *Iris;* it was she that took *Trumbull* in 1781. All the earlier converted navy had been captured or destroyed by the end of 1779, and most of the officers not languishing in British jails had turned to privateering for want of another command. By the end of the war the United States Navy consisted of only one or two ships larger than an armed schooner.

Captain John Paul Jones and Robert Morris, who in addition to his financial burdens became Congress's first secretary of the navy, wished to organize the Continental navy in task forces to make diversionary raids on the British Isles or the West Indies. This was actually done only by exceptional leaders like Jones; for the British broke up most attempts of American warships to assemble, and, owing to the competition of privateers, naval ratings had to be kept happy by taking prizes. A privateersman had little discipline and not much danger, since these ships were built for speed and could escape any enemy that looked powerful. On the other hand, they had ample opportunity to get rich out of prize money—or rather, only thought they did, for most of them were eventually captured and the sailors spent the rest of the war in English prisons. Nevertheless, few men could be recruited for the Continental navy unless the captain made it clear that his major job was to capture prizes. There was no money in raiding British ports, as John Paul Jones found out to his sorrow.

Thus the only results effected by these private, state, and Continental navies were to annoy British commerce and supply the American war market with consumer goods at enemy expense. The real naval accomplishments of the war, for America, were effected by the royal navy of France.

5. *The Loyalists*

The War of American Independence was a true civil war. In America itself a strong minority who called themselves Loyalists, and by their enemies were called Tories, supported the mother country; and there was much fighting between Loyalist and Patriot partisan (guerrilla) bands. In England itself there was no fighting, apart from the exploits of John Paul Jones in coastal waters; yet sympathy with the American cause was widespread. Vice Admiral Augustus Keppel and General Sir Jeffrey Amherst refused to serve against America; General Harry Conway refused to "draw his sword in that cause"; the Earl of Effingham, colonel of a regiment ordered to America, turned in his commission because "the duties of a soldier and a citizen" had become "inconsistent." He was publicly congratulated on his stand by the city corporations of Dublin and London. Charles James Fox adopted blue and buff for the colors of the Whig opposition because they were those of General Washington's uniform.

The Loyalist party in America persisted throughout the war, although it never managed to get properly organized outside New York City. Socially, it was top-heavy. The royal office-holders, about half the councillors in the royal and proprietary colonies, and many wealthy merchants, went Tory. The pacifist sects—Quakers, Moravians, and Mennonites—stayed neutral if they could. Most of the Anglican ministers in New England and the Middle colonies remained loyal to the king, the head of their church; and when British troops evacuated New York, the rector of Trinity Church and his entire congregation went with them. Families everywhere were divided. Almost every leading American—Adams, Otis, Lee, Washington, Franklin, Jefferson, Randolph, and Rutledge—had Loyalist kinsmen. But there were also many thousand farmers, artisans and shopkeepers, on the king's side; and it is probable that a majority of the back countrymen in the Carolinas, initially, at least, were loyal, since the Regulator troubles had created bitter enmity toward local Whigs. Many who started as good Whigs could not swallow the Declaration of Independence, and others were so outraged by mob action as to repudiate it.

The number of the Loyalists varied from colony to colony. They were strongest in New York, partly because the city was occupied by the British after the Battle of Long Island and held by them throughout the war; partly because New York had an aristocratic social structure. They were weakest in Connecticut, Massachusetts, and Virginia, where the radical leaders were talented, respectable men and good organizers. Governor Dunmore of Virginia drove to the Patriot side many who otherwise would have been Tory, by a proclamation inviting slaves to desert their masters. Estimates of as high as 50 per cent of the total population have been made for New York and as low as 8 per cent for Connecticut. My guess is that not more than 10 per cent of the white population of the United States was actively Loyalist; that about 40 per cent was actively Patriot, and about 50 per cent indifferent or neutral. The significant fact is that nowhere, except in Georgia and in occupied seaports, were the British able to organize a Loyalist civil government.

One factor that had no visible effect on a man's choice was race and language. Blacks in general remained faithful to their masters, and many served in the Continental army and navy. German-Americans contributed their share to George III who, after all, was a German king; and the only place during the war where German was recognized as a second official language was in New York City under British rule. Even the Irish were far from unanimous on the Patriot side. Loyal Irish volunteers were organized during the siege of Boston to help defend that town against Washington; and a big Loyalist corps, Lord Rawdon's Volunteers of Ireland, did valiant work for several years. The first New York St. Patrick's Day parade on record was staged by 500 members of this corps in 1779. Conversely, many English, Irish, and Scots who had been but a short time in America became ardent Patriots and fought for the cause. Among these were Generals Montgomery, Gates, and St. Clair, and Captains Barry and Paul Jones.

Wherever a British army held firm, Loyalists flocked to its protection; but when the troops evacuated, they had to leave too or suffer vengeance from the Patriots. But by far the greater number of Loyalists stayed in the United States. There was no general purge, concentration camp, gas chamber, forced-labor battalion, or other cruelty with which we are recently familiar. If a Loyalist was discreet, kept his mouth shut, paid his taxes, refrained from spying or enlisting in partisan raids, it was possible for him to stay at home with no damage other than to his pride; and thousands did. But Loyalists afforded aid and comfort to the enemy. Scattered throughout the country, they acted as secret service for the king. After Sir Henry Clinton had consolidated his army in New York City, he began enrolling special Tory units; New York State furnished more troops to the king than she did to Congress.

The persecution that Loyalists suffered early in the war aroused the liveliest resentment; and their tactics when they were enrolled in military units were to wage war with the utmost severity. The massacre of the garrison of Fort Griswold, New London, in 1781, was the work of Loyalist battalions from New York and New Jersey, led by Benedict Arnold. Colonel John Butler's Tory Rangers and Sir John Johnson's Loyal Greens, with 500 Seneca auxiliaries, perpetrated the Wyoming Valley massacre of peaceful farmers. Loyalist units directed by former Governor Tryon would dash over to the New Jersey or Connecticut shore, burn houses and crops, and seize booty and prisoners. In the Carolinas the civil war between Patriots and Loyalists was most severe and prolonged. Oaths and tests were applied by both sides, only to be violated at the first opportunity. Prisoners were hanged by one side for treachery, and the other side retaliated in kind. Thus the War of Independence was a civil war in which the contending parties were not mainly sectional, as in the war of 1861–65; they lived side by side throughout the length and breadth of the land, and, naturally, they fought tough.

6. The Commander in Chief

Although the Thirteen States lacked a great political leader to call forth a spirit of sacrifice, Washington did his best to fill the political as well as the military role. He was more than a general: the embodiment of everything fine in the American character. With no illusions about his own grandeur, no thought of the future except an intense longing to return to Mount Vernon, he assumed every responsibility thrust upon him, and fulfilled it. He not only had to lead an army but constantly to write letters to Congress, state leaders, and state governments, begging them for the wherewithal to maintain his army. He had to compose quarrels among his officers and placate cold, hungry, unpaid troops. Intrigues against his authority he ignored, and the intriguers came to grief. In his relations with French officers he proved to be a diplomat second only to Franklin. Refusing to accept a salary, he dipped into his modest fortune to buy comforts for the soldiers and to help destitute families of his companions in battle. Thus Washington brought something more important to the cause than military ability and statesmanship: the priceless gift of character.

Although Washington was scrupulous in his respect for the civil power, there was a certain jealousy of him in Congress and the state governments, largely from fear that he would be too successful and become a dictator. Yet, inconsistently, several members, especially Richard Henry Lee of his own state, and James Lovell of Massachusetts, thought he was not successful enough and played with the idea of relieving him by Charles Lee, or Gates, or the French Duc de Broglie. Just how far the "Conway cabal" of 1777 intended to go; whether it was an officers' plot to supersede Washington, or mere grumbling by ambitious malcontents, is still a mystery. But it is certain that the commander in chief was regarded by the rank and file, and by people in all parts of the country, with deep respect and affection. He did not have the personality of a Napoleon, a Nelson, or a Stonewall Jackson to arouse men to fanatical loyalty; but the soldiers knew that they could depend on him for valor, for military wisdom, and for justice.

WAR AND WASHINGTON

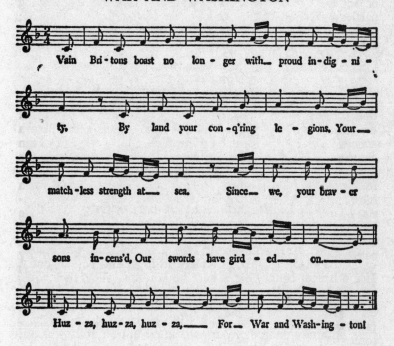

Vain Bri-tons boast no lon - ger with proud in-dig - ni -
ty. By land your con-q'ring le - gions, Your match-less strength at sea. Since we, your brav - er sons in-cens'd, Our swords have gird - ed on.
Huz - za, huz-za, huz - za, For War and Wash-ing - ton!

XVI

The Northern Campaigns

1776-1778

1. *Long Island and New York City*

NEW YORK CITY, with about 22,000 inhabitants, was second only to Philadelphia as an American town and port of entry. If the British could hold it and the Hudson valley, they could cut off New England from the rest of the rebel colonies.

If General Sir William Howe had lifted his army from Boston directly to New York City, he could doubtless have held both city and colony for the king. But Sir Billy was one of the greatest bus-missers in British military history. After evacuating Boston on 17 March 1776, his army was escorted by the fleet of his brother Admiral Lord Howe to Halifax, to await reinforcements. Not until 7 June did the Howe brothers sail from Nova Scotia to New York, and their first transports arrived in the Narrows on 2 July. Washington had transferred his Continental army to New York directly after the siege of Boston, so Sir Billy had to fight for New York instead of having it fall into his lap.

Washington now had 18,000 men in and around Manhattan, almost the top strength attained by the Continental army during the war. General Howe landed 25,000 men on Staten Island without opposition, and the British fleet acquired complete control of New York harbor, the East river, and the Hudson.

Washington transferred most of his army to Brooklyn and fortified the Heights, hoping that he could force the enemy to evacuate. But Sir Billy, in an unusual spasm of energy, shifted a large part of his army by ships' boats across the bay and challenged Washington on 27 August 1776 in the Battle of Long Island. That battle very nearly crushed both Washington and the cause. Instead of taking a stand on the Heights, Washington drew up his forces on the plain, where the British had the advantage. They were used to European methods of open-field ,fighting, which Americans were not; and Howe fought his army skillfully. The American commander in chief's dispositions were defective, the New England militia panicked, and the result was a bad defeat for the Americans. They lost over 1000 men killed, wounded, and captured, including two general officers. But Howe's failure to pursue enabled Washington to execute a strategic retirement. Nine thousand men, with field artillery, provisions, cattle, horses, and wagons were transferred across the East river to Manhattan in thirteen hours. Skillful retirements do not win wars; but this one, like that of the British from Dunkerque in 1940, saved an army from annihilation and allowed the war to continue.

Washington's situation on Manhattan was still bad. He now had fewer than 15,000 effectives, constantly diminishing by desertion and expiring enlistments, against 20,000 to 25,000 British regulars and German mercenaries, constantly augmented by reinforcements from England and supported by a naval force unopposed by anything Congress could set afloat. Manhattan was impossible to defend without Brooklyn Heights. The most sensible military measure would have been to burn the city and retire, which Washington proposed to do; but Congress forbade. So he withdrew to Harlem Heights in the north end of Manhattan. In the meantime, Admiral Howe sailed his warships up both flanks of the island, threw a cordon across it at the site of 34th Street, and took possession of the city.

New York remained in British hands throughout the war. This was a tremendous asset. By concentrating their main military force in New York, the British were able to strike out in three directions—into New England, up the Hudson, and down through the Jerseys. And since the Royal Navy commanded the Atlantic except for a few months in 1778 and 1781, troops could be shifted from New York to any part of the

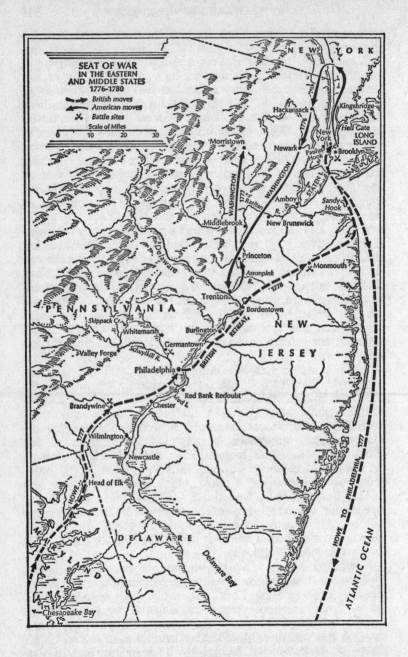

SEAT OF WAR
IN THE EASTERN
AND MIDDLE STATES
1776-1780

- ⇢ British moves
- ⟵ American moves
- ✕ Battle sites

Scale of Miles
0   10   20   30

NEW YORK

Hackensack

Morristown

Newark

Kingsbridge

Hell Gate

LONG ISLAND

New York

Paulus Hook

Brooklyn

STATEN I.

Amboy

Sandy Hook

Raritan R.

WASHINGTON

Middlebrook

New Brunswick

Princeton

Monmouth

Delaware R.

Assunpink R.

Trenton

1778

PENNSYLVANIA

Bordentown

NEW

Skippack Cr.

Whitemarsh

Burlington

BRITISH RETREAT

JERSEY

Germantown

Valley Forge

Schuylkill R.

Philadelphia

Red Bank Redoubt

Mud I.

Brandywine

Chester

Wilmington

Newcastle

HOWE TO PHILADELPHIA, 1777

1777

Head of Elk

MARYLAND

DELAWARE

Delaware Bay

ATLANTIC OCEAN

Chesapeake Bay

318

Atlantic coast by sea. The food problem was not serious, because the British also held Staten Island, parts of Long Island,
and most of Westchester County, and were able to bring in
army rations from Europe.

Washington did not immediately give up Manhattan. At
the upper end, near where 180th Street meets the Hudson,
he built Fort Washington, and Fort Lee across the river on
the Palisades. After beating off an attack on his left flank at
White Plains, he decided to retire further up the Hudson
and establish stronger lines behind the Croton river. General
Howe now forced his hand by moving the British army up to
Dobbs Ferry, which placed it between Washington's army and
the two forts, and in a position to march across New Jersey
to Philadelphia.

Washington countered by sending 5000 men under General
Israel Putnam into New Jersey, leaving 7000 under General
Charles Lee at North Castle, where the Croton flows into the
Hudson. Before so doing he advised General Nathanael
Greene, commander at Forts Washington and Lee, to abandon them as useless enclaves inside the British lines. Greene
made the valiant but unwise decision to defend Fort Washington and lost it, together with 2500 men taken prisoner.
Howe's subordinate, General Lord Cornwallis, then transferred 5000 men across the Hudson, mounted cannon on the
Palisades, and forced Greene to abandon Fort Lee too; but
this time the garrison made a successful retreat. Fort Washington was renamed Fort Knyphausen, after the Hessian general who led the assault; it was, in fact, a German victory on
American soil. "This sort of glory, won by German mercenaries against free-born English subjects, has no charms for
me," said Edmund Burke.

2. The Campaign of the Jersies

Washington with 5000 men had crossed into New Jersey
before Cornwallis. The first phase of this Campaign of 1776
in the Jersies was a race for the bridge over the Raritan at
New Brunswick. Washington won, getting there on 1 December. His immediate objectives were to preserve the Continental
army intact and to cover and defend Philadelphia. Howe's
objective should have been to destroy Washington's divided
army. It was the time of times for a British commander to go
all out, while Washington's small army was split three ways.
Yet, at this juncture, Howe chose to send a large part of his
force, in 70 transports, escorted by 11 warships, to Newport,
Rhode Island. Not until 7 December did Howe himself cross

into New Jersey and take personal command of Cornwallis's force in hope of bringing Washington to decisive action.

New Jersey was a problem for Washington. The Jerseymen waited to see who would win before committing themselves. When the British entered the state, they encountered no countryside in arms; rather, a countryside that took to the cellar. General Howe offered British protection papers to all and sundry who would come in and take an oath of allegiance; and so many did so that the blanks gave out. "The conduct of the Jerseys has been most infamous," wrote Washington to his brother Augustine. "Instead of turning out to defend their country, and affording aid to our army, they are making their submissions as fast as they can. If they had given us any support, we might have made a stand at Hackensack and after that at Brunswick, but the few militia that were in arms, disbanded themselves . . . and left the poor remains of our army to make the best we could of it."

So Washington's little army, with no help from Charles Lee's division, plodded wearily across wintry New Jersey, keeping one jump ahead of Howe. On 7–8 December they first crossed the Delaware river. There were no bridges above Philadelphia, which made the river an excellent defense; but it was a difficult stream for an army to cross. Foreseeing everything, Washington sent men and officers ahead from as far back as New Brunswick, to collect every boat within twenty miles of Trenton. General Lord Stirling[1] held up Howe at Princeton, then made a forced march to Trenton and got his last man on board just as a Hessian brigade entered Trenton with brass bands playing.

Naturally the Americans kept all the boats on the Pennsylvania side of the river, so there were none for the British to use. And Howe on 13 December decided to call off the campaign for that year. The Jersies were very cold and wet, he had a charming mistress in New York City, and gentlemen did not wage war in winter. Washington's ragged army might melt away before spring; surely the Americans now realized that Britain was invincible? So Howe distributed his army in houses and cantonments all the way from Burlington to Hackensack.

General Howe, by wintering in New Jersey, succeeded in curing the Jerseymen of their neutralist attitude. About half the forces strung from Burlington to Hackensack were German mercenaries, and Germans have been notorious looters from the days of Tacitus to those of Hitler. Protection papers

[1] William Alexander, son of a New York lawyer who defended John Peter Zenger, and a claimant to the earldom of Stirling.

issued to loyal Jerseymen did them no good because the Germans couldn't read; even so, they stole books out of the Princeton library and ransacked shops and houses indiscriminately. So many trains of army wagons moved into New York laden with plate, furniture, and clothing that it looked as though all Jersey were moving to town. The officers were generous in letting their men have a piece of every load. Those not so fortunate stole horses and saddlebags and loaded them with valuables; one Hessian private even got a grandfather clock into New York on horseback.

So far as General Howe was concerned, the campaign of 1776 was over. But Washington had different ideas. He had a touch of the gambler in him, as have all great military leaders. He had been retreating for almost six months; to do nothing all winter but watch the ice cakes float down the Delaware would about finish his army. "You can form no idea," he wrote his brother Augustine on 18 December, "of the perplexity of my situation. No man, I believe, ever had a greater choice of difficulties, and less means to extricate himself from them . . . under a full persuasion of the justice of our cause I cannot entertain an idea that it will finally sink."

He had to do something, and that soon, because the enlistments of half his army would expire with the year 1776, and few replacements were coming. To protect his position on the west bank of the Delaware, he had spread his line regiments thin along 25 miles of the river. A Hessian brigade was in Trenton; if it were allowed to take the offensive it might crash through and march into Philadelphia. So Washington took the offensive, with 2400 men whom he led nine miles upstream to cross at McKonkey's Ferry, where most of the boats were assembled. Pan ice was floating down the river. For landing craft Washington had a fleet of Durham boats, 30 to 40 feet long, whose peace-time employment was to carry freight on the Delaware. Each was manned by four or five men of Colonel Glover's webfooted Marblehead regiment.

The crossing started at 7:00 p.m. Christmas Day. By 3:00 a.m. all the men and 18 fieldpieces were across. It took an hour to form the regiments on the east bank. At 4:00 o'clock December 26, the advance began in two columns through snow and in a biting wind. Sunrise found the columns a mile from Trenton, where Colonel Rall's Hessians were sleeping off Christmas. They were completely surprised, their retreat cut off, and when General Knox's artillery fired briskly down the two main streets of the village, the German officers decided to surrender. At a cost of none killed, four wounded, but two frozen to death, Washington captured over 900 prisoners, 1200 small arms, 6 brass cannon, and the colors of the Hessian brigade.

"All our hopes," wrote Lord George Germain the British secretary at war, "were blasted by the unhappy affair at Trenton." American enlistments at once increased. Pennsylvania militia swarmed into Washington's camp, delighted at an opportunity to invade New Jersey. Three New England line regiments, whose enlistments had expired, were persuaded by a personal appeal from the General to remain six weeks longer.

Washington now established headquarters at Newtown, hoping to advance before New Year's and drive the enemy from New Jersey. Congress responded by granting him—for six months,—the authority to raise a new army and to appoint all officers under rank of brigadier general. He now had 5000 men, partly new recruits but including many veterans. Lord Cornwallis, leaving strong rear guards at Princeton and Lawrenceville, took up a position with about 5500 men before Trenton on the left bank of Assumpinck Creek. Washington evaded this main enemy force and on the night of 2–3 January 1777 advanced on Princeton. At dawn an advance column under General Hugh Mercer encountered a small British force marching south to reinforce Cornwallis, and the Battle of Princeton took place. General Mercer was killed, and the battle almost became an American rout; but Washington personally rallied his men within thirty paces of the enemy and held them in check until Pennsylvania riflemen and veteran New England troops could deploy. Once again Washington proved that he was as good a field commander as he was a planner and strategist. The British were routed and chased into the college town, where one of the regiments barricaded itself in Nassau Hall but surrendered after Washington's artillery fired a few cannon balls into the building.

Washington wished to march on to New Brunswick, but his men were dog-tired, falling asleep by the roadside, and Cornwallis was on his trail. So, five miles out of Princeton, he marched by the left flank, again eluded Cornwallis, and by the end of the first week of January took up winter quarters at Morristown. Cornwallis retired to the New Brunswick-Perth Amboy-Paulus Hook triangle. From Morristown, Washington could maintain communications with Philadelphia, Albany, and New England; and by sending out raids he captured Hackensack, Elizabethtown, and Newark in the course of the winter. In a campaign lasting only three weeks, at a time of year when gentlemen were not supposed to fight, the military genius of America's greatest gentleman, and the fortitude of some five thousand of his men, had undone everything Howe accomplished, recovered the Jersies, and saved the American cause.

Thomas Paine struck the keynote, not only for that day but for every time of tribulation, in his *Crisis* paper which appeared 23 December 1776:

These are the times that try men's souls. The summer soldier and the sunshine patriot will, in this crisis, shrink from the service of their country; but he that stands it now deserves the love and thanks of man and woman. Tyranny, like hell, is not easily conquered; yet we have this consolation with us, that the harder the conflict, the more glorious the triumph. What we obtain too cheap, we esteem too lightly; it is dearness only that gives everything its value. Heaven knows how to put a proper price upon its goods; and it would be strange indeed if so celestial an article as freedom should not be highly rated.

3. *The Saratoga Campaign*

The small Northern American army under Benedict Arnold, after failing to capture Quebec, fought a series of stubborn retiring actions from the St. Lawrence to Lake Champlain that consumed most of the summer of 1776. Arnold's opponent, Governor Sir Guy Carleton, was a capable officer; but Arnold's energy in building a fleet on Lake Champlain, and his skill in handling it in the Battle of Valcour Island (11 October 1776) delayed the British long enough to keep them off Washington's neck in the critical summer of 1776.

The season for gentlemanly campaigning closed earlier in Canada than in the Jersies. Carleton, after recovering Crown Point, retired on 2 November to winter quarters in the loyal Province of Quebec. Major General John Burgoyne now sold the North ministry a plan for invading New York and New England by way of Lake Champlain and the Hudson, under his command. This sounded good because the same route had so often served during the colonial wars; and Sir Guy supported it, even though "Gentleman Johnny" Burgoyne would reap the glory. Sir John Johnson, son of old Sir William of the Mohawks, promised to bring in thousands of Mohawk valley Loyalists and Iroquois braves to support any British army that marched thither.

Nevertheless, the plan made very little sense, owing to the

existence of another potential countryside in arms. Since the conquest of Canada, the "Hampshire Grants," the future State of Vermont, had been settled by thousands of New England farmers and frontiersmen. They organized a *de facto* independent state which was not represented in the Continental Congress, owing to the opposition of New York. The British government appears not to have heard of these Green Mountain Boys, or else assumed them to be of the same breed as the amiable Jerseymen.

General Howe had no fewer than 27,000 men in and near New York City in the spring of 1777, doing nothing. Admiral Howe had a sizable fleet; and the sensible way for the British to secure the line of the Hudson and Lake Champlain would have been to thrust up the Hudson. But this sound strategy was not adopted, because Sir Billy wished to retrieve his poor performance in the Jersies by taking Philadelphia, which he imagined would put an end to the war. The British war department ordered Howe to send a substantial force up the Hudson and rendezvous with Burgoyne near Albany, but it approved his sending the bigger force to Philadelphia, and left him the choice of route.[1] He selected the longest ocean route, via Chesapeake Bay, because his brother's fleet could escort him, and Congress had set up strong points on the Delaware below Philadelphia. He was uncommonly slow in getting started, wasting May and June in marches and countermarches between Hoboken and New Brunswick, hoping to draw Washington into a pitched battle; Washington, with an army greatly inferior in numbers, naturally declined. On the first anniversary of the Declaration of Independence, General Howe loaded in transports all the troops he could spare from holding down New York. There ensued one of those long spells of July calm that are the despair of Long Island yachtsmen, and not until the 23rd did a fair wind enable the fleet to sail through the Narrows.

Leaving Sir Billy's army, miserable and seasick as the transports rolled in a heavy ground swell off the Jersey coast, let us follow Burgoyne. Around the first of June he jumped off from the St. Lawrence with about 4000 British regulars, 3000 Germans, and 1000 Canadian militia and Indians. These Indi-

[1] The story was current in England that the dispatch ordering Howe to help Burgoyne failed to reach him in time because the war minister had to enjoy his Christmas holidays before signing it. This was not true, but George Bernard Shaw used it effectively in his play *The Devil's Disciple*. In defense of Howe, when he first received word from London to help Burgoyne, on 16 August, he ordered Sir Henry Clinton, in command at New York City, to start north; but Clinton, too, got the slows and did not start until 3 October.

ans, Burgoyne expected, would put the fear of God and King George into any rebel frontier settlements they might encounter, and he amused himself by making grandiloquent speeches to them:—"Warriors! Go forth in the might and valor of your cause!" etc. Burgoyne so relished his own oratory that he sent copies of these speeches to the London papers. Horace Walpole wrote a friend, "Have you read Burgoyne's rhodomontade, in which he almost promises to cross America in a hop, step and jump? He has sent over, too, a copy of his 'talk' with the Indians, which they say is still more supernatural. I own I prefer General Howe's taciturnity who, at least, if he does nothing, does not break his word." The "talks" may have amused the Indians, but they made the Green Mountain Boys grimly determined to stop Gentleman Johnny at first opportunity.

Burgoyne's campaign opened well for him and ill for the Americans. Fort Ticonderoga was held by a small garrison under Major General Arthur St. Clair. Assaulted by an overwhelming force of redcoats, Indians, and the Canadian freshwater navy, St. Clair evacuated Ticonderoga in good order on 6 July and marched his men by forest trail to Fort Edward on the Hudson, where they reinforced the American Northern army under General Philip Schuyler.

At this juncture the morale of the American Northern army was jeopardized by congressional shillyshallying about the command. A controversy over the respective merits of Generals Schuyler, Arnold, and Gates, which their partisans have continued to this day, has obscured the events of the campaign. In the promotions of general officers by Congress in the spring of 1777, Brigadier Benedict Arnold, who deserved a second star for his brilliant work in the Canadian campaign, missed out because New England's allowance of major generals was already filled. Consequently he could not command the Northern army, which should then have been placed under General Philip Schuyler of Albany, who had done very well under Arnold in the retreat. But the New England troops refused to serve under Schuyler. An aristocrat like Washington, he was not a great enough gentleman to be effective as a leader of plain people, and had made himself unpopular by insisting on excessive military punctilio. Moreover, Schuyler belonged to the class of New York patroons who had opposed the settlement of Vermont by New Englanders, contested their titles, and endeavored to have them ejected. So the leaders of the Green Mountain Boys threatened to do nothing to stop Burgoyne if General Schuyler were given the command. Congress, on 4 August, then gave command of the Northern army to General Gates.

Horatio Gates, as a man and a soldier, is something of an enigma. He seems to have been pushed by circumstances and an ambitious wife into positions too great for his merits. He had served in the British army in America during the French and Indian War, after which he bought a plantation in Virginia, raised thoroughbred horses, and reflected the politics of his neighbors. Washington made him adjutant general of the Continental army, an administrative command similar to that of a modern chief of staff. His brother officers never liked him, and soldiers observed that, unlike Washington, he never exposed his person to bullets. But he had a way with politicians, especially those of New England, who, when disappointed in Charles Lee, made Gates their favorite son.

It took Burgoyne's army, encumbered by officers' wives and children and enormous quantities of baggage, nearly a month to reach Fort Edward, which Schuyler had abandoned. The problem of logistic supply was insoluble. To carry one month's provisions to the army at Fort Edward required 180 Canadian batteaux, hauled by relays of oxen and horses over the portages between the two lakes and the Hudson, a job that required five weeks. While waiting for food to arrive from Canada, Burgoyne made two diversions, each of which ran into a countryside in arms.

Colonel Barry St. Leger commanded the first. He moved up the St. Lawrence to Oswego, then across country to Fort Stanwix, the Mohawk country where Sir John Johnson had promised a big turnout of Loyalist militia and Mohawk braves. But there was a bigger turnout of Patriot militia under General Nicholas Herkimer. On 7 August St. Leger reached Fort Stanwix. Herkimer, marching to relieve the garrison, was ambushed by the Mohawks at Oriskany and badly cut up. A small force under Benedict Arnold now marched up the Mohawk to relieve Fort Stanwix. He managed, by spreading false rumors, to panic the Mohawks. St. Leger then gave up the siege of Fort Stanwix on 22 August, and retired through the woods to Canada.

Burgoyne's second diversion went into Vermont in search of food. The general's ideas of American geography were so hazy that he imagined his raiders in two weeks could march across Vermont to Bellows Falls, down the Connecticut to Brattleboro and back by the Albany road, collecting hundreds of horses and cattle and wagonloads of grain. For this incursion he chose 375 dismounted German heavy dragoons under Colonel Baum, and 300 Canadians and Indians. They did not even reach the Vermont line; for, as Burgoyne complained, "Wherever the King's forces point, militia to the number of three or four thousand assemble in a few hours." General John Stark, hero of the rail fence at Bunker Hill, led a force of Green Mountain Boys out from Bennington to meet them, and on 16 August captured or killed the entire raiding force.

In militia warfare, nothing succeeds like success. The Battle of Bennington brought Vermont militia by the hundreds to the headquarters of General Gates, who took command of the Northern American army on 19 August. And the British delay at Fort Edward gave Washington time to send important reinforcements from New Jersey, in the shape of Morgan's Rifles. General Burgoyne, still jaunty despite the failure of his two diversions (which cost him a good 1000 men), marched south and crossed to the west bank of the Hudson. He was now in a rich farming country where ripe wheat and corn were available for men and horses. The Americans felled trees across the roads and destroyed bridges, slowing his advance to about one mile a day.

Although Gates's army now outnumbered Burgoyne's almost two to one, Gates almost lost the campaign by constructing a strong entrenched camp on Bemis Heights (12 September) and refusing to budge, even when it became evident that Burgoyne was about to occupy a hill commanding his position. Arnold begged to lead an attack with Morgan's brigade and a New England regiment, and Gates grudgingly consented. Through leadership, audacity, and tactical skill, Arnold beat Burgoyne badly in the First Battle of Freeman's Farm, 19 September. One Yankee soldier said of Arnold, "There wa'n't no waste timber in him. It was 'Come on, boys!' not 'Go on, boys!' He didn't care for nothin'. He'd ride right in." He rode right in on Gates, too, when the commanding general neglected to mention his name in the official report of the action. Gates then suspended Arnold from command.

Burgoyne's situation worsened daily. General Benjamin Lincoln, with a force of New England militia, cut his communications with Canada. Burgoyne could no longer retreat, his Indian allies were slipping away, his foraging parties were being bushwhacked by militia, his field hospital was crowded with the sick and wounded. On 7 October Burgoyne made a bold attempt to turn the Americans' left. During this Second Battle of Freeman's Farm,[2] Arnold, without Gates's permission, rushed into the fray, took command of the New England regiments, turned a British defeat into a rout, and was badly wounded. One week later, when his force had fallen to less

[2] Also called Battle of Bemis Heights, or Stillwater.

than 6000, Burgoyne sent a flag of truce to American headquarters and asked for terms. On 17 October Gates granted Burgoyne very favorable terms of surrender. His army was allowed to return to England, on the promise not to serve again.

This was a turning point in the war. Burgoyne surrendered six generals and 300 other officers, and about 5500 enlisted men. Gates, as top commander, received credit which should have gone to Benedict Arnold, who now began to think that his talents would be better appreciated by the king than by Congress.

4. From the Brandywine to Monmouth

Shortly before Burgoyne marched south from Fort Edward, General Howe disembarked 18,000 troops at Elkton near the head of Chesapeake Bay, 50 miles from Philadelphia. To oppose his advance, Washington had 12,000 men, including militia. So few had uniforms that he ordered each man to wear on his tattered jacket a sprig of green, as a symbol of hope. Since Philadelphia could not be abandoned without a fight, the best Washington could do was to delay the enemy, whose navy commanded all sea approaches.

Washington made his first stand, on 9 September 1777, at a ford of Brandywine creek, which flows into the Christiana at Wilmington. Howe used excellent tactics. The Americans lost 1000 men killed and wounded, and Congress had to retire to Lancaster. On 26 September Howe occupied Philadelphia. He made no move to pursue Washington, but decided to take the two American forts on the Delaware. While so engaged, Washington attempted to exploit Howe's temporary weakness in Philadelphia by attacking his main encampment at Germantown (5 October). Everything that can go wrong in an attack, went wrong in that one; and Washington lost over 1000 more men. He then retired to Valley Forge.

Two weeks after Washington's defeat at Germantown came the triumphant news of Burgoyne's surrender. It is not surprising that a movement (the Conway cabal) began, to replace retreating Washington by victorious Gates. Members of Congress and a few general officers were involved, but the whole thing fizzled out and nobody thereafter would admit having had anything to do with it. The fact that the country and the army stood by Washington is a tribute to their appreciation of a really great man. In no other major revolution has a loser of so many battles been supported to the point where he could win.

Sir Billy Howe now settled down for the winter in Philadelphia. He cared not to risk arousing another countryside to arms. The British army, numbering on 1 April 1778 some 19,500 men in Philadelphia, 10,500 in New York, and 3700 in Newport, Rhode Island, was completely stymied by the example of what had happened to Burgoyne.

Capture of the "rebel capital" brought the war's end no nearer. Shortly there arrived news of the French alliance with the United States. The North ministry relieved Howe on 8 May by Sir Henry Clinton whose instructions were to evacuate Philadelphia, concentrate on New York, and prepare to fight a French expeditionary force. He decided to retire across New Jersey. Washington followed on a parallel line, watching for an opportunity to attack. It came on 28 June 1778 when Clinton was at Monmouth County Court House. There followed one of those battles that are difficult to untangle. The essential thing is that Charles Lee (who had been exchanged and commanded the van) was ordered by Washington to attack. He disobeyed, and retreated with so little reason as to be suspected of treason. Washington brought up the main

THE BATTLE OF THE KEGS

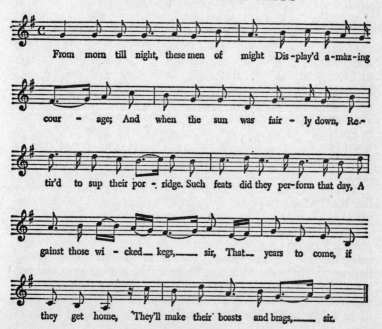

From morn till night, these men of might Dis-play'd a-maz-ing cour - age; And when the sun was fair - ly down, Re-tir'd to sup their por - ridge. Such feats did they per-form that day, A-gainst those wi - cked— kegs,— sir, That— years to come, if they get home, 'They'll make their' boasts and brags,— sir.

body and prevented the retreat from becoming a rout, but could not prevent Clinton's reaching New York.

The Commander in Chief then did the only thing he could do; he half encircled the city on the north side, hoping that a French fleet would appear to break the stalemate. He had to wait almost three years for that.

XVII

Diplomacy, Carolinas, Yorktown, and Peace

1778-1783

1. *The French Alliance*

THE CONTINENTAL CONGRESS began fishing for foreign aid even before declaring independence. In November 1775 it appointed a committee to correspond secretly with Great Britain, Ireland, "and other parts of the world," meaning France. Thither Silas Deane, Arthur Lee, and Franklin were sent to buy munitions and hold out the advantages of direct support. In a debate on the advisability of asking for a French alliance, John Adams, our original isolationist, said, "We ought not to enter into any alliance with her, which would entangle us in any future wars in Europe." He wanted only something equivalent to the lend-lease of 1940. His view prevailed for a time, but before long the military situation became so desperate that Congress instructed the commissioners to conclude alliances with France and Spain, if necessary to obtain their participation in the war.

Louis XVI, amiable but stupid, and even younger than George III, was then king of France. His able foreign minister, the Comte de Vergennes, had been following American revolutionary movements with the keenest interest, and showed his

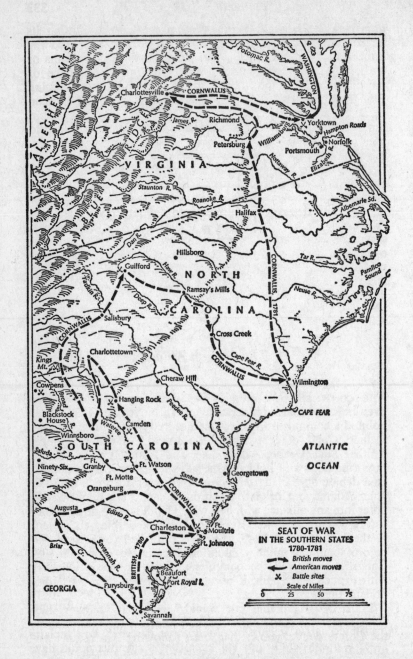

SEAT OF WAR
IN THE SOUTHERN STATES
1780-1781

- - - British moves
---- American moves
✗ Battle sites

Scale of Miles
0   25   50   75

approval of Thomas Paine's *Common Sense* by putting its author on a secret French payroll. All France approved the American Revolution. The government saw in it a means of weakening the British empire and restoring the balance of power which had been upset by the previous war. Rising French industrialists craved more direct access to the American market than they could obtain under the taut imperial system inaugurated by Charles Townshend. The bourgeoisie wished to get even with "perfidious Albion," and the intelligentsia admired America on idealistic grounds.

For a generation the dominant intellectual movement in France had been directed toward the reconstruction of society. Everyone was talking about scrapping feudalism, disestablishing the church, and starting fresh on the basis of liberty and "reason." The *philosophes* found inspiration in Pennsylvania, where one could lead the good life without a nobility or an established church. Voltaire admired the Quakers, who really meant peace when they talked peace; Rousseau regarded American Indians as unspoiled "children of nature"; Condorcet was so charmed with what he read about Connecticut that he signed one of his tracts "Un Bourgeois de New Haven." The *économistes*, especially Dupont de Nemours whose sons established an industrial empire in Delaware, found Virginia an illustration of their theory that agriculture is the sole source of wealth; that commerce, manufacturing, and finance are so many parasites on the farmer's back. Turgot, finance minister of Louis XVI, wrote that Americans were "the hope of the world. They may become its model."

All these generous, hopeful people boiled over with enthusiasm for America. The Virginia Declaration of Rights and the state constitutions embodied eternal principles of liberty; Washington was a modern Cincinnatus, with a volunteer army of free and virtuous republicans. Instead of fearing that royalist France might be contaminated by the radical example of America, the French intellectuals warned America not to let French opulence undermine republican simplicity.

This atmosphere explains the remarkable success of our republican commissioners in monarchical Paris. Thomas Carlyle describes the amusing spectacle of those sons of the Puritans, "sleek Silas, sleek Benjamin," consorting with the gay, sophisticated, Roman Catholic society of the French court. Ben Franklin, wilier than the cleverest diplomat of Europe, was a brilliant choice. The homely quips of his *Way to Wealth*, translated as *La Science du Bonhomme Richard*, won acclaim from liberal Catholics as evidence that a scientist could have sound moral principles. His inventions proved that science was not negative and destructive but offered a positive program to a better life. As a freemason, he was welcomed to French lodges where liberals congregated, and his contributions to the knowledge of electricity won him admission to the Academy of Sciences. At the same time his suit, unadorned by gold lace because he hadn't the money for court dress, and his unpowdered hair, in which he appeared before Louis XVI because the hired wig didn't arrive, made a great hit as the embodiment of republican simplicity. Franklin took care to play up to this image. He did not drive about Paris waving his arms and soliciting cheers; he held receptions at his lodgings in Passy, dined with courtiers, and became almost a legend in his lifetime. But he could not have accomplished this but for his genuine love of people. Of the French he later wrote, "I have spent several years in the sweet society of a people whose conversation is instructive, whose manners are highly pleasing, and who above all the nations of the world, had in the greatest perfection the art of making themselves beloved by strangers."

Franklin's difficulties in France came not from the French, but from fellow Americans. Deane and John Adams, who came over in 1777, were jealous of him; Arthur Lee jumped to the conclusion that he was a thief, and through Richard Henry Lee and Samuel Adams, tried to undermine Franklin in Congress. Often without funds, Franklin had to borrow money from the French to feed his staff; his first loan for the colonies was raised against future deliveries of Virginia tobacco. But he kept a constant eye on his main mission, to obtain French military aid and, if possible, an alliance. And he returned to Philadelphia poorer than when he left home.

For France to recognize American independence would have meant instant war with England, for which Louis XVI was not prepared. But his government, through the intermediary of the playwright Beaumarchais (author of *Le Mariage de Figaro*), sent valuable cargoes of munitions and clothing to Congress, and allowed American privateers and naval vessels to use French ports while the country was still officially neutral.

The surrender of Burgoyne at Saratoga on 17 October 1777 brought a change in French policy. Vergennes, subtly steered by Franklin, became fearful that this signal defeat might persuade Lord North to offer generous terms which Congress would accept, and the empire be restored. North very nearly did so. He introduced a new conciliatory bill in November 1777 which, if passed promptly, might have changed our entire history; but the country M.P.s had to have their Christmas holidays and Parliament adjourned without passing it. In the meantime, Franklin so worked on French fears of an accommodation with Britain that on 6 February 1778 Vergennes signed two treaties with the United States, one of amity and commerce, and one of alliance.

Vergennes allowed Franklin to write his own terms, which consequently were very liberal. The main thing was a promise that neither nation would lay down arms until Great Britain recognized American independence. France renounced designs on Canada, so the way was still open to making that British possession the fourteenth state. In return, the United States guaranteed French possession of those West Indian colonies which she then held. And commerce was to be on the basis of most favored nation.

Eleven days later, on 17 February, Lord North's conciliatory bill passed Parliament. It offered even more than the Second Continental Congress had demanded; as much as Adams, Wilson, and Jefferson had suggested in their dominion proposals of 1774–75. A royal commission headed by the Earl of Carlisle was sent over to negotiate with Congress on this basis. It was authorized to conclude an armistice, to promise repeal of the Coercive acts and all revenue acts since 1763, to cancel overdue quitrents, taxes, and claims arising from the war; even to renounce parliamentary regulation of imperial trade. It could concede any other insistent American demands "short of open and avowed Independence." These terms were to be secured by an intra-imperial treaty like that, over a century later, which recognized the Irish Free State. Had this plan gone through, the revolted colonies would have returned to British allegiance, leaving only war and foreign relations to the crown.

It was too late. News of the French treaties, which reached New York on 2 May 1778, engaged the honor of the country to France. Washington even earlier advised Congress in vigorous terms to pay no attention to the Carlisle mission, and Congress refused to meet it unless American independence were first recognized, the one thing that the commissioners were forbidden to do. They tarried in New York until late in the year, hoping that a change in the military situation might soften up Congress, and even offered £10,500 and a fat job to a congressman if he would help them. But they got exactly nowhere.

The French treaties said nothing about the amount or kind of warlike aid to be furnished to the United States. At the time they were signed, John Paul Jones's plan for a French fleet to attack Lord Howe's fleet in Delaware Bay and then recapture New York was adopted by the French minister of marine, but executed so slowly that the fleet, under Rear Admiral the Count d'Estaing, only reached the Delaware on 8 July, after Howe had left for New York. D'Estaing followed him thither, but the local pilots were so unnerved by the sight of the British fleet drawn up in line, ready to rake the French ships fore and aft, that they refused to pilot them through the Narrows. D'Estaing then sailed to Newport, where Washington arranged for a detachment of his army to co-operate in wresting that base from the British. Just as the French marines were about to land, a summer gale blew down Narragansett Bay and the fleet put out to sea. There they encountered Lord Howe's fleet, reinforced by that of Commodore Byron, which had just arrived from England. The summer gale became a line storm, and both fleets were kept so busy cutting away masts and avoiding collision, that no battle developed. The British ships returned to New York; the French put in at Boston, where their sailors on liberty were beaten up by Sam Adams's waterfront mobsters. D'Estaing then sailed for the West Indies, a more profitable theater for a winter campaign than the coast of New England.

Georgia in the meantime had been reconquered by the British. General Robert Howe, in command of the American Southern army at Savannah, had only 700 Continentals and 150 militia under him. In November 1778 a British amphibious operation under Colonel Sir Archibald Campbell, mounted in New York, landed some 3500 men unopposed on Tybee Island, advanced on Savannah, routed Howe's force, and took the Georgia capital. Campbell then pressed inland to Augusta, while Sir George Prevost, advancing overland with the garrison of loyal East Florida, occupied Sunbury. Loyalists flocked to the British colors, the royal governor was reinstated, an assembly summoned; and by the spring of 1779 it looked as though Georgia were back in the empire.

Congress relieved Robert Howe by General Benjamin Lincoln, who brought reinforcements south by land and took command at Charleston. Prevost then advanced on the South Carolina capital. That expedition, for looting, vandalism, and savagery by Tories and Cherokee Indians, makes Sherman's march through Georgia in 1864 seem a picnic in comparison. Charleston was only protected from capture by the prompt arrival of Pulaski's Legion, which helped Generals Lincoln and Moultrie to win an engagement. Prevost then retired to Savannah.

At this juncture appeared Admiral d'Estaing, gallantly answering a call for help. The French fleet of 20 ships of the line, 13 frigates, and transports carrying 6000 troops, arrived off Tybee Island on 8 September 1779. The British had only 3200 men to defend Savannah. It was just such a situation that led to the surrender of Cornwallis at Yorktown. But, with no safe anchorage for his big ships, and autumn gales threatening, D'Estaing insisted on launching a premature assault on 9 October. Casualties were heavy, Pulaski was killed, and the Admiral wounded. The French re-embarked and returned to France without anything to show for fifteen months in American waters. The Bailli de Suffren, who served under D'Estaing, summed him up in a phrase—"Had only his seamanship equalled his courage!"

2. *Hit-and-Run Raids*

A year and a half had elapsed since the conclusion of the French alliance, and victory still seemed far away. The war had reached a stalemate. Washington, without sea power, could not force the British out of New York City; Sir Henry Clinton dared not invade the interior for fear of running into another Bennington. So each side resorted to raids and to desultory, haphazard operations that had no useful military result but aroused bitterness and hatred.

The British did most of it, to employ the thousands of soldiers and scores of ships that were idling at New York. Sir Henry Clinton was instructed by the war office, on 8 March 1778, to make no offensive land operations into the interior (a tribute to the "countryside in arms") but to raid seaports and destroy rebel property, especially ships. That year there were British raids on Egg Harbor in New Jersey, New Bedford and Fairhaven in Massachusetts, and Vineyard Haven on Martha's Vineyard. Commodore Sir George Collier in May 1779 ravaged the shores of Chesapeake Bay, capturing many American merchant ships and burning Portsmouth; he then returned to New York, sailed up the Hudson, and attacked Stony Point. Having secured that good military objective, Sir George resumed the pitiful strategy of burning defenseless villages. Commanding a fleet of 50 vessels, carrying 2600 troops (mainly Loyalists and Germans), he sailed through Hell Gate into Long Island Sound and on 4 July issued a proclamation to the people of Connecticut who, he hoped, had "recovered from the phrensy which has distracted this unhappy country," and were about to "blush at their delusions." Next day, the soldiers landed to attack New Haven; but the unblushing countryside rallied and forced the troops to re-embark without indulging in their anticipated pleasure of burning Yale College. On 8 July the village of Fairfield was looted and completely destroyed, and on the 11th, Norwalk received similar treatment. There was no military purpose in these exploits except to terrify the Yankees. Congress, in retaliation, discussed ordering Franklin to hire incendiaries to burn London, starting with Buckingham Palace; but they thought better of it and left retaliation in the able hands of Captain John Paul Jones.

That accomplished officer, in sloop-of-war *Ranger*, raided the English port of Whitehaven to burn shipping, tried to kidnap his former Scots neighbor Lord Selkirk, and captured H.M.S. *Drake*. In 1779, Franklin and the French admiralty fitted out for him a task force consisting of an old East Indiaman which Jones renamed *Bonhomme Richard*, the new Continental frigate *Alliance*, French frigate *Pallas*, and two smaller French vessels, all under the American flag. Eleven different nationalities were represented in *Bonhomme*'s crew of 380, but the officers were almost all Americans; and Jones's genius whipped this motley collection of professional sailors, beachcombers, and peasants into as stout a force as ever served under the Stars and Stripes.

Jones sailed around the British Isles, took many prizes, scared the daylights out of Edinburgh and Newcastle, and on 23 September 1779 in the North Sea fought his greatest fight, against H.M.S. *Serapis* off Flamborough Head. In a hot ship-to-ship battle between *Bonhomme Richard* and *Serapis*, lasting from 6:30 to 10:30 p.m., Jones fought his almost disabled ship long after any other captain would have struck, and had the satisfaction of ·receiving the British captain's surrender. *Bonhomme Richard* was so badly shot up that she went down; but Jones, transferring his flag to *Serapis*, sailed her and the rest of the squadron, including a sloop-of-war captured by *Pallas*, into the neutral Dutch port of the Texel.

3. Fall of Charleston; Carolinas Campaign

Paul Jones's victory shone the brighter because the years 1779–80 were very dark for his cause. The Massachusetts state navy was wiped out in an abortive attack on the British base at Castine, Maine. And the worst American defeat of the entire war was the loss of Charleston, South Carolina.

Charleston has always been a hard nut for an enemy to crack, as General Lord Cornwallis had found in June 1776; but he was eager to try again. Cornwallis despised the hit-and-run strategy that Sir Henry Clinton had been employing. In the fall of 1779 he sold Sir Henry the plan of an amphibious expedition against Charleston, to be followed by the conquest of the Carolinas with the help of local Loyalists, and a joint military and naval campaign in Virginia to secure that state and Chesapeake Bay. There was nothing wrong with this strategy, but two unexpected factors wrecked it. The Carolina Loyalists were neither numerous nor strong enough to counteract the local Patriots, and the French navy intervened at a crucial point.

The campaign opened brilliantly for Britain. General Benjamin Lincoln, after failing to recapture Savannah, was now based on Charleston, commanding about 1200 men of the South Carolina and Virginia Lines, and some 2000 militia. Clinton organized a formidable expedition against Charleston, with Cornwallis as second in command. Some 8500 troops, about one-third of them American Loyalists, were embarked in 90 transports and escorted by 14 men-of-war. To meet this overwhelming naval force, Congress dispatched to Charleston the only available vessels of the Continental navy, three frigates and sloop-of-war *Ranger,* under Commodore Abraham Whipple USN. Whipple adopted the fatuous plan of anchoring his ships close to the city, in the hope that their guns might sink British landing craft. But Clinton and Cornwallis were much too smart to try a frontal assault. They landed most of their troops south of Charleston and advanced against its land side, which Lincoln had left almost undefended, while the British light-draft frigates crashed through the fire of Fort Moultrie and anchored off the city (8 April 1780). Clinton then summoned the Americans to surrender. Lincoln might have cut his way out; but too long he hesitated, and on 12 May he surrendered unconditionally. The British took the town, with about 5500 prisoners, captured the three Continental ships which had not been scuttled, and set up a Loyalist government.

Clinton now returned to New York and left Cornwallis in charge. Using mainly his Loyalist units, especially Colonel Banastre Tarleton's Legion, which seldom gave quarter, he overran almost the whole of South Carolina within three months. The Patriot militia under General Sumter were overwhelmed. Cornwallis set up a line of fortified posts between Camden and Ninety-Six to protect the state from attack from the north, and placed garrisons at Savannah, Port Royal, and Charleston to protect the coast. Expedient Charleston merchants resumed trade with England, the former royal governor took over, and to all appearances the Palmetto State was back in the empire along with Georgia.

American reinforcements, however, were coming. In April

1780 Washington dispatched the Maryland and Delaware line regiments southward under General de Kalb, to succor the Carolinas. These veteran outfits had fought in every northern campaign, but took their new and difficult mission without a murmur. On 22 June they reached Hillsboro, North Carolina, after incredible hardships owing to the failure of the states through which they passed to furnish supplies. Soldiers went without food for days, then gorged on peaches, green corn, and raw beef, with devastating results to their digestive tracts. When news of the fall of Charleston reached Congress, it appointed Horatio Gates, the politicians' favorite general, to command the Southern Department, over De Kalb's head and against Washington's advice. Gates, when he took command at Hillsboro, decided to advance on Camden; and, against everyone's advice, insisted on taking the direct route through the pine barrens where there wasn't enough food to support a hog, instead of following the longer wagon road along which were many farms and well-affected people. This march, too, was attended by hunger and dysentery.

Near Camden, Gates's army with between 2600 and 3000 men fit for duty (only 1000 of them Continentals) was attacked by Cornwallis. The British were inferior in numbers, but all were regulars except the Royal North Carolinians and Rawdon's Volunteers of Ireland. And Cornwallis was an outstanding leader, beloved by his men, which Gates was not. The Battle of Camden, 16 August 1780, was one of the fiercest fights of the war. American militia panicked at the first British bayonet charge; De Kalb, mortally wounded, held the field with the Maryland and Delaware Line. These famished but courageous soldiers stood their ground until all, except Major John Eager Howard's threescore who cut their way out, were killed or captured. General Gates, mounted on one of his Virginia thoroughbreds, galloped at the head of the fleeing militia and never stopped until he reached Charlotte, North Carolina, sixty miles from the battlefield. This battle finished his army career and scattered most of his troops to the woods and swamps.

Bad news indeed for America; and worse was to come. On 25 September 1780, Benedict Arnold went over to the enemy. For over a year he had been providing Sir Henry Clinton with military intelligence and dickering for the price of treason. Only the capture of their go-between, the unfortunate Major André, prevented Arnold from delivering West Point to the enemy.

North Carolina now lay open to Cornwallis. He marched deliberately into that state, hampered only by attacks of Colonel

William R. Davie's dragoons and other hastily organized volunteer units. At the same time, Major Patrick Ferguson, who had organized and armed 4000 South Carolina Loyalists, was ordered by Cornwallis to march north on a route parallel to his own. Ferguson, a gallant Scots veteran, uttered a foolish threat that brought out a countryside in arms. He sent word to the frontiersmen of the Watauga country that in retaliation for their having taken part in the South Carolina fighting he would soon lay waste their settlements and hang their leaders to the nearest tree. So they decided to get him first; and in this enterprise they were joined by rangy militia from western Virginia.

Major Ferguson, with a force of 1400 Loyalists, took his stand on the top of a wooded ridge called Kings Mountain and sent word that "he defied God Almighty and all the rebels out of hell to overcome him." There then took place (7 October) a Bunker Hill in reverse. Frontier militia swarmed up the forested slopes. Twice they were driven down by bayonet charges; but their long rifles, fired from behind trees, forced the Tories into a huddled mass, killed Ferguson, and slaughtered everyone who did not surrender.

Kings Mountain was the Trenton of the Southern campaign, giving new life to an apparently lost cause. Since Cornwallis's advanced position at Charlotte was now untenable, he hurriedly retreated to Winnsboro, South Carolina. There he remained all winter while his dashing cavalry officers, Tarleton and Wemyss, indulged in a series of skirmishes with the Patriot partisan leaders Pickens, Marion, and Sumter.

Congress, thrice having failed to pick winning generals in the South, now allowed Washington to choose a successor to galloper Gates. He appointed Nathanael Greene, who took command of the Southern Department at Charlotte in December 1780. Greene's army comprised fewer than 950 Continental infantry, 150 Continental gunners and troopers, and about 530 militia. "The appearance of the troops," wrote Greene early in January 1781, "was wretched beyond description, and their distress, on account of lack of provisions, was little less than their suffering for want of clothing and other necessities." But Greene, who like Knox had been selected from the ruck of New England militia officers by the discerning eye of Washington, was a great strategist. Only thirty-eight years old, mild and serene in manner, there was something about him that inspired confidence in troops.

He not only reorganized the army but adopted the audacious strategy of dividing his inferior force into two columns, one under General Daniel Morgan, the other under himself, in order to harass Cornwallis and live off the country. Washington managed to send reinforcements, notably "Light Horse Harry" Lee's elite cavalry legion, every man a disciplined scout and raider. Cornwallis, too, had been reinforced from New York. He now divided his army into three parts, hoping to knock out both Morgan and Greene with a swift left-and-right, then march north with the third division. On an open plain at a place near Kings Mountain called the Cowpens, Morgan took his stand and awaited attack by Tarleton's Tory troopers and a Scots infantry regiment. Morgan's tactics were so sound and his men, both militia and Continentals, fought so well that, at a minimum cost, they killed or captured nine-tenths of the British force.

Victory at the Cowpens gave Greene opportunity to show his strategic skill in a shifty compaign that puzzled Cornwallis. The Englishman was too stubborn to do the prudent thing, retire to Charleston; pride led him again to invade North Carolina. Morgan and Greene kept well ahead of him, hauling boats on wheels to expedite the crossing of rivers. Greene crossed the Dan river into Virginia, leaving Cornwallis momentarily elated, since he imagined that both Carolinas were now in the royal bag. But Greene, without even waiting for reinforcements, struck back across the Dan, chose his ground at Guilford Courthouse, and awaited attack. On 15 March 1781 it came: one of the bloodiest and most bitterly contested battles of the war. Cornwallis forced Greene to retreat after all his militia and one line regiment had panicked. But it proved to be an empty and barren victory. British casualties were almost 30 per cent, whilst Greene saved the bulk of his army. Cornwallis, having outrun his supplies, and unable to live off the country, had to retire to the coast, at Wilmington. Logistics won when arms failed.

Already Greene had profited by the retreat of Cornwallis to lash back into South Carolina. This general had an amazing record of losing battles but winning campaigns. Although beaten in a number of small engagements during the summer of 1781 and in the Battle of Eutaw Springs on 8 September, Greene always inflicted greater losses on the enemy than he suffered himself. And in the fall he drove all British and Loyalist units back into Charleston.

Cornwallis on the day of the Guilford battle wrote to General William Phillips, then operating in Virginia, "If we mean an offensive war in America, we must abandon New York, and bring our whole force into Virginia; we then have a stake to fight for, and a successful battle may give us America. If our plan is defensive, mixed with desultory expeditions, let us quit the Carolinas (which cannot be held defensively while Virginia can be so easily armed against us) and stick to our salt pork at New York, sending now and then a detachment to steal tobacco, etc."

Sound strategy indeed; but cautious Clinton could not be persuaded to abandon comfortable New York. The most he would allow Cornwallis to do was to march north into Virginia.

The Old Dominion was now in almost as unhappy a condition as Carolina. Benedict Arnold, now a British general, invaded Virginia with a force of about 1700 Tory volunteers in January 1781. No countryside rose in arms against him, partly because so many militia had already been sent south, but mostly owing to the incompetent administration of Governor Thomas Jefferson, whom Arnold had the satisfaction of chasing out of Richmond. Washington detached Lafayette's light infantry corps to handle Arnold; but the Marquis, lacking naval support, could accomplish nothing in that land of many and deep rivers. Arnold and his relief, General Phillips, made a particular point of burning tobacco, as the only export which paid for military supplies in France and Spain. That was the reason for Cornwallis's gibe about "a detachment to steal tobacco."

Cornwallis, with fresh supplies obtained by sea, started north from Wilmington, North Carolina, on 25 April 1781. He marched unopposed to Petersburg, Virginia, where he was joined by Phillips's force and by reinforcements from New York. These brought his numbers up to 7200, including a fair number of cavalry under the redoubtable Tarleton, who raided the interior as far as Charlottesville, where he nearly captured Jefferson. On 6 July Lafayette fought a brisk engagement with Cornwallis at Greenspring (old Governor Berkeley's plantation) and was defeated, but saved his little army by a timely retreat to Malvern Hill—scene of a greater battle in 1862. Cornwallis now brought his entire force into Yorktown and began turning that little town into a naval and military base.

There we shall leave Cornwallis, while we describe the mighty events by sea and land which forced him within three months to surrender.

4. Sea Power and Yorktown

The winter of 1780–81 marked the nadir of the American cause. England, controlling the sea, could throw in troops anywhere she chose. If Cornwallis managed to establish another military and naval base on Chesapeake Bay, she would possess every major American seaport except Boston. On the other side, the French alliance had proved a bitter disappointment. Congress seemed impotent to raise men or money. Many Americans began to accept the probability of defeat. Desperate diplomatic deals were proposed in Congress: to cede Spain everything west of the Appalachians in return for an alliance; to offer Catherine II of Russia a slice of Western territory if she would attack England! Rochambeau's French expeditionary force had been in Newport since the summer of 1780, but for want of sea power Washington knew not how or where to employ these 6700 French regulars. He was more discouraged than at any other period of the war.

In his diary for 1 May 1781 Washington thus summarized the situation:

> Instead of having magazines filled with provisions, we have a scanty pittance scattered here and there in the different States. Instead of having our arsenals well supplied with military stores, they are poorly provided, and the workmen all leaving them. Instead of having the various articles of field equipage in readiness to deliver, the Quartermaster General (as the denier resort) . . . is but now applying to the several States to provide these things for the troops. . . . Instead of having a regular system of transportation . . . all that business, or a great part of it, being done by military impress. We are daily and hourly oppressing the people—souring their tempers—and alienating the affections. Instead of having the regiments compleated to the new establishment and which ought to have been so by the 1st of February . . . scarce any State in the Union has, at this hour, an eighth part of its quota in the field and little prospect, that I can see, of ever getting more than half. In a word—instead of having everything in readiness to take the field, we have nothing; and instead of having the prospect of a glorious offensive campaign before us, we have a bewildered and gloomy defensive one—unless we should receive a powerful aid of ships, land troops, and money from our generous allies; and these, at present, are too contingent to build upon.

Yet presently a new and radiant light shone from France. Louis XVI decided to commit the major part of his navy to support Washington and Rochambeau. Twenty line-of-battle ships under a great fighting sailor, Rear Admiral the Count de Grasse, departed Brest in March 1781 for the West Indies. There he drove off a British blockading squadron, captured an island or two, and escorted a convoy of 200 merchantmen to Cap Haitien, Hispaniola, where four more battleships joined, and the combined fleet took on board 3000 soldiers of the Saint-Domingue garrison commanded by General the Marquis de Saint-Simon. It was now July, time to "stand by" for hurricanes, and the French fleet must make haste.

It did, and Washington was expecting it. On 21 May he held a conference with Rochambeau at Wethersfield, Connecticut, to decide on their objective. Washington was eager for a combined attack on New York City; but, as he wrote to Rochambeau in a letter that shows his strategic savvy, "In any operation, and under all circumstances a decisive Naval superiority is to be considered as a fundamental principle, and the basis upon which every hope of success must ultimately depend." He agreed with Rochambeau that they move against whatever target Admiral de Grasse chose, assuming it would be Yorktown if not New York.

There followed a faultless pattern of co-operation between two allied armies on the continent, and two French fleets, at Newport and the West Indies. Rochambeau sent word by frigate *La Concorde* to De Grasse of his and Washington's intentions, and begged the French admiral to inform them promptly of where he decided to strike. He chose the Chesapeake rather than New York, because of D'Estaing's failure to break through the Narrows three years earlier, whilst within the Chesapeake his ships would have room to maneuver. *La Concorde* on 12 August brought this dispatch to Newport, whence it was forwarded to Rochambeau, who had already pulled up stakes and marched his army across Connecticut to join Washington at White Plains.

Thus, all allied forces converged on Cornwallis's army at Yorktown, not on Clinton's at New York. On 19 August Washington and Rochambeau broke camp at White Plains and ferried 6000 men across the Hudson at King's Ferry. Commodore the Count Barras de Saint-Laurent, stationed at Newport, loaded his ships with Rochambeau's siege artillery, too heavy for overland haulage, and prepared to pop into the Chesapeake as soon as De Grasse had cleared the ocean lanes. By this time the big French fleet was off Cape Hatteras, sailing north before prosperous southwest winds.

In contrast to this beautiful co-ordination between the allied armies and fleets, the British were making a mess of their communications. Rear Admiral Thomas Graves was in command at New York. Rear Admiral Sir Samuel Hood's fleet sailed north from the West Indies to reinforce him, but the frigate that should have brought the word got into a fight, and not until 28 August, when Hood's flagship entered New York, did the British there know that De Grasse was coming north.

Two days later De Grasse's fleet anchored in Lynnhaven Bay within the Chesapeake Capes. On 1 September Graves and Hood sailed from New York for the same destination. Washington, who had long since lived down his alleged disinclination to tell a lie, set up an elaborate deception to make Clinton believe that he and De Grasse were planning to attack New York City via Staten Island. He left 4000 men at White Plains, gave out a series of false intelligence to British spies, and even constructed fake hardtack bakeries in New Jersey to make Clinton think that this would be his most advanced base. Clinton was completely fooled; he never sent one man to reinforce Cornwallis.

On 31 August Washington's and Rochambeau's armies began marching through Philadelphia. Everything now depended on whether De Grasse could keep the British fleet out of the Chesapeake long enough to allow the Franco-American army, and Lafayette's contingent, to surround Cornwallis at Yorktown. Washington was very, very anxious. On 2 September he wrote to Lafayette, "I am distressed beyond expression, to know what is become of the Count de Grasse, and for fear the English Fleet, by occupying the Chesapeake . . . should frustrate all our flattering prospects in that quarter." Three days later, when he reached Chester, Pennsylvania, he received news that De Grasse had arrived at Lynnhaven Bay. The French officer who brought the word said that he had never seen a man express such joy. "Washington acted like a child whose every wish had been gratified."

At that very moment the decisive naval battle was being fought off the Capes. At 8:00 a.m. 5 September, a picket frigate off Cape Charles sighted a fleet of 19 ships bearing down before the wind, and identified it as that of Admiral Graves. De Grasse was in a critical situation. About 2000 sailors were absent in landing craft, engaged in setting ashore Saint-Simon's troops near Jamestown. The tide was on the flood, and he had to get his cumbersome ships under way, beat out against both wind and tide, and form a line of battle. Graves missed the opportunity (which Jones or Nelson would have grasped) to attack the French while their ships were in confusion. He wore ship (turned every vessel on the other tack), waited for the French to sortie, and bore down on a course diagonal to that of De Grasse, to deliver a classic line-of-battle attack.

The wind was so light that not until 4:15 p.m. did the two fleets clash. The British had so poor a system of flag signals—

the only method, except shouting, to send orders ship-to-ship—
that Hood, in command of the British rear, did not understand
what Graves wanted of him, and sheered off. De Grasse maneuvered his fleet so expertly that when the two came together,
sixteen of his ships engaged eleven of the British. For over two
hours it was "Fire-away-Flanagan" between these units. By the
time darkness fell and gunfire ceased, the British had suffered
heavy casualties and two ships were in a sinking condition, but
all French vessels were in good shape. The decisive Battle off
the Capes of the Chesapeake was over, and the French had
won.

For four days, 6–9 September, De Grasse steered southerly,
luring the British away so as to give Barras a chance to enter
with the siege artillery. He then broke visual contact with the
British and squared away for the Capes, and found Barras's
ships within, while Graves's fleet limped down-wind to New
York for repairs. These took over a month; and when Graves
next arrived off the Capes, all was over.

Washington and Rochambeau conferred with De Grasse on
board his 110-gun flagship *Ville de Paris* in Lynnhaven Bay on
17 September, to make plans for the investment of Yorktown.
The small French vessels—for every fleet in those days was
accompanied by a squadron of frigates, corvettes, and light
craft—helped ferry the Allied troops down the Bay from Elkton and Annapolis, and delivered naval gunfire support during
the siege of Yorktown which began on 28 September. De
Grasse was eager to depart for the West Indies. These were his
orders from France, and he was apprehensive of hurricanes.
But Washington persuaded him to stay, and wrote to him (27
September), "The resolution that your Excellency has taken in
our circumstances proves that a great mind knows how to
make personal sacrifices to secure an important general good."

The siege of Yorktown was conducted according to the
book, with redoubts, trenches, horn-works, saps, mines, and
countermines. Cornwallis had about 8000 men in the little
town on the York river, which French ships patrolled so that
he could not break away. The armies of Rochambeau and
Saint-Simon were almost as numerous as his, and in addition
Washington had 5645 regulars and 3200 Virginia militia. The
commander in chief, profiting by D'Estaing's error at Savannah, wasted no men in premature assaults. There were gallant
sorties and counterattacks, one led by Lieutenant Colonel Alexander Hamilton. Casualties were light on both sides, fewer than
in the naval battle; but Cornwallis, a good professional soldier,
knew when he was beaten. On 17 October he sent out a white
flag, and on the 19th surrendered his entire force. Pleading ill-

ness, he sent his second in command, Brigadier Charles
O'Hara, to make the formal surrender to General Lincoln,
whom Washington appointed to receive him. One by one, the
British regiments, after laying down their arms, marched back
to camp between two lines, one of American soldiers, the other
of French, while the military bands played a series of melan-
choly tunes, including one which all recognized as "The World
Turned Upside Down."

Lafayette announced the surrender to Monsieur de Maurepas
of the French government in terms of the classic French
drama: "The play is over; the fifth act has come to an end."
Lieutenant Colonel Tench Tilghman carried Washington's dispatch to Congress at Philadelphia, announcing the great event.
Arriving at 3:00 a.m. on 22 October, he tipped off an old
German night watchman, who awoke the slumbering Philadelphians by stumping through the streets with his lantern,
bellowing, "Basht dree o'glock und Gornvallis ist gedaken!"

Windows flew open, candles were lighted, citizens poured
into the streets and embraced each other; and after day broke,
Congress assembled and attended a service of thanksgiving.

5. *Conclusion of the War*

When Lord North heard the news of Yorktown at 10 Down-
ing Street, on 25 November, he threw up his arms as though
hit in the breast by a musket ball and cried, "O God! it is all
over!" But it took more than a year and a half to end a war
that had extended to almost every part of the world, and in
which Britain was fighting not only the United States but
France, Spain, and the Netherlands.

Washington was keen to follow up his Yorktown victory by
a combined attack on Wilmington or Charleston, but De
Grasse obeyed orders from his government to return to the
West Indies with the French troops. Early in 1782 he recaptured several islands from the English. England then reinforced
her West Indies fleet with a dozen ships of the line under Admiral Rodney, who on 12 April beat the French badly in the
Battle of the Saints, capturing De Grasse in his flagship.

Rodney's victory prevented France from sending another
fleet to North America for months. In the meantime, British
warships and privateers based on New York and Halifax were
sweeping American coastal waters, capturing most of the few
merchantmen still at sea, and wiping out the New England
privateering and fishing fleets. General Washington, who had
been vainly urging the states to reinforce his army, on 18 July
wrote to James McHenry, "At present, we are inveloped in

darkness . . . Providence has done much for us in this contest, but we must do something for ourselves." But the British will to victory, feeble at best, had completely evaporated.

The only fighting on American soil in 1782 was in the West. By that time the British there were in the ascendant, owing largely to better treatment of the Indians. Colonel William Crawford, Washington's old associate in land speculation, was ambushed and killed by a force of Loyalists and Indians at the site of Sandusky, Ohio, on 4 June 1782. This brought into the war many more Indians, who began raiding deep into Pennsylvania, western Virginia, and Kentucky. It was a situation much like that after Braddock's defeat, or during Pontiac's rebellion. Bryan's Station, a fort near Lexington, Kentucky, was besieged in August by Tories and Indians, who routed a relieving force of frontier militia at the Lower Blue Licks. George Rogers Clark then collected 1100 mounted riflemen and on 10 November 1782 routed the Shawnee and burned their villages near Chillicothe, Ohio. That was the last land battle of the War of American Independence.

Lord North had long been in favor of ending the war by recognizing American independence. Rockingham was willing to form a ministry with that end in view; but George III said he would rather lose his crown than call in "a set of men" who would make him "a slave." It took several months' tearful pleading by Lord North to persuade the king to do just that. In March 1782 George had to let his favorite resign and accept an Old Whig ministry, including Shelburne and Charles James Fox. That opened the way to peace negotiations.

The Count de Vergennes, the French foreign minister, wished to keep these negotiations under French control. He persuaded Congress, in 1781, to order the American envoys in Paris to negotiate with England only under French direction, and to conclude nothing without his consent. At the same time Congress appointed John Jay and John Adams, together with Franklin, who was already minister to France, as the peace commission.

Formal negotiations began at Paris in April 1782 between Franklin (since the other two had not arrived) and Richard Oswald, a liberal Scots merchant sent over by Shelburne. John Jay, arriving on 23 June, raised objections to the wording of Oswald's commission, "To treat with the Thirteen Colonies . . . or any parts thereof." He insisted on Oswald's obtaining a new commission to treat with "The United States of America." This wasted time, during which the British position grew stronger by winning the Battle of the Saints and raising the Franco-Spanish siege of Gibraltar. But for this quibbling over words, the United

States might have obtained preliminary articles making no mention of Loyalists or debts, and giving her the Canada boundary of 1763. Shelburne, the prime minister, was anxious to conclude peace at almost any terms.

Shelburne now sent Oswald new instructions, authorizing him to treat with "Commissioners of the Thirteen United States," thus acknowledging independence before the negotiations began. These were received in September 1782. John Adams, the third commissioner, arrived in Paris in October after obtaining a commercial treaty from the Netherlands. In the end, Britain consented to the present northern boundary because Shelburne had the good sense to see that it would allow the United States and Canada to expand on parallel lines. The United States promised nothing for the Loyalists, except to "earnestly recommend" that the states restore their property, and that "no future confiscations" be made. American debts, owed to British subjects before the war, would be paid; and, at Yankee Adams's insistence, Britain conceded that American fishermen enjoy their ancient liberty to land and dry fish on the coast of Newfoundland.

The preliminary treaty of peace was signed on 30 November 1782, more than thirteen months after Cornwallis's surrender; the definitive treaty on 3 February 1783, the same day as the treaties between Great Britain and France, Spain, and the Netherlands. The entire transaction was called the Peace of Paris. Britain kept Gibraltar, which she had successfully defended, but ceded Minorca and the Floridas to Spain. France got nothing but Tobago in the West Indies and Senegal in Africa. The United States won the West to the Mississippi, north to Canada, and south to the Floridas. This was more territory than she actually controlled at the war's end, when Britain still had garrisons on the Atlantic coast at Castine, New York City, Wilmington, Charleston, and Savannah; and six different points on the northern border. And Spain still controlled the east bank of the Mississippi up to the Walnut Hills at the site of Vicksburg.

Franklin now wrote to the English ambassador at Paris, "What would you say to a proposition of a family compact between England, France, and America? America would be as happy as the Sabine girl if she could be the means of uniting in perpetual peace her father and her husband." That was too much to expect. An effort to conclude a commercial treaty failed, owing to the resignation of Shelburne and the formation of a less liberal ministry, who wished to prove that the Americans had been foolish to attempt independence. In the French government there was a feeling that the Americans had let them down by signing a preliminary treaty without French consent. Thus, on the morrow of achieving independence, the United States was a lone lamb in the society of nations.

The new republic, however, was hailed with enthusiasm by all liberal elements of England and Europe. The Old Whigs felt that Washington's valor had saved them from a royal despotism; and no later British monarch ever aspired to the power that George III exercised between 1774 and 1781. The French intelligentsia hailed the triumph of liberty and reason over tradition and autocracy; they looked forward to doing the same thing for their own country, and had not long to wait. European liberals everywhere, filled with an unsatisfied longing for liberty, equality, and the rule of reason, felt that the triumph of the American Republic portended a new order for old Europe.

They were right. As the English historian Lord Acton stated, "It was from America that the plain ideas that men ought to mind their own business, and that the nation is responsible to Heaven for the acts of the State—ideas long locked in the breast of solitary thinkers, and hidden among Latin folios—burst forth like a conqueror upon the world they were destined to transform, under the title of the Rights of Man . . . and the principle gained ground, that a *nation can never abandon its fate to an authority it cannot control*." Many, alas, have done so, but their people have always suffered for it.

News of the preliminary treaty of 30 November 1782 did not reach America until 12 March 1783. Since the treaty included an armistice, the war in America ended then and there, to the "inexpressible satisfaction" of General Washington. Recently, by a personal appeal, the General had dissuaded his officers from presenting a rude ultimatum to Congress about pay and pensions. The Continental treasury was so empty that the soldiers had to be sent home with no pay, only chits for three months' arrears, signed by Robert Morris; and with their muskets as a gift.

General Sir Guy Carleton, now British commander in New York City, completed the evacuation of his garrison on 25 November 1783. General Washington marched in, his ill-clad troops a contrast to the smart, scarlet-uniformed regulars who had departed. But, as a spectator remarked, "They were *our* troops . . . and I admired and gloried in them the more, because they were weather-beaten and forlorn."

At the Fraunces Tavern on 4 December, the commander in chief and the few remaining officers of his vanishing army dined together for the last time. Filling a wineglass, he held it up and said, "With a heart full of love and gratitude, I now take my leave of you. I most devoutly wish that your later days may be as prosperous and happy as your former ones have been glorious and honorable." With tears in his eyes, Washington invited each officer to come forward and shake his hand. First to do so, because nearest to the commander in chief (as he had been throughout the war), was Henry Knox, the one general officer who in eight years' service had never given Washington a moment's trouble. When Knox held out his hand, the commander in chief not only grasped it but embraced him and kissed him on the cheek, both shedding copious tears; for in those days strong and brave men were not ashamed to weep on suitable occasions. Washington passed between the ranks of a guard of honor and then past throngs of citizens, to a wharf on the North river, whence a barge rowed him to Paulus Hook. There he mounted a horse to ride south and resign his commission to Congress.

Hurrying on, in the hope of keeping Christmas at Mount Vernon, Washington reached Annapolis, where Congress was sitting, on 19 December. The Marylanders, true to form, insisted on giving the General a ball before he retired, so Congress set the public ceremony in the State House for the 23rd. Congress's address was written by James McHenry, who described the moving scene in a letter to his fiancée, Peggy Caldwell:

It was a solemn and affecting spectacle. . . . The spectators all wept, and there was hardly a member of Congress who did not drop tears. The General's hand which held the address shook as he read it. When he spoke of the officers who had composed his family, and recommended those who had continued in it to the present moment to the favorable notice of Congress he was obliged to support the paper with both hands. But when he commended the interests of his dearest country to almighty God . . . his voice faultered and sunk, and the whole house felt his agitations. After the pause which was necessary for him to recover himself, he proceeded to say in the most penetrating manner, "Having now finished the work assigned me I retire from the great theatre of action, and bidding an affectionate farewell to this august body under whose orders I have so long acted I here offer my commission and take my leave of all the employments of public life." So saying he drew out from his bosom his commission and delivered it up to the president of Congress. He then returned to his station, when the president read the reply that had been prepared.

By very hard riding, which meant little to a man of his splendid physique, George Washington reached Mount Vernon in time to keep Christmas Eve with Martha and her grandchildren.

THE WORLD TURNED UPSIDE DOWN

XVIII

Revolutionary Constitution Making

1775-1781

1. *The Bills of Rights*

ONE OF THE MOST REMARKABLE things about the American Revolution is the fact that the radicals of 1774–76 who started it, also saw it through to a point—that point being 1787, when younger men took over to put a capstone on the edifice. All modern history proves that it is easy enough for a determined minority to pull down a government, but exceedingly difficult to reconstruct, to re-establish law and order on new foundations. And in no other great revolution have the initial agitators long survived liquidation by their successors. Dozens of nations since World War II have won independence—but how many have secured liberty?

According to the natural history of revolutions, we would expect the American Confederation to fall apart, or that the army or some outstanding leader would set up a military despotism. What actually happened was the establishment of government under law. The reasons for this noteworthy outcome lie, first, in the political experience of Americans. As Emerson wrote, "We began with freedom." Secondly, they believed in the importance of political institutions as a guarantee of liberty. Thomas Jefferson, for instance, wrote to a member of the Virginia assembly on 16 May 1776 that constitution making "is the whole subject of the present controversy; for should a bad government be instituted for us in future, it had been as well to have accepted . . . the bad one offered to us from beyond the water, without the risk and expense of conflict." Moreover, the principles of the American Revolution were essentially conservative; the leaders were thinking of preserving and securing the freedom they already enjoyed rather than, like the Russians, building something new and different. As John Dickinson said in the Federal Convention, "Experience must be our only guide, reason may mislead us." One cannot imagine such a thing being said by a French or a Russian revolutionist.

Thus, when the Americans risked law and order to attain liberty, they made every effort to win them back. Their political experience before 1775 set the pattern for their new institutions. Unlike the French, who had little or no experience with representative government when their revolution opened in 1789, Americans needed merely to maintain, develop, and correct the state of things political and religious, which already existed. Americans had enjoyed more freedom than any other people in the world, and so large a measure of self-government that they were competent to make it complete. Certain conservative patriots feared lest the people take up revolutionary slogans with such enthusiasm that all government would be threatened. But there was really very little danger of that. The typical feeling was expressed by the Massachusetts farming town of Medfield: "While we profess ourselves advocates for Rational Constitutional Liberty we don't mean to patrionise Libertinesm and Licenteousness we are sensible of the necessety of Government for the Security of Life Liberty and property." That tiny community had grasped the principle that the rule of law is perhaps the greatest achievement in the long struggle for liberty, and that if it is lost, liberty is lost; that the use of orderly, "due process" to change the law is essential for an orderly society.

Most of the American state and federal constitutions were the work of college-educated men who had studied political theory in Aristotle, Plato, Cicero, Polybius, and other ancient writers, and had given deep thought to problems of political reconstruction. Men such as George Mason and Thomas Jefferson, James Madison, John Adams, and James Bowdoin knew exactly what they were doing. And most of these were relatively young men. Jefferson was thirty-three years old and Madison twenty-seven when they helped draft the Virginia constitution. John Adams, when he did the same for Massachusetts, was a mature forty-four; of the same age was John Dickinson when he drew up the Articles of Confederation. The

New York constitution was drafted by three graduates of King's College (now Columbia): Gouverneur Morris, Robert R. Livingston, and John Jay, aged respectively twenty-four, thirty, and thirty-two. These men were familiar with what ancient and modern publicists had written on government; yet they were no mere doctrinaires. Every one had had political experience in colonial assemblies, local conventions, or the Continental Congress. This synthesis of classical discipline with practical politics accounts for the striking success of the Americans at constitution making. Their efforts won the admiration of the Old World, and from them the New World still benefits today.

Everyone assumed that the new states must have written constitutions, limiting and defining the powers of government. They were used to colonial charters, had felt the want of a written British constitution defining the respective powers of Parliament and the colonial assemblies. The objects of these state constitutions were, to establish the rule of law which they believed that George III had violated, to secure life, liberty, and prosperity, and to set up a practical frame of government.

Liberty was no vague term with our revolutionary forebears. It had not yet acquired the fuzzy overtones of economic choice and social welfare that have accrued in the course of a century and a half. To the Americans of 1776, liberty meant, first, freedom under laws of their own making; and, second, the right to do anything that did not harm another. One of the crisp sayings of John Locke, with whom all reading Americans were familiar, was "Wherever law ends, tyranny begins." The proper way, they felt, to secure liberty to posterity was to set up a representative government, limited in scope by a statement of natural rights with which no government may meddle. Consequently, every state constitution included a bill of rights. The first, Virginia's, was drafted by George Mason and adopted by the Virginia convention on 12 June 1776.

This Virginia Declaration of Rights is one of the great liberty documents of all time. It applied the past experience of free-born Englishmen, and parented not only all other American bills of rights, but the French *Déclaration des droits de l'homme et du citoyen* of 1789 and, the Universal Declaration of Human Rights adopted in 1948 by the General Assembly of the United Nations. Virginia begins by asserting, "That all men are by nature equally free and independent, and have certain inherent rights of which, when they enter into a state of society, they cannot . . . deprive or divest their posterity; namely, the enjoyment of life and liberty, with the means of acquiring and possessing property, and pursuing and obtaining happiness and safety."

Certain clauses of the Virginia Declaration came down from the Magna Carta of 1215—the right to a jury trial, the right not to be deprived of liberty except by the law of the land or the judgment of one's peers. Others are derived from the Petition of Right with which Charles I was confronted in 1628: that a man cannot be compelled to give evidence against himself, that standing armies in peace time should be avoided as dangerous to liberty, "and that in all cases the military should be under strict subordination to and governed by the civil power." The prohibition of excessive bail and of cruel or unusual punishments was derived from the English Bill of Rights of 1689 which concluded the Glorious Revolution. Others were developments from principles merely hinted at before, such as freedom of the press, and religious liberty.

These rights were valid, not only as derived from American and English experience, but because they were based on the ancient theory of natural law; the principle of Western civilization that laws must have divine sanction. Blackstone, the English legal writer most widely read in America, in his *Commentaries* declared, "This law of nature, being coëval with mankind and dictated by God himself, is of course superior in obligation to any other . . . no human laws are of any validity if contrary to this." These "unchangeable, unwritten laws of Heaven," as Sophocles called them in the *Antigone*, twenty-one centuries before Blackstone, must be the foundation of human enactments which are to endure. They became the basis of the American constitutional system.

The other states, in general, followed Virginia in their bills of rights. Pennsylvania had stronger statements than Virginia on religious liberty, added freedom of speech to Virginia's freedom of the press, protected conscientious objectors to military service, and gave foreigners "of good character" the right to buy land and to become citizens. An amusing difference between the two constitutions was Virginia's declaration that no government separate from Virginia's should be erected or established within the limits thereof; whilst Pennsylvania declared, "All men have a natural inherent right . . . to form a new state in vacant countries." For Virginia then claimed the future Kentucky and Northwest Territory, whilst Pennsylvania had a definite western boundary.

The Massachusetts Declaration of Rights, declaring "All men are born free and equal," was construed by the courts of that commonwealth as freeing all slaves from bondage. And a separation of powers between the legislative, executive, and judicial departments was enjoined, "to the end it may be a government of laws and not of men."

2. The Frames of Government

Most of the state constitutions were drafted by legislative bodies and placed in effect without consulting the voters. John Adams felt that this was not the right way to do it. In the Congress he urged that we "invite the people to erect the whole building with their own hands, upon the broadest foundation . . . by conventions of representatives chosen by the people." The first instance in which he managed to have a specially elected convention and popular ratification was in his own commonwealth in 1780.

State governments during this era followed three main types: the Virginian or legislative supremacy, the Pennsylvanian unicameral, and the Massachusetts "mixed" types. Virginia, impressed by John Locke's dictum that the legislative should be the chief power in a commonwealth, gave hers most of the power. The governor, chosen by joint ballot of both houses, could do nothing without the advice and consent of a council, which was elected by joint ballot of the legislature, as were the judges. This constitution was a bad example of seeking political guarantees against past dangers, in this instance the arrogant royal governors; and Virginia suffered from that mistake during the war. Owing, however, to the prestige of Virginia, her constitution was imitated by a majority of the Thirteen States.

Pennsylvania adopted a different type of constitution, reflecting an internal revolution; the Philadelphia artisans, the Scots-Irish frontiersmen, and the German-speaking farmers were now on top. George Bryan and Dr. Thomas Young, a former leader of the Boston Sons of Liberty, drafted this constitution, with the blessing of Benjamin Franklin who presided over the provincial congress that adopted it. It was the most democratic of American revolutionary constitutions, except that of Vermont, which was a copy. Every male taxpayer and his adult sons could vote. Rotation in office was enjoined; none could serve as representative for more than four years in every seven. A single-chamber legislature was set up, the only qualification for membership being that one must be a Christian. Membership was apportioned according to population, as the back-country people had always wanted. Instead of a single governor, this constitution provided an elective executive council, with rotation of office to prevent "the danger of establishing an inconvenient aristocracy." The president of the council, chosen annually by joint ballot of council and assembly, acted as chief executive. A peculiar feature of the Pennsylvania and Vermont constitutions was the election every seven years of a Council of Censors, whose duty was "to enquire whether the Constitution has been preserved inviolate in every part," to order impeachments, and to summon a constitutional convention if necessary.

This type of constitution worked well enough in the homogeneous frontier community of Vermont; but in Pennsylvania, where there were deep class, racial, and religious divisions, it established the nearest thing to a dictatorship of the proletariat that we have had in North America. A Pennsylvanian wrote to Thomas Jefferson, "You would execrate this state if you were in it. . . . The supporters of this government are a set of workmen without any weight of character." The legislature managed to disfranchise Quakers by a loyalty test oath to which they could not subscribe; and the assembly, controlled by the leather-aproned boys, frontiersmen, and the less prosperous Germans, expended more energy during the war in plundering Tories, jailing profiteers, and persecuting conscientious objectors than in supporting the army. Eventually Pennsylvania turned against this "popular front" government, and in 1790 elected a convention which drafted a new constitution with a bicameral legislature and a proper governor.

Nevertheless, the Pennsylvania constitution, introduced by Franklin to the French intelligentsia, was hailed in Europe as well-nigh perfect, because it was "rational." If the people were to rule, there was no logic in a second chamber or in checking a legislative power by a governor or judges. Turgot wrote a treatise attacking the American state constitutions for compromising with custom and privilege, and for adopting "mixed" forms; but he gave that of Pennsylvania a clean bill of health. John Adams replied in a more lengthy treatise, defending the bicameral system as necessary to protect the people against unwise, hasty, and proscriptive legislation, and defending a strong executive as necessary to enforce the laws and give the government leadership. The events of the American Revolution period showed unmistakably that John Adams was right and Turgot wrong; yet, in 1791, the very year after the "rational" Pennsylvania constitution had been superseded, the French Constituent Assembly adopted a unicameral constitution for France.

Around 1780 a mildly conservative reaction set in throughout the United States. It was reflected in some of the early radicals being dropped out of the Continental Congress, in giving greater authority to General Washington and to Franklin, in appointing Robert Morris superintendent of finance, and creating the office of secretary of foreign affairs for Robert R. Livingston. And the reaction was reflected in the constitution of Massachusetts.

This most conservative of the state constitutions was adopted through a completely democratic process. A constitutional convention, elected by manhood suffrage, met in the fall of 1779, appointed a committee to prepare a draft, and adjourned. The committee of three—James Bowdoin and both Adamses—wisely let John Adams do it. His draft was submitted to the convention in 1780, amended, and then tossed back to the town meetings. They voted on the constitution clause by clause, and stated their objections. A surprising popular interest was shown; many town meetings debated the constitution clause by clause, and some made original proposals such as the popular initiative and referendum, which were adopted many years later. But the people did ratify the constitution as a whole, as an adjourned session of the convention, after counting the votes, declared on 15 June 1780.

John Adams's Massachusetts constitution was based, not on Locke's principle of legislative supremacy, but on Polybius' theory of "mixed government" (which Governor Winthrop pointed to in the seventeenth century), which by this time had been renamed "checks and balances." The theory was this: any "pure" governmental form degenerated into something else —pure democracy into class tyranny or anarchy, pure aristocracy into a selfish oligarchy, pure monarchy into absolutism. Hence, to secure the happiness of the people, a government must be a mixture of the three: a strong chief executive to represent the principle of authority, a senate to represent property, and a lower house to represent the multitude. These "mutually keep each other from exceeding their proper limits," as Blackstone wrote in his *Commentaries*. Finally—John Adams's own contribution—you needed an independent judiciary as a balance wheel. Thus, Massachusetts was given a popularly elected house of representatives; an "aristocratic" senate apportioned according to taxable wealth, not population; and a governor, re-eligible indefinitely, with a veto (which only one other state governor enjoyed) over legislation, and power to appoint most of the state officials. The governor of Massachusetts was intended to assume leadership, and to that end he too was chosen by popular vote, as were the governors of only three other states.

Connecticut and Rhode Island, which had popularly elected governors under their old royal charters, made the transition from colony to state simply by altering the name of the body politic, declaring that the "excellent constitutions of government" derived from their "pious ancestors" were still in force, and tacking on a bill of rights. These amended colonial charters served Connecticut until 1818, and Rhode Island until 1842. The Massachusetts constitution of 1780, though never formally superseded, has been so amended from time to time as to make it more democratic, supporting one of the least efficient and most corrupt of modern state governments.

Other features were common to all state constitutions. Several forbade the granting of titles of nobility. One-year terms for governors and assemblymen were the rule in every state except South Carolina; since it was a common American belief that "where annual elections end, tyranny begins." In seven states, every male taxpayer could vote; elsewhere there were moderate property qualifications. Women could vote in New Jersey, if they could meet the property requirement, and free blacks in general had the same political privileges as white men.

In most states there was a high property qualification, about $4000 in New Jersey and Maryland, for membership in the upper house. In all states, judges were appointed for long terms, or during good behavior—no more "pleasure" tenure for free-born Americans. Test oaths of allegiance, designed to exclude from office Loyalists and (in some instances) Roman Catholics, were common. And, whilst the principle of freedom of worship for all religions was generally adopted, church and state were not completely separated. The Church of England was not disestablished in Virginia until 1785, and in Connecticut and Massachusetts a modified official preference to the Congregational churches continued until 1818 and 1833, respectively.

In addition to the Old Thirteen and Vermont, several American communities beyond the mountains established temporary states during or shortly after the war. Transylvania was organized in 1775 by pioneers of Kentucky who had emigrated to the blue-grass country or had been brought there by a land company organized by Judge Henderson of North Carolina.

The several thousand settlers scattered along the banks of the Watauga, Holston, and other tributaries of the Tennessee river took care of themselves throughout the war and, as we have seen, "took care" of Major Ferguson at the Battle of Kings Mountain. But in 1784, owing partly to the Cherokee going on the warpath, frontier leaders called a convention at Jonesboro which adopted the constitution of the State of Franklin. Taxes were payable in beaver skins, well-cured bacon, clean tallow, rye whisky, peach and apple brandy. After a few years North

Carolina asserted her jurisdiction, and Franklin eventually became part of Tennessee. Another isolated group in central Tennessee formed in 1780 the Cumberland County Compact for self-government and protection from Indian attack.

Thus, political maturity was common to every section and class. The people had a genius for self-government. They followed leaders who were political scientists, not with docility but critically. And even the rough frontiersmen realized that liberty could only be secured under law.

3. The Articles of Confederation

While framers of state constitutions were wrestling with that perennial problem of government, balancing liberty with authority, the Continental Congress grappled with a vital question which colonials and British had long been squabbling about—federalism. This, another aspect of the *libertas* vs. *imperium* problem, is to find a balance between a central government and the rights of member states. The federal question has bedeviled American history to the present day.

The central problem of federalism is to distribute sovereign powers in layers, as it were, between a central government and member states. A federal constitution should draw the line, but it is impossible to make a clean-cut distinction. Before 1763, the government of the British empire was *de facto* federal. But the colonies found that they had no security for their rights in this informal arrangement unless it became *de jure* as well; if Parliament had the sovereign power that it asserted in the Declaratory Act and applied in the Coercive Acts, colonial reserved rights were worthless. That is why Adams, Jefferson, and Wilson suggested a federal constitution for the British empire; but nobody in England except Camden and Shelburne seemed to understand what they were talking about. Now the controversy was transferred to Philadelphia. All the old problems: war and peace, taxation, Indians, the West, commerce, were crying for solution in an expanding continental area.

The Articles of Confederation were another American attempt, following the New England Confederation and the Albany Plan, to grapple with this central problem of government. It is no wonder that the Articles were imperfect; even so, they were the best instrument of federal government adopted anywhere up to that time. The Articles would have secured American union for many years but for unfavorable circumstances and certain defects, which could not be removed because only a unanimous vote of the member states could carry an amendment.

John Dickinson, chairman of a congressional committee to draft a confederation, reported it to Congress in July 1776. Congress, in the meantime, had assumed sovereign powers and was in no hurry to confirm by law what it had assumed of necessity. Dickinson's draft provided representation of the states in Congress in proportion to their population, but the small states would have none of that. So it was agreed that each state have one vote. But, as Congress was too busy directing the war to spend much time debating federal union, it was not until 15 November 1777 that it adopted the Articles in their final form and submitted them to state legislatures for ratification. These also took their time; but by February 1779 all states had ratified except Maryland, which held out until 1 March 1781. Consequently, the United States fought the war almost to the Yorktown campaign with no federal constitution, only an informal union. The Continental Congress simply exercised powers that by common consent seemed necessary to wage war and conduct foreign affairs.

The essential reason for the long delay in ratifying the Articles of Confederation was land-grabbing. Virginia claimed the entire West north of her southern boundary and west of Maryland and Pennsylvania. The land companies that were lobbying at London for enormous grants in the 1760's, now transferred their activities to Philadelphia. The Indiana Company (formerly the Vandalia) tried to persuade Congress to insist on Virginia's ceding her Western land claims to the Confederation, which they hoped to get. Franklin wrote a tract for this company, and Tom Paine wrote an attack on Virginia's land claims which was published under the persuasive title *The Public Good*. But the old Ohio Company of Virginia, in which Washington was mildly interested, naturally blocked any cession of land to the Confederation until its claims were honored.

Most powerful, however, of the land companies was the Illinois-Wabash, which before the Revolution, in defiance of royal proclamations, purchased land from the Indians both north and south of the Ohio. Among influential stockholders were Robert Morris, James Wilson, four Maryland signers of the Declaration of Independence, and the first two French ministers to the United States. The Wabash Company engaged in tortuous negotiations with Congress, with Maryland, and with France and Spain; an intrigue which, could it be unraveled, might prove more fascinating than the story of Arnold's treason or Burr's conspiracy. The influence of this group at Annapolis caused Maryland to declare that she would never ratify the Articles of Confederation until the states with Western lands, especially Virginia, ceded all land claims west of the mountains to the Confederation, which the Illinois-Wabash Company hoped would then validate its purchases from the Indians. The Virginia speculators countered by inducing their state to set on foot the George Rogers Clark expedition of 1778, a patriotic version of Governor Dunmore's War. Colonel Clark floated his Virginia force down the Ohio to the mouth of the Cumberland, then made a bold march across the wilderness to the British post of Kaskaskia in the Illinois country, and in February 1779 bagged Vincennes too. Thus Virginia implemented her old charter claims to the whole Northwest.

The next move of the Illinois-Wabash Company was to turn to Spain. In 1780 one of its stockholders, the French minister at Philadelphia, urged Congress to cede all territory between the Appalachians, the Ohio and Mississippi rivers to Spain, in return for a Spanish alliance. The most prominent member of Congress to support this proposal was another stockholder, Daniel of St. Thomas Jenifer. The Company felt they would get a better land deal from Spain than from Virginia or Congress.

This particular intrigue was defeated in Congress, and about the same time the states, starting with New York, began ceding their western land claims to Congress. A congressional resolution of 10 October 1780 promised that any western lands ceded to the United States would be "settled and formed into distinct republican States, which shall become members of the Federal Union, and shall have the same rights of sovereignty, freedom and independence, as the other States." Here was the beginning of a new federal colonial policy.

Virginia was first to respond. The assembly on 2 January 1781 offered to cede claims north of the Ohio, under several conditions—that the state be repaid expenses of Colonel Clark's expedition; that 150,000 acres north of the Ohio river be reserved for Clark and his soldiers; and that all other purchases from the Indians be considered null and void—a slap at the Illinois-Wabash crowd. This was too much for Congress to accept. Nevertheless, Maryland voted to ratify the Articles of Confederation, because her assembly had become tired of playing the speculators' game.

Consequently, this first Constitution of the United States, the Articles of Confederation, went into effect on 1 March 1781. The church bells of Philadelphia pealed the good news; sloop-of-war *Ariel*, commanded by John Paul Jones, dressed ship and fired a 21-gun salute; Samuel Huntington, president of Congress, gave a reception and "the evening was ushered in by an elegant exhibition of fireworks."

Actually the adoption of the Articles made no perceptible change in the federal government, because it did little more than legalize what the Continental Congress had been doing. That body was now taken over as the Congress of the Confederation; but Americans continued to call it the Continental Congress, since its organization remained the same. Each state was represented by not less than two or more than seven members, as it preferred, but each state had one vote. The new provisions were: (1) assent of nine out of thirteen states was required for decisions on important matters such as making war or concluding treaties, borrowing money, raising armed force, and appointing a commander in chief. (2) Congress acquired the power to appoint executive departments, and shortly created five: foreign affairs with Robert R. Livingston as secretary; finance with Robert Morris as superintendent; war with General Lincoln as secretary; a board of admiralty of which Robert Morris was the only effective member, and a post office department. (3) A committee consisting of one delegate from each state sat between sessions of Congress to exercise all powers except those that required the consent of nine out of the thirteen.

A guiding principle of the Articles of Confederation was to preserve the independence and sovereignty of the states. The federal government received only those powers which the colonies had recognized as belonging to king and parliament. Thus, Congress was given all powers connected with war and peace, except the important one of taxation to support a war. It could conclude no commercial treaty limiting the states' rights to collect customs duties. It had power to establish post offices and charge postage (the only taxing power it possessed), to set standards of weights and measures, and to coin money. It had power to regulate the trade and manage all affairs with "Indians, not members of any of the states," a recognition that Western Indian affairs must be under federal control. In view of the land cessions by the states to Congress, a strange oversight was the failure to give the new government power over federal territory; but as somebody had to do that, Congress went ahead and did, and the greatest permanent success of the Confederation was in working out a new territorial policy.

The only colony outside the Thirteen expressly invited to join the Confederation was Canada, and Canada declined. None other could be admitted unless agreed to by nine states. Vermont, whose war record entitled her to admission, never got into the Confederation because New York and New Hampshire claimed her territory.

Of powers that the Articles did not make federal, the most important was the touchy one of taxation. Congress was not even allowed to tax imports, since colonial experience had shown that customs duties could be used against liberty. The colonial system of requisitions continued; all expenses of the federal government were to be assessed "in proportion to the value of all land within each state"; but the taxes to pay these requisitions had to be laid by the states. Congress had no power to regulate domestic and foreign commerce, because it was felt that Parliament's power to pass the Acts of Trade and Navigation had been abused. No federal judiciary was set up. Instead, a complicated machinery was provided to determine boundary and other controversies between the states. And finally, its greatest weakness, the Confederation was given no means to enforce such powers as were granted; it rested on the good will of the states. In his "Vices of the Political System of the United States" (1786) James Madison wrote: "A Sanction is essential to the idea of law, as coercion is to that of Government. The federal system being destitute of both, wants the great vital principles of a political constitution. Under form of such a constitution, it is in fact nothing more than a treaty of amity and of alliance between independent and sovereign states."

For all that, the Confederation might have met the needs of the Union for many years, could its powers have been increased by amendment. The unanimous consent of the member states was required for amendment, and that wrecked it.

Congress hoped that the Articles would constitute a "perpetual union"; and in a sense they did. The Great Seal of the United States, adopted on 20 June 1782, continues as the official seal to this day. Although some members wished to adopt a distinctly American bird like the wild turkey, or a dove of peace, Congress chose the eagle, symbol of imperial Rome. Over his head is a "glory" of thirteen stars, a new constellation in the galaxy of nations. In one talon the eagle grasps an olive branch and in the other a sheaf of arrows, to represent peace and war. In his beak is a ribbon inscribed *E Pluribus Unum*, and on his breast a shield with thirteen vertical stripes for the states, surmounted by a horizontal "chief" for Congress. On the reverse of the seal is a pyramid of thirteen courses of stone, to indicate permanence, with room for a few more at the top; and over it, in another "glory," the all-seeing eye of Divine Providence. On this reverse are two Latin mottoes: ANNUIT COEPTIS, meaning, "He has favored our undertakings"; and NOVUS ORDO SECLORUM, "A New Cycle of Centuries." Both were suggested by the poetry of Virgil: *Aeneid,* ix.625 and *Eclogues,* iv.5–7, best known by Shelley's paraphrase:

> The World's great age begins anew,
> The golden years return.

The classically trained leaders of the American Revolution were very fond of this prophecy. They believed that the Declaration of Independence had inaugurated a new order; and they hoped that they themselves were the *nova progenies,* the new Heaven-born generation predicted by the Latin poet.

ODE TO THE FOURTH OF JULY

'Tis done, the e-dict past, by Hea - ven de-creed,__ And Han - cock's__ name con-firms the glo-rious deed. On this au-spi-cious morn was__ In-de-pen-dence born: Pro - pi - tious day! Hail the U-ni-ted__ States of__blest A - mer - i - ca!

XIX

The Creative Period in Commerce and the Arts

1782-1789

1. *The Revival of Commerce*

JOHN ADAMS IN PARIS was overwhelmed by the painting, the statuary, the architecture, and the gardens of Versailles. But to his "dear Portia" Abigail he wrote a prophetic letter to the effect that, for America, political problems must long take precedence over the arts and sciences. He predicted that two generations must elapse before Americans would have opportunity to study poetry, music, and the fine arts.

John's countrymen were not so patience. Peace and independence, they felt, should bring prosperity at once, and cultivation of the arts would soon follow. Americans were now free to develop their own arts and industries. They hoped to enjoy free trade with the world; and with that end in view, Congress concluded commercial treaties with four European countries. But for several years the results were disappointing. The main trouble was the double adjustment that the country had to make—from a war to a peace economy, and from a favored position within the British empire to an independent status in a competitive world. A secondary cause of slow recovery was the right of each state to set up its own customs service. This not only deprived the Confederation of bargaining power with Europe, but permitted local protective tariffs.

Jefferson, who succeeded Franklin as American minister to France in 1784, wished to strengthen economic relations with our ally in order to free America from the commercial domination of Great Britain. During the war, France enjoyed a favorable trade balance with the United States, and intended to keep it. But, after a few years, the French realized that the American profits from selling to France were being used to pay their bills for English manufactures. Official France became vexed with American "ingratitude." But the real reasons for this situation were the lack of credit facilities in France, a natural preference of Americans for English consumer goods, and French protective tariffs. The only United States products that France wanted in large quantities were rice and tobacco. A French corporation which had the monopoly of importing tobacco made a contract with Robert Morris at such a low price that he could not meet his quota, and the French had to buy American tobacco in the English market.

It was much the same with rice. Before the Revolution, Britain had been the entrepôt for American rice, as for tobacco. During the British occupation of Charleston and Savannah, British and Loyalist export firms sent almost the entire rice crop to England, whence it was re-exported to the continent of Europe. Jefferson exerted himself to send seeds of an improved strain of rice to South Carolina, and persuaded French commercial houses to pay in advance for shipments; but he could not loosen the hold that British merchants had acquired on the Carolina trade through their credit facilities.

French efforts to persuade Americans to alter their drinking habits in favor of French wines likewise failed. Shortly after the war, the French consul at Boston entertained leading citizens in a champagne party. The Boston gentry, thinking champagne to be a sort of sparkling cider, got merrily drunk; but the experience did not change their preference for sherry and Madeira. And the common people continued to drink rum. Consequently, the only commercial advantage France obtained from American independence was the facility to export directly, instead of through England, silks and other articles of feminine adornment.

Although England got back most of her trade with the United States, she recovered little good will with it. John Adams, when received by George III as the first American minister in 1785, expressed his hope that "the old good nature and the old good humor" between the two countries would be restored; and the king appeared to agree. But British shipping interests prevented the admission of American ships to the British West Indies, and the government refused to conclude a commercial treaty, feeling that it could get back all the American trade it wanted without making concessions. That is about what happened. New Jersey, Connecticut, and New Hampshire, trying to steal foreign trade from New York, Rhode Island, and Boston, conceded more favorable rights of entry to British ships and goods than to those of their sister states.

The South recovered prosperity earlier than the North, since she produced tobacco, indigo, rice, and naval stores which Britain could buy nowhere else so cheap. Virginia's prewar exports, in value, were restored by 1786; but in the same year the exports of Massachusetts were only one-quarter of what they had been in 1774. New England's West Indies trade, deepsea whaling, and offshore fishing had been almost completely wiped out; Nantucketers emigrated to Milford Haven and Dunkerque to build up a whaling industry for England and France. Under the old Navigation Act, the Northern colonies had built hundreds of ships for British owners; now they no longer had this privilege. Here, as in other ways, Americans learned too late that the old imperial system had not been so oppressive as their political leaders loudly asserted.

To compensate for lost imperial trade, America showed enterprise in establishing new lines of business and commerce. Before the Revolution there was not a single bank in the Thirteen Colonies. If a man wanted capital, he borrowed from an individual. Robert Morris established the Bank of North America at Philadelphia in 1781; Boston and New York followed suit in 1784. Local paper factories prospered, and farmers made nails out of rod iron imported from Sweden. The Cabot family set up a small cotton-spinning factory at Beverly in 1784, and the same year began to trade with the Baltic, exporting tobacco, flour, and rum, and bringing back Swedish iron and Russian duck and hemp for ships' sails and cordage.

The boldest new trade to be established was with the Orient. Robert Morris and a number of New York merchants built the ship *Empress of China* and sent her to Canton in 1784. She was laden largely with borrowed silver and ginseng, an herb which the Chinese believed to be a restorative for male virility. She brought back a valuable cargo of tea, porcelain, silk, and nankeen, the cotton cloth which gentlemen of that period favored for their breeches. The difficulty about trading with China was to find a product that the Chinese wanted. Silver was scarce, and American ginseng did not produce the desired results. New England solved the problem by the Northwest

Coast-Hawaii-China trade. In 1787 Bostonians fitted out ship *Columbia* and sloop *Washington*, each less than 100 feet long, and sent them around Cape Horn laden with iron tools, looking-glasses, and all manner of knickknacks, to trade with the Indians of Vancouver Island for sea-otter fur, then in great demand among Chinese mandarins. The outward passage took eleven months. After spending a winter trading on the Northwest Coast, the *Columbia*, Captain Robert Gray, proceeded to Canton where she exchanged her cargo for China goods, and returned to Boston around the world, the first American ship to do so. This curiously complicated trade, which usually included a call at the Hawaiian Islands to pick up sandalwood for the China market, continued to be profitable for some thirty years. On her second voyage, in 1792, the *Columbia* sailed into the mouth of the great river named after her, and established the United States claim to the Oregon country.

In the meantime the merchants of Salem, Massachusetts, had been approaching the Canton market by way of the Cape of Good Hope, trading also with India and Indonesia. Salem, through her Oriental, Baltic, and West Indies trade, became a worthy rival to Boston, New York, and Philadelphia before the turn of the century. During a period of twenty days in 1790, the Salem custom house (where, 50 years later, Nathaniel Hawthorne could spend whole days dreaming) entered from Canton three ships, paying more than $53,000 customs duties; seven from the West Indies, and seven from Lisbon and Cadiz.

By that time the West Indies trade was in a measure restored because France, owing to Jefferson's efforts, admitted American ships and products to her Antilles; and because the people of the British islands badly needed North American produce. Local authorities were always ready to certify that a Yankee schooner put in "under distress." Captain Horatio Nelson of H.M.S. *Boreas* on the West Indies station gave up in despair his attempts to enforce the British Acts of Trade. The islanders, he said, were "as great rebels as ever were in America," and Yankee skippers would "swear through a nine-inch plank" for permission to sell cargoes illegally.

Even the horse kind contributed to the postwar revival. "Royal Gift," a big jackass sent to General Washington by the king of Spain, was a slow starter; and (wrote the General to Lafayette), performed with a "majestic solemnity supposed to be the example of his late Royal Master." But, having become "a little better acquainted with republican enjoyment," Royal Gift decided to "amend his manners" and began covering mares not only locally but on tours all the way to Charleston, siring strong, heavy mules which proved a boon to American farmers and to the army.

In England during the war, several of the new classics of the turf, such as the Derby, the St. Leger, and the Oaks, began; and after the war some of the winning stallions were imported into the United States. Messenger, a gray thoroughbred descended from the Darley Arabian, landed at Philadelphia in 1788, and sired the Hambletonian race of trotters. Ten years later Diomed, in whose veins ran the blood of all three of England's Oriental stallions, began serving mares in Virginia. Toward the end of his life he begot Sir Archie, whom General Davie bought for the then unprecedented sum of $5000, and whose stud fees made a fortune for his subsequent owners.

These imported thoroughbreds imparted a magic touch to American mares, but the all-American sire of the period was a horse of unknown ancestry named Justin Morgan. This stallion, named after his first owner, a school-teacher who brought him as a two-year-old to Randolph, Vermont, was better known for a quarter-century than any two-legged citizen of the Green Mountain State. He was a dark red bay with black points, 14 hands tall, with a compact body, small, fine ears, a large bright eye, long, thick mane and tail, and a sweet disposition. Justin Morgan transmitted both conformation and characteristics to his descendants for a century and a half. No American horse ever began to touch the Morgan breed as the people's choice; they could win quarter-mile running races, pull stone boats, work in wagon teams, carry the children to school and the family to church—anything that a horse could do except compete with thoroughbreds in four-mile races or with hunters timber-topping. Justin Morgan came on the scene just in time for his get to replace the Narragansett pacers, no longer in demand for road work.

2. Debts, Loyalists, and Western Posts

The resumption of friendship with Great Britain, that both John Adams and George III wished, did not come about; and Adams left London in 1788 feeling frustrated. There were several bones of contention. Congress recommended the states to restore Loyalist property, as the treaty required, but few states complied, except Pennsylvania which paid the heirs of William Penn $650,000; and Maryland, which generously compensated the Calverts for the loss of their proprietary rights. The treaty also provided that "no future confiscations" be made. Except in New York and South Carolina, where the civil war between Whigs and Tories had been particularly vicious, this was complied with. A New York confiscatory law was invalidated by a decision of the state supreme court, after a trial in which Alexander Hamilton defended the Loyalists; a similar law in South Carolina was repealed in 1786.

Although British historians such as Arnold Toynbee continue to assert that Loyalists "were expelled bag and baggage, men, women, and children, from their homes after the war was over," this is incorrect. None were expelled after the war, and only a few royal officials were exiled during the war. Tory migration was almost completely voluntary; about 80,000 departed with the British garrisons to which they had flocked for protection. The loss to the United States was the British empire's gain, since most of these exiles settled in New Brunswick, Nova Scotia, or Ontario, where they became leaders in their communities and helped to keep them loyal to England. The great majority of Loyalists never left the states, but became good American citizens; and a surprisingly large number who did leave, drifted back. Cadwalader Colden returned from self-imposed exile and was elected mayor of New York City. Henry Cruger, a member of Parliament during the war, came back and was elected to the New York state senate. Dr. John Jeffries of Boston, a surgeon in the British army during the war, made the pioneer balloon crossing of the English Channel; he then returned to Boston and built up a large practice. Philip B. Key, uncle of the author of *The Star Spangled Banner,* served as officer in a Maryland Loyalist regiment; after the war he was admitted to the Maryland bar and received an appointment to the federal bench while still receiving his British pension. Isaac Coffin of Boston, an officer of the Royal Navy when the war began, remained in the king's senior service and rose to be Admiral Sir Isaac Coffin, but he founded a school at his ancestral home, Nantucket, and exported English thoroughbreds to improve the breed of horses in New England. In general, the only Loyalists who were not allowed to return to their homes after the war were those who had indulged in partisan warfare and Indian raids.

In the matter of prewar debts owed by American citizens to British subjects, Britain had good reason to complain. The treaty of peace required that "no legal impediment" be placed in the way of recovering such debts. Most states complied, but Virginia, whose citizens owed the most, insisted that those debts had been cancelled by state legislation during the war, and no longer existed. This subject was not settled until 1802, when the United States paid to the British government the lump sum of £600,000 as compensation to individual creditors. The amount would have been greater, but for deducting the value of hundreds of Negro slaves that the British armies either sold in the West Indies or carried off when evacuating, which was also contrary to the treaty of peace.

Canadian border posts on territory ceded to the United States in the peace treaty caused the most ill feeling. British garrisons of Atlantic coast ports from Castine to Savannah were evacuated "with all convenient speed," as the treaty required; but those on the northern border, at two points on Lake Champlain; at Ogdensburg, Oswego, and Niagara; and at Detroit and Michilimackinac, refused to budge. At the request of the governor of Canada, his superiors held these posts "to secure the fur traders in the Interior Country." Several Scots firms had built up a fur trading empire in the Old Northwest, producing peltry to the value of a million dollars a year; and the Western posts were the keys to keeping the Indians quiet and loyal; or, from the United States point of view, warlike and hostile. Although this retention of the posts was originally conceived as a temporary measure to help the fur traders to wind up their affairs, the longer they were retained, the more reluctant Canadians became to give them up. So, under the convenient excuse that Americans broke the treaty first in the matters of debts and Loyalists, the British government held on until 1796, narrowly escaping a war on that issue.

Equally troublesome to the infant republic was the attitude of Spain, whose government was determined to check American expansion to the south or west. As a result of the war, Spain recovered both Floridas and posted garrisons at Natchez and the Walnut Hills (Vicksburg), denying Britain's right to cede the east bank of the Mississippi to the United States. In 1784 the Creek, Choctaw, and Cherokee nations, or parts of them, made treaties placing themselves under Spanish protection. With ammunition obtained from former Loyalists at Pensacola, these Indians began raiding American settlements on the Cumberland and Tennessee rivers.

Possession of New Orleans and posts on the Mississippi enabled Spain to put pressure on Western pioneers. Without any better system than the pack mule to cross the Appalachians, Western farmers had to send their bulky products down the Mississippi and its tributaries to reach the sea and foreign markets. A surprising number of American backwoods politicians, notably General James Wilkinson of Kentucky, accepted pensions from Spain in return for a promise to promote the secession of trans-Appalachia and make it a satellite to the Spanish empire. This movement became especially strong after 1786 when John Jay, the Confederation's secretary for foreign

affairs, failed to persuade Spain to recognize the "right of
deposit," which meant the privilege to transit New Orleans,
where the Spanish empire straddled both banks of the Mississippi. And this Western secession movement continued even
after the federal government was established in 1789. We shall
later find a former Vice President of the United States fishing
in these troubled waters—the lagoons of Louisiana and the
Gulf of Mexico.

Vermont, too, was threatening secession because denied a
place in the Confederation. Levi Allen, Ethan's brother, journeyed to London to seek a treaty with Great Britain. With
suitable encouragement, which he did not obtain, he might
have persuaded the veterans of Bennington and Saratoga to
vote for annexation to Canada.

Thus, the War of the American Revolution settled American
independence, but little else. Unless American statesmen played
their cards cannily and well, the United States might long be
confined to a comparatively narrow strip between Canada, the
Appalachians, the Floridas, and the Atlantic. And the indications were that it would be a very poor country at that.

3. *Literature and Education*

This was the bright dayspring of republican culture. Many
young Americans, despite John Adams's prediction, turned to
arts, letters, and science as soon as the war was over. They
accomplished nothing great; but we now look on their efforts
with tolerant appreciation.

The keynote was struck in 1778 by Noah Webster, a twenty-
five-year-old schoolmaster at Hartford: "America must be as
independent in *literature* as she is in politics, as famous for *arts*
as for *arms*." He did his best to make her so with his famous
bluebacked speller, his first American reader, and the monthly
American Magazine, which he edited. That failed within a
year, but the books were astounding successes. *The American
Spelling-Book,* which simplified the king's English by omitting
the *u* from words like *labour* and *colour,* and spelling *wagon*
with one *g,* became an all-time best seller, and remained in
print for over a century. Webster's *American Dictionary,* first
to record colloquial words and Americanisms, is still being
published in both enlarged and condensed editions not far from
Noah's old home. His reader, *An American Selection of Les-
sons in Reading and Speaking* (1785), was compiled "to Improve the minds and refine the Taste of Youth." It is a true
anthology, culled from American orations, American history
and politics, as well as from classic English literature. These

are interspersed with amusing bits such as a recommendation of square dancing to "excite a cheerfulness of mind, and producing copious perspiration," and "a Dialogue between Mr. Hunks and Mr. Blithe," representing the older generation and the new. Mr. Hunks complains, "There's no living in this prodigal age—the young people must have their bottles, their tavern dinners, and dice, while the old ones are made perfect drudges to support their luxury."

Similar works were Caleb Bingham's *The Young Lady's Accidence; or, A Short and Easy Introduction to English Grammar* (Boston, 1785); *The Sister's Gift; or, The Naughty Boy Reformed* (Worcester, 1786), an attempt to cure juvenile delinquency; and Eleazar Moody's *The School of Good Manners, Composed for the Help of Parents Teaching Children How To Behave* (Portland, 1786).

The Reverend Jedidiah Morse (father of the artist who invented the electric telegraph) brought out the first edition of his *Geography Made Easy* in 1784, the year following his graduation from Yale; it became almost as popular as Webster's speller. Most agreeably, Morse did not confine his book to mere facts and statistics. For instance, "The refreshing sea breezes . . . render Charleston more healthy than any part of the low country in the southern states. On this account it is the resort of great numbers of gentlemen . . . who come here to spend the *sickly months,* as they are called, in quest of health and of the social enjoyments which the city affords." One Yankee product Morse refused to promote. "New England rum is by no means a wholesome liquor," he observed. "It has killed more Indians than their wars and sicknesses. It does not spare white people, especially when made into flip, which is rum mixed with small beer, and muscovado sugar."

American schoolboys needed new arithmetic books, now that they had to reckon in dollars and cents, even though the dollars were still Spanish "pieces of eight," and the copper cents hard to come by. Nicholas Pike brought out *A New and Complete System* of that science at Newburyport in 1788. It ran through many editions and became the standard American text.

These works were intended as schoolbooks or manuals; but creative literature was not altogether wanting. Joel Barlow, Noah Webster's Yale classmate, was no sooner out of college than he began an epic poem which eventually ran to over 5000 lines and was printed at Hartford in 1787 as *The Vision of Columbus.* Timothy Dwight, tutor of both these young poets at Yale, sparked off a group called the "Hartford Wits" who contributed squibs to the newspapers, of which the best known are Barlow's *Anarchiad* (1786–87), a satire on Shays's Rebellion;

and John Trumbull's *McFingal,* a lengthy and heavily humorous attack on the Tories. Royall Tyler, after serving as a major in the war, brought out in 1787 *The Contrast,* the second play to be produced by a native American,[1] and in which Jonathan, the first stage Yankee, provided most of the laughs.

Philip Freneau, a Princeton graduate, was the first poet of the American Revolution. In 1786 he brought out a sizable volume of his collected poems, including the humorous doggerel *Sketches of American History* containing amusing cracks at the New England Puritans and Dutch Knickerbockers. But the public neglected Freneau's *Sketches* while enthusing over his odes to heroes of the Revolution, and his poem on an Indian Burying Ground.

The girl wonder of this age was Phillis Wheatley, a slave born in Africa and owned by a Boston tailor. Before the war she exhibited such versifying talent that her master took her to London where her *Poems on Various Subjects* was published. Returning to Boston free, she married a member of her race and celebrated her country's emancipation and her own with *Liberty and Peace, A Poem* (1784), ending:

> Auspicious Heaven shall fill with fav'ring Gales,
> Where e'er *Columbia* spreads her swelling Sails:
> To every Realm shall *Peace* her Charms display,
> And Heavenly *Freedom* spread her golden Ray.

There was soon enough native poetry by this time to fill an anthology—*American Poems, Selected and Original,* which appeared at Litchfield, Connecticut in 1793.

John Trumbull, cousin to the like-named poet, aspired to be a painter, but was packed off to Harvard by an unsympathetic father, the governor of Connecticut. He served for two years in the Continental army, then resigned his commission and set up a studio in Boston. Finding neither teacher nor customers there, he obtained a safe conduct from the British to London, where he studied under Benjamin West, an expatriate artist from Philadelphia. There Trumbull painted his "Battle of Bunker Hill" and "Death of Montgomery," and began his famous "Declaration of Independence."

Another American pupil of Benjamin West was the prolific Charles Willson Peale of Annapolis, who lived in Philadelphia during the war, and as captain of Pennsylvania militia fought at Trenton and Princeton. During the war he undertook to paint all the distinguished generals and naval officers from life;

---

[1] The first was Thomas Godfrey's *The Prince of Parthia,* produced at Philadelphia in 1767.

Washington sat for him at least seven times, and from these sittings Peale produced no fewer than sixty portraits of the commander in chief. This artist depicted the Continental uniform in careful detail, but unfortunately used a standard face so that his portraits of Washington and Lafayette, who differed greatly in physiognomy, look like father and son; and even John Paul Jones looks like a member of the same family.

After the good start made by Franklin and the colonial *cognoscenti,* this period became fruitful in natural science. David Rittenhouse, a self-educated Philadelphian, became the first American professor of astronomy, at the University of Pennsylvania. A practical science in great demand in a growing country was surveying. For want of competent American surveyors, Mason and Dixon had come from England to survey the line that has made their names immortal; but Rittenhouse and Andrew Ellicott continued the line from the spot where the two Englishmen dropped it in 1767. Ellicott, with the aid of an amateur black astronomer named Benjamin Banneker, surveyed the ten-mile square for the District of Columbia. Manasseh Cutler, one of many scientifically inclined New England ministers, compiled the first flora of New England, and measured the height of Mount Washington—very inaccurately—by carrying a huge mercury barometer to the summit on his back. Dr. Benjamin Rush of Philadelphia began lecturing on medicine at the University of Pennsylvania in 1780, and six years later established the first free medical dispensary in the United States. And he devoted a large part of his energy and fortune to promoting the abolition of slavery, and better education for women.

Franklin's colonial Junto of Philadelphia was reorganized in 1780 as a learned academy, the American Philosophical Society. The same year, Harvard professors and several New England parsons founded the American Academy of Arts and Sciences at Boston; and the same group founded the first American historical society, that of Massachusetts, ten years later. Several valuable histories of the American states were written, and one, the Reverend Jeremy Belknap's *History of New Hampshire* (1784), has literary merit. George Richards Minot, extravagantly called "the American Sallust" by his admirers, picked up the history of Massachusetts where Governor Hutchinson had been forced to leave off, and brought out a *History of Shays's Rebellion* in 1788. Mrs. Mercy Warren, gifted sister of James Otis, after writing satires on Tories during the war, now began a fresh and original *History of the Rise, Progress and Termination of the American Revolution,* which finally appeared in 1805. This lively presentation of the "pure republican" and antifederalist point of view delighted Thomas Jefferson but infuriated John Adams. Equally unorthodox was *A History of New England, with Particular Reference to the Baptists* (3 vols., 1777–96) by a robust minister of that denomination, the Reverend Isaac Backus, who had led the movement for religious liberty in Massachusetts.

This creative activity resulted from a feeling that Americans could know and love their country better through scientific investigation of her natural resources, by studying her past, and by writing poetry on native themes. Even those writers who began with something imitative turned "American." For instance, Peter Markoe of Philadelphia, after writing *The Patriot Chief*, a tragedy of ancient Lydia which he had printed in 1784 but never managed to produce, wrote a pungent satire on American affairs, *The Algerine Spy* (1787), in the form of "Letters Written by a Native of Algiers." The Reverend Timothy Dwight, after producing a dreary Old Testament epic, *The Conquest of Canaan* (1785), wrote a charming pastoral about the Connecticut countryside, *Greenfield Hill*, printed in 1794. By contrast, during the subsequent Federalist and Jeffersonian periods, the leading American literary men, Joseph Dennie and his circle, abandoned local themes in favor of pallid imitations of *The Spectator* and "Gothic" novels of mystery and horror.

After the war, when paper became more available, newspapers and periodicals increased in number. The *Pennsylvania Packet and General Advertiser* of Philadelphia, which started in 1784, was the first daily newspaper to last more than a few weeks; and by 1789 over eighty weekly or bi-weekly gazettes and a few monthly magazines were being published.

In education, this period was marked by the founding of new colleges in the South, and privately endowed secondary schools such as the two Phillips academies of Andover and Exeter. All Northern colleges suffered from the war, but Yale forged ahead with a graduating class of seventy in 1785, more than twice Harvard's. In William and Mary College, where the first intercollegiate fraternity, Phi Beta Kappa, was founded during the war, two chairs of theology were converted to law and history by Governor Jefferson, and by 1787 this college was offering an excellent liberal arts course.

Impressive is the list of colleges and universities founded in the South shortly after the war, in some cases before it was over. Religious bodies were responsible for most of them. Presbyterians founded four colleges in 1782–87: Hampden-Sydney, Liberty Hall which has been renamed Washington and Lee, Transylvania in the frontier state of Kentucky, and Dickinson at Carlisle, Pennsylvania. The Episcopalians founded three colleges in 1782–85: Washington at Chestertown, Maryland, St. John's at Annapolis, and Charleston College, South Carolina. The first Roman Catholic college in the United States was Georgetown, founded in 1789 by Bishop Carroll. It was typical of the liberal spirit of the South in this era that she pioneered in state universities free from sectarian control. The University of North Carolina, first state university to be established, was chartered in 1789 and opened in 1795.

Even in music this era was far from silent. William Billings, the Boston psalm singer who had written patriotic odes during the war, was still producing hymns and choruses which have been revived in the present century. Secular song and dance books were Daniel Bayley's *Essex Harmony* (Newburyport, 1785), John Griffiths's *Collection of the Newest and Most Fashionable Country Dances and Cotillions* (Providence, 1788), William Brown's *Three Rondos for the Piano Forte* (Philadelphia, 1787), and the *Charms of Melody, A New Collection of Songs* (Philadelphia, 1788). Oliver Holden of Massachusetts wrote hymn tunes of which the best known is *Coronation*, to which is sung "All Hail the Power of Jesus' Name." The Moravians of Bethlehem, Pennsylvania, had already established their festivals devoted to Johann Sebastian Bach. Francis Hopkinson, signer of the Declaration of Independence, judge, poet, painter, and organist of Christ Church, Philadelphia, composed an oratorio *The Temple of Minerva*, which was performed before General and Mrs. Washington in 1781. And the German Reformed Church of Philadelphia, in 1784, sold over 2000 tickets to a concert by 50 instruments and 250 choristers, at which works of American composers were performed. The concert concluded with a lusty rendering of Handel's Hallelujah Chorus, an appropriate celebration for achieving American independence.

4. Religion and Reform

Throughout the country one encountered the same complaints that are heard after every war, that moral and religious standards had declined; and frequent advertisements in the newspapers of quack cures for social diseases indicate that they had indeed. But independence was a distinct gain for the institutional aspect of religion, since it put many sects on their own resources. And a general spirit of mutual tolerance and religious liberty was in the air. Least affected were the Congregational churches of New England, and the Quaker meetings, which had always been independent of those in the old country. The Presbyterians, who had numbers, wealth, and a great leader in Dr. John Witherspoon, held a series of synods between 1785 and 1788 which drew up a confession of faith and a form of government and discipline for the Presbyterian Church of America. The Dutch Reformed, the Lutherans, and the German evangelical sects broke loose from their old-world organizations.

The French alliance led to a favorable attitude toward the Roman Catholic church on the part of American Protestants, and this was encouraged by Washington, Franklin, and other leading men. The Roman communion in 1785 counted only 24 priests and about 25,000 souls, mostly in Maryland and Philadelphia. The first mass to be celebrated openly in Boston was on 2 November 1788 by a former chaplain in the French navy; the first Catholic church in New York was St. Peter's, consecrated in 1785. The small number of Roman Catholics in the English colonies had been under the jurisdiction of a vicar apostolic in London. Now that that bond was broken, Pope Pius VI in 1784 appointed the Reverend John Carroll of Baltimore his apostolic prefect. Upon hearing that the Gallican church was endeavoring to have him replaced by a Frenchman, the Maryland clergy petitioned to have Carroll made a bishop; and as such he was consecrated in 1790, by a Roman Catholic bishop in England. His see covered the entire United States until 1804. During that era, the Catholic churches in the United States usually presented their own priests for ordination, almost as if they had been Congregational.

Two important developments took place among the Anglicans. The Methodists or Wesleyans, who had never formally separated from the Anglican communion, did so in 1784 when the Reverend Francis Asbury of Delaware, John Wesley's superintendent, called a conference at Baltimore. It chose him and the Reverend Thomas Coke joint superintendents, and organized the Methodist Episcopal Church in the United States. Asbury, who styled himself "The Bishop," and apparently was accepted as such by the brethren, gave an example of his church's favorite method of proselytizing, by circuit riding far and wide. "My horse trots stiff," he complained, "and no wonder when I have ridden him upon an average of 5000 miles a year for five years."

Before 1776 the Anglican church was supported by taxation, and enjoyed a monopoly of performing marriages in all Southern colonies and in parts of New York. It was disestablished in New York, Maryland, and the Carolinas, and complete religious liberty adopted in those states, during the war. In Virginia, however, it took a ten-year contest, which Jefferson called the severest of his life, to separate church from state. Finally the Virginia Statute of Religious Liberty, drafted by Jefferson, passed the assembly on 16 January 1786. The exercise of religion, it declares, is a "natural right" which has been infringed by "the impious presumption of legislators and rulers" to set up their own "modes of thinking as the only true and infallible"; and "to compel a man to furnish contributions of money for the propagation of opinions which he disbelieves," which "is sinful and tyrannical." The statute roundly declares, "No man shall be compelled to frequent or support any religious worship, place or ministry whatsoever." It even warns later assemblies that any attempt on their part to tamper with this law "will be an infringement of natural right." None, to this day, have ventured to do so; the statute is still in force.

At the close of the War of Independence the Anglican church reached its all-time low in America, partly owing to loss of support from taxes, partly because many Anglican clergymen went Tory. But there were enough patriotic laity left to demand an independent episcopate. The Reverend Samuel Seabury, former rector of Westchester, New York, was elected bishop of Connecticut and sent abroad in 1784 to obtain consecration. This was no easy matter, since the Archbishop of Canterbury still regarded the Americans as rebels and traitors; but the Scots bishops were more liberal, and through them Bishop Seabury transmitted apostolic succession to the American episcopate. The Protestant Episcopal Church of America was organized at a series of conventions between 1784 and 1789. These conventions adopted the Book of Common Prayer, omitting prayers for the royal family, and gave more power to the laity than churchmen enjoyed in England.

In the meantime John Adams, as American minister to the Court of St. James's, obtained an act of Parliament allowing bishops to be consecrated without taking an oath of allegiance to the king. Consequently the Reverend Samuel Prevoost and the Reverend William White, elected respectively bishops of New York and Pennsylvania, were consecrated by the Archbishops of Canterbury and York at Lambeth in 1787. Shortly after the Reverend James Madison, president of William and Mary College, was consecrated bishop of Virginia. The Reverend Edward Bass, elected bishop of Massachusetts, missed out on this occasion because he remarried within six months of the death of his first wife, which was thought to be a bit brisk for a sixty-three-year-old bishop; but he finally obtained his consecration from Bishop White in Philadelphia in 1797.

Just as Noah Webster maintained that there should be an American language and literature, so there were freethinkers who aimed at a republican religion. The apostle of this group was Colonel Ethan Allen, leader of the Green Mountain Boys of Vermont. In 1784 he brought out a long, dreary tract entitled, *Reason the Only Oracle of Man, or a Compendious System of Natural Religion*. Therein he denied that the Bible was the Word of God, and attempted to substitute a vague deism for Christianity. When relighted by Thomas Paine's *Age of Reason* this cult shot up into a flame that for a time frightened the clergy, but died out when the French Reign of Terror seemed to point out the consequences of abandoning the Christian religion.

Although a political revolution, like war, may speed things up socially—"Revolution is the locomotive of history," said Karl Marx—this does not necessarily occur, and did not happen here. American patriots wanted no social upheaval. No flaming demagogues, no radical reformers, emerged from the revolutionary ferment. The abolition of primogeniture (leaving one's entire property to the eldest son) and entails (making it illegal for an heir to sell his estate) in Virginia and other states has been cited as social reform; but in reality amounted to little. Primogeniture was abolished for the heirs of people who died intestate—without making a will—and entails, in a country expanding westward with wide economic opportunities, were a burden rather than a privilege.

The confiscation of Loyalists' estates has been called a social revolution. Loyalist patroonships in New York were divided up, but not excessively; and in North Carolina the purchasers of Henry McCulloh's 40,000 acres acquired up to 5000 each, and the 3600-acre estate of Tom Hooper, Tory, passed intact to John McKinsey, Patriot. But for the most part, Loyalists' estates were of average size, and the result of confiscation was simply to substitute new owners for the old.

A social revolution indeed was the abolition of slavery, but this did not extend to any state where slaves were numerous or slavery was considered essential to the economy. In Rhode Island, a participant in the African slave trade, the assembly of 1774 resolved that, whereas Americans were now contending for rights and liberties, all slaves henceforth imported into that colony would be free. In Massachusetts a black named Quork Walker won his freedom in 1781 on the ground that the state constitutions said "All men are born free and equal"; and that ended slavery in Massachusetts. The other New England states and Pennsylvania did not free existing slaves, fearing lest their support fall on the taxpayer, but gave freedom to all children thenceforward born of slave parents. New York and New Jersey, where slavery was more of an economic factor than in New England, did not begin gradual abolition until 1799 and 1804, respectively.

South of Mason and Dixon's line, the efforts of liberals such as Jefferson and George Mason to put slavery on the way to extinction were defeated, precisely because this would have meant a social revolution. Many Southern leaders declared publicly that slavery was morally wrong and contrary to Revolutionary principles, but they could not convert the voters. The Virginia assembly in 1783 freed slaves who had served in the armed forces. Two years later, when Methodists petitioned the Virginia assembly to begin a general emancipation on the ground that slavery was "contrary to the fundamental principles of the Christian religion" and a violation of the Declaration of Rights, their petition was unanimously rejected. Had it been acted upon, there might have been no American civil war.

The African slave trade, however, was prohibited by Delaware, Maryland, Virginia, and all Northern states by 1783. North Carolina placed a heavy tax on slave imports, and in South Carolina the trade was prohibited between 1787 and 1803, when the act was repealed as unenforceable. But abolishing the direct trade from Africa merely shifted it to the border slave states as source of supply for plantations of the lower South.

Discussion of slavery was still completely free and every Southern state nourished one or more abolition societies. The general American expectation seems to have been that slavery would fade away in competition with immigrant white labor. Oliver Ellsworth of Connecticut predicted in the Federal Convention that "as population increases, our laborers will be so plenty as to render slaves useless. Slavery in time will be a speck in our country." Alas, if only it had turned out that way! But for the coming convulsions in Europe, indentured labor from Ireland and the Continent might have come in such numbers as to fulfill Ellsworth's prophecy. There were fewer than 700,000 slaves in the United States in 1790. The emancipation of these blacks, their becoming domestic servants, common laborers and small farmers, even the return of many to Africa, would then have been possible. But the Revolutionary generation lacked the imagination to foresee the tragic consequences of perpetuating an institution which denied the very premises upon which American independence was based.

XX

The Creative Period in Politics

1785-1788

1. *Some Western Problems Solved*

ALMOST EVERY WESTERN SETTLEMENT that we have described suffered during the war from Indian raids and cattle thieves. Nevertheless, the attraction of blue-grass and hardwood, and desire to escape the war, brought in thousands from Virginia and the Carolinas. When in 1780 Virginia set up a land office in Kentucky, it was flooded with prospective settlers and speculators, and the movement increased after news of peace arrived. Congress now became eager to obtain control of the West north of the Ohio (it never had any chance to get anything south of that river), in order to sell land and put something into the empty Confederation treasury.

When Virginia again offered to cede her land claims north of the Ohio, with reserves for veterans but no other strings, Congress accepted (1 March 1784). Massachusetts and Connecticut followed two years later. Connecticut retained a tract of land on Lake Erie, known to this day as the Western Reserve. She had agreed with Pennsylvania to give up her claim to the Wyoming valley, where there had been clashes between rival settlers, if Pennsylvania would support her claim to this section of Ohio. William Grayson of Virginia cynically remarked that the Connecticut cession was "nothing but a state

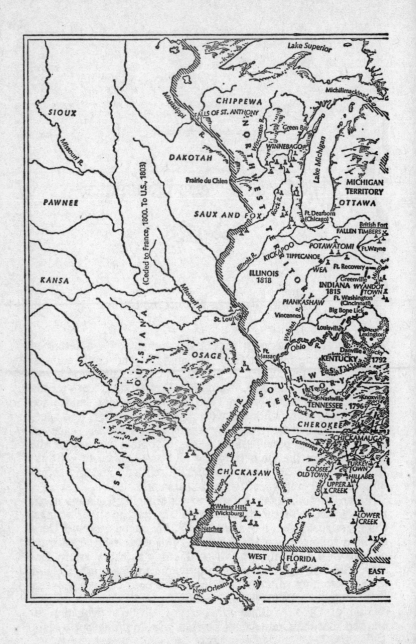

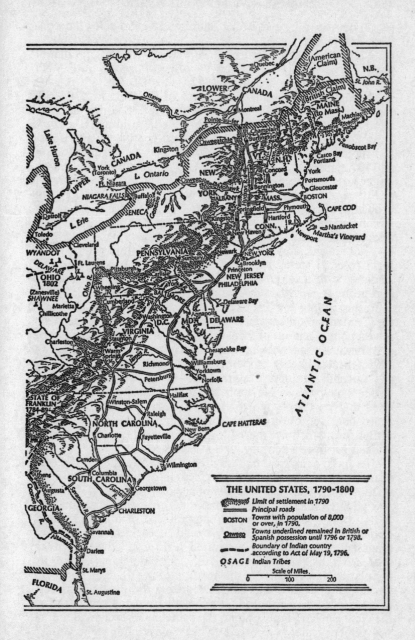

THE UNITED STATES, 1790–1800

Limit of settlement in 1790

Principal roads

BOSTON Towns with population of 8,000 or over, in 1790.

Oswego Towns underlined remained in British or Spanish possession until 1796 or 1798.

Boundary of Indian country according to Act of May 19, 1796.

OSAGE Indian Tribes

Scale of Miles
0   100   200

juggle contrived by old Roger Sherman to get a sidewind confirmation to a thing they had no right to." Anyway, Connecticut got it, and the Western Reserve was governed as an integral part of that state (like Maine by Massachusetts) until Ohio was admitted to the Union in 1802.

Through these state cessions north of the Ohio in 1784–86, the United States became a colonial power; or, to use another word which has recently been denigrated, an imperial power. John Paul Jones referred to his adopted country as an "imperial republic"; and Joel Barlow, in his Fourth of July Oration of 1787 remarked, "Every free citizen of the American empire ought now to consider himself the legislator of half mankind."

But before going that far, the new "Empire" had its own problems. Congress was confronted with Western questions which had been debated or decided in London before the war. Should white settlement in the Indian country be encouraged or discouraged, and how? Should Congress anticipate a long-term colonial status for the West to protect Indians and fur traders, or encourage white settlement, abandon the Indians, and promise eventual admission of the West to the Union?

Responsibility for this territory was the main bond that held the Confederation together. In 1783–84 Congress reached its lowest point. Run out of Philadelphia by mutineers of the Pennsylvania line regiments, it wandered from place to place in the Middle states like an emperor of the Holy Roman Empire in the fifteenth century. Congress moved to Princeton in June 1783, Annapolis in November, Trenton in 1784, and a year later to New York, where it stayed until the Confederation faded out. Yet, during this period Congress passed a series of ordinances which set the pattern of federal land and colonial policies for over a century.

The basic principle, that any lands ceded to the Confederation would "be settled and formed into distinct republican states, which shall become members of the Federal Union," was adopted in 1780. Next came the Territorial Ordinance of 1784, drafted by Jefferson in consequence of Virginia's land cession. United States territory would be divided into ten rectangular territories, each promised territorial government as soon as it had 20,000 inhabitants, and statehood when its population equaled that of the smallest of the original Thirteen. On 20 May 1785 Congress decided how the public land was to be divided and disposed. It adopted, from the precedent of the New England land system, the principle of rectangular survey prior to sale, in contrast to the "indiscriminate location" that the Southern states had copied from colonial Virginia. The land was surveyed into townships six miles square, each containing 36 sections of 640 acres, one mile square. Section number 16 in each township was reserved for the maintenance of public schools. When surveyed, the land must be sold by public auction; even-numbered townships by sections, and odd-numbered townships as a whole. Surveying promptly began, and four "ranges" or tiers of townships, beginning at the western boundary of Pennsylvania, were ready for sale in 1787.

Congress badly needed money, and land speculators were ready to oblige. The older companies, like the Illinois-Wabash, had spent their initial capital in lobbying and disappeared; but a vigorous new one, the Ohio Company, organized by New England veterans such as General Knox, came into the picture. This company proposed to buy 1,500,000 acres for the same number of dollars in Continental currency. Congress had now fallen so low that the number necessary to do business was seldom present, but the prospect of raising money induced enough members to attend early in July 1787 to make a quorum of eight states. Nathan Dane of Massachusetts then drafted the Territorial or Northwest Ordinance, wanted by the Ohio Company as a prerequisite for its purchase. Congress passed it on 13 July by vote of eight states, represented by only eighteen members; but no more important enactment was ever made by the Confederation. The Northwest Ordinance laid fundamental principles of the American colonial system which have been followed, even through the admission of Alaska and Hawaii. A territorial assembly, under a governor appointed by Congress, was promised as soon as a "district" had a population of 5000 free males. Statehood was promised as soon as any one of three districts attained 60,000 people. A bill of rights was established "as articles of compact between the original States and the people and States in the said territory," forever to remain inalterable. And one of the articles in this bill of rights stated, "There shall be neither slavery nor involuntary servitude in said territory."

This was the greatest triumph for antislavery in the Creative Period. It dedicated the entire West north of the Ohio and east of the Mississippi to free soil. And, although the authority of Congress to legislate for the West was doubtful, both state and federal courts have held that the Northwest Ordinance is still superior to all constitutions and laws subsequently adopted by the five states—Ohio, Indiana, Illinois, Michigan, and Wisconsin—carved out of the Northwest Territory.

Thus the main lines of federal land and territorial policy were adopted by the Congress of the Confederation before the Federal Constitution was adopted. These were: the principle of future statehood after an intermediary stage as a partly self-governing territory, and division into six-mile-square townships and one-mile-square sections, reserving a portion for education.

So wrote Philip Freneau in his contemporary poem "On the Emigration to America and Peopling the Western Country."

> Far brighter scenes a future age,
> The muse predicts, these States will hail,
> Whose genius may the world engage,
> Whose deeds may over death prevail,
> And happier systems bring to view,
> Than all the eastern sages knew.

2. Shays's Rebellion and the Movement Toward Stronger Union

> My name is Shays; in former days
>   In Pelham I did dwell, Sir.
> But now I'm forced to leave the place
>   Because I did rebel, Sir.
>
> Within the State I lived of late,
>   By Satan's foul invention,
> In Pluto's cause against the laws
>   I raised an insurrection.

So runs a ballad about Shays's Rebellion in Massachusetts, which stimulated local bards, as the War of the Regulation had inspired those of North Carolina. There was much in common between these movements, and Shays's followers were often called Regulators. Both were revolts of poor farmers against intolerable conditions; both were relatively bloodless, and both were put down in the name of law and order. Shays's Rebellion, moreover, gave an emotional fillip to the movement for stronger union.

There were "combustibles" of revolt, as Washington put it, in almost every state; but only in Massachusetts did they catch fire. The basic causes were the postwar readjustment and consequent poverty, which made the poor and discontented seek relief from their state governments. As John Jay wrote, "New governments have not the aid of habit and hereditary respect, and being generally the result of preceding tumult and confusion do not immediately acquire stability and strength."

In states where conditions were better than in Massachusetts, legislatures relieved debtors and poor farmers by unorthodox financial expedients which had earlier been quashed by the British government. A favorite device was the old land bank scheme in which the state lent script to farmers up to the value of their real estate, and made it legal tender for taxes, sometimes for all payments. Another was the stay law, postponing the collection of all debts and mortagages for a number of years. The Rhode Island assembly, worst offender against sound finance, provided that if a creditor refused to accept state paper currency at par, the debtor could discharge his debt simply by depositing the script with the nearest judge. The reverse of the usual situation took place—harassed creditors were pursued by implacable debtors eager to tender a wad of depreciated paper for the full value of their debts! Rather than sell goods for worthless paper, merchants shut up shop, hid their stock, or loaded it on a vessel and escaped to New York or the West Indies.

In Massachusetts, where the farmers' situation was worse, the political setup brought about an explosion. In the state constitution, as we have seen, the senate represented property, so that the maritime counties had a majority and were able to defeat all relief measures passed by the lower house. Mercantile influence had been strong enough to put the state on a specie basis in 1782, which meant a rapid deflation. Following the old Puritan adage, "A bargain's a bargain and must be made good," the commonwealth paid off old bills and notes in specie at the market value of the time of issue, instead of following Virginia's example of discharging state debts at the depreciated value of a thousand to one. Heavy taxes had to be laid to support this sound money policy, and the taxes were not justly apportioned; 40 per cent of the total was collected by poll taxes, which fell equally on rich and poor.

Merchants in the seaports, pressed by foreign creditors to pay for imported goods, tried to collect from country storekeepers and they from the farmers. A situation was created somewhat like the old nursery tale which begins, "The stick began to beat the dog." With trade at a standstill, farm produce a drug in the market, no employment for common labor, and little specie in circulation, court judgments for debts or overdue taxes could in most cases be enforced only by stripping a farmer of his real estate, his cattle, and his furniture. In Worcester County alone, 92 persons were imprisoned for debt in 1785. The situation was very bad, and rumor made it seem worse; stories flew about that the wealthy men of Boston and Salem were trying to get all the land into their hands and convert the free farmers of Massachusetts into a dependent peasantry.

The people now resorted to the measures which they had employed against the Coercive Acts. They prevented the county courts from sitting, so that there would be no more judgments for debts; they held county conventions to state grievances and draft petitions, and appointed committees of correspondence between counties. This was a grim joke on the leaders of the American Revolution who were now running the state government. Samuel Adams, now a respectable member of the state council, proposed to hang anyone who used the methods he had empoyed in 1774.

In the fall of 1786, mobs of farmers prevented the courts from sitting in the four western counties of Massachusetts, and in Middlesex County at Concord. Annual state elections at that time came in the spring; and the main object of the insurgents was to stop executions for debt and taxes until they could elect a new legislature to grant legal relief, as had been obtained in other states. James Bowdoin, a staunch conservative, was now governor of Massachusetts. In September 1786 he issued a proclamation against unlawful assemblies and called out the militia to disperse them. This made the insurgents desperate. Daniel Shays was now thrust forward as a leader, against his will. He had served with distinction as captain in a Massachusetts line regiment, and settled at Pelham after the war. He was a poor man; a few years earlier he had been unable to raise twelve dollars to pay a debt. He now served as chairman of a committee which resolved to prevent the sitting of the state supreme court at Springfield, fearing lest it indict their leaders for treason. Major General Shepherd, at the head of loyal militia, undertook to defend both the courthouse and the federal arsenal where the insurgents hoped to get arms. He defeated an attack on Springfield by 1100 men led by Shays, with Luke Day and Eli Parsons as lieutenants. Shepherd had artillery and they none, so it is not surprising that after one volley the insurgents broke and ran (25 January 1787). A fresh militia army from the eastern counties then arrived on the scene, impressively led by General Benjamin Lincoln, and pursued the rebels through the snow to Petersham, where their force was scattered, and many prisoners taken. A few skirmishes occurred elsewhere, but the rout of Shays's main force at Petersham on 4 February broke the back of the rebellion. Shays escaped to Vermont.

Massachusetts, fortunately, reacted with wisdom and mercy. Fourteen leaders were captured and sentenced to death, but all were either pardoned or let off with prison terms. The newly elected legislature, in which a majority sympathized with the rebels, granted some of their demands, such as allowing soldiers' notes to be tendered for taxes. And the return of prosperity in 1787 caused the eruption to subside, leaving no bitter slag. Law and order had been maintained without the mass murders which have characterized the suppression of revolts by desperate people in our day.

Shays's Rebellion had a great influence on public opinion. News of it delighted the English Tories, as proof that Americans were incapable of self-government. It alarmed all American leaders except Jefferson, who, from his snug retreat in the Paris legation, remarked, "A little rebellion now and then is a good thing; the tree of liberty must be refreshed from time to time with the blood of patriots and tyrants." When Massachusetts appealed to the Confederation for help, Congress was unable to do a thing. That was the final argument to sway many Americans in favor of a stronger federal government.

Washington and almost all military leaders of the war, and many civilians as well, had long felt that the Confederation could never become a respectable government without the power to tax. It could not even apportion requisitions as the Articles required, according to the assessed value of real estate in each state, because it had no money to make a survey. Congress could only obtain taxing power by amendment, which required unanimous consent of the member states. The first attempt, the impost amendment of 1781 which granted Congress power to levy an import duty of not more than 5 per cent, failed because Rhode Island refused to ratify, and Virginia reneged on her ratification. In 1783 a second attempt, limited in operation to twenty-five years, was ruined by the selfishness of New York landowners who feared higher land taxes if their state gave up customs revenue. An amendment proposed in 1784, to give the Confederation limited power to regulate domestic and foreign commerce, did not even pass Congress. The prospect of getting money by any means, except selling Western land to speculators, seemed hopeless. Only New Jersey refused absolutely to pay her annual requisition, but other states did so in fact, by applying their shares to pay interest on federal debts owed to their own citizens.

There were enough interstate brawls to cause great disquiet. The New York assembly in 1787 assessed heavy entrance and clearance fees on all vessels coming from or bound to New Jersey and Connecticut; New Jersey retaliated by taxing the lighthouse on Sandy Hook £30 a month. But another interstate conflict furthered the cause of more perfect union. Virginia and Maryland, long at loggerheads over the oyster fishery, made a settlement at a joint conference in Alexandria. Pennsylvania and Delaware were also concerned, because some of their commerce had to pass through Virginia's territorial waters. Virginia's assembly, which at this juncture was in a nationalist mood, invited all the states to send delegates to a convention at Annapolis, "to take into consideration the trade of the United States."

This Annapolis Convention, which met in September 1786, was attended by delegates from only five states. Two of its youngest members, Alexander Hamilton and James Madison, took the lead in persuading the delegates that nothing could be accomplished by so slim a body, and in adopting a report which Hamilton drafted. This report pointed up the critical situation of the Confederation, and proposed that all thirteen states choose delegates to a convention, "to devise such further provisions as shall appear to them necessary to render the constitution of the federal government adequate to the exigencies of the Union." This was the genesis of the Convention of 1787.

Congress took its time to consider the Annapolis invitation. On 21 February 1787 it invited the states to send delegates to a convention at Philadelphia in May, "for the sole and express purpose of revising the Articles of Confederation," to "render the federal constitution adequate to the exigencies of government, and the preservation of the Union."

3. The Federal Convention of 1787

The Federal Convention, which sat in Philadelphia from 25 May to 17 September 1787, drafted the most successful constitution in history, now covering fifty instead of thirteen states, and a population approaching 200 million as compared with fewer than four million enrolled in the census of 1790.

At Philadelphia twelve states (Rhode Island having sulkily declined the invitation) were represented by fifty-five delegates. Two (William S. Johnson and Abraham Baldwin) were college presidents; three (George Wythe, James Wilson, and William C. Houston) were or had been professors; twenty-six others were college graduates. Four delegates had read law at the Inns of Court in London; nine were foreign-born. Twenty-eight had served in Congress, and most of the others in state legislatures. The most surprising thing about the delegates is their youth. Five, including Charles Pinckney, were under thirty years old; Alexander Hamilton was thirty-two; in the next oldest group James Madison, Gouverneur Morris and Edmund Randolph were within a year of thirty-five. Wilson, Luther Martin, Oliver Ellsworth, and William Paterson were between forty-one and forty-five. General Washington who, much against his desire, had been "drafted" for the Convention, was now fifty-five, the same age as Dickinson and Wythe. Only four members had reached or passed the age of sixty; and Benjamin Franklin at eighty-one was the oldest member by fifteen years. Practically every American who had useful ideas on political science was there except John Adams and Thomas Jefferson on foreign missions and John Jay, busy with the foreign relations of the Confederation. Jefferson contributed indirectly by shipping to Madison and Wythe from Paris sets of Polybius and other ancient publicists who discoursed on the theory of "mixed government" on which the Constitution was based. The political literature of Greece and Rome was a positive and quickening influence on the Convention debates.

The Convention had been summoned to meet on 14 May, but not until the 25th did enough delegates report at the place of sessions, the State House next to Independence Hall, to enable it to organize. George Washington was chosen president of the Convention, and it was decided to keep all proceedings secret until the results were known.

In the meantime, the national-minded Virginia delegation, led by young Randolph and Madison, who arrived in mid-May, held several informal meetings with Robert Morris and other Philadelphia nationalists. At these caucuses the important decision was made not to try to amend the Articles of Confederation but to start fresh. An outline plan for a new nationalist government was presented by Edmund Randolph of Virginia on the third day of the Convention's sessions, 29 May. The essential principles of these Virginia resolutions, as they were called, were a "national legislature" of two houses, members of both to be apportioned according to population, and those of the upper house to be elected by the lower; a "national executive" and a "national judiciary," both to be appointed by the national legislature; provision for amendment, and for binding members of state governments by oath to support the new constitution.

The Convention immediately resolved itself into a committee of the whole to debate this national plan. Roger Sherman and Elbridge Gerry, still trembling over the recent Shays's Rebellion, opposed popular elections. "The evils we experience flow from the excess of democracy," said Gerry. But George Mason, with the serenity of a liberal Southern gentleman, "argued strongly for an election of the larger branch by the people," and was supported by Madison and by James Wilson, who "was for raising the federal pyramid to a considerable altitude, and for that reason wished to give it as broad a basis as possible." Popular election "of the first branch of the National Legislature" was adopted by a vote of six states to two, with two divided.

The Convention then debated whether the national executive power should be vested in one man or several. Wilson argued for "a single magistrate, as giving most energy, dispatch and responsibility to the office." Randolph opposed it as "the foetus of Monarchy." Oliver Cromwell, Julius Caesar, and every "man on horseback" of ancient and modern history were prancing in the members' minds.

The Convention then debated the method of election and apportionment of the second branch, which it agreed to call the Senate, following Roman precedent. Madison made a great speech on "the use of the Senate"—to proceed "with more coolness, with more system, and with more wisdom, than the popular branch." He wished to have the Senate, too, elected by the people (as it has been since 1913); but Gerry insisted that the commercial and monied interests would be more secure in the hands of the state legislatures than of the people at large; and Mason agreed that to have senators elected by the states would be the best way to make these "a constituent part of the national establishment." The Convention so voted, unanimously.

This realistic appreciation of distinct economic but sectional interests in the United States was shared by many members. How were the rival interests of seaboard merchants and back-country farmers (expressing the age-old antagonism between town and country), creditors and debtors, produce-exporting Southerners and trading Yankees, to be reconciled? Madison observed that the larger the political unit, the less likelihood of class or sectional injustice; he pointed out that Rhode Island was the place where one class had been riding roughshod over every other. "All civilized societies," he said, were "divided into different sects, fashions, and interests, as they happened to consist of rich and poor, debtors and creditors, the landed, the manufacturing, the commercial interests, the inhabitants of this district or that district. . . . Why was America so justly apprehensive of Parliamentary injustice? Because Great Britain had a separate interest. The only remedy is to enlarge the sphere, and thereby divide the community into so great a number of interests and parties, that a majority will not likely to have a common interest separate from that of the whole or of the minority."

Enlarge the sphere, and balance the interests: has not American history proved Madison's wisdom? And has not the completely contrary communist theory, of recognizing no interests except those of the "workers" and the state, brought an end to personal liberty wherever put into effect?

The Convention was still happily debating the Virginia national plan when William Paterson of New Jersey exploded a bomb in the form of the New Jersey plan. The essential feature of it was one state, one vote; it was little more than an amended Articles of Confederation. The New Jersey plan naturally appealed to delegates from smaller states, who feared having their interests overridden by majorities formed out of big ones. Paterson introduced it with a long speech on state sovereignty, to which young Charles Pinckney retorted, "Give New Jersey an equal vote, and she will dismiss her scruples, and concur in the National system." And Hamilton remarked, "It is a contest for power, not for liberty."

Delegates from the four larger states, Massachusetts, Pennsylvania, Virginia, and Connecticut, in alliance with the Carolinas, defeated the New Jersey plan on 19 June and brought the national plan back as order of the day. But the wisest members reflected that their task was not to draft a theoretically best constitution, but as good a one as could probably get ratified; that they must make concessions to state rights. So, as a starter, the words "national government" in the Virginia plan were replaced by "Government of the United States."

Hot weather now set in, tempers flared, and the Convention seemed to be getting nowhere. So, on 28 June, Benjamin Franklin made his famous speech recommending that sessions be opened with prayer:

> The small progress we have made after four or five weeks . . . is methinks a melancholy proof of the imperfection of Human Understanding. We indeed seem to feel our own Want of political wisdom, since we have been running about in search of it. . . . In this situation . . . groping as it were in the dark to find political truth . . . how has it happened, Sir, that we have not hitherto once thought of humbly applying to the Father of lights to illuminate our understanding? . . . I have lived, Sir, a long time, and the longer I live, the more convincing proofs I see of this truth, *that God governs in the affairs of men.* And if a sparrow cannot fall to the ground without his notice, is it probable that an empire can rise without his aid?

Franklin's motion was lost, not because the delegates disbelieved in prayer, but because they had no money to pay a chaplain. The states which elected them provided neither salary nor expense account.

The deadlock was broken on 16 July when the Convention adopted the great compromise of the Constitution, by some called the Connecticut compromise because it was suggested by Roger Sherman. The House of Representatives would be popularly elected, and apportioned according to the number of free inhabitants, plus three-fifths of the slaves (the so-called federal ratio); but the Senate would consist of two members from each state, elected by the state legislatures.

All decided points were now turned over to a large committee, which reported on 6 August a series of propositions which the Convention debated one by one. Franklin spoke in favor of a liberal admission of foreigners. Irish-born Pierce Butler of Georgia opposed this, as did Gouverneur Morris, who wanted no "philosophical gentlemen, those citizens of the world as they call themselves . . . in our public councils." He would not be polite to foreigners at the expense of prudence. "He would not carry the complaisance so far as to bed them with his wife," as the hospitable Indians did with strangers. Gouverneur Morris was the "bad boy" of the Convention. Hamilton once bet him a dinner if he would slap Washington on the back and say, "How are you today, my dear General?" Morris took him up; but declared that after the look Washington gave him, he wouldn't do it again for a thousand dinners. Morris was a wit but no clown; it was his pen that put the final, taut touch to the language of the Constitution, and on 5 July he made one of the most eloquent and prophetic speeches of the session. As reported by Madison, Gouverneur Morris said, "He came here as a representative of America; he flattered himself he came here in some degree as a Representative of the whole human race; for the whole human race will be affected by the proceedings of this Convention. He wished gentlemen to extend their views beyond the present moment of time; beyond the narrow limits of place. . . . Much has been said of the sentiments of the people. They were unknown, they could not be known. All that we can infer is that if the plan we recommend be reasonable and right; all who have reasonable minds and sound intentions will embrace it. . . . This country must be united. If persuasion does not unite it, the sword will."

Elbridge Gerry, seconded by Luther Martin, wished to restrict the members of the United States Army to 3000 in time of peace, and made a humorous comparison (transmitted by oral tradition) of a standing army to a standing member— "an excellent assurance of domestic tranquillity, but a dangerous temptation to foreign adventure." But he got no support; it was agreed that the President be commander in chief of the army and navy, and that the size of each be left to Congress.

As the debates continued, the proposed constitution lost the legislative supremacy character of the original Virginia resolutions, and became more and more a "mixed government," in which the democratic, aristocratic, and authoritarian elements were balanced, as John Adams had done in the constitution of Massachusetts. Luther Martin even sneered at the Federal Constitution as "a perfect medley."

It is not, however, correct to say that the sentiment of the Convention was undemocratic. Members did not propose to set up an unlimited democracy like the Pennsylvania constitution; but they insisted on giving democracy its share in what they intended to be a balanced government. Apart from using the Senate "to protect the minority of the opulent against the majority," there were no built-in safeguards to property in the Constitution. Certain confiscatory practices of the states during the last few years, such as breaking contracts and issuing paper money, were forbidden to them, but not to the federal government—as the Civil War period and our own have learned. The Constitution gave Congress power to pay the national debt but did not require it to do so, as Gerry and other members of the Convention demanded it should. And in one respect the Constitution was more democratic than that of any state except Pennsylvania. No property qualifications were imposed for any federal office, although several Southern delegates argued that not only officials but voters should be men of property. George Mason, whose alleged democratic principles did not go very deep, wished congressmen to have the same landed requirements as those imposed on members of the House of Commons in the reign of Queen Anne. Charles Pinckney wanted a property qualification of at least $100,000 for the President, and $50,000 for federal judges, congressmen, and senators. But Gouverneur Morris hinted that any such requirement would exclude George Washington from high office; and John Dickinson, reverting to his original character as the Pennsylvania Farmer, "doubted the policy of interweaving into a Republican constitution a Veneration for wealth." Franklin, consistently democratic, expressed his dislike of everything that tended "to debase the spirit of the common people," or to discourage the emigration of such to America. Thus, a proposal to make the federal government "high-toned" was emphatically defeated.

The odd method of choosing a President of the United States was the result of several compromises. It was assumed that

Washington would be the first President, and the number of terms was not limited; but the Convention, not anticipating the rise of a two-party system, expected a free-for-all after the General, each state voting for a "favorite son," and none obtaining a majority of electoral votes. Hence it provided for a final election by the House of Representatives where the voting would be by states, a majority of states being necessary to elect.

An interesting sectional struggle took place over three subjects that had no logical connection: the African slave trade, export taxes, and the power to pass a navigation act. George Mason made a prophetic speech against continuing the slave trade: "Slavery discourages arts and manufactures. The poor despise labor when performed by slaves. They prevent the immigration of whites, who really enrich and strengthen a country. They produce the most pernicious effect on manners. Every master of slaves is born a petty tyrant. They bring the judgment of Heaven on a country." General Charles Cotesworth Pinckney, however, insisted that his state and Georgia could not "do without slaves"; and John Rutledge threatened that the three states of the lower South would secede unless permitted to continue this traffic. The Southern states, since their main profits came from exporting agricultural products, also insisted that export taxes be outlawed; and they wanted free competition in freight rates, having very little shipping of their own. Thus, they demanded the exceptional requirement of a two-thirds majority in Congress for passing a navigation act restricting shipping to the American flag. These three proposals on exports, slave-trading, and shipping were then committed and compromised. There could be no federal interference with the slave trade for twenty years. A navigation act could be passed like any other law by a bare majority; but federal taxes on exports were absolutely forbidden. That is why the United States today is almost the only nation that cannot impose export duties.

Finally, all agreed propositions were embodied in twenty-three resolutions and submitted to a committee on detail, of which Gouverneur Morris was chairman. Their report contained the significant Article VI on sanctions, which may be traced to the New Jersey plan. Paterson proposed that if any state ignored or failed to enforce an act of Congress, the executive should have power "to call forth the power of the Confederate States . . . to enforce and compel an obedience." Hamilton and Madison objected: "The larger states will be impregnable, the smaller only can feel the vengeance of it. . . . It was the cobweb which would entangle the weak, but would be the sport of the strong." One of the signal achievements of the Convention was to reject this "coercion by force," as Ellsworth called it, and substitute "coercion by law."

That principle is embodied in two key clauses of the Constitution. In Article VI, section 2, we find: "This Constitution, and the laws of the United States, which shall be made in pursuance thereof; and all treaties made, or which shall be made, under the authority of the United States, shall be the Supreme Law of the land; and the judges in every State shall be bound thereby, any thing in the Constitution or laws of any State to the contrary notwithstanding." And Article III, section 2, gives federal judges jurisdiction over "all cases, in law and equity, arising under this Constitution, the laws of the United States, and treaties made . . . under their authority."

These clauses give the Constitution a different character from that of earlier federal governments. They afforded the new federal government, in contrast to that of the Confederation, "complete and compulsive operation" on the individual citizen. State officials are expressly bound to enforce acts of Congress; and, as Madison pointed out, the federal judiciary may declare null and void any law "violating a constitution established by the people themselves."

Luther Martin objected, in a speech lasting over three hours, with "arguments too diffuse, and in many cases desultory." "The General Government," he said, "was meant merely to preserve the State Governments, not to govern individuals." That was true of the Confederation, as it is now true of the United Nations. But the genius of the Convention of 1787, its greatest contribution to political science, was to get away from this horizontal separation between the state governments and federal government, and give the latter a direct line to each individual citizen. Nevertheless, events in the South as recently as 1964 have proved that if a state government is firmly opposed to a federal measure, it becomes almost unenforceable.

By mid-September the work of the Convention neared its end. The New York members, except Hamilton, had already withdrawn in disgust; others, for various reasons, declared they would never sign. Gouverneur Morris cleverly devised a form to make it seem unanimous: "Done in Convention, by the unanimous consent of the States present the 17 September." At 4:00 p.m., 17 September 1787, "The Members adjourned to the City Tavern, dined together, and took cordial leave of each other."

During the four months of sessions in a muggy Philadelphia summer, they had thrashed out great issues in political theory and practical politics, and produced a constitution which has gathered prestige with age. When the Convention adjourned, most members felt that the compromises had vitiated the result. Alexander Hamilton called the Constitution a "weak and worthless fabric," certain to be superseded. Luther Martin regarded it as a stab in the back of the goddess of liberty. Daniel Carroll called it "the Continental Congress in two volumes instead of one." Madison accepted Carroll's criticism as a factor in the new government's strength; it was not a clean break with the Confederation. "The change which it proposes consists much less in the addition of *New Powers* to the *Union,* than in the invigoration of its *Original Powers.*" The most that Madison and the majority of delegates hoped, was that this practical, workable constitution, planned to meet the immediate needs of Thirteen States with approximately four million people, would last a generation.

The Federal Constitution gave new meaning to the term "federal," by setting up a "sovereign union of sovereign states." This federal government is supreme and sovereign within its sphere; but that sphere is defined and limited by the Constitution. Explicit in the Constitution is the statement (Article VI, section 2) that laws "which shall be made in pursuance thereof," and none other, are the supreme law of the land; and implicit is the principle that the Tenth Amendment of 1791 made clear: "Powers not delegated to the United States by the Constitution, nor prohibited by it to the States, are reserved to the States respectively or to the people." The states are co-equally sovereign within the sphere of their reserved powers; in no sense are they subordinate corporations as the British insisted that the colonies must be. Both federal and state governments rest on the same broad bottom of popular sovereignty.

The balance that the Constitution created has been upset by time and circumstances, and other successful federal constitutions have been adopted—notably that of Canada. But the Constitution of 1787 is still unique in many respects; above all, in meeting the test of over 175 years. It is still imperfect, creaky in vital spots, as the segregation struggle has recently proved; but Ben Franklin's prophecy that, with all its faults, no better one could be obtained, has proved to be correct. The philosopher Alfred North Whitehead well said:

> The men who founded your republic had an uncommonly clear grasp of the general ideas that they wanted to put in here, then left the working out of the details to later interpreters, which has been, on the whole, remarkably successful. I know of only three times in the Western

world when statesmen consciously took control of historic destinies: Periclean Athens, Rome under Augustus, and the founding of your American republic.[1]

4. *The Ratification Contest*

The Convention, anticipating that the influence of many state politicians would be Antifederalist, provided for ratification of the Constitution by popularly elected conventions in each state. Suspecting that Rhode Island, at least, would prove recalcitrant, it declared that the Constitution would go into effect as soon as nine states ratified. The convention method had the further advantage that judges, ministers, and others ineligible to state legislatures, could be elected to a convention. The nine-state provision was, of course, mildly revolutionary. But the Congress of the Confederation, still sitting in New York to carry on federal government until relieved, formally submitted the new constitution to the states and politely faded out before the first presidential inauguration.

In the contest for ratification the Federalists (as the supporters of the new government called themselves) had the assets of youth, intelligence, something positive to offer, and the support of Washington and Franklin. Everyone knew that the General favored the Constitution, and the Philosopher promptly made it clear that he did too. This was unexpected, since Franklin believed in unicameral constitutions like that of Pennsylvania. But on the last day of the Convention he made his famous harmony speech, saying, "The older I grow, the more apt I am to doubt my own judgment." Not only was he astonished that a constitution the result of so many compromises could be as good as this one but, he predicted, "It will astonish our enemies, who are waiting with confidence to hear that our councils are confounded. . . . Thus I consent, Sir, to this Constitution *because I expect no better, and because I am not sure that it is not the best.*" He hoped that every member who disliked the Constitution would do the same, and keep his mouth shut.

Nevertheless, only thirty-nine of the fifty-five delegates signed the Constitution. A few non-signers, such as Martin, Yates, and Lansing, were completely opposed to it. Mason, Randolph, and Gerry abstained largely from wounded vanity, since their pet projects were not adopted. All delegates who opposed, except Randolph, who saw the light, worked hard against the Constitution. This Federalist-Antifederalist contest

[1] Lucien Price, ed., *The Dialogues of Alfred North Whitehead* (Reprinted by permission of Atlantic-Little, Brown & Co., 1954), p. 203.

was largely personal; it was not a class, a sectional, or an economic cleavage. Some of the wealthiest men in the country were Antis. George Mason, who looked down his nose on Washington as an "upstart surveyor," and James Winthrop, scion of New England's most aristocratic family, wrote pamphlets against the Constitution. Delegates to the Virginia ratifying convention from the old tidewater region were mostly Antifederalist; those from the recently settled valley, Federalist. And so it went, all over the country. The only generalization that can stand the test of fact is that the cleavage was one of age against youth. Old political war horses such as Gadsden and Willie Jones of the Carolinas, Henry and the Lees of Virginia, Martin of Maryland, George Bryan of Pennsylvania, George Clinton of New York, and (for a time) Samuel Adams and John Hancock of Massachusetts, were Antifederalist; but the warmest advocates of the Constitution were eager young men such as Madison, Morris, and McHenry, all within a year of thirty-five, Rufus King and Hamilton who were thirty-two, and Charles Pinckney who was twenty-nine.

Antifederalists appealed to Tom Paine's sentiment, "That government is best which governs least." They viewed with alarm the omission of annual elections and rotation in office. And there is little doubt that the Antifederalists would have won a Gallup poll. Elderly radicals such as General James Warren and his gifted wife Mercy, who believed that the states were the true guardians of "Republican Virtue," predicted that the new Constitution would encourage vice and speculation, and that under it America would soon go the way of imperial Rome. This prediction is repeated every four years.

The Federalists were the realists. They had learned from experience that the natural rights philosophy, taken straight, would go to the nation's head and make it totter, or fall. Had not half the commonwealth of Massachusetts gone on a terrific binge? Federalists believed that the slogans of 1776 were outmoded; that America needed more national power, that the immediate peril was not tyranny but dissolution, that certain political powers such as foreign affairs, war, and commerce were national by nature, that the right to tax was essential to any government, and that powers wrested from king and parliament should not be divided among thirteen states.

Supporters of the Constitution promptly opened a campaign of education through pamphlets and newspaper articles. Most famous and effective were the essays that appeared in a New York newspaper, written by Madison, Hamilton, and John Jay over the common signature "Publius," later republished under the title *The Federalist*. Numerous editions of this collection have been published in many languages, and it has been a mine of arguments as to the nature of the Constitution and what the founding fathers thought of it. Important as these essays were, the knowledge that Washington and Franklin were in favor of the new Constitution probably did more to affect public opinion than all the pamphlets and oratory.

Even so, the struggle for ratification was tough. Only in a few small states was there no contest, since their leaders knew that with an equal vote in the Senate and two extra votes for presidential electors they were getting more than their share of power. Delaware ratified unanimously in December 1787. Pennsylvania, second state in population, was second to ratify since the Federalist policy there was to rush things through before the Antis could organize. Next came Massachusetts, where the situation was critical, since a rebellion had just been suppressed. Shortly after the ratifying convention met on 9 January 1788, a straw vote polled 192 members against the Constitution and 144 in favor. John Hancock, elected president of the convention, refused to take his seat, pleading "indisposition" until the three leading Federalists promised to support him for Vice President if the Constitution were ratified—a promise that they never fulfilled. Samuel Adams, so far Anti, was reached through a backfire kindled by the Federalists among his old cronies, the shipwrights of Boston. After leading merchants had promised to build new ships when and if the Constitution was ratified, these and other artisans possed strong Federalist resolutions, and Sam listened to *vox pop*.

The most important strategy by the Bay State Federalists was to propose a bill of rights to supplement the Constitution. This had not been provided by the Federal Convention, partly because the Constitution set forth limited and specific powers for which no bill of rights was logically necessary; but mostly because members were worn out and wanted to go home when they got around to the subject. Lack of a bill of rights, however, was a strong Antifederalist talking point. So the Massachusetts Federalists agreed to support a set of amendments, to be recommended to the states, and Hancock presented these as a bill of rights. That settled it; the Massachusetts convention ratified on 6 February 1788, 187 for to 168 against.

The Maryland convention, also proposing a bill of rights, ratified on 28 April by an emphatic vote; partly, it seems, because the members grew weary of listening to Luther Martin's three-hour Antifederalist speeches. South Carolina came next. Charles Pinckney made strong arguments in favor of union, which he lived long enough to repudiate; and on 23 May his state ratified the Constitution by a strong majority. New Hampshire had the honor of being the ninth state, whose ratification put the Constitution into force.

But four states, with about 40 per cent of the population, were still undecided. In Virginia, the most important, there took place a bitterly contested struggle. On the Federalist side were Washington, Madison, Colonel Henry Lee, John Marshall, and Edmund Randolph, who had been converted. Antifederalist leaders were Mason, Richard Henry Lee, and Patrick Henry, who disliked the entire Constitution. It was too consolidated. It "squints toward monarchy." The President will "make one push for the American throne." Congress, with power of taxation, will "clutch the purse with one hand and wave the sword with the other." The time-honored system of requisitions would be abolished. "Never will I give up that darling word requisitions!" These withering blasts of oratory were patiently met with unanswerable logic by Madison and Edmund Pendleton, and the objections were disposed of, point by point. John Marshall, thirty-two years old in 1788, defended the federal judiciary which he was later to adorn. Someone brought in a "red herring" proposal to ratify on condition that a bill of rights be adopted; it was voted down, and the convention ratified unconditionally on 23 June by the close vote of 89 to 79.

Immediately before this vote was taken, Patrick Henry, seeing that his cause was lost, set a fine example of the good loser: "I will be a peaceable citizen. My head, and my heart, shall be at liberty to retrieve the loss of liberty, and remove the defects of the system in a constitutional way." Antifederalist leaders without exception followed his example. There was no attempt to sabotage the new government, or to set up a "Confederation in Exile" in Providence or Quebec.

Three states were still outside. In New York, as Washington remarked, there was "more wickedness than ignorance" in Antifederalism. Governor Clinton opposed the Constitution, as did most of the big landowners, who feared heavier taxation if the state lost her right to levy customs duties. John Jay and Hamilton led the Federalist forces in the state convention with great skill, and the convention ratified by a vote of 30 to 27. Willie Jones, who dominated the North Carolina convention, prevented a vote at the first session, but it met again in November 1789 and decided to go along. Rhode Island, still controlled by the debtor element, called no convention until 1790, and then came in.

The Confederation Congress declared the new Constitution duly ratified, arranged for the first presidential and congressional elections, and appointed 4 March 1789 for the first presidential term to begin. But this had to be postponed. The new House of Representatives, which had no quorum until 1 April, counted the electoral ballots on the 6th. It took another week for Washington to learn officially that he had been chosen. The old Congress selected New York as the first capital of the new government.

Thus ended happily the most active and tumultuous quarter-century in the entire history of the United States. It was a period of little social change, but of a violent war and a turnover from a dependent colonial status to that of an independent federal union. The Federal Constitution was the capital

ODE ON SCIENCE

achievement of this creative period; a work of genius, since it set up what every earlier political scientist had thought impossible, a sovereign union of sovereign states. This reconciling of unity with diversity, this practical application of the federal principle, is undoubtedly the most original contribution of the United States to the history and technique of human liberty.

But, would the Constitution work? Nobody then knew the answer. This question was a major challenge to the age that was waiting before.

INDEX

Vermont: Revn. War, 287, 324–8; *de facto* state, 324; const., 358–9; land claims, 365; secession threat, 375

Verrazzano, Giovannia, 75–6, 84

Vespucci, Amerigo, 64

Vinland, 51–2

Virginia: colonial, 81–2, 85–6, 86–93; government of, 87–93, 130–2, 138–9; Bacon's Rebellion, 161–6; Seven Years War, 224–33; Two Penny Act, 239; Resolves of *1765*, 253–4; committees of correspondence, 273, 277; in Revn. War, 286, 292, 339, 342–3, 349; logistics, 304, 307–8; Loyalists, 312;

COMMONWEALTH: Bill of Rights and Const. as prototype, 354–8; land claims, 357; cession, 363–4, 385; debts, 373–4; anti-federalism, 403–4, 406;

CONDITIONS IN: land systems, 88, 89, 90, 125, 131; Indians, 87–93, 161–5, 265–6, 281–2, 349, 363–4, 385; trade and finance, 88, 90, 132–4, 139, 239, 267, 368–70; farming and tobacco, 91–3, 131–4, 135–6, 139, 239; slavery, 128, 131, 135, 207, 208 *n.*, 294–5; population, 131, 136, 186, 198, 199, 207; religion, 135, 136–8, 239, 361; 382; culture and society, 134–9, 205–7, 238–9; expansion, 220–1, 265–6, 282, 363–4, 385; slave trade, 384

Voltaire, 183, 333

W

"Walking Purchase," 183–4

Walpole, Horace, 252; *quoted*, 325

War of Independence

ARMY: American, make-up of, 298–303; logistics, 303–7; foreign volunteers, 306–7; weapons, 307–9; Tories, 311–4; Washington's role, 314–5;

CAMPAIGNS: of *1775*, 283–91, 292; Northern campaigns: Long Island and New York City, 316–9; the Jersies, 319–23; Saratoga, 323–8; Brandywine to Monmouth, 328–9; raids, 337–8; Yorktown, 343–8; Southern: Georgia and the Carolinas, 336–7, 338–43; Western, 349; West Indies, 344–5, 348;

FRENCH AID, 305, 331–4; volun-

teers, 306; Franklin mission, 333–6; treaties, 355–6; naval, 343–8;

SEA POWER, 309–11; French support, 343–8;

PEACE NEGOTIATIONS, 349–50

Warren, Joseph, 260, 272, 278; *quoted*, 281

Washington, Augustine (I), 200; (II), 320, 321

Washington, George, 198, 207, 221, 223, 333, 394–5; Seven Years' War, 225, 227; 2nd Cont. Cong., 287, 359; commands Cont. Army, 288, 289–90, 298–314, 314–5; Valley Forge, 303–4, 307, 328; ability and character, 314–5; New Jersey campaign, 319–23; Saratoga campaign, 323–8; sea power and, 343–8; Yorktown campaign, 343–8; farewell to troops, 351–3; Const., 403, 406; chosen President, 406–7; *quoted*, 304, 320, 321, 344, 348–9

Washington, Col. John, 132, 134, 162

Washington, Martha, 353

Watts, Capt. John, 82

Wayne, Gen. Anthony, 299, 302, 308

Webster, Noah, 376, 383; *quoted*, 375

Wesley, Rev. John, 210, 238, 381

West, American

RIVALRY FOR, 220–4; population, 236–7; English policy, 226, 249, 265–6; 281–2; back country revolts 262–6; in Revn., 349;

U.S. ACQUISITIONS: Peace of Paris, 350; state claims, 363–4, 385–8;

FEDERAL POLICY, 385–90; Northwest Ordinance, 289–90;

SLAVERY AND, 389

West, Benjamin, 183, 377

West Indies, 46; discovery and Spanish, 55–61; 69–71; French, English, and Dutch, 75, 82, 85, 98–100, 127, 145–9; in Queen Anne's War, 193, 194; in Revn., 283, 311, 344–6; slavery in, 146–9, 283; trade, 107, 116, 135, 145–8, 182, 199–200, 217, 241, 249, 267; post-Revn., 370, 371; population, 186, 283

Wheat: production, 197, 239; export, 199, 257

Whig Party, 254, 256, 265, 272, 276, 277, 281, 287, 312;

NOTES

NOTES

NOTES

NOTES

NOTES

NOTES

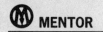 **MENTOR**  **MERIDIAN**

MEN WHO SHAPED A NATION

(0452)

☐ **WITNESS AT THE CREATION: Hamilton, Madison, Jay, and the Constitution by Richard B. Morris.** Two hundred years ago, the groundbreaking document that made the thirteen colonies into a unified country was ratified after a bitter explosive fight. Leading the battle were three brilliant and very different statesmen—Alexander Hamilton, James Madison, and John Jay. "A shifting web of ideas and personalities . . . skillfully rendered with an estimable style and scholarship."—*Booklist* (626869—$4.50)

☐ **CHRISTOPHER COLUMBUS, MARINER by Samuel Eliot Morison.** This saga of Columbus, told by a modern scholar who was himself an accomplished sailor, recreates the terror and excitement of the first Atlantic voyage, the discovery of land, the loss of the Santa Maria, and the tragedy of the subsequent voyages with all the intensity of a firsthand account. (009928—$9.00)

☐ **ABRAHAM LINCOLN: THE MAN BEHIND THE MYTHS by Stephen B. Oates.** His politics, his morals, and everything else about Abraham Lincoln has been clouded by time and distorted by both the devotion and the enmity which he inspired. Now Stephen Oates uses his pioneering research and dramatic new findings to offer us a picture of Lincoln as he truly was.
(009391—$10.00)

☐ **WASHINGTON: THE INDISPENSABLE MAN by James Thomas Flexner.** This award-winning biography looks at the man behind the legend to reveal a noble, hot-tempered, strong, sometimes flawed, and always imposing human being whom we come at last to know as he really was. (628381—$5.99)